THE OXFORD HISTORY OF THE BRITISH EMPIRE

COMPANION SERIES

THE OXFORD HISTORY OF THE BRITISH EMPIRE

Volume I. *The Origins of Empire*
EDITED BY Nicholas Canny

Volume II. *The Eighteenth Century*
EDITED BY P. J. Marshall

Volume III. *The Nineteenth Century*
EDITED BY Andrew Porter

Volume IV. *The Twentieth Century*
EDITED BY Judith M. Brown and Wm. Roger Louis

Volume V. *Historiography*
EDITED BY Robin W. Winks

THE OXFORD HISTORY OF THE BRITISH EMPIRE

COMPANION SERIES

Wm. Roger Louis, CBE, D. Litt., FBA

*Kerr Professor of English History and Culture, University of Texas, Austin
and Honorary Fellow of St Antony's College, Oxford*

EDITOR-IN-CHIEF

∿

Australia's Empire

∿

Deryck M. Schreuder

*Visiting Professor and
former Challis Professor in
History, The University
of Sydney.
Adjunct Professor, Humanities
Research Centre, Australian
National University*

and

Stuart Ward

*Associate Professor
at the University
of Copenhagen*

OXFORD
UNIVERSITY PRESS

OXFORD

UNIVERSITY PRESS

Great Clarendon Street, Oxford OX2 6DP

Oxford University Press is a department of the University of Oxford.
It furthers the University's objective of excellence in research, scholarship,
and education by publishing worldwide in

Oxford New York

Auckland Cape Town Dar es Salaam Hong Kong Karachi
Kuala Lumpur Madrid Melbourne Mexico City Nairobi
New Delhi Shanghai Taipei Toronto

With offices in

Argentina Austria Brazil Chile Czech Republic France Greece
Guatemala Hungary Italy Japan Poland Portugal Singapore
South Korea Switzerland Thailand Turkey Ukraine Vietnam

Oxford is a registered trade mark of Oxford University Press
in the UK and in certain other countries

Published in the United States
by Oxford University Press Inc., New York

British Library Cataloguing in Publication Data

Data available

Library of Congress Cataloging in Publication Data

Data available

Typeset by Laserwords Private Limited, Chennai, India
Printed in Great Britain
on acid-free paper by
Biddles Ltd, King's Lynn, Norfolk

ISBN 978−0−19−927373−7

1 3 5 7 9 10 8 6 4 2

FOREWORD

The purpose of the five volumes of the Oxford History of the British Empire was to provide a comprehensive survey of the Empire from its beginning to end, to explore the meaning of British imperialism for the ruled as well as the rulers, and to study the significance of the British Empire as a theme in world history. The volumes in the Companion Series carry forward this purpose. They pursue themes that could not be covered adequately in the main series while incorporating recent research and providing fresh interpretations of significant topics.

Wm. Roger Louis

CONTENTS

ILLUSTRATIONS

LIST OF CONTRIBUTORS

ALAN ATKINSON (Ph.D., Australian National University) is Australian Research Council Professorial Fellow at the University of New England, in New South Wales, and Honorary Professor at the University of Sydney. He is author of *The Europeans in Australia*, of which volumes one and two appeared in 1997 and 2004 respectively. A third volume is in progress.

GEOFFREY BOLTON (D. Phil., Oxford) is Emeritus Professor and former Chancellor, Murdoch University, Western Australia. He has been General Editor of the Oxford History of Australia and ABC Boyer Lecturer for 1992 and has published extensively in Australian history.

HILARY M. CAREY (D.Phil., Oxford) is Associate Professor of History at the University of Newcastle, NSW, and a former Keith Cameron Professor of Australian History, University College Dublin (2005–6). She has published *Believing in Australia* (1996) and edited special issues of the *Journal of Religious History* on Indigenous Religion, vol. 22 (1998), Millennium, vol. 24 (2000), and Religion and Memory, vol. 31 (2006).

ANN CURTHOYS (Ph.D., Macquarie University) is Manning Clark Professor of History and an Australian Research Council Professorial Fellow at the Australian National University and the author of *Freedom Ride: A Freedom Rider Remembers* (2002), and *Is History Fiction?* (with John Docker, 2005). She has recently completed *Rights and Redemption: History, Law and Indigenous People* (2008, with Ann Genovese and Alexander Reilly).

JOY DAMOUSI (Ph.D., Australian National University) is Professor of History and Head of the School of Historical Studies at the University of Melbourne. She has published in the fields of feminist history, the history of war and grief, and the history of psychoanalysis. Her works include *The Labour of Loss: Mourning, Memory and Wartime Bereavement in Australia* (1999); *Living With the Aftermath: Trauma, Nostalgia and Grief in Post-War Australia* (2001), and *Freud in the Antipodes: A Cultural History of Psychoanalysis in Australia* (2005).

HOBBLES DANAIYARRI (c.1925–1988) was born on Wave Hill Station (Northern Territory). He grew up on the station and worked for much of his life as a stockman. During most of this time he was a ward of the state. In 1966 he was among the pastoral workers who walked off the station demanding land and justice. Following the walk-off he went with his wife to her country, and was one of the founders of the community of Yarralin. By this time he had become a senior Lawman and ceremony leader, and travelled widely in the NT and WA on Law business. He was a moral leader with a gift for political analysis told in stories. He had no time for regrets, nostalgia, or recriminations; his stories express his passionate desire to see his people achieve a better future.

ANNE GRAY (Ph.D., Melbourne) is Head of Australian Art at the National Gallery of Australia. She has co-authored *Letters from Smike: The Letters of Arthur Streeton* (1989) and *The Edwardians: Secrets and Desires* (2004). She has also edited *Australian Art in the National Gallery of Australia* (2003) and has written extensively on Australian art.

JOHN HIRST (Ph.D., University of Adelaide) is Reader in History at La Trobe University, Melbourne, and author of *The Sentimental Nation: The Making of the Australian Commonwealth* (2000); *Australia's Democracy: A Short History* (2002); and *Sense and Nonsense in Australian History* (2006).

MARK MCKENNA (Ph.D., University of New South Wales) is International Research Fellow in History at the University of Sydney. He is the author of *The Captive Republic: A History of Republicanism in Australia, 1788–1996* (1996); *Looking for Blackfellas' Point: An Australian History of Place* (2002); and *This Country: A Reconciled Republic?* (2004).

NEVILLE MEANEY (Ph.D., Duke) is Honorary Associate Professor at the University of Sydney. He has published widely on the history of Australia and the world. He is the author of *Search for Security in the Pacific, 1901–1914* (1976); *Under New Heavens: Cultural Transmission and the Making of Australia* (1989); and *Towards a New Vision: Australia and Japan Across Time* (2007).

ERIC RICHARDS (Ph.D., Nottingham) is Professor of History at Flinders University, Adelaide. He has published extensively in the field of British social history and migration studies, including *The Highland Clearances: People, Landlords and Rural Turmoil* (2000) and *Britannia's Children: Emigration from England, Scotland, Wales and Ireland since 1600* (2004).

DEBORAH BIRD ROSE (Ph.D., Bryn Mawr College) is a senior fellow at the Fenner School of Environment and Society at the Australian National University. She is author of *Dingo Makes Us Human: Life and Land in an Australian Aboriginal Culture* (1992); *Hidden Histories: Black Stories from Victoria River Downs, Humbert River, and Wave Hill Stations, North Australia* (1991); *Country of the Heart: An Indigenous Australian Homeland* (2002), and *Reports from a Wild Country: Ethics for Decolonisation* (2004).

DERYCK M SCHREUDER (D. Phil., Oxford) is Visiting Professor (and formerly Challis Professor of History) at The University of Sydney, as well as Adjunct

Professor at the Australian National University. He has been an Australian vice chancellor, and President of the Vice Chancellors' Committee, the Australian Academy of the Humanities, and the Australian Historical Association. He has published widely in British and imperial history, including *Gladstone and Kruger* (1969), *The Scramble for Southern Africa* (1981), and (with John Eddy) *The Rise of Colonial Nationalism* (1989). He has edited (with Brian Fletcher) John Manning Ward's unpublished study of *The State and the Nation: Australian Federation and Nation-Making 1870–1901* (2001); and (with Jeff Butler), *Sir Graham Bower's Secret History of the Jameson Raid and the South African Crisis, 1895–1902* (2002). He has also recently been an Associate Editor of the New Oxford Dictionary of National Biography.

HSU-MING TEO (Ph.D., University of Sydney) teaches history at Macquarie University, Sydney. Her books include the Australian Vogel award winning novel, *Love and Vertigo* (1999), *Behind the Moon* (2005), and *Cultural History in Australia* (2003, co-edited with Richard White).

STUART WARD (Ph.D., Sydney) is Associate Professor at the University of Copenhagen. He is the author of *Australia and the British Embrace: The Demise of the Imperial Ideal* (2001) and has edited *British Culture and the End of Empire* (2001). He is the 'Australasia and Pacific' Editor of *History Compass*, and has also edited a special issue of *The Australian Journal of Politics and History* on Post-Imperial Australia (with Graeme Davison, 2005).

RICHARD WATERHOUSE (Ph.D., Johns Hopkins) is Bicentennial Professor of Australian History at the University of Sydney. His most recent books include *Private Pleasures, Public Leisure: A History of Australian Popular Culture Since 1788* (1995), *A New World Gentry: The Making of a Merchant and Planter Class in South Carolina, 1670–1770* (revised edition, 2005), and *The Vision Splendid: A Social and Cultural History of Rural Australia* (2005).

RICHARD WHITE teaches history at the University of Sydney. His books include *Inventing Australia: Images and Identity 1688–1980* (1981); *Cultural History in Australia* (2003, co-edited with Hsu-Ming Teo), and *On Holidays: A History of Getting Away in Australia* (2005).

ANGELA WOOLLACOTT (Ph.D., University of California, Santa Barbara) is Professor of Modern History at Macquarie University. Her books include *On Her Their Lives Depend: Munitions Workers in the Great War* (1994); *To Try Her Fortune in London: Australian Women, Colonialism, and Modernity* (2001); and *Gender and Empire* (2006).

Introduction: What Became of Australia's Empire?

DERYCK M. SCHREUDER AND STUART WARD

> 'The great question, What became of the British Empire? is one which, in 1957–8, it seems proper and timely to ask.'
>
> A. P. Thornton, *The Imperial Idea and its Enemies* (London, 1959)

The question remains. The fall of the British Empire and the complexity of its legacies have generated historical debate in Britain for half a century. Thornton's work was to be among the first of many attempts to view the imperial past through a post-imperial lens.[1] The loss of the extensive colonial dependencies throughout Asia, Africa, and the West Indies suddenly redrew global political maps and transformed international politics. And this inevitably transformed the way imperial historians approached their subject, raising questions about the enduring influences—political, social, and cultural—of imperial decline. In recent years, historians have sought to identify all kinds of contemporary resonances of Empire in Britain, from devolution in Scotland and Wales to Euroscepticism, the resurgence of 'Englishness', a 'missionary zeal' in foreign policy, changing attitudes to immigration, and even the break-up of 'Britishness' itself.[2]

---

[1] The literature is vast but see, for example, John Strachey, *The End of Empire* (London, 1959); David Goldsworthy, *Colonial Issues in British Politics* (Oxford, 1971); Wm Roger Louis, *Imperialism at Bay: The United States and the Decolonization of the British Empire* (Oxford, 1977); B. R. Tomlinson, *The Political Economy of the Raj, 1914–1947: The Economics of Decolonization* (London, 1979); John Gallagher, *The Decline, Revival and Fall of the British Empire* (Cambridge, 1982); R. F. Holland, *European Decolonization, 1918–1981* (Basingstoke, 1985); John Darwin, *Britain and Decolonization: The Retreat from Empire in the Post-War World* (London, 1988) and *The End of the British Empire: The Historical Debate* (Oxford, 1991); W. David McIntyre, *British Decolonization, 1946–1997* (London, 1998).

[2] See variously Norman Davies, *The Isles: A History* (London, 1999), p. 1053; Richard Weight, *Patriots: National Identity in Britain, 1940–2000* (London, 2002), p. 727; Krishan Kumar, *The*

Yet all these questions about imperial legacies have not had the same sense of immediacy or urgency in the former migrant settler societies of the Empire. Here it is as though the experience of 'losing an Empire and finding a role'—such a prominent theme in contemporary British history[3]—has had something of a forgetful quality, exhibiting a curious communal amnesia. As one of the few Canadian historians to address this question suggests, it has become more a case of 'Whatever happened to the British Empire?'[4]

In Australia, the question has proved to be particularly elusive as historians are fundamentally faced with trying to explain an absence, rather than a loss, of Empire. To earlier generations of Australians, 'Empire' was a key conceptual anchor of their identity and security in a fast-expanding world of modernity. To some it even remained 'home' well into the twentieth century. But in more recent times the Empire has quietly dropped through the trapdoor of history, without any heroic anti-imperial struggle. As early as 1968, Geoffrey Serle observed that the younger generation no longer appreciated the immense weight of the imperial past in Australia. Foundational works like Ernest Scott's *Short History of Australia* (which had assured Australian readers that 'British history is their history'[5]) or Keith Hancock's *Australia* (with its maxim that 'among the Australians pride of race counted for more than love of country'[6]) were no longer compulsory reading. Serle proposed that the time had come 'for what is no longer obvious to be restated and explained'.[7]

Finding an appropriate language and imagery to depict Australia's imperial experience proved, however, to be an elusive task. Previous generations had portrayed Empire through the familiar family image of the Mother Country

Making of English National Identity (Cambridge, 2003); Andrew S. Thompson, *The Empire Strikes Back: The Impact of Imperialism on Britain from the Mid-Nineteenth Century* (Harlow, 2005); Wendy Webster, *Englishness and Empire, 1939–65* (Oxford, 2005); Stuart Ward, ed., *British Culture and the End of Empire* (Manchester, 2001).

[3] As in Dean Acheson's December 1962 verdict that Britain had 'lost an Empire, and not yet found a role'. See for example David Sanders, *Losing an Empire, Finding a Role: British Foreign Policy Since 1945* (London, 1990).

[4] Philip Buckner, 'Whatever happened to the British Empire?' *Journal of the Canadian Historical Association*, Vol. 4 (1993), pp. 3–32.

[5] Ernest Scott, *A Short History of Australia* (London, 1916), p. 336.

[6] W. K. Hancock, *Australia* (London, 1930), p. 56.

[7] Geoffrey Serle, 'Australia and Britain', in Richard Preston, ed., *Contemporary Australia: Studies in History, Politics and Economics* (Durham, 1969), pp. 3, 17.

and her developing offspring. 'The present phase of relations to our colonies is transitional and therefore critical—not unlike the period in domestic life when the sons of a family are just grown up to manhood', as the Reverend Alfred Barry wrote in 1890 (having been a Sydney Anglican bishop); but warning that they were now 'too old and too mature for discipline and dependence of earlier days and yet not properly ready for separation to an absolute independence'. In the era of global decolonization and colonial national liberation movements, these ideas were adapted by a 'radical nationalist' school of historians who saw the growth to maturity and national distinctiveness as the core dynamic of Australian history. But as influential as these ideas were, the 'dependence to maturity' metaphor has proved to be as unreliable as it is simplistic. Ultimately, Australians did not so much leave home in some adolescent rebellion against the authority of the parent state as adapt quietly to the changing external realities of an Empire in decline. In the meantime, the Empire itself ultimately morphed from Great Power to relatively benign memory, even to no memory at all.

It needed particular events—such as the notorious 'Methods of Barbarism' debate in the South African War years, or the divisions over conscription during the Great War, or even the aggressive 'Bodyline' Test-cricket series (1932–3)—to exacerbate incipient tensions in the colonial–imperial relationship. But these events did not unfold along a progressive scale of ever-greater maturity—in the eyes of contemporaries they were generally regarded as isolated and aberrant. Australia proudly went to war with the Empire in 1914; Empire markets revived in the later 1930s; and after Munich and Appeasement, Australia also declared war on Germany, almost by loyal reflex action. The Second World War itself was to find deeper fissures underlying the Anglo-Australian alliance war strategy, not least over the fall of Singapore and the British south-east Asian military deployments in general. But again the bonds of sentiment and Empire survived these traumatic years. A major surge of British emigration to Australia followed the war; and a young Queen Elizabeth II could still make her extraordinarily popular post-war royal tour in the Australian high summer of 1954. Yet as Don Aitkin has commented, 'That was the high point; thereafter Britishness simply declined until it was akin to a relic. The stimulus to decline came as much from the United Kingdom as it did from Australia, and the two sources of change reinforced each other.'[8] As the

---

[8] Don Aitkin, *What Was It All For? The Reshaping of Australia* (Sydney, 2005), p. 215.

Empire itself shuffled off the global stage (and the British then joined the European Union), so the imperial mindset in Australia was fatally fractured.

To visit Australia in the first decade of the twenty-first century is to find a modern state and international society where the trappings of Empire have been quietly relegated to the museum (and, in the case of the new Australian National Museum in Canberra, rather discreetly so). Some external observers have pointed to a culture of classless hedonism, careless of history, as the really pervasive new ethos in contemporary Australian civic life. Australians now live in a major and successful OECD economy, ranked eighth in the world by per capita income (well ahead of the old imperial state of Great Britain at fourteenth). But beyond the comforts of conspicuous consumption, other observers of contemporary Australia have claimed to detect a newly self-confident patriotism in changing civic values, perhaps even 'a new nation on the move', as the Queen herself remarked in Perth during her 2003 Australian visit. That sense of community pride is most evident in sporting contests, but it is becoming manifest in a wider array of public rituals and display—from the revival of Anzac Day, to new citizenship ceremonies, the visual spectacle of state funerals, and an increasing public use of symbols like the flag and anthem. While these ritualized expressions of nationhood continue to draw on a sense of the past, the Empire is invariably conspicuous by its absence.[9] As Stuart MacIntyre suggested in Volume Five of the *Oxford History of the British Empire*, 'There is something in Australia's present disposition, it would seem, that resists the Imperial past.'[10]

*   *   *

In one sense, this seems perfectly understandable. If the Empire was understood as inherently 'British' then it followed that its history and legacy would seem of less immediate relevance to the successor nations of the post-colonial world. A history that celebrated the transplantation of British customs, institutions, values, and, above all, people to the Antipodes, had

---

[9] Jim Davidson 'The De-Dominionization of Australia', *Meanjin*, Vol. 63, no. 3 (September 2004) and 'De-Dominionization Revisited', *Australian Journal of Politics and History*, Vol. 51, no. 1 (March 2005).

[10] Stuart MacIntyre in Robin Winks, ed., *The Oxford History of the British Empire. Vol. V: Historiography* (Oxford, 1999), p. 164.

little place in an era when the Empire was in rapid decline and Britain itself in transformation. On the contrary, the changing ideological climate of the 1950s and 1960s raised difficult questions about the moral foundations of Australia's British history. But rather than confront these historical questions directly, Australian historians generally sought to displace them by identifying and elaborating new myths of national distinctiveness—a phenomenon that Stephen Howe has likened to 'trying to escape the history of Empire'.[11]

This is not to say that issues relating to colonization disappeared from Australian historical consciousness—simply that historians increasingly resorted to national paradigms in order to generate meaningful questions and themes. In some instances, this involved a self-conscious anchoring of the national past in the native soil, borrowing implicitly from the ideology and rhetoric of colonial national liberation. As Manning Clark reflected on his own 'discovery' of Australian history in the 1950s, 'Australians were about to become Australian-centred. Our history was not a branch of British colonial history, or the story of the beginning of British civilisation in the ancient continent of Australia.'[12] And of course, many of the new national histories *were* liberating, in the sense of breaking down the debilitating colonial presumption that 'history' was something that happened elsewhere. The new 'contact histories' of Aboriginal dispossession that began to emerge in the 1970s are a good example of how colonial history was invested with a new urgency and vitality, precisely because the self-legitimating blinkers of an imperial perspective had been replaced by a more insistently national, post-colonial framework.[13]

But the vibrancy of a new self-awareness and self-discovery came at the cost of a more constrained intellectual horizon. In a synoptic essay in *Past and Present* in 1999, A. G. Hopkins charged that historical scholarship in Australia and Canada had become so inward-looking and self-referential that it was 'scarcely studied elsewhere'.[14] Conversely, John Hirst decried the proliferation of undergraduate programmes in Australian History where

[11] Stephen Howe, 'The Slow Death and Strange Rebirths of Imperial History', *Journal of Imperial and Commonwealth History*, Vol. 29, no. 2 (2001), p. 137.

[12] Manning Clark, *The Quest for Grace* (Ringwood, Vic., 1990), p. 159. See also Clark's 1976 Boyer Lectures, *A Discovery of Australia* (Sydney, 1976).

[13] See for example C. D. Rowley, *The Destruction of Aboriginal Society* (Canberra, 1970); Henry Reynolds, *The Other Side of the Frontier* (Townsville, 1981); Lyndall Ryan, *The Aboriginal Tasmanians* (St Lucia, Qld, 1981).

[14] A. G. Hopkins, 'Back to the Future: From National History to Imperial History', *Past and Present*, 164 (1999), p. 216.

'students can major in history without having to study the history of anything else.'[15] What was at stake was not where Australian history was studied or by whom, but the sense in which historical change in Australia had been geared to the wider, transformative dynamics of Empire.

One primary reason for reassessing Australian history in the light of its imperial antecedents is simply to do with history and the importance of each generation forming its own view of the national past. The last comprehensive, collaborative study of the Empire in Australia took the form of a weighty special volume in the major interwar series *The Cambridge History of the British Empire*, published as long ago as 1933.[16] The Empire had then not only a long history behind it, but an apparently long history in front of it, as 'Commonwealth'. Unsurprisingly, Australia was portrayed as a great British enterprise and historic achievement. 'A century has passed since Gibbon Wakefield and his collaborators projected a new age and art of English colonization in the far seas; they dreamed great things … yet not more splendid than have come from the anvil of time', as the General Series Editors declared. More still: it was the 'independent spirit of the pioneer community' which had not only sponsored a 'national consciousness and self-assertion' over time; but which had contributed to the 'building of nations which has transformed the British Empire into the Commonwealth of Nations'.[17]

This Oxford volume is hardly too soon a successor: the mere fact that the Empire is long gone invites reappraisal. In every sense, 'history' has moved on. Yet this volume shares a certain goal with its predecessor: an opportunity, as Geoffrey Bolton has remarked of the Cambridge project, 'to bring together a group of scholars from across the continent and set them reflecting on what it meant to be Australian'.[18]

Beyond the rationale of revising and updating the record of Empire, there is moreover the fundamental contemporary issue of ensuring that the vanishing traces of Empire are still appropriately aired, debated, and interpreted. David Malouf has challenged his fellow citizens to engage in just

---

[15] John Hirst, 'Australian History and European Civilisation', *Quadrant*, Vol. 37, no. 5 (1993), p. 28.

[16] Edited by Ernest Scott (who also wrote two of the chapters) together with contributions by T. Griffith Taylor, J. A. Williamson,, A. C. V Melbourne, S. H. Roberts, A. Grenfell Price, G. V. Portus, E. O. G. Shann, E. A. Benians, K. H. Bailey, Robert Garran, W. Harrison Moore, W. K. Hancock, F. W. Eggleston, H. S. Gullet, D. B. Copland, Fred Alexander, and Archibald Strong.

[17] *Cambridge History of the British Empire, Australia*, pp, xxiii–iv,

[18] In his Introduction to the 1988 re-issue Vol. VII, Part I.

such critical reflections in a luminous essay, 'Made in England' (2004). Here he subtly argues the case for locating Empire at the very core of language and civic discourse: 'Australia was founded at a particular turning point in the evolution of English, and the form of English we inherited has been a strong shaping influence on what happened here, and on the way it happened.' He has even detected a powerful 'habit of mind' in the British legacy, a kind of purposeful pragmatism that created the common law and parliamentary system, as well as promoting scientific and industrial revolutions which shaped a new state and Empire.[19]

Knowing the past is clearly a form of self-knowledge, as applicable to a community as to an individual. This is the context of the current, highly politicized public argument about contemporary Australian culture and the past. The widely debated 'History Wars' have often taken the form of a rather *unhistorical* set of ideological skirmishes over simplified moral interpretations of a complex past.[20] The imperial experience has been evoked as a significant aspect of those arguments, including ideological positions over whether Australia's foundational history is ultimately something to celebrate or to excoriate. Blunt assertion and counter-assertion, with little deepening of historical knowledge itself, has been a feature of the media coverage, allowing precious little rhetorical space for historical nuance or complexity.[21] Yet the sheer intensity of the media coverage and the public debate indicates that the ethical dilemmas about the legitimacy of the colonization of Australia have acquired a new edge. And the recent discussion over the teaching of history in Australian schools has had as its subtext the reclamation of Australia's past for lessons in civic pride. In reality what is actually needed is a wide-ranging reassessment of Australia's imperial experience across a broad front—and not merely those aspects that have excited politicians and the opinion writers in the broadsheet press of recent years.

That process of critical enquiry really begins outside Australia, with a recognition of the global forces that have driven modern history itself. The British Empire was to become a transforming agency for historic trans-oceanic change which came to touch all corners of the globe. And the making of Australia has to be seen within that international history which,

---

[19] David Malouf, 'Made in England: Australia's British Inheritance', in *Quarterly Essay*, 12 (2003), p. 43.

[20] See generally Stuart MacIntyre, *The History Wars* (Melbourne, 2003).

[21] See Bain Attwood, *Telling the Truth about Aboriginal History* (Sydney, 2005).

as C. A. Bayly has powerfully suggested, points to 'the interconnectedness and interdependence of political and social changes across the world well before the supposed onset of the contemporary phase of "globalization" '.[22] For not only does modern Australia exist within the natural environment of an ancient continent (and incorporate by conquest Indigenous peoples with a deep past and cultural complexity), but its very historical processes reflect the underlying forces which have shaped modern history itself since the later eighteenth century. This has involved no less than the birth and global expansion of an industrial and market economy, originating in Great Britain itself; a radical philosophical revolution concerning the constitutional 'Rights of Man' in the age of the democratic revolution in Europe and North America; and a transforming cultural revolution in manners and sensibilities which brought 'conscience' into public life, so affecting human relations from slavery to legal punishments, through to social reform movements and religious revivalism. Simply by being a projection of the British metropolitan state, 'Empire' in Australia meant not just the imperialism of power and sovereignty but also a social imperialism of radical and transformative change.

Australian settlers were also an integral part of a 'liberal Empire' of deliberately devolved power onto qualified forms of local constitutional democracy.[23] In terms of its migrants, here was an Empire of increasing colonial 'home rule', in which settlers became the 'ideal pre-fabricated collaborators' in the project of a Greater Britain.[24] The effect was a subtle process of imperial devolution—not least for fiscal reasons—which relied on the bonds of sentiment, where elsewhere the British magistrate and the military sustained Empire. In short, in the settler Dominions, Empire had lost its absolute authority well before the challenge of an age of anti-colonial nationalisms; while the British 'official mind' itself had come to see the value of Empire as being best advanced by more subtle constitutional arrangements than that of direct government.

For this reason, any consideration of the dynamics of Empire in Australia needs to take account of the capacity of Australian migrants—

---

[22] C. A. Bayly, *The Birth of the Modern World, 1780–1919* (Oxford, 2004), p. 1.

[23] As J. M. Ward established long ago in his *Colonial Self-Government: The British Experience, 1759–1856* (London and Cambridge, 1976).

[24] R. E. Robinson, 'Non-European Foundations of European Imperialism: Sketch for a Theory of Collaboration', in Roger Owen and Bob Sutcliffe, eds, *Studies in the Theory of Imperialism* (London, 1972), pp. 117–42.

overwhelmingly but by no means exclusively 'British'—to make their own versions of modernity far distant from Old Europe itself. Australian migrants were both colonists and citizens at one and the same moment. By sentiment and racial conviction they long remained attached to their British imperial beginnings, or at least an increasingly mythologized version of Britain. But by identification and interests, by experience and community, by opportunity and aspiration, they increasingly shaped the new social entity that became 'Australia'. Through the impact of that growing sense of local agency and local capacity over time, it is not unreasonable therefore to speak of the formation of not only 'Empire in Australia', but of 'Australia's Empire'.

* * *

A perceptive twenty-six-year-old Edwardian traveller and radical imperialist, Richard Jebb, visited Australia as part of a global tour of 'Greater Britain' at the start of the twentieth century, and discovered the existence of distinctive local societies under the umbrella of Empire. 'New nations are bursting out of the colonial chrysalis', he pronounced just a little breathlessly in his best-selling travel book of May 1905, *Studies in Colonial Nationalism*. But his central message was in fact to interpret such 'colonial nationalisms' as being expressions of local vitality not incompatible with a pluralistic Empire of peoples and cultures. Jebb's 'Citizens of the South', as he called them with an affectionate admiration, had begun to behave and look and sound like an identifiable community of modern Australians, but who were also still at their core 'British imperial subjects'.[25]

Historians, and especially those of a more nationalist outlook, have sometimes expressed considerable difficulty in reconciling those apparently entwined, even contradictory, outlooks. But contemporaries had little sense of cultural schizophrenia. Writing from Adelaide University during the Depression, a young professorial W. K. Hancock (born 1898) opened his own central chapter in the *Cambridge History of the British Empire* with the statement that 'the architects of the Australian Commonwealth looked upon their work, and saw it was good. They believed they had built a dwelling-place spacious enough to house a nation—a nation that was to be new and old; Australian, yet still British. They did not fear a conflict between

[25] J. J. Eddy and D. M. Schreuder, eds, *The Rise of Colonial Nationalism: Australia, New Zealand, Canada and South Africa First Assert their Nationalities 1880–1914* (Sydney, 1988) works from Jebb's 1905 text in analysing the 'Empire of settlement' before the Great War.

the two elements of their ideal.' Hancock's citizens (like those of Richard Jebb) fitted Alfred Deakin's memorable characterization of 'Independent Australian Britons'. As Hancock concluded: 'These phrases suggest the essential qualities of Australian nationalism, and the essential facts about the Australian people. In 1901, 95% of the population was British, and was uneasy about the existence of the other 5%.'[26]

Perhaps, as Carl Berger has suggested for the Canadian colonists, so too for the Australian settlers: their imperialism was also their nascent nationalism. Commenting on his grand portrayal of the opening of the first Australian Federal Parliament (by the Duke of York, in Melbourne's Exhibition Hall), Tom Roberts unhesitatingly declared: 'that's the Empire … And that's what I'm painting!'[27] Here were a global people (the 'British race' was their idiom), within a global system of Empire itself.

'Happy Englands abroad' was the slogan of British 'colonial radicals' in the age of Wakefield and Roebuck. Yet the harder social reality was that colonial societies were but a partial and fragmentary reflection of the metropolitan society and its cultural norms. Their elites were to be different in wealth and esteem, as well as being more open to 'new money' and new social mobility. While Australia's foundational university in Sydney (1851) had an appropriate imperial motto, *Sidere Mens Eadem Mutato* (roughly, 'the same under another hemisphere'), the institution soon had a professional and vocational momentum of its own. A popular material mass culture was also fuelled by higher wages and better standards of living than 'back home'. Studies of the global economy over the last century now indicate that at 1900 Australian citizens enjoyed the highest per capita GDP of any people in the world. In that sense, they had joined other colonists of Greater Britain who did not actually see themselves as 'colonized' people of the Empire (to follow the perceptive idiom of the Canadian scholar Philip Buckner).[28]

In this context, an Australian 'nationalism' in the face of Empire was always likely to be an unusual political animal. At the heart of the evolving Australian sense of nationality was a hybrid ideology, one that drew from both a tenacious race identity of Britishness, together with an increasingly

---

[26] Hancock in the *Cambridge History of the British Empire*, p. 491.

[27] Quoted in John Rickard, 'The Big Picture', in David Dunstan, ed., *Victorian Icon: The Royal Exhibition Building, Melbourne* (Melbourne, 1996), p. 272.

[28] See the Introduction to the Canada volume in this OHBE Companion Series edited by Philip Buckner. In addition, there is still real value in the analysis of Carl Berger's *The Sense of Power: Studies in the Ideas of Canadian Imperialism, 1867–1914* (Toronto, 1970).

assertive sense of material self-interest, and an environmental sense of place. Rousseau saw 'love of one's own' as the heart of nationality. Yet what constituted 'one's own' for the independent Australian Briton? Henry Parkes invoked the 'crimson thread of kinship' as a rallying cry for Federation, but his imagery invoked a collective British rather than exclusively Australian ethnicity. He called on Australian colonists to unite *because* of their common British ancestry, not in defiance of it. At the same time, the architects of Federation proved to be tenacious in defending their draft Constitution from the legislative scrutiny of Westminster. This was a species of nationalism that relied heavily on the language, culture, and heritage of an imagined community of Britishness, while insisting on the distinctive interests and aspirations of a people who, by virtue of their physical displacement from Britain, had an outlook and perspective all their own. The problem of reconciling the inherent tensions between these two conceptual pillars of Australia's Empire would become a defining theme of twentieth-century Australian history.

✳ ✳ ✳

To make sense of that complex story, it is crucial to comprehend the core historical dynamic of the British imperial system. Without that elemental lodestone of Empire, Australian history becomes an unsecured narrative, robbed of the power of its deepest forces and atavisms. Indeed, a history which has ironically been de-historicized.

But this is not just a question of 'putting the Empire back in'—or alternatively, given the scope and ambition of this Oxford series, of putting Australia 'back in the Empire'. Rather we wish to emphasize how *Australia's* Empire was as much the project of the colony as of the metropole, as much the product of the Australian imagination as of the British Colonial Office. This is not to make some proprietary boast, but rather to highlight four crucial points. Most fundamentally, there is the enduring theme of European culture, material, and ideas transmitted to a colonial setting and thereby transformed. The Australian colonies were never mere 'repetitions of England' as Anthony Trollope would have it ('English life all over again'), but places with their own internal dynamic and agency.[29]

---

[29] David Cannadine's *Ornamentalism: How the British saw their Empire* (London, 2001) contains Trollope's comment and other such representative Victorian views of the settlement colonies as merely extensions of the Mother Country (pp. 27–40).

Secondly, 'Australia's Empire' reflects the many ways in which 'Empire' simply meant different things to Australians in comparison with their British (and for that matter, other settler-colonial) counterparts. While settlers inevitably brought metropolitan attitudes and orientations with them (most obviously in persisting with the 'Far East' as a short-hand for their near-northern neighbours), they would nonetheless adopt a conception of Empire and Britishness that was subtly attuned to their colonial coordinates. Thirdly, the volume foregrounds the role of Australians as Empire-builders themselves, not only in asserting their sovereignty over the Australian continent and its Indigenous owners, but also in promoting an imperial programme of their own in the Pacific. Had it been left to the British alone, the entire Pacific basin (with the exception perhaps of Norfolk Island) and even large portions of Australia itself, may never have fallen under the Empire's sway. And finally, 'Australia's Empire' reminds contemporary Australians that the imperial legacy is as much theirs as Britain's. Exploring the after-effects of Empire is not about shifting the focus 'back to Britain', but about making sense of Australia's own imperial inheritance.

For analytical purposes this book is divided into three parts, dealing respectively with the origins, inner workings, and culture of Australia's Empire. The first part is devoted to 'Contact' in its various forms, from the first encounters between colonists and Indigenous peoples to the appropriation of land, the dynamics and ideology of conquest, the broad patterns of White settlement, the subjugation of the Aborigines, and, finally, the imaginative encounter between settlers and their new environment.

From the outset the volume emphasizes that there was always more than one version of 'Australia's Empire'. While it is impossible to recapture fully how Aboriginal communities experienced conquest and its consequences, there survives enough evidence in the oral tradition to suggest that theirs were powerful histories, with their own narrative structure and logic. The volume accordingly opens with an account that represents one of many Indigenous oral traditions: 'The Saga of Captain Cook'—as recorded in the Northern Territory in March 1982 from the memory of Hobbles Danaiyarri, a remarkable Aboriginal cultural custodian and cattle-station stockman. In Hobbles' version, Cook's 'discovery' of Australia is depicted as a recurring cycle of violence, destruction, and dispossession, in which Cook himself reappears across time and space as the mythological symbol of the greed and insensitivity of 'Big England'. In its departure from the western conventions of historical writing, Hobbles' account suggests that 'history' itself is part of Australia's imperial legacy. In the 'Saga', it is not only Cook's material advantages but his 'big book' that is central to the colonizing project—a 'book' that embodies both the legal instruments of Aboriginal dispossession and the historical narratives that legitimated them. Hobbles' voice powerfully and movingly evokes an Aboriginal sense of the burden of colonization, and the unfinished business of bridging the gulf that separates Aboriginal from 'Oxford' histories of the British Empire.

The meaning, method, and practice of conquest in Australia are then the focus of Chapter 2 by Alan Atkinson. The age-old liberal dilemma of the British as a 'free though conquering people' had its own peculiar trajectory in Australia:[30] as Atkinson argues, 'the idea of Australia as a moral and legal vacuum was essential to the business of conquest.' For this reason, conquest was more often than not understood as a triumph over the land itself, rather than over the Indigenous people. It was the 'imaginative power' of cartography, as much as the material and technological advantages of the colonists, that both inaugurated and gave meaning and purpose to the appropriation of the continent. An admixture of Enlightenment philosophy and frontier violence provided the core dynamic of a continuous process of conquest which never seemed entirely complete, and which remains contested to this day. In contrast to the British, Australians have never really thought of themselves as a 'conquering people'—such was the pervasiveness of the myth of original vacancy.

'Settlement', by contrast, was a term that came more readily to colonial Australians, and Chapter 3 examines the means whereby rural Australia became tethered to the Empire. In an age of rapid industrialization in the old world, metropolitan forces were paramount in providing the economic rationale for an expanding frontier of White colonization. Yet these factors could not determine the pattern or nature of land settlement and Richard Waterhouse emphasizes the rural agencies of Empire-building in Australia—how it was precisely the *loss* of centralized, imperial control that brought the continent under the Empire's sway. The imperial

---

[30] The phrase is from P. J. Marshall's inaugural lecture, citing John Bruce (1793), the official historiographer of the East India Company. P. J. Marshall, 'A Free Though Conquering People': Eighteenth-Century Britain and its Empire', Inaugural Lecture in the Rhodes Chair of Imperial History, King's College London, 1981, p. 3.

reach was invariably two steps behind the self-appointed pastoralists who determined both the distribution of land resources and how these should be put to use. The inevitable violence with the prior Indigenous inhabitants therefore differed significantly—in causation, scope, and outcome—from the imperial wars over New Zealand's Taranaki or the Xhosa of the Eastern Cape. Finding an appropriate means of describing those conflicts has proved particularly vexing for historians—not least because they cannot easily be anchored in some comparable 'British' experience.

In the following chapter the focus shifts to the subjectivity of Indigenous peoples at the interface of colonial contact. Again, in contrast to much of the imperial experience elsewhere, Australia's Empire was one where the status of Indigenous peoples was highly ambiguous from the outset. As Ann Curthoys argues, Aboriginal peoples were regarded as both 'British subjects entitled to the protection of British law', but also a 'subjected people' who posed an ever-present threat to colonial authority. Aborigines, too, adopted these various standpoints, at times drawing on their limited means to resist the incursion of an alien force, at other times petitioning the Crown for protection of their rights as subjects vis-à-vis settlers and missionaries. Metropolitan humanitarianism and evangelicalism, which, from the 1830s, sought to exercise a moderating influence over settler–Indigenous relations, brought an added layer of complexity to the concept of Aboriginal subjecthood. For Aborigines, the Empire not only brought the threat of destruction but also furnished the tools of adaptation and survival.

The first section of the volume concludes with a chapter on contact and accommodation with the new environment as depicted in the work of Australian artists. Here again, the emphasis is on how the continuities between European and colonial artistic styles and techniques produced 'new visions from old'. The earliest colonial artists were attached to the European South Sea voyages of the seventeenth and eighteenth centuries, and their work was an extension of the logic of exploration and colonization. This was equally true of the first generation of landscape painters, who sought to harness the Australian environment to contemporary British conventions. Anne Gray argues that the reliance on imperial borrowings was not the hallmark of an inauthentic, derivative culture, but the key to an original vision of Australia's Empire. She questions the 'colony to maturity' school of art history as itself an outdated remnant of a colonial mindset. In the eyes of contemporaries, the 'nationalism' of painters like Tom Roberts, Arthur Streeton, and Fred McCubbin was in no way at odds with the networks of Empire within which they worked. Even later artists, like Margaret Preston who rejected imperial influences, were essentially part of a long-standing tradition of adapting those influences to Australian experience.

Part II of *Australia's Empire* turns to the inner-workings of Empire itself—the institutions and agencies that were crucial in establishing and consolidating an imperial presence in Australia. The dynamics of any imperial system are inevitably complex and multifaceted, but we have sought to isolate and elaborate five key 'instruments of Empire': the state, migration, the churches, money, and the means of securing Australia's Empire from external threats. These processes not only provided the pillars of imperial power in Australia, but also served to tie the Australian colonies into wider imperial networks.

The first of these chapters examines the central issue of governance and the formation of the Australian State. John Hirst argues that nineteenth-century liberalism, and the mythological version of British history which nurtured it, provided the foundations of the Australian polity even before the achievement of self-government in the 1850s. He suggests that it was the liberal inclinations of an earlier tradition of 'enlightened despotism' that paved the way for a smooth, relatively strife-free transition to parliamentary democracy. In this way, liberal principles 'were applied to the colonies well in advance of Britain' as Australia's Empire acquired its own characteristics and its own 'British' history. The same is true for the Federation of the Australian colonies—an expression of political will that affirmed liberties for Australians that were yet to be secured in Britain. The advocates of the Australian Constitution were invariably 'Empire loyalists', but they were also moved by a desire to protect and enlarge British principles of governance by and for themselves. It is argued here that the unravelling of Empire and Britishness since the 1960s has left a legacy of British institutions, grafted onto Australian experience, but without 'the history and myth to explain and sustain them'.[31]

Migration from Britain, as Eric Richards maintains in the following chapter, was the 'unquestioned assumption' of Australia's Empire. Yet the flow of people to the Australian colonies in the nineteenth and

---

[31] Page 143.

twentieth centuries was neither steady nor inevitable. Migration was historically contingent—its causes often incidental to the project of 'Empire-building'—and it was subject to wild fluctuations in supply and demand. But it was widely understood, particularly from the late-nineteenth century, as fundamental to securing the British claim over the continent. Assumptions about race, community, and culture took on a special urgency and agency that were peculiar to Australia. The social engineering that underpinned the White Australia Policy represented a departure from British practice designed—ironically—to keep Australia British. These aspirations underpinned successive schemes for State-sponsored migration, which over the course of the twentieth century became subject to the law of diminishing returns. As the certainties of Empire, and the appeal of Britishness, faded in the 1950s and 1960s so too did assumptions about the absolute imperative of racial purity. These assumptions have nonetheless left one of the most enduring legacies of Empire in the composition of the Australian population and the hesitant embrace of multiculturalism.

In Chapter 8 Hilary Carey addresses the role of religion and the missionary impulse. She considers the activities of the 'colonizing clergy' in Australia, not only in relation to Australian Aborigines but also in enlarging the scope of Australia's Empire into the Pacific. Australian-based missionaries were among the first to establish themselves in New Zealand, and later became active in Melanesia, Fiji, and the New Hebrides. Theirs was an ambiguous dual role: on the one hand advocating the expansion of the frontiers of Empire into the Pacific as a means of securing their spiritual gains, while at the same time acting as the 'voice of conscience' in the face of exploitation by European settlers and traders. Beyond the proselytizing activities of missionaries, religion also had an enormous influence over the structure and character of colonial society. While Protestantism was a defining influence on the idea of Britishness in the eighteenth and nineteenth centuries, it was subject to 'distinct limitations' in the Australian colonies by virtue of an 'effective separation of Church and State'. Catholicism, with its strong Irish following, and the prevalence of dissenting Protestant churches, ensured that religion was as much a source of sectarian division as national or imperial unity. Although the churches remained active in instilling notions of loyalty in their congregations, religion never acquired the potency of race in the Australian conception of the British world.

In a chapter on 'Money', Geoffrey Bolton argues that British finance played only a minor role in the first half-century of colonization. He takes issue with an earlier tradition (influenced not least by J. A. Hobson's radicalism), which viewed British capital as the governor of the imperial engine, dictating the terms of colonization, and effectively reducing Australian colonists to a subordinate role serving British capital interests. In fact, while Britain inevitably became the dominant source of foreign investment and trade, for much of the nineteenth century the Australian colonies remained undercapitalized. Moreover, colonial politicians and financial institutions were able to manipulate the system to their own ends—or at least more so than the 'gentlemanly capitalism' model has allowed.[32] A free-trading Empire brought great advantages to Australian exporters to Britain; while membership of the Empire benefited Australian entrepreneurs by offering loans on the London markets at highly favourable secured rates. Moreover, to the extent that Australia was financially dependent on the City of London and the mills of Lancashire, this was as much the product of Australian fiscal and trade policies as imperial conceit.

This section concludes with that most indispensable instrument of Empire: defence. Securing the colonies against perceived threats was crucial to the viability and credibility of colonization. From the 1850s, survivalist anxieties became a feature of colonial political culture as rival European powers made their presence felt in the Pacific. These dangers were often more imaginary than real, as the succession of Russian invasion scares indicates; but this did not curtail their capacity to influence colonial attitudes and defence strategies. Reliance on imperial naval protection became the *sine qua non* of colonization, serving to reinforce and popularize late-nineteenth-century assumptions about Australia's inherent 'Britishness'. By the 1880s, instinctive fears of France and Russia began to give way to even greater anxieties about an 'awakening Asia'. Thus, defence strategies acquired distinctive racial overtones, which only served to strengthen the colonial governments' insistence on a viable network of imperial naval defence. Yet it was a relationship fraught with tension and uncertainty. The imperative of Empire-building in the Pacific—a recurring theme of colonial dispatches to Britain—seemed less urgent or even necessary from London,

---

[32] P. J. Cain and A. G. Hopkins, *British Imperialism: Innovation and Expansion 1688–1914* (Harlow, 1993) and *British Imperialism: Crisis and Deconstruction 1914–1990* (Harlow, 1993).

and doubts were thus constantly raised in the colonies about the efficacy of the British defence guarantee. An underlying divergence of material self-interest would bedevil imperial defence planning for more than a century, subtly undermining ingrained assumptions about the indissoluble unity of the British race. It is argued here that it was the very distinctiveness of the evolving Australian conception of Empire that contributed ultimately to its dissolution.

Finally, Part III is concerned with the culture of Australia's Empire. If the dynamics of Empire ensured that Britain was more crucial to Australia's existence than vice versa, it followed that Empire loomed larger in the Australian imagination. Family ties, business affiliations, institutional links, information flows, transport networks, and cultural connections all underlined the immediacy of Empire in Australia in ways that were never so self-evident to contemporary Britons. As a result, Australians began to acquire their own distinctive culture of Empire, albeit a culture sustained by the presumption of a shared ethos with Britain.

Perhaps the most striking illustration of this is the Australian conception of the Monarchy. No symbol has been more potent in conveying ideas of Australia's inherent unity and fraternity with Britain and Empire. Yet as Mark McKenna argues in Chapter 11, from the very first 'King's Birthday' celebration in 1788, the meaning and rituals of Monarchy took on their own Antipodean inflection. Distance from Britain tended to 'exaggerate affection and loyalty'.[33] Royal tours would be greeted with scenes of unbridled enthusiasm that were never matched in Britain where the mere presence of Royalty was not, in itself, a cause for celebration. Moreover, in Australia, the institution of Monarchy became detached from the ancient hierarchy of aristocracy and privilege on which it rested in Britain. Because the distant Monarchy was not widely regarded as the preserve of a particular class, it was more readily available as a symbol of the people. Down to the 1950s, the Monarchy persistently evoked an imperial Britishness edged with Australia's peculiar racial sensibilities. At the same time, royal tours underlined the 'foreignness' of Britain in the sheer novelty and strangeness of the rituals, etiquette, curtseys, and customs. This dimension came increasingly to the fore as the perceived need for racial unity waned, and the Empire itself receded in popular memory. It is argued here that this has produced a 'symbolic void' at the heart of Australian political culture. So powerful and

---

[33] See p. 262.

pervasive has been the Monarch's hold on the Australian imagination that it has proved exceedingly difficult to come up with home-grown alternatives to the Queen as the symbol of a sovereign people.

Imperial wars were fought, revered, and remembered in terms of a deep sense of community with fellow Britons overseas. But these too became key reference points for highlighting Australia's distinctive contribution to imperial Britishness. In Chapter 12, Joy Damousi surveys the crucial role Australia's experience of war and commemoration from the Sudan expedition in the 1880s to the recent revival of interest in Anzac Day. The meaning and memory of warfare in Australia were determined not only by notions of duty, service, and loyalty imported from Britain, but also by a more local insistence on the reciprocal nature of Australia's obligation to defend the Empire. In order for this promise to be made good, it was deemed essential that Australia's role in the Empire's wars should stand out from the crowd. A nagging feeling that Australian nationhood lacked a tangible legacy of martial Britishness underpinned C. E. W. Bean's lifetime work of chronicling and elevating the achievements of the 'Australian Imperial Force' in the First World War. For Bean, the Australian 'diggers' at Gallipoli and other theatres provided the stuff of national legend because they embodied qualities 'as purely British as the people of Great Britain—perhaps more so'.[34] This amalgam of imperial loyalty and Australian achievement was carried over into the Second World War, and weathered the tensions and contradictions of Britain's abandonment of Singapore in 1942. With the rapid decline of Empire in the post-war era, however, Australians were left with a national martial tradition stripped of the imperial assumptions on which it was founded. But, in contrast to the Monarchy, the Anzac legend has held up well in the post-imperial era, due to subtle but decisive shifts in the relative weighting of nation and Empire in Australian commemorative culture.

Beyond the more visible, symbolic importance of royal tours and Anzac Day, the culture of Empire penetrated deeply into Australian society, not least in the realm of gender and sexuality. Chapter 13 documents the distinctive attributes of colonial gender relations across a broad spectrum, from the culture of frontier masculinities to the early successes of women's struggle for equal citizenship rights. Angela Woollacott argues that the material realities of Empire produced new assumptions about gender identities in Australia. Australian middle-class manliness, for example, was defined in

---

[34] See p. 295.

opposition to Aborigines, Asians, the Australian climate, environment, and indeed the English themselves, thus placing an idealized colonial manhood at one remove from its British origins. These assumptions, in turn, fed back into colonial perceptions of the Empire as a male preserve. Women were not easily incorporated into gendered images that celebrated men's freedom from the fetters of domesticity. Yet it was precisely colonial ideas about masculine excess that, paradoxically, helped to secure the early achievements of an Australian 'feminism built on temperance'. In other words, the gendered assumptions that were integral to colonization helped produce political outcomes for colonial women well in advance of their metropolitan counterparts. This is just one of many examples detailed here of the material and cultural interactions between Empire and gender. While these legacies continue to manifest themselves, it is argued that the gradual decoupling of imperial and gender identities from the 1950s also contributed to an era of radical transformation in Australian gender relations.

The popular culture of Empire in Australia is the subject of Chapter 14. Despite a lively and long-standing debate in Britain on the question of 'how the British saw their Empire', historians have been less inclined to ask questions about the scope or nature of 'popular imperialism' in the colonies themselves, not least in Australia. Richard White and Hsu-Ming Teo point to some of the underlying structural reasons for the emphasis on 'the popular' in the creative output of the colonies, and evaluate the imperial myths and meanings which animated the popular pastimes of the colonists. It was a complex mix, an example indeed of the hybrid nature of the colonial society. On the one hand, there is the ubiquity of imperial popular culture. Even popular ephemera that are normally associated with the promotion of a distinctive Australian nationalism were often 'created against imperial culture and even determined by it'.[35] Empire thus remained part and parcel of the inner workings of the colonial cultural exchange—which partly explains why it has generally been so overlooked by historians. On the other hand, the analysis in this chapter cautions against an overly schematic reading of imperial popular culture: popular tastes and attitudes cannot be reduced to an undifferentiated display of imperial loyalty. Australians had begun to create the ways of life, tastes, and public values which ultimately expressed a distinctive community. Ambivalence and ambiguity abounded in the hazy distinction between imperial and colonial identities in all the settler societies;

[35] See p. 342.

and here we have a subtle exposition of this theme for Australia's Empire told through engaging case studies of popular fiction and sporting culture. Any assessment of popular imperialism in Australia will need to consider the limits of popular identification with Empire, as the effects of countless other influences on everyday life came to shape a new society.

The final chapter in Part III turns to history itself—the many ways that Australians evoked a British past as a corollary to their sense of themselves as an offshoot of the British race. Neville Meaney considers this issue not only in the work of academic historians, but also through the historical myths that informed political discourse, public debate, newspaper editorials, education, popular histories, ballads, and songs (including the national anthem, *Advance Australia Fair*). The chapter identifies and elaborates three distinct phases in the evolution of Australia's 'British' history. First, the early colonial era was typified by a liberal republicanism which emphasized Australia's inheritance of British liberties, from Magna Carta through the English Civil War, the Glorious Revolution, and the great reform movements of the nineteenth century. This conception of Australia's Empire did not baulk at the idea of separatism—on the contrary it looked optimistically to the future promise of a 'new Britannia in another World'. From the 1850s, however, this tradition was superseded by a new era of 'race patriotism'—itself the product of the rapid modernizing forces which produced mass nationalism and which compelled the Australian colonists to conceive of themselves in more overtly racial terms. The social Darwinism that accompanied (but by no means caused) these tendencies meant that republicanism gave way to a new emphasis on the indissoluble unity of the British peoples.

In keeping with one of the persistent themes of this volume, it is argued here that these ideas took root more readily and radically in Australia than in Britain itself. This was often recognized by contemporaries, who felt bound to conclude with the educator W. H. Fitchett, and the politician W. M. Hughes, that Australians were 'more British than the people of Great Britain'.[36] Australian historians in this era had their own peculiar preoccupations, not least an emphasis on the constitutional and cultural ties that bound the 'Dominions' organically to the Mother Country. But these scholarly pursuits were unlikely to survive the demise of Empire and Britain's withdrawal into Europe, and there thus ensued a third, post-imperial phase where Australian historians have sought to make sense of their national

[36] See Chapter 10, p. 246.

origins outside British or imperial frameworks. In a sense, this brings the volume back to its point of departure—the problem of how to unearth and elaborate the material and cultural legacies of Australia's Empire, without falling prey to the colonial mindset that produced those legacies or indeed to a nostalgia for an Empire on which the sun has well and truly set.

* * *

Here, surely, lies the real challenge for post-imperial historians in Britain; and for their post-colonial counterparts who see Empire 'from the outside in'. Histories have long functioned as repositories of power and legitimacy for the communities they serve, and there will inevitably be concerns that a renewed attention to Australia's British and imperial antecedents will work to revive and sustain a complacent, outdated, Anglo-Celtic vision of the nation. At a time of widespread calls for the moral certainties of a more 'structured narrative' in high school history curricula (in place of what the former Prime Minister, John Howard, regarded as an ambiguous 'stew of themes and issues'), there is perhaps good reason to approach the task of reinterpreting Australia's Empire with an eye of healthy scepticism.[37] But it would be absurd to dismiss the sheer weight of British and imperial agency in Australian history as a conservative fantasy. The authors assembled here write from a variety of political, regional, and generational perspectives; but they share an emphasis, not on reviving a moth-eaten imperial vision, but on understanding the significance of Empire in Australia's past and how the unravelling of that phenomenon brought its own tide of radical change.

In 1964 Donald Horne (1921–2005) published his noted polemic on Australian history and society, famously describing his native land in acerbic terms: a 'lucky country, run by second-rate people who share its luck'. His progressive intellectual agenda for a modern Australia focused on developing 'new theories of itself'—the first of which he identified as providing 'new histories'. *Australia's Empire* is as much a contribution to that debate as it is an extension to the existing scholarly literature in the *Oxford History of the British Empire*. Colonial Australians remain our contemporaries even in our conceits of modernity. The social realities which endured from the imperial foundations of the New World cannot be ignored. The contemporary historian of *The Isles*, Norman Davies, remarked on a visit

---

[37] See John Howard's Australia Day Address, 26 January 2006; Michelle Grattan, 'Beyond the History Wars', *The Age*, 23 July 2006.

to Sydney: while we will always seek to recognize the distinctiveness which is modern Australia, 'nothing will be able to alter the fact that Australia was born and nurtured in the British orbit ... [and] when the very word of "Britishness" has been consigned to the past ... the memory will remain.'[38] But Davies only gets it half-right: Australia's political and social fabric may well be indelibly marked by the legacies of Empire, but the memory of that experience can never be taken for granted.

Historical writing is indeed at its heart about memory—both that which lives in popular imagination, and that which is put in place by careful and critical analysis of the past in all its protean and sometimes painful complexity. It becomes a civic memory which can be contested. It is also a memory which can be evoked for reasons of power, authority, and cultural hegemony. It is not neutral territory, no matter how much we might yearn for a simplified past which legitimizes the present. The process itself is complicated. 'We dream the past', in Louis Namier's memorably ironic aphorism, just as we engage in 're-constructing the future'.

[38] Norman Davies, unpublished public lecture, University of Sydney, August 2001.

PART I

CONTACT: THE PROJECTION OF EMPIRE

1

The Saga of Captain Cook

HOBBLES DANAIYARRI
(AS TOLD TO DEBORAH BIRD ROSE)[1]

Right. Well, I'm speaking today. I'm named Hobbles Danaiyarri. And I got a bit of troubling. Long way back beginning, I think, right back beginning.

[1] Hobbles Danaiyarri thought deeply about history, race relations, and moral philosophy. I met him in the Aboriginal settlement of Yarralin in the Northern Territory of Australia in 1980 when I went there as a novice anthropologist to conduct research for a Ph.D. Hobbles took me in hand, as did a number of senior well-regarded teachers. Almost immediately he started telling me about Captain Cook, injustice, and alternatives. Having worked as a stockman for most of his life, he spoke from his own experience of 'Captain Cook's law'. Alongside of his station life, Danaiyarri was one of the main bosses for a ceremony line relating to young men's initiation. He travelled from the desert areas of Western Australia through to the desert, river, and salt water country of the Northern Territory. He observed, he assessed, he told stories, and sometimes he exhorted. He was an activist as well as a philosopher, and his activity was aimed primarily towards unsettling people from any acceptance of unjust structures of relations between 'White' and Aboriginal peoples. He wanted to awaken the conscience of Settlers, and to provoke remembrance among Aboriginal people.

Danaiyarri dictated this narrative in March 1982. It is the introduction to a full history of the region which he dictated to me in sections during March and April 1982. I taped his narratives, and the transcriptions are taken directly from the tapes. The full document constitutes the core of an Aboriginal history of the region. In this introductory section Danaiyarri offers a moral analysis of the structure of domination. Later segments take up events in much greater detail. The Saga was first published as 'The Saga of Captain Cook: Morality in Aboriginal and European Law', *Australian Aboriginal Studies*, 2 (1984), pp. 24–39 (D. Rose). More recently, a version was reprinted in 'The Saga of Captain Cook: Remembrance and Morality', in B. Attwood and F. Magowan, eds, *Telling Stories: Indigenous History and Memory in Australia and New Zealand* (Sydney, 2001).

Danaiyarri was a fluent speaker of Gurindji, Mudbura, Ngarinman, Kriol, and Aboriginal English. He spoke Aboriginal English in order to present the Saga to a non-Aboriginal audience; when the Saga is recounted for an Aboriginal audience it is usually told in Kriol. I have used English spelling in my transcription. However, since Danaiyarri's English has some Kriol characteristics, the English spelling may sometimes encourage incorrect interpretations. I have included translations in brackets where I think this may assist people who are unfamiliar with Aboriginal English.

When him been start, that Captain Cook, still thinking about to get more land. From London and Big England, that's his country. Lotta man in Big England, and they start there and looking for nother land. And get the sailing boat and get a lotta people and have a look at it: Australia. And when that Captain Cook been come through down to Sydney Harbour, well he's the one been hit the Sydney Harbour. And lotta people, lotta women, lotta children, they're owning that city. That's his country. And he don't askem, that man. Too frightened. He never look whitefella coming longa his place and start a fight. And he don't askem for land. He don't say 'good day'. No. He say to him, ask him, 'this your country?' 'Yeah, this my country.' 'Ah, yeah!' He didn't askem really. 'Pretty country,' Captain Cook reckoned. 'It's a good country. Any more people around here?' 'Yeah, plenty people round here in Sydney Harbour!' That mob still in the bush, looking for a bit of fish and tucker. And lot of food old people getem.

He got a bit of jetty. And putem out those people, takem out them guns, and bullock, and man. And roll up all his swag and a bit of food, everything. Captain Cook been shooting there for, I think, nearly three weeks' time. Shooting all, all the people. Women get shot, kids been get knocked out. That means Captain Cook getting ready for the country, going to try to take it away. But he's the one been start up shooting them there now. Three weeks' time and pack his gear and put it in the sailing boat and keep going right round follow the sea. Every pocket him go in and have a look around on another people. Same thing. Shooting right round like that and every pocket some fellow been running away.

When him got to Darwin, that's the biggest place. Lot of people been there, another people. He's belong to Darwin mob. People been born in this country. Whatever building up in Darwin now, he belong to Aboriginal. Darwin only been sit down no house, nothing. There the people been havem lotta food again. Lotta fish and lotta tucker. Getembad [get], people been getembad anything, crocodile, anything. Makembad [make] spear. And Captain Cook come up, see that old fellow sit down makembad spear there, hunting fish. And he don't ask him. Same thing. Ask him one bit of a story: 'By Christ, that's good land here. Your country, it's big one? Many people around here?' 'Oh, lotta people round here. We big mob people here,' he said. 'Big big mob Aboriginal people. This we country. We never look whitefella come through here. That's first time you coming. We can be ready for you. Got a big mob spear. We don't want whitefella!' He start to hear that story. Captain Cook been hear that story. 'Get ready for this, old fellow. We might start here!' [He] Start to put the bullet in the magazine, start to shooting people, same like Sydney. And everything: 'Really beautiful country,' Captain Cook reckoned. 'That's why I'm cleaning up people, take it away. And after that I'm going to sailing boat, pack up gear, and gone [keep going, enjoy freedom of movement].' He gone every bit of pocket and leave that sailing boat there and walk around. He might see two or four or six people on that country. Country for that every one of them people. Captain Cook been jealous [envious]. And he clean up and they been come running around.

When him been shooting and going back, straight back. Follow that sea right around again. Right over to Sydney Harbour. Straight back. Captain Cook reckoned, 'I been want to clean that people right up. That's good country. I like to put my building there. I like to put my horses there. I like to put my cattle there. I going to take all my book to make a bit of an office in Sydney Harbour.'

All right. When him been start to building Sydney Harbour, that means he get all the books from London, Big England. Bring a lot of man, coming back again and bring lotta horse and lotta man longa big sailing boat. Loading boat. Bring lotta horse and bring lotta rifle, bullock.

'When that people been settle down, if you can see people little bit cheeky [hostile], you might be hitem them. And if you ready, all right, come up with the horses. Some of them no good, fight for land!' They been fight for land. No good whitefella come up here, he'll have to reckon with these blackfellas. And some of those whitefellas been get a spear [killed by it]. That's one big country longa Northern Territory. They been get a spear. When that old people come up, gotem horse, and that Captain Cook been sendem over. Sendem over here shooting lotta people. Some couldn't get a man, followem up, and that's why these Aboriginal people make an army. They been shooting all over, people gotem horse. Horse been galloping all over Australia, hunting all those people. Still, people been running away, still. Can't catch up. Horse can't gallop over rough place or them caves. And this country, sandstone country, people been plantem meself [hiding themselves] there.

That's right. We been ready for whitefellas all right. They don't wantem come up whitefellas through here. And they been really, really cranky [angry], my people. They been knock some of them whitefellas now straight away. Hitem with spear, killem. They been fight whitefella. Blackfella been fight, and another whitefella been shot the whole lot. Because they been have a spear, and whitefella been have a rifle. That been beat him. If whitefella been come up got no bit of a gun, couldn't been roundem up, killing all the people. They never been give him fair go. I know Captain Cook been little bit wrong for these people. 'This no more blackfella country. No more. Belong to me fellow [it's our] country,' he said. That means, to bring all buildings, houses. They bring all the buildings now. 'I'm going to put my place. Anywhere I can put him.' He start to put this station. Him bring lotta book from Big England right here now. They got that book for Captain Cook from England. And that's his law, book belong Captain Cook, they bring it Sydney Harbour. And lotta government got it in there from Big England.

Gilruth,[2] he's the one been in Darwin, nother government bloke took over from Captain Cook. Lotta man there, man from Big England. Same book he been havem. And that Captain Cook, when them two stations [Darwin and Sydney] been get big enough, that means all belong to Captain Cook.

Right. And my people been start to work around, old people. And really frighten for the white people coming from Big England. They didn't ask. And they been really, really sad, poor buggers. And when that Gilruth, well Gilruth [had] the same book from the Captain Cook. All right. Anybody sick, anybody sick in the guts or in the head, Captain Cook orders: Don't give him medicine. 'Don't give him medicine. When they getting crook [sick] old people, you killem him first. When they on the job, that's right, you can have them on the job. But don't payem him. Let him work for free. While we run that station. Any children come round, you can have the stockman killem him. We'll still hold that people and don't letem go. Any man come sick, boy, anything like that, blind man, don't give him medicine. You take him in a dry gully and knock him [kill him]. And after that, women, women got a bit of a baby, don't let him grow that baby. Just kill that baby. And whatever man been work, people round there eating tucker, tucker with the kerosene, flour with the kerosene [food placed in discarded kerosene tins]' ....

And still that book never finish. He still belong to Gilruth and Gilruth been have that book from Captain Cook. That's why grow along and building up. And that man, this one Gilruth, said to all the people, Aboriginal: 'This not your land. This mine. This here my building. Here my cattle and horse. This

---

[2] John Anderson Gilruth, first Commonwealth Administrator of the Northern Territory, (1912–19).

my land.' Really, belong to him [Aboriginal people], it's just for Aboriginal. But that book was go new way, coverem over.

Same book. Not only one book, book all over. And he still got it today. Sort of a, cut at one end [truncated]. But still we got it today. But I think that was finished now for the Captain Cook. And belong to Gilruth. That time been gone. It's finished now. But really, it [the land] belongs to Aboriginal people. Captain Cook and Gilruth, that two fellow been on Darwin, been on Sydney Harbour, all right. I think you two fellow been stealing this country. You, Captain Cook, and Gilruth. They really crook men. Steal it and make it them land. Because why Gilruth didn't ask them what people been live over to Darwin. And Captain Cook went longa Sydney Harbour and people been live over there. And why didn't you ask them? You, Captain Cook, when you come through. When that Captain Cook been bring you bit of a man in Darwin, put your manager, company. Because I know you Gilruth, in Darwin. He's the manager. I think they been take the wrong book. Steal. Kill my people no reason. You, Captain Cook, and Gilruth, you kill my people. You been look around, see the land now. People been here, really got their own culture. All around Australia. Really Australia, because Aboriginal people with different, different language. Different, different language, lot of people.

And right up to Gurindji now we remember for you two fellow Captain Cook and Gilruth. I know. Why didn't you look after London and Big England? Why didn't you stop your government, Captain Cook? You're the one been bring him out now, all your government from Big England. You been bring that law. My law only one. Your law keep changing. I know you keep changing lotta law. You, Captain Cook, you the one been bringing in new lotta man. Why didn't you give me fair go for my people? Why didn't you give it me fair go? Should have askem about the story. Same thing, I might go on another place, I must askem. I might stay for couple of days. You know. That's for the me fellow Aboriginal people. But you, Captain Cook, I know you been stealing country belong to me fellow. Australia, what we call Australia, that's for Aboriginal people. But him been take it away. You been take that land, you been take the mineral, take the gold, everything. Take it up to this Big England.

Select Bibliography

BAIN ATTWOOD and FIONA MAGOWAN, eds, *Telling Stories: Indigenous History and Memory in Australia and New Zealand* (Sydney, 2001).

CHRIS HEALY, *From the Ruins of Colonialism: History as Social Memory* (Cambridge, 1997).

ERICH KOLIG, 'Captain Cook in the Western Kimberley', in R. M. and C. H. Berndt, eds, *Aborigines of the West, Their Past and Their Present* (Perth, 1981), pp. 274–82.

CHIPS MACKINOLTY and PADDY WAINBURRANGA, 'Too Many Captain Cooks', in Tony Swain and Deborah Bird Rose, eds, *Aboriginal Australians and Christian Missions* (Adelaide, 1988), pp. 355–56.

DEBORAH BIRD ROSE, 'The Saga of Captain Cook: Morality in Aboriginal and European Law', *Australian Aboriginal Studies*, no. 2 (1984), pp. 24–39.

—— *Hidden Histories: Black Stories from Victoria River Downs, Humbert River, and Wave Hill Stations, North Australia* (Canberra, 1991).

—— *Dingo Makes Us Human: Life and Land in an Australian Aboriginal Culture* (Cambridge, 1992).

—— 'Ned Kelly Died for Our Sins', *Oceania*, Vol. 65, no. 2 (1994), pp. 175–86.

2

Conquest

ALAN ATKINSON[1]

The continent and islands of Australia were claimed for the British Empire in an interlinked chain of ritual—of military drill, gold braid, and parchment—extending over more than fifty years.

On 22 August 1770 James Cook, commander of HMS *Endeavour* and one of the world's great explorers, having travelled northward along the entire east coast of the mainland to the tip of Cape York, hoisted the British flag on Possession Island and claimed all the territory he had seen in the name of King George III. Then, on 12 October 1786, Cook's claim was reinforced by the King himself, when he commissioned a Governor, Captain Arthur Phillip, for this remote part of the world, a region which—so it was thought—no other European had so far seen. According to Phillip's commission, the King's government was to extend over two-thirds of the continent (then known as New Holland), from the east coast to the 135th degree of longitude, and include 'all the islands adjacent in the Pacific Ocean'.[2] This was a vast space of earth and water, and largely unknown. When Pope Alexander VI divided the New World between Spain and Portugal, in 1494, his effort had been only a little more abstract.

Governor Phillip made the next move in this dance of appropriation when, on 26 January 1788, having landed at Sydney Cove, Port Jackson, within the new territory of New South Wales, he raised the flag, took the prescribed oaths, and began the process by which a British population was to make a living from the soil.

The western half of New Holland was still unclaimed, but in 1826 a settlement was formed from Sydney at King George Sound, on its south

---

[1] Bain Attwood and David Andrew Roberts kindly read and commented on this chapter.

[2] Arthur Phillip's first commission, 12 October 1786, *Historical Records of Australia* (hereafter *HRA*), 1st series, Vol. 1, p. 1. Phillip's second and permanent commission, 2 April 1787, used the same description (ibid., p. 2).

coast, and in 1829 another, from Britain itself, was laid out along the lower reaches of the Swan River, on the west. Finally, in 1832, the Governor at Swan River was given a commission from the Crown like Phillip's. His rule was to extend far beyond the likely reach of settlement for many years to come, up to the 129th degree (altered from the 135th degree in 1825), the boundary of his brother-Governor in Sydney. This completed the British appropriation of Australia.

Or rather, it completed it in theory. The real conquest of the country and its people took many generations more. Ten years after the Federation of the Australian colonies the journalist and historian Charles Bean remarked that much of the centre of the continent could not 'reasonably be called Australia … The law of Australia is just about as applicable there', he said, 'as at Timbuktu'.[3] Frontier battles, involving serious loss of life, continued as late as the 1920s. The last Indigenous community to live in full independence, the Pintupi people of the Western Desert, only began to move onto government reserves in the 1940s. As for the land itself, new species of indigenous plants and wildlife, and truly long-term methods of management, were still being discovered in the early years of the twenty-first century. It is well known that the independence of the country, as a nation-state, has been a gradual process, the work of three generations or more. The same is true of its conquest, which in a sense still continues.

And yet the dance of ritual has sometimes seemed to be all that matters. Especially during the twentieth century, stories of the Australian past were often told as if all the blood and trouble were cancelled by a single shining moment—when Cook raised the flag on Possession Island or when Phillip took the oaths at Sydney Cove. Cook, Phillip, and those who came after them, belonged to a cartographic age, an age when maps were beginning to be familiar at least to educated Europeans, and when common cartographic knowledge was vastly extending the range of European thought. Such imaginative power simplified dreams of territory. As a result, the conquest of Australia has sometimes seemed as easy as the sketching or colouring of a map.

There had been considerable overseas exploration by Europeans since the fifteenth century. Stories of these remote parts of the world were in wide circulation in Europe, but mainly in anecdotal and mythical form. However, it was one thing to be entertained by exotic information from

---

[3] C. E. W. Bean, *The 'Dreadnought' of the Darling* (London, 1911), p. 4.

abroad and quite another to use it as a means of conquest and control.[4]
Only a few skilled in the use of maps could think of them as a means of
managing remote places. Geography was not commonly taught in European
schools and the small number of children who learnt it did not often see
their subject matter laid out in cartographic form. Until the early nineteenth
century, maps were made by the expensive process of engraving, so that
they were not often drawn and published, and they were even less frequently
updated.[5] Narratives and lists of places were much more commonly used
by the teachers of geography. As a result, Australia (*Terra Australis*) was
not a delineated territory but a place of fable. It was a land as vague and
insubstantial as the 'Big England' that Hobbles Danaiyarri spoke of in his
account of Captain Cook. It might be wondered at, but it could hardly be
conquered, even in dreams.

Only from about the 1820s, with advances in lithography, was the making
of maps cheap enough for them to become, in theory, part of the curriculum
in schools. Among large numbers of educated individuals, imagination
began to be shaped by maps, and some of the ordinary problems of life
were considered from a cartographic point of view—as if from the serene
and predatory perspective of the eagle. Hitherto cartography had been
useful mainly for long-range commercial and military purposes. Now it
began to shape a great variety of far-sighted activity, from the creation
of steam-transport networks to the planning of town water and sewerage.
Weather maps were still to come—perhaps the supreme example of the
way daily experience might be broadcast to the mass in cartographic form.
These were the law and lore of the colonial invader. They were all 'books'
in Hobbles Danaiyarri's terms: 'Same book. Not only one book, book
all over.' Mapping became in itself an act of conquest, a declaration of
appropriation.

In his pamphlet *A Letter from Sydney* (1829), Edward Gibbon Wakefield
showed how intellectual authority might be underwritten by cartographic
literacy. In a fictional account of his leaving England for Australia, Wakefield

---

[4] J. B. Harley, 'Maps, Knowledge, and Power', in Denis Cosgrove and Stephen Daniels, eds,
*The Iconography of Landscape: Essays on the Symbolic Representation, Design and Use of Past
Environments* (Cambridge, 1988), pp. 277–312.

[5] Ibid., pp. 280–3; Avril M. C. Maddrell, 'Discourses of Race and Gender and the Comparative
Method in Geography School Texts 1830–1918', *Environment and Planning D: Society and Space*,
16 (1998), pp. 84–7; Anne Coote, 'Space, Time and Sovereignty: Literate Culture and Colonial
Nationhood in New South Wales up to 1860', Ph.D. thesis (University of New England, 2004),
pp. 163–6.

told of explaining his destination to his grandmother. He showed her a world map.

'Why,' she ... [said], 'it is terribly out of the way—down in the very right hand corner of the world'. The chart being mine, I cut it in two through the meridian of Iceland, transposed the parts laterally, and turned them upside down. 'Now,' I asked, 'where is England?' 'Ah! boy,' she replied; 'you may do what you like with the map; but you can't twist the world about in that manner, though they *are* making sad changes in it.'[6]

Those who were making the 'sad changes' most effectively were those who knew how to read and interpret maps, not only through careful training but also, ideally, by walking over the ground with paper in hand. Wakefield himself was a theorist. And yet he was to be one of the leading exponents of what was called 'systematic colonization'—the settling of communities within well-defined and carefully subdivided spaces. This was an approach used during the 1830s, especially in South Australia and New Zealand, but cartographic skill everywhere informed the first stages of the conquest of Australia.

*   *   *

To begin with, in 1788 it still seemed possible that the settlement at Port Jackson might be positioned on some massive archipelago. The discovery of Bass Strait in 1798, by George Bass and Matthew Flinders, showed that there were at least two quantities of dry land, one large and one small, the latter being Van Diemen's Land, or Tasmania, but further expeditions by Flinders revealed no more intervening seas. Others made themselves gradually familiar with the coastline and interior.

Conquest was not only the work of government. Whaling and sealing had begun from Sydney as early as the 1790s and as the trade flourished miscellaneous individuals began to live for long periods, or even for good, throughout the waters to the south and south-west, on Kangaroo Island, the islands of Bass Strait, and the south-west coast of New Zealand. Others began to understand how to live in the bush. In 1798 John Wilson, an ex-convict bushman, led a party south-west over the Blue Mountains to within sight of the Goulburn Plains, an extraordinary achievement which pre-dated by

---

[6] Edward Gibbon Wakefield, 'A Letter from Sydney', in *A Letter from Sydney and Other Writings* (London, 1929), pp. 54–5.

fifteen years the more famous crossing of the gentlemen-settlers Gregory Blaxland, William Lawson, and W. C. Wentworth.[7]

From 1788 Australia was a place of transportation for British and Irish convicts. For some of them the Antipodean landscape was a prison wall, but for others it was a means of escape. Transportation was itself a lesson in geography, and the way convicts came to terms with new spaces and distances helps to explain the process of conquest. It was impossible to subdue the country without knowing how to live in it. Irish convicts were especially keen to escape and, given the fact that on average they were less literate than the English, they were probably even more ignorant of the way they were shut in by distance. Large numbers thought they were within walking distance of China. There was also talk of a land inhabited by 'a copper-coloured people, who would receive and treat them kindly', and many died in the bush trying to find it.[8]

Though unsure about its shape and size, some convicts seem to have had a strong sense of Australia as a British space. In order to escape they made for the East Indies, the nearest region governed by a foreign but still European power. In 1791 a party of eleven, including a woman (Mary Braund or Bryant) and two children, set sail up the east coast. A number were seamen, and they managed to reach the Dutch settlement on Timor, but only the woman and four men survived to see England. In 1794 a party of Irish made a similar plan to get to Batavia (now Jakarta) in a stolen longboat, but they were caught before they could leave. Such hopes were long-lived. Charles Sturt, the explorer, tells of two Irish convicts who, in 1829, set off from one of the western inland settlements of New South Wales with a fortnight's provisions and headed for Timor.[9]

Growing acquaintance with the bush led many to think of it as a place of liberty. Convict stockmen working in remote parts might use

[7] Chris Cunningham, *The Blue Mountains Rediscovered: Beyond the Myths of Early Australian Exploration* (Sydney, 1996), pp. 78–85.

[8] John Hunter to Duke of Portland, 15 February 1798, *HRA*, 1st series, Vol. 2, p. 129; David Collins, *An Account of the English Colony in New South Wales*, ed. Brian H. Fletcher (Sydney, 1975; first pub. 1798, 1802), Vol. 1, pp. 154–5, 304; Watkin Tench, *A Complete Account of the Settlement at Port Jackson* (first pub. 1793), in L. F. Fitzhardinge, ed., *Sydney's First Four Years* (Sydney, 1979), pp. 243–4, 246.

[9] Collins, *An Account of the English Colony*, Vol. 1, pp. 126–30, 309; Charles Sturt, *Two Expeditions into the Interior of Southern Australia*, 2 Vols. (London, 1833), Vol. 1, p. 114; C. H. Currey, *The Transportation, Escape and Pardoning of Mary Bryant* (Sydney, 1963); Cunningham, *The Blue Mountains Rediscovered*, pp. 58–61.

the term 'inside' for the Sydney district. Being 'outside' the main area of settlement made them relatively free. According to a rural magistrate, escapees 'almost invariably follow the Abercrombie and the Lachlan [Rivers], to the Murrumbidgee'. In other words, they used the southern and western flowing streams as a highway to the frontier, where law and order were less in evidence.[10]

These people themselves had to be reconquered by the imperial state. In 1794 some former convicts took up land in the rich valley of the Hawkesbury, beyond the existing limits of the Port Jackson settlement. '[T]hey did not care for the Governor', they said, 'or the Orders of the colony—they were free men, and wou'd do as they pleas'd'. In fact, they relied on the government for title to their land and for protection against the Dharug people, and they were soon drawn within the official embrace.[11] However, escaped convicts living in the bush were a constant challenge to government. In Van Diemen's Land the reach of the Crown was limited during the first fifteen years, while bushrangers moved about in gangs, living off the land and trading vast quantities of kangaroo skins. Their most famous chief, Michael Howe, addressing the Lieutenant-Governor in Hobart, called himself 'Lieutenant-Governor of the Woods'. Like an independent ruler, he relied, he said, on divine favour and public opinion. In Howe's time the process of conquest in Van Diemen's Land seemed to hang in the balance, with fears that the convicts might shortly desert to him en masse.[12]

As late as the 1830s Kangaroo Island, and some of the islands of Bass Strait, were inhabited by small, independent communities of White men. They captured Aboriginal women, lived off fish and wildlife, and traded in skins. On Kangaroo Island, Henry Wallen, a former seaman, called himself 'Governor'; 'and to his rule', so it was said, 'the others yielded such obedience as was necessary in so primitive a state of society'.[13] About the same time,

[10] W. H. Dutton, evidence before committee on police and gaols, 9 June 1835, NSW Legislative Council Votes and Proceedings, 1824–37, p. 335; William Hobbs, evidence during the first inquiry into the Myall Creek massacre, 30 July 1838, Archives Office of NSW 4/5601.

[11] Hunter to Portland, 20 June 1797, HRA, 1st series, Vol. 2, p. 23; Alan Atkinson, The Europeans in Australia: A History, Vol. 1 (Melbourne, 1997), pp. 171–2.

[12] Thomas Seals, evidence, 10 July 1816, and Michael Howe and others to Thomas Davey, [November 1816], HRA, 3rd series, Vol. 2, pp. 162–3, 643–4; Atkinson, The Europeans in Australia: A History, Vol. 2 (Melbourne, 2004), pp. 69–71.

[13] W. H. Leigh, Reconnoitering Voyages, Travels and Adventures in the New Colonies of South Australia (London, 1839), pp. 124–6.

pastoralists in the Port Phillip district similarly argued, 'we are on the border and can do as we like.'[14]

Such communities were absorbed by the state with minimal violence. And yet the long-term process of conquest—even the conquest of White men—sometimes seemed uncertain. The British government was now satisfied that its claim to the entire continent was good in international law, against attempts, say, by the French. But on the ground much still looked like no-man's land, free of officials and open for appropriation by the people themselves. This opinion was reinforced by the maps generally available, which implied that New South Wales, in particular, was merely the surveyed country, within the 'limits of location'.[15]

Bass Strait offered especially complicated challenges. It was an avenue for seaborne traffic and yet out of the way of government. Until the mid-1830s Launceston was its only official town and even there leading men asserted themselves against Hobart and Sydney.[16] At Launceston in 1835 the most elaborate attempt at government independent of the Crown was planned for the northern shore of Bass Strait (later Victoria), when John Pascoe Fawkner sketched the constitution of a small republic, with an elected president and council of three. In the same spirit, John Batman, acting on behalf of a party of local entrepreneurs, sought to make an independent treaty with the Wurundjeri people, bordering Port Phillip, aiming to secure title in the land, not from the Crown but from its ancient owners. However, the Governor in Sydney asserted his own authority, republican hopes vanished, and the treaty was overridden.[17]

＊　＊　＊

Independence at the outskirts of settlement deeply compromised the way the business of conquest was understood. Thomas Livingston Mitchell was both an energetic explorer and surveyor-general of New South Wales. And

[14] G. A. Robinson, n.d. (1845–8), quoted in Henry Reynolds, *Frontier: Aborigines, Settlers and Land* (Sydney, 1986), p. 52.

[15] Coote, 'Space, Time and Sovereignty', pp. 167–80. Here I am much indebted to Anne Coote's work.

[16] J. E. Calder, 'Early Troubles of the Colonists' (pub. *Mercury* (Hobart), 17, 27 November 1873), collected in the Mitchell Library, Sydney, as 'Scraps of Tasmanian History', Vol. 1, p. 202; Atkinson, *The Europeans in Australia*, Vol. 2, p. 69.

[17] John Pascoe Fawkner, 'Constitution and Form of Government', n.d. (*c.* 1835), State Library of Victoria, La Trobe MS 13273; Atkinson, *The Europeans in Australia*, Vol. 2, pp. 145–6, 159–61.

yet, he too failed to imagine that the British dominion which centred on Sydney included everything westward to the 129th degree. He crossed what he described as the boundary of 'the colony' as he travelled north-west over the Liverpool Range, at the head of the Hunter valley. He and his men then became, as he put it, 'rather unceremonious invaders of [Aboriginal] … country'.[18]

This view was inconsistent with the maps in Downing Street. In our own day, it clashes with long-standing historical tradition. The fundamental myths of Australian nationhood include stories, or at least assumptions, about an original vast vacancy and its almost instantaneous possession by a single, united people. The dazzling image of a pristine, sun-lit space to which only agents and subjects of the British Crown might lay claim dates from the beginning of settlement, and the legal term 'terra nullius' has been used by historians to pinpoint the common belief, obvious in the words and actions of colonial administrators, that this was a land hitherto belonging to no one.[19] 'Terra nullius' encapsulates a legal fiction, but its origins also lie in a certain cartographic understanding, in the type of knowledge expressed by maps as distinct from grounded knowledge, whereas schemes such as Fawkner's and Batman's, and language such as Mitchell's, were thoroughly anchored in the soil. In fact, all settlers knew that, whatever the theory of Empire, they had to beat back the current owners of the land, its Indigenous people.

Ideas of vacancy, and of instantaneous possession, were especially potent during the first two-thirds of the twentieth century, the age of Australian nation-building. Unity and the assimilation of difference were then all-important. During the first century of settlement, on the other hand, it was a patent fact that conquest was unfinished.

Conquest involved copious bloodshed, but it was also an intellectual effort, and this intermixture of violence and enlightenment is one of the most remarkable aspects of Australian history. During the first decades, there were numerous men and women of high intellectual pretensions in and around the capital towns, especially Sydney. Arthur Phillip and several of his young officers (David Collins, William Dawes, John White, Watkin Tench) had come in a spirit of intellectual adventure. During the 1820s and

---

[18] T. L. Mitchell, *Three Expeditions into the Interior of Eastern Australia* (London, 1839), Vol. 1, pp. 217, 247.

[19] Henry Reynolds, *The Law of the Land* (Ringwood, Vic., 1987); Bain Attwood, 'The Law of the Land or the Law of the Land?: History, Law and Narrative in a Settler Society', *History Compass*, 2 (2004), pp. 1–30.

1830s a professional class began to form in all of the colonies and policy was mediated by meticulous public debate. Nearly all the Governors were men of ideas and several Governors' wives—Anna King, Elizabeth Macquarie, Eliza Darling, Jane Franklin—did work of social and cultural importance. Government surgeons, surveyors, and clergy were active agents in shaping local policy. Penal administration on such a large scale posed moral, legal, and logistical challenges new to British experience and important for the whole business of settlement.

Newspaper editors now made it their business to tackle complex public issues. In Sydney, Edward Smith Hall's *Monitor* (1826–41) was one of the most widely read papers in the Australian colonies.[20] Hall wrote of an 'extirpating war' and of a country which was by no means vacant. Like any kingdom in Europe, it had what he called its 'ancient proprietors', and yet, as he said, 'we ... treat their laws with derision, violate all their national prejudices, and exasperate them at our pleasure.'

What would our Readers say [he asked] if we were to state, that a Black of intelligence, *acting as a Constable*, was, upon a mere suspicion of having taken part in the war, and because he could not give certain information which our English butchers *presumed* he could give, was ... tied hand and foot, and thrown into a pond, where he perished! If this be true is not our land defiled with blood?

Thus, while he talked of 'English butchers', Hall also appealed to English humanity and justice.[21] He constructed for his colonial readers a world of considerable moral complexity.

At this point, in 1826, Hall seems to have thought that justice was still possible. Twenty years later Alexander Harris, an observer with similar principles, was much less optimistic. 'The blacks cannot be conciliated', said Harris, 'unless by giving up their country.'[22] During the 1820s and 1830s, in short—a period of continuously expanding settlement and continuous public debate—it became clear that the conquerors, for all their idealism, had to shed blood and live with hatred.

On the one hand, the government and the settlers worked from a position of extraordinary strength, using a degree of military and technological power which the Indigenous people could hardly begin to imagine. Capable

---

[20] Erin Ihde, *A Manifesto for New South Wales: Edward Smith Hall and the Sydney Monitor 1826–1840* (Melbourne, 2004).

[21] *Monitor* (Sydney), 2 June 1826 (original emphasis).

[22] Alexander Harris, *Settlers and Convicts: Recollections of Sixteen Years' Labour in the Australian Backwoods* (Melbourne, 1953; first pub. 1847), p. 222.

of reaching beyond the horizon of both time and place, of debating each frontier within the context of Empire, the British easily believed that they were responsible for the welfare of the communities they encountered. From the beginning the Governors were ordered to protect the property of 'the natives': 'And if any of our subjects shall wantonly destroy them, or give them any unnecessary interruption in the exercize of their several occupations, it is our will and pleasure that you do cause such offenders to be brought to punishment according to the degree of the offence.'[23] These original instructions distinguished between 'our subjects' and the Aborigines. However, by the 1820s all the inhabitants of British territory in Australia, both Black and White, were officially deemed to be British. All were as much entitled to the benefits of British law and order as the inhabitants of Britain itself.

On the other hand, the intellectual challenge was deeply complicated by the fact that the imaginative range of the Blacks overlapped very little with that of the newcomers. Aboriginal notions of conquest were straightforward. Many put themselves in a position to kill and be killed, as Hall remarked, in defence of 'their laws', 'their national prejudices', their land, and their way of life.

Governor Phillip himself had been anxious to maintain good relations with the Aborigines. He was genuinely interested in them as a people who might benefit from the European presence. However, the settlement was his main responsibility, and the spearing of his own servant, John McEntyre, in December 1790, forced him to act in its defence. He ordered a party of soldiers to go in search of some of the Eora of Botany Bay who were thought to be responsible, and to kill ten. Hatchets and bags were supplied so that the desired number of heads might be brought back. In anxious self-justification, Phillip explained himself at length to Watkin Tench, who was in charge of the expedition. He had used no violence so far, he said, in spite of seventeen Whites having been killed by Blacks, but 'against this tribe he was determined to strike a decisive blow, in order, at once to convince them of our superiority, and to infuse an universal terror, which might operate to prevent further mischief'.[24]

Tench easily persuaded him that it would be better to capture six, and then execute two. But no one showed much warlike purpose. Tench and his men went out twice without success, and the project was dropped.[25] In 1792

---

[23] Governor Phillip's Instructions, 25 April 1787, *HRA*, 1st series, Vol. 1, pp. 13–14.

[24] Tench, *A Complete Account*, pp. 207–8.

[25] 'Comments by Governor Phillip', n.d., enclosed with Phillip to Lord Grenville, 7 November 1791, *HRA*, 1st series, Vol. 1, p. 294; Tench, *A Complete Account*, pp. 208–15.

garrison duties passed from the Marines to the New South Wales Corps, whose officers were less idealistic. Also, settlement was now spreading quickly beyond the immediate control of government. David Collins spoke of 'open war ... between the natives and the settlers'. Troops were stationed on the Hawkesbury valley frontier, and there the Dharug developed systematic methods of harassment, not only attacking the settlers but destroying buildings, crops, and other property.[26] And yet the Governors, one after the other, continued to believe that they were duty-bound to limit the damage involved in conquest. Aware of the lawlessness of convict and ex-convict men living on the frontier, they easily concluded that the Blacks were not always to blame.

Lachlan Macquarie was Governor from 1810 to 1821. He thought of the Aborigines as a category of the King's subjects similar to the Highlanders of his native Scotland. He began annual Christmas-time conferences with them, he established a school where their children might learn the rudiments of English civilization, and he was the first Governor to hang a White man for killing a Black.[27] However, he was also the first to launch a proper military campaign on Australian soil. By April 1816 there was trouble to the south as well as to the west, among Dharug, Tharawal, and Gundungurra, and detachments of light infantry were sent out. Each side now appreciated the skills of the other. British soldiers had become better bushmen, moving more quickly and using guides and mounted messengers. They won only one skirmish, at Appin, near Campbelltown, where seven Aboriginal men were killed. But nothing could make Macquarie think in narrowly defensive terms. No Governor since Phillip had such an expansive idea of his own authority—such a map-based imagination—and the Blacks remained for him individuals within the King's dominion. His soldiers were told 'to Punish the guilty with as little injury as possible to the innocent', and they were given a list of named men whom they were entitled to capture or kill.[28]

Macquarie's tactics even included an order to the Indigenous people to stop fighting among themselves, 'not only at and near the British Settlements but also in their own wild and remote Places of Resort'. Similarly, in July

---

[26] Collins, *An Account of the English Colony*, Vol. 1, p. 348; John Connor, *The Australian Frontier Wars 1788–1838* (Sydney, 2002), pp. 38–42.

[27] *Sydney Gazette*, 16 and 23 December 1820; Christine Bramble, 'Relations between Aborigines and White Settlers in Newcastle and the Hunter District', B.Litt. thesis (University of New England, 1981), pp. 41–3.

[28] Connor, *The Australian Frontier Wars*, pp. 49–52 (Lachlan Macquarie to W. J. B. Schaw, 9 April 1816, quoted p. 49).

he issued a proclamation against 'certain *Banditti* or *Tribes* of the *Black Natives*', outlawing ten men among them.[29] He apparently imagined that at every campfire and along every bush-track, from Port Phillip to Cape York, legitimacy belonged to the Crown alone.

This sweeping approach took its most sophisticated Australian form in the mind of Saxe Bannister, Attorney General of New South Wales 1824–6. Bannister belonged to a family of Empire idealists. His brother, Thomas, as sheriff of Van Diemen's Land, was an associate of John Batman in his attempts to settle Port Phillip. In that scheme, said Thomas Bannister, the aim was 'not possession and expulsion, or what is worse extermination, but possession and civilization'. It was 'the only chance for the natives'. By treating them as rational beings, capable of engaging with the settler economy on their own terms, he and his colleagues aimed, he said, to 'substitute real benefits for them, in the place of the *verbal* benevolence heretofore bestowed'.[30]

Saxe Bannister paid considerable attention to 'real benefits'. His mind was keenly exercised by the way in which conquest might be a means of good and he thought in terms of individual grievances and benefits. We must, he said, be 'just at every step'—just in spreading and absorbing ideas, just in offering opportunity, just in all matters of commercial engagement, employment, and landed property. In his reading about the colonization of North America he had 'shuddered', as he put it, 'with indignation and sorrow upon hearing accounts ... of the barbarous personal tyranny' suffered by the original inhabitants. In New South Wales he found 'frequent and gross injustice' in dealings with the Blacks: 'common right, in matters of life and death, ... constantly outraged, by our neglecting the plainest principles of equity'.[31]

As Attorney General, Bannister was behind the decision by Governor Brisbane, in August 1824, to declare martial law on the frontier around

---

[29] Governor Macquarie, proclamation, 4 May, 20 July 1816, *HRA*, 1st series, Vol. 9, pp. 143, 362 (original emphasis).

[30] Thomas Bannister, Memoranda, 1835, and Thomas Bannister to Sir Charles Burrell, 22 June–3 July 1835, Bannister Papers, 45–51 (original emphasis), State Library of Victoria; Thomas Bannister to George Arthur, 8 December 1835, and Arthur to Sir Richard Bourke, 13 January 1836, *Historical Records of Victoria*, Vol. 1, pp. 21–2.

[31] 'Philadelphus' [Saxe Bannister], *Remarks on the Indians of North America, in a Letter to an Edinburgh Reviewer* (London, 1822), p. 31; Saxe Bannister, *Humane Policy: Or Justice to the Aborigines of New Settlements Essential to a Due Expenditure of British Money, and to the Best Interests of the Settlers* (London, 1830), pp. 2–3, 7, 40–1, 81, 87, 162.

Bathurst. Brisbane's proclamation was designed to authorize 'summary justice' and 'the Use of Arms against the Natives beyond the ordinary Rule of Law in Time of Peace'. And yet its broader purpose was to stop 'mutual bloodshed', including 'the Slaughter of Black Women and Children and unoffending White Men'. The government was to act with maximum force, not in order to wage war against aliens but to prevent grievous personal injury to both Black and White. The moral and legal bases of this step were carefully explained in the body of the proclamation: 'the Shedding of Blood is only just, when all other Means of Defence or of Peace are exhausted; … Cruelty is never Lawful; and … when personal Attacks become necessary, the helpless Women and Children are to be spared.'[32] Governor Macquarie, in his efforts to establish peace, had attempted to draw a more precise line between the guilty and the innocent. Bannister seems to have thought this impossible. Under martial law all Aboriginal men, whatever their known behaviour, were to be legitimate targets. He envisaged brief violence, including a type of justice which was sweeping and summary, for the sake of a long-term, general peace. Such peace would guarantee fair dealing among individuals of all kinds.

Bannister was prepared to interrupt justice 'at every step' in order to ensure, in the end, the common citizenship of Black and White, and Brisbane seems to have been persuaded by his logic. However, Brisbane's successor, Governor Darling, thought it unnecessary to use such complicated methods 'to put down a few naked Savages', and martial law was not used again on the mainland for such purposes.[33] Bannister's was a generalizing, imperial, and intellectual perspective. Idealism like his might well have existed among other high-minded men and women on the ground, but it seldom survived the fear and brutality involved in frontier violence. According to Tacitus, in his account of the Roman conquest of Britain, 'new manners … sweeten slavery'.[34] Many Aborigines had not yet learnt this fact. As long as they saw fit to resist, there was a fundamental contradiction between the idea of justice 'at every step' and the ongoing conquest of Australia.

* * *

[32] Proclamation of martial law, 14 August 1824, enclosed with Sir Thomas Brisbane to Earl Bathurst, 2 November 1824, *HRA*, 1st series, Vol. 11, pp. 410–11.

[33] Ralph Darling to Bathurst, 6 October 1826, *HRA*, 1st series, Vol. 12, p. 609.

[34] Tacitus, 'The Life of Cnaeus Julius Agricola', in *Tacitus: Historical Works*, 2 (trans. Arthur Murphy) (London, 1908), pp. 366–7.

Saxe Bannister relied on military power. Justice, he said, depended on peace, and peace often depended on 'the Government putting forth an overwhelming force'.[35] This was also the attitude of George Arthur, Governor of Van Diemen's Land in the crucial years 1824–36. During the 1820s and 1830s the numbers of convicts and free settlers arriving in eastern Australia were far greater than ever before, and land was occupied with extraordinary speed. In New South Wales, Saxe Bannister and E. S. Hall were perhaps the most trenchant commentators on this process. In Van Diemen's Land, intellectual authority belonged mainly to Arthur, an Evangelical Christian who had made his name as a military administrator. In dealing with the Aborigines, Arthur was not only an idealist and a bureaucrat but also a soldier.

It has been estimated that rather more than 187 Tasmanian settlers were killed by Aborigines between 1824 and 1831. Black fatalities were very poorly documented, but the total was probably two or three times that number. The size of the original Indigenous population is likewise unknown. However, recent estimates range from about 6,000 to a little under 2,000, and by the early 1830s, from various causes, only three or four hundred remained. Meanwhile, settler numbers had grown to more than 10,000.[36] These were the statistical dimensions of conquest in that part of Australia.

With the hope of limiting bloodshed in the long term, in November 1828 Arthur declared martial law. However, unlike the New South Wales proclamation his did not quite admit the legal equality of Black and White. It referred to 'His Majesty's Subjects' being under attack from 'the Black or Aboriginal Natives of this Island', a crucial differentiation now abandoned in Downing Street. Arthur also used geography in his own distinctive way. Brisbane's proclamation had created a state of emergency from the Blue Mountains westward, but Arthur's drew an outer rather than an inner boundary, cutting off the Tasman Peninsula, the north-east corner, and the far south and west of the island.[37] Brisbane's announcement, shaped by

[35] Saxe Bannister to Darling, 5 September 1826, *HRA*, 1st series, Vol. 12, pp. 577–8.

[36] Henry Reynolds, *Fate of a Free People: A Radical Re-Examination of the Tasmanian Wars* (Ringwood, Vic., 1995), pp. 76–82; Keith Windschuttle, *The Fabrication of Aboriginal History*, Vol. 1, *Van Diemen's Land 1803–1847* (Sydney, 2002), pp. 388–95 (Windschuttle argues for a maximum of 101 Aborigines killed, but his logic confuses maximum with minimum); James Boyce, 'Fantasy Island', Lyndall Ryan, 'Who Is the Fabricator?', and Tim Murray and Christine Williamson, 'Archaeology and History', in Robert Manne, ed., *Whitewash: On Keith Windschuttle's Fabrication of Aboriginal History* (Melbourne, 2003), pp. 32, 251–4, 314.

[37] Proclamation of martial law, 1 November 1828, enclosed with George Arthur to Sir George Murray, 4 November 1828, *HRA*, 3rd series, Vol. 7, p. 631.

Saxe Bannister, had affected Black and White together, even on the extreme frontier. Arthur's left a refuge for the Aborigines, and it might appear that in doing so he wanted to drive them beyond his own rule, back into what he conceived to be the moral and legal vacancy of their old way of life. But while the Aborigines were to be divided from the settlers, they were, of course, still within the limits of the island. They remained under Arthur's eye. Their future was to depend not on British justice in a legal sense, as Bannister might have hoped, but on something more important to Arthur—the *moral* reach of Empire. They were to rely on the humanity of administrators. This was a symbolic step of vast importance in the conquest of Australia. Far into the twentieth century we see the same variation in legal standing between Black and White.

When this plan in turn failed, Arthur applied the same principles in another way. Thirty years before, Phillip had captured three Aboriginal men with the hope of persuading them and their tribespeople about his benign intentions and unavoidable authority. Capture was a telling means of conquest. The captives were thus persuaded that all their circumstances now depended on a power far greater than their own. Capture was conquest writ small. In Van Diemen's Land in 1830, 2,200 men were organized, as the 'Black Line', to move through the centre of the island, herding the Aborigines towards the Tasman Peninsula where they were to be caught and managed as a people apart.[38] This plan also failed, and Arthur turned at last to George Augustus Robinson—a former builder who had tried his hand successfully as a local missionary. In an extraordinary effort of diplomacy, Robinson gathered up nearly all the remaining Tasmanian Aborigines (1830–1) and took them to Flinders Island, in Bass Strait, where they lived and died in the hands of government.

On the Australian mainland the frontiers were much longer and more difficult to police than they were in Van Diemen's Land. Indigenous people could hardly be captured in useful numbers in a land whose limits were so remote. Negotiation was less easily forced upon them and, for a time, some settlers placed their hopes in more open and even-handed methods, including the learning of local tongues. Saxe Bannister had thought that with a knowledge of Indigenous language would come a merging of moral and legal priorities, which he saw as a fundamental means of justice. In Western Australia the

---

[38] Lyndall Ryan, *The Aboriginal Tasmanians* (St Lucia, Qld, 1981), pp. 10–12; Reynolds, *Fate of a Free People*, pp. 114–19.

linguist Robert Menli Lyon called it 'utter folly' to try to govern conquered peoples without such understanding.[39] But the effort, bedevilled by the number of languages in existence, was beyond British patience and skill.

In theory, the law was available for ordinary emergencies. But it frequently failed. In 1840 a passenger vessel, the *Maria*, was wrecked near Lacepede Bay, in South Australia, some distance beyond the limits of settlement, and the survivors were massacred by the local people, the Milmenrura. Governor Gawler sent an expedition to enforce summary justice, and two Aboriginal men were hanged. Some in Adelaide were outraged by the execution, without proper trial, of two British subjects. Others, on the other hand, said that circumstances could make the rights of subjects irrelevant. Even the Chief Justice, Charles Cooper, took the latter approach, contradicting imperial policy as it had evolved since Macquarie's time. Cooper argued that people like the Milmenrura, in spite of living within British territory—as outlined on the map—were beyond the jurisdiction of the courts. Aborigines, he said, might be taken to be the Queen's subjects only where there was 'some submission or acquiescence on their part, or at least, some intercourse between us and them'.[40] The Milmenrura were not yet caught or conquered, in other words, and summary justice was all they could hope for.

The same principle applied in the operations of the Native Mounted Police, a force of Aboriginal men commanded by White officers which operated in northern New South Wales from the late 1840s, before being taken over by the Queensland government when that colony was established in 1859. The Native Police did not operate under martial law, and while they killed large numbers of Indigenous people over several decades, their officers were not required to give any exact account of the deaths. The victims were certainly people who had made no 'submission or acquiescence'. But within any large scheme of Empire it was hard to deny that the work of the Native Police was illegal. As a Queensland squatter remarked, to make it otherwise 'You would have to pass a law to render killing no murder'.[41] This

---

[39] Robert Lyon, 'A Glance at the Manner and Language of the Aboriginal Inhabitants of Western Australia; With a Short Vocabulary', 1833, in Neville Green, ed., *Nyungar—The People: Aboriginal Customs in the Southwest of Australia* (Perth, 1979), p. 156; Atkinson, *The Europeans in Australia*, Vol. 2, pp. 40–4.

[40] Charles Cooper's address to grand jury, *South Australian Register*, 7 November 1840; Kathleen Hassell, *The Relations Between the Settlers and Aborigines in South Australia, 1836–1860* (Adelaide, 1966), pp. 52–62.

[41] John Ker Wilson, evidence before the select committee on the Native Police Force, 18 June 1861, p. 72, Queensland Legislative Assembly Votes and Proceedings, 1861; Mark Finnane and

force was nevertheless part of the logic of conquest. From the perspective of the eagle, cartographic vacancies might be filled with justice 'at every step'. On the ground, however, at every step principles were formed by an excess of imperial power on one side and by Indigenous resistance on the other.

*   *   *

At first it seems strange that the story of European settlement in a country as large and open as Australia should be so much fraught with issues of capture and detention. Even E. G. Wakefield's scheme of 'systematic colonization' involved drawing a line on the landscape within which colonists would be happily confined. However, the British brought to Australia ideas of government that came directly from the European Enlightenment. The application of those ideas could work only within a community subject to a single power and living within obvious boundaries. It was therefore the very vastness of the country that made it important for the authorities to draw limits on its surface. And, on the other hand, its isolation, 'in the very right hand corner of the world', made the business of escape, in fact or imagination, a vital challenge.

Some of the most engaging Australian stories take up such issues. The 'crawling' shepherd, the impoverished farmer and the docile wife, are set in contrast with the bushranger and larrikin. Some of the most important arguments about Australia, since 1788, have likewise circled around questions of looking inwards on a confined order, and of looking outwards to some bright horizon. The conquest of the continent has involved making sense of a tightly governed people. But it has also involved exploring routes towards a world beyond.

Historians themselves, for instance, have argued since the 1950s about why the British government chose, in August 1786, to make Australia a place of convict transportation. Some stress the abundant evidence that ministers wanted a place of perfect isolation. The transportation of convicts to a site close to Europe would defeat its own purpose—escape would be too easy—and within the known world there were few places so remote and so little visited as New South Wales. In fact, traffic soon increased, especially from the 1820s. But a closed-in remoteness continued throughout

Jonathan Richards, ' "You'll Get Nothing Out of It"? The Inquest, Police and Aboriginal Deaths in Colonial Queensland', *Australian Historical Studies*, 123 (April 2004), pp. 84–105.

the nineteenth and most of the twentieth centuries to be one of Australia's
defining characteristics.

And yet, according to those on the other side of the debate, the original
decision is also proof of foresight and efficiency in the extension of Empire.
They argue that Sydney was meant from the beginning as a port, and that
transportation was contingent on the needs of a potentially unlimited ocean-
bound traffic. The penal settlement was meant to be efficiently linked to the
rest of the world. From this approach there unfolds a certain type of national
story—a faith in the overriding importance of human energy, intellect,
enterprise, and broad horizons. Under this rubric, Australians have always
been an 'international' people, their character most clearly demonstrated by
their enthusiasm for communications technology, from the telegraph to the
internet, and by their extraordinary achievements in worldwide competitive
sport.

The contradictory evidence fuelling debate among scholars is a result of
the fact that from the very beginning there were two equally inconsistent
ambitions for a British Australia. The minister in charge of the project
in 1786, Lord Sydney, hoped for a community of peasant proprietors, a
quasi-republic whose members would learn to live in mutual trust. On the
other hand, some of his colleagues recognized very early that the settlement
at Sydney Cove might be a means of opening up the Pacific to British
commerce and naval power.[42] The same contest of principle appears in
the management of New South Wales during the 1790s. Governor Phillip
imposed a centralized discipline and his successor, John Hunter, worked to
create a self-sufficient farming people. And yet, the officers of the New South
Wales Corps, who managed the settlement from 1792 to 1795, succeeded
in making Sydney a place of trade. 'Little other conversation is heard but
buying, selling, bartering, &c.', said the chaplain, Richard Johnson, in 1794.
This conversation reached to India, China, the Cape of Good Hope, and the
United States.[43]

Both types of ambition were peculiarly challenging. Set against each other,
they inspired a conflict of principle that has lasted many generations. It

---

[42] Alan Frost, *Convicts and Empire: A Naval Question 1776–1811* (Melbourne, 1980), pp. 78–84,
121–6, 137–41; David Mackay, *A Place of Exile: The European Settlement of New South Wales*
(Melbourne, 1985); Atkinson, *The Europeans in Australia*, Vol. 1, pp. 44–58.

[43] Richard Johnson to Jonathan Stonard, 11 August 1794, in G. Mackaness, ed., *Some Letters of
Rev. Richard Johnson, B.A. First Chaplain of New South Wales* (Dubbo, 1954), pt 2, p. 7; Atkinson,
The Europeans in Australia, Vol. 1, pp. 207–10, 231–4.

was a conflict, once again, born of the European Enlightenment, and it was similar to the division of ideas associated in the United States with the name of Thomas Jefferson on the one hand (with his love of deeply rooted agricultural life) and of Alexander Hamilton on the other (stressing urban ambition and mobile trade). The American Revolution and the initial invasion of Australia were part of a single movement of thought, a movement nourished by internal contradiction.

This movement also included the creation of a body of law, most clearly within the British Empire, tailored to the needs of worldwide monetary investment. Lord Chief Justice Mansfield (famous also for his part in limiting slavery in Britain, in Somersett's case, 1776) established the central principles of British commercial law. The result was a single code which was all at once predictable and flexible, uniform and various. Its success ensured confidence among merchants in distinct times and places. It involved a profound elaboration of trust, guaranteeing financial credit into the future and throughout the world. And it reinforced the great leap forward in cartographic literacy outlined at the beginning of this chapter. Commercial law was to be effective everywhere. The moral regime that was to fill the seeming vacancies of the world, including Australia and the Pacific, depended on this great creation.

The conquest of Australia involved both cartographic and legal innovation. Activity on the Australian frontier was intermeshed with the demands of a global market—the energy of the individual with the prosperity of the world. It depended on ingenuity like Mansfield's, on reconciling the particular with the general—the peculiarities of each bounded community with fluid, far-reaching patterns of communication. The convicts, for instance, had to be managed in two, apparently contradictory ways. On the one hand, they were criminals, subject in theory to a centralized regime of welfare, reform, and punishment, as if in a prison. On the other hand, they were a workforce on which depended the growth of fine wool for export to Britain. This contradiction exercised some of the leading minds in the colonies, including supreme courts judges who sought to establish not only settled principles of criminal justice and common rights, but also secure patterns of trade and a consistent relationship between master and servant.

In fact, by the 1830s some aspects of the contradiction were proving too much. Convict labour was likened to slavery, and that alone put it at odds with advanced commercial thinking. Slavery itself was abolished throughout the British Empire in 1833. Transportation ceased to New South Wales in

1840 and to Van Diemen's Land in the early 1850s and, while Western
Australia took convicts during the 1850s and 1860s, it did so without the old
system of private assignment.

Nor was it easy to apply these principles, even in their most subtle form, to
the government of the Indigenous people. Saxe Bannister was a commercial
lawyer. He saw every Black man and woman as a rational being, an individual
with material and moral concerns. He was devoted to the idea of variety
within the system and by the 1830s his hopes for New South Wales had grown
into a scheme for the Empire as a whole, comprehending all its Indigenous
languages and legal systems. These hopes he explained to a parliamentary
select committee in London, but they exhausted the imaginative powers
even of his immediate listeners.[44]

To most educated minds, in other words, the idea of Australia as a moral
and legal vacancy was essential to the business of conquest. However, it
was not the only means of justifying the extension of Empire. Among the
conquerors there were some who could see imprinted on the landscape the
living work of 'ancient proprietors' and who thought in terms of conflicting
rights. Britain was a global power of high intellectual and moral pretensions,
and for a time, at least, it was possible to hope that conquest was compatible
with justice.

Australia has never been a country governed by any sense of 'manifest
destiny'. Unlike the United States, which gradually expanded to fill the space
allowed by Providence, and where hopes remain today of some perfect
future, this was a territory theoretically possessed all at once, almost within
a single moment, and long ago. Historical enquiry might say otherwise,
suggesting that the conquest of Australia continues even now. But the myth
of original vacancy remains enormously powerful. Even those who argue
(as in this chapter) that it never existed are indirectly caught up with the
idea that it did, with ideas of authority expanding like smoke from shore to
shore, and with ideas about place which dwell on containment and escape.

Australians, unless they take the point of view of a Hobbles Danaiyarri,
rarely talk about the conquest of their country. But the notion of conquest
in fact lies at the heart of the Australian imagination. Confronting the
moral ambiguities of conquest is another matter. It seems to have been
easy for Edward Smith Hall, Saxe Bannister, and others in their time to do

---

[44] Saxe Bannister, evidence before select committee on Aborigines (British settlements),
14 March 1837, *Parliamentary Papers*, 1837 (425) VIII, pp. 14–20.

so, but more recently the task has been far more challenging. Confined as Australians within the idea of 'Australia', later generations have found it very difficult to think that the conquest of the country might have been at once both brutal and intelligent, bloodthirsty and benign.

Select Bibliography

ALAN ATKINSON, *The Europeans in Australia: A History*, 1 (Melbourne, 1997).
—— *The Europeans in Australia: A History*, 2 (Melbourne, 2004).
BAIN ATTWOOD, '*The Law of the Land* or the Law of the Land?: History, Law and Narrative in a Settler Society', *History Compass*, 2 (2004), pp. 1–30.
DAVID DAY, *Conquest: A New History of the Modern World* (Sydney, 2005).
ERIN IHDE, *A Manifesto for New South Wales: Edward Smith Hall and the Sydney Monitor 1826–1840* (Melbourne, 2004).
HENRY REYNOLDS, *The Law of the Land* (Ringwood, Vic., 1987).
—— *Fate of a Free People: A Radical Re-Examination of the Tasmanian Wars* (Ringwood, Vic., 1995).
LYNDALL RYAN, *The Aboriginal Tasmanians* (St Lucia, Qld, 1981; Sydney, 1996).

3

Settling the Land

RICHARD WATERHOUSE

The settlement of British colonies in Australia from 1788 reflected an older Empire of conquest and migrations. The common portrayal of the colony at Botany Bay as essentially a penal settlement provided only a partial characterization of this founding society: and it obscured the deeper role which British experience in the Americas and Caribbean played in shaping the regional Empire that became 'Australia'.[1]

Driven by a determination to acquire wealth, migrants settled England's southern and Caribbean colonies in the seventeenth century. They quickly developed into monocultural economies, based on the cultivation of staples, economies that were heavily dependent on the labour of imported African slaves. Planters with large holdings of land and slaves dominated their economic, political, and social life. But it was notions associated with 'possessive individualism'—emphasizing the right of every individual to seek his own interest—that underpinned the manner in which the English occupied and exploited the southern and Caribbean colonies. In contrast, New England was settled in 1630 and after by Puritan family groups intent on recreating in the New World the village and rural communities that they had left behind in England. In the Puritan settlements land was allocated in small and more or less even lots and, to ensure a stable and static society, each inhabitant was assigned a place or calling.

---

[1] The material on which this chapter is based consists in part of the MS letters, diaries, and autobiographies of those who lived in rural Australia—squatters, farmers, itinerant workers, their wives and female co-workers—held in the National Library of Australia (Canberra) and the State Libraries of New South Wales, Victoria, and Queensland. The *Australasian Pastoralists' Review*, which cogently articulated the views of squatters, the *Australian Town and Country Journal*, which was more sympathetic to the interests of small farmers and town businessmen, and *Walkabout*, a travel industry magazine which commented shrewdly on both rural progress and the dangers which this represented to the natural environment, are vital sources for historians of rural Australia.

In New South Wales the European occupation of the interior thus reflected a significant measure of continuity with the complex story of the plantation colonies of the Americas. The pastoralists, or squatters, ruthlessly pursued their own interests, at first relying on the forced labour of convict 'servants' to produce an Antipodean staple in the form of wool. However, the alternative vision of Australia, as a land of small-scale farmers, exerted increasingly powerful influence in the course of the nineteenth century, in the end shaping government policies designed to bring about closer, agricultural settlement. The final triumph of large- over small-scale agricultural production reflected recognition of economic and environmental reality and the triumph of one British colonization model over another. In a very special historical sense, the development of Australia constituted a strand in a larger British imperial scheme.

*   *   *

From the early days of European settlement the British Colonial Office encouraged the Governors of New South Wales to experiment with agri-cultural staples—both as a means of encouraging self-sufficiency in food production, and in the expectation that the infant colony would produce crops to compete with those grown in the North American possessions 'lost' by the Revolution of 1776. Blight, fire, flood, and drought regularly decimated the grape, maize, and wheat crops, while the lagoons of the Hawkesbury River west of Sydney proved unsuitable for rice. As a consequence, leading colonists like Samuel Marsden and John Macarthur turned to promoting wool as a more reliable staple. It was this commodity that eventually stimu-lated the expansion of European settlement across the ranges, and brought a degree of prosperity to a small and privileged number of colonists.

The crossing of the Blue Mountains in 1813 by Blaxland, Wentworth, and Lawson, men whose main concern was to find new pasturage for sheep and cattle, was later mythologized as a feat that allowed the transformation of the colony from a small outpost of Empire to a prosperous and progressive province. The reality was that the expedition did not lead to an immediate and massive population exodus westwards. Governor Macquarie used his authority to control settlement, preventing colonists moving into the Hunter, limiting the occupation of land near Bathurst to a few large- scale pastoralists, although allowing larger numbers of owners of small herds of cattle to move south-west into the Sutton Forest, Argyle, Goulburn Plains, and St Vincent districts. Despite the proclamation of the Limits of Location in 1826, 1829, and 1835—which defined boundaries beyond which occupation was not permitted—his successors failed to contain a significant movement of pastoralists, their workers, and stock. Beginning in the 1820s, this expansion took place westward across the Blue Mountains onto the western slopes and plains, south-west towards Goulburn and Australia Felix (Victoria); and north-west through the Hunter, onto the Liverpool Plains, and quickly as far as the Darling Downs in what is now southern Queensland. In 1840, Governor Gipps acknowledged that not only the poor emancipists had defied Government Orders, but also the wealthiest men in the land, including former navy and army officers, merchants, traders, and lawyers.

Accordingly, as the early scholarship of Stephen H. Roberts first established, British imperial policy attempted to make a virtue out of a loss of local control: far-ranging squatters now became licensed agents of Empire.[2] These crossings and further exploratory expeditions also increasingly confirmed that the immediate future of NSW lay with grazing, not with agriculture. Government officials, in both London and the colonies, accepted that most of the newly 'discovered' land was suited to 'pasturage rather than tillage'.[3]

The early sheep runs beyond the Limits of Location shared a number of characteristics. Until the Orders in Council legalized them in 1847, pastoralists held no legal title to their runs and so were naturally reluctant to make improvements to them. And so the squatters and their employees lived in primitive, makeshift huts, shearing took place in the open air, and fences were rare. But this absence of improvements also resulted from the fact that these were men on the make. For them the bush was a place to exploit and leave. They did not conceive of establishing permanent and stable communities, of calling it home. Such patterns of behaviour were not dissimilar from those of the Virginia and Caribbean planters of earlier centuries.[4] Nor were they obliged to create comfortable domestic surroundings for wives and children, for most were single men. Writing in the 1870s, the English novelist Anthony Trollope observed that the typical Victorian squatter was now a rich man 'but he is rich because in all his expenditure he has thought more of a return on his capital than the

<hr />

[2] Stephen H. Roberts, *History of Australian Land Settlement, 1788–1920* (Melbourne, 1924).

[3] J. T. Bigge, *Report of the Commissioner of Inquiry into the State of the Colony of New South Wales* (London, 1822), p. 92.

[4] Jack P. Greene, *Pursuits of Happiness: The Social Development of Early Modern British Colonies and the Formation of American Culture* (Chapel Hill, 1988), passim.

adornment of the place'.[5] And so their acquisitive behaviour retarded capital investment. The use of hut-keepers and shepherds to raise and guard sheep reflected traditional practices, while the practice of washing sheep by forcing them into creeks and rivers (and holding them under water with forked sticks) was crude and, indeed, wasteful for in the process a high proportion of the animals died. Finally, the early runs did not make use of skilled labour. In the late nineteenth century workers specialized as shearers or rouseabouts (shedhands); but in this earlier time the shepherds and hut-keepers, as well as itinerant workers, shared the washing and shearing.

As the squatters moved their cattle and sheep onto Aboriginal lands they caused immediate and significant changes to the environment. Introduced stock monopolized local water supplies, sometimes draining them dry. They also competed with native animals for fodder and ate the roots that Aborigines collected as tucker (food). As a result, wallabies, kangaroos, and emus, often a key source of food for Aborigines, were driven from the area. Usually the squatters simply assumed ownership and insisted that Aborigines remove themselves from the runs. 'They seem to fail to understand our method of stock raising and consider the animals are imported here for their own convenience', claimed the explorer and pastoralist William Hovell, without any sense of Aboriginal rights and needs, 'every effort is made to convince them their place is outside of the fence'.[6] But Aborigines had to return to land claimed by the squatters to access food and water.

With their traditional sources of food now scarce, they now hunted sheep and cattle and carried off wheat from cultivated fields. In the process, Aborigines attacked the shepherds, driving them off or killing them. Accounts of conflict over stock were commonplace in NSW and Australia Felix in the 1830s and 1840s; and they were still regularly recorded in Queensland, the Northern Territory, and Western Australia in the early twentieth century. Although turn-of-the-century commentators sometimes claimed the Aborigines did not lack food and took the stock from 'mischief', it is more likely they did so from the need to eat, indeed in some cases to escape starvation.

Even when they tried to maintain traditional hunting practices, Aborigines antagonized the interlopers because their practice of setting fire to the grass—to flush out the game—destroyed what the pastoralists considered their sheep pastures. What intensified the animosity between Europeans

---

[5] Anthony Trollope, *Australia and New Zealand* (London, 1876), p. 304.

[6] William Hilton Hovell, Diary of My Travels Within the Colony of New South Wales, 1825, MS Safe 1/9a, Mitchell Library, Sydney (hereafter ML).

and Aborigines was the practice of the former of seizing Aboriginal women for the purpose of sexual 'relations'. If Aborigines picked off the shepherds in part because they were the most vulnerable, it was also because of their records of sexual abuse. Later in the century, the abduction of Aboriginal women by European pastoral workers in Queensland, Western Australia, and the Northern Territory resulted in further conflict and killings.

One of the most notorious retaliatory raids by Europeans took place at Myall Creek in New England in 1838, a raid allegedly prompted by Aboriginal cattle stealing. Encouraged by the son of a local squatter, eleven European station workers attacked a group of Aborigines camped in the bush, killing at least twenty-eight of them.[7] There was nothing unusual about this except that eventually seven of the perpetrators were sentenced to death. The impact of Myall Creek and its consequences was not to end the attacks on Aborigines but to make the Europeans more careful and surreptitious. Squatters may have come to rely more extensively on poisoning, because it allowed them to claim that the Aborigines died accidentally from eating sheep treated with arsenic for the cure of scab. Visiting Queensland in the 1870s, the English novelist Anthony Trollope was informed that squatters still shot Aborigines to 'protect' their families and stock, but that, 'No one but a fool would say anything about it.'[8]

Pastoralists who excluded Aborigines from their properties claimed that it resulted in 'peaceful' relations and the loss of fewer European lives. After the killing of nineteen Europeans, including members of the Wills family at Cullinlaringo on the Nagoa River in central Queensland in 1861, the supporters of this policy insisted that the killings proved the necessity of such segregation policies. Allowing members of a nearby tribe to camp near where he had established his station, Horatio Spencer Wills had also set out to befriend, 'civilise' and 'make use of the Aborigines', and became, in the view of his critics, a victim of his own 'kindness and over-confidence'.[9]

Yet from the early days of pastoralism other squatters had followed different policies, those which promoted some form at least of accommodation. In part their motives were pragmatic because they concluded, unlike the majority of their contemporaries, that excluding Aborigines from their runs promoted rather than prevented conflict and violence. Some

[7] Richard Waterhouse, *The Vision Splendid: A Social and Cultural History of Rural Australia* (Fremantle, 2005), pp. 42–51.

[8] Trollope, *Australia and New Zealand*, p. 48.

[9] Oscar De Satge, *Pages From the Journal of a Queensland Squatter* (London, 1901), p. 154.

squatters were also motivated by a sense of humanitarianism, underpinned by recognition that the land they now occupied was usurped from the Aborigines. The Archers, who first settled in southern Queensland before subsequently taking up a run on the Fitzroy River, accepted the Aborigines 'as the hereditary owner[s] of the soil' and considered it an injustice to drive them from their hunting grounds. The Aborigines were encouraged to work for the Archers as well as to hunt kangaroos and to grow corn and sweet potatoes.[10]

The relations between Europeans and Aborigines early on were marked by violence, hatred, and mutual distrust, with just a dash of paternalism. Yet what also developed were patterns of interdependence, which produced transcultural exchanges with significant ramifications for both Aboriginal and European societies. Aborigines played an important role in teaching Europeans how to find their way and survive in the bush. As the pastoralists fanned out across the slopes and plains in New South Wales, Australia Felix, and (what was to become) Queensland, it was Aborigines who led them to water, showed them where to ford rivers, and who tracked and caught straying horses.

In the early days of British settler occupation of the inland some squatters employed assigned servants for the purposes of shepherding sheep and droving cattle, while hiring Aborigines to carry out 'supplementary' tasks. Indeed, Aborigines filled an astonishing variety of roles. On many runs they were employed primarily for the purposes of hunting game, especially ducks, and catching fish using lines and hooks provided by their employers. Because of their tracking abilities they were used, in preference to European labour, to find lost stock and runaway servants. They also laboured on improvements, cutting and erecting fence posts, clearing ground for crops (and protecting them from caterpillars and crows), grubbing stumps, and cutting bark to build huts for both the squatters and their European workers. Although some squatters argued that Aborigines were unreliable workers because they could 'never settle', others employed them as an alternative and indeed preferred source of labour to convicts and emancipists. And so Aborigines became shepherds, drovers, and sheep washers, although in this period they were not usually employed as shearers. Although some Aborigines, especially those who worked as shepherds, received wages, most

[10] Charles Archer to William Archer, 28 April 1845, Archer Papers, MS OM 80-10, Oxley Library, Brisbane.

were 'paid' in clothing, food, and tobacco, which meant they were a cheap source of labour. Because of the heavy drinking habits of many assigned servants, Aborigines were also considered more reliable workers. European employers also discovered that because of their knowledge of the landscape both male and female Aborigines made excellent shepherds and drovers, for they knew where water and the best grass were to be found.

With the coming of the gold rushes beginning in 1850, the pastoralists became even more reliant on Aboriginal labour because of the labour shortages caused as the European bush workers deserted the runs to pan for gold near Bathurst and Bendigo. Aborigines now took on trades previously reserved for Europeans, notably shearing. Throughout the second half of the century Aborigines continued to find employment in the pastoral industries of the southern colonies, and most continued to be paid in food and clothing. On the eve of the First World War some Aborigines in NSW had become expert shearers and earned union rates. Some had also become entrepreneurs, engaging in such diverse occupations as owning pubs and operating fishing boats.

As the sheep and cattle industries expanded into the remote areas of central and northern Queensland, the northern areas of Western Australia, and the Northern Territory in the late nineteenth century, the pastoralists discovered that, with European labour almost non-existent, Aboriginal labour was essential. Those Europeans who ventured into the Deep North were astonished to discover that on most stations Aborigines undertook virtually all the work. The men were to be found as stockmen and shearers as well as general station hands responsible for erecting and maintaining fences and yards. On the cane fields too, Aborigines worked beside Pacific Island labourers. Many Aboriginal women worked as servants both on the sheep and cattle stations as well as on the sugar cane farms. On the more remote stations they also worked as drovers, shepherds, vegetable gardeners, and fence builders. In the south, the number of Aborigines turning up on the Queen's Birthday to collect blankets was diminishing rapidly from year to year, which Europeans claimed was evidence that the Aborigines were a 'dying race'. But what Europeans discovered in northern Australia, somewhat to their consternation, was that the Aboriginal population was not 'dying out'; and that, in fact, the pastoral economy was heavily dependent on Indigenous labour. The large numbers of Chinese working on the Queensland and Northern Territory goldfields in the late nineteenth century also contributed to the creation of a multicultural society that was at odds with the 'Little England' ideal to which English colonists in the Americas and Australasia had traditionally aspired.

The second half of the nineteenth century was marked by the emergence of an impressive number of large sheep (and cattle) runs. By 1895 more than forty stations in NSW alone were each shearing more than 100,000 sheep. Whereas cattle stations continued to operate in traditional ways, using a minimum of labour and machinery, wool-growing underwent a revolution. The erection of fences, which became commonplace in the 1850s, not only rendered shepherds obsolete but also allowed the introduction of more sophisticated management practices: now, wethers, ewes, and rams were kept in separate paddocks and careful breeding practices followed. The Peppin merinos (bred in the 1860s in the Riverina by the Peppin family), which dominated flocks by the end of the century, were hardy and produced high yields of medium fine wool. Mechanization also came to the industry. Washing was replaced by machine scouring; baling was done by mechanical presses rather than by tramping or spade pressing it; and, most important of all, in the 1880s machine shears, which allowed sheep to be shorn quickly and evenly, were first used in place of hand shears. And the large sheep stations came to resemble factories. Their equipment included pumps to irrigate feed for the sheep, electric generators to drive the shears, conveyor belts to carry the wool from the shearing sheds to the wool classing room, scouring machines, and wool presses. Visitors compared their operations to those of 'a well-regulated machine'. In Australia, the machinery and form of labour organization associated with modern factory production were more typical of rural than they were of urban industry.

By the twentieth century sheep properties had acquired more permanent characteristics, reflected in the introduction of improvements in the form of more substantial homesteads and woolsheds, fences, and machinery. Married squatters became more common too, and so many properties became more homely and domestic. The introduction of advanced technology to the wool industry from the 1870s onwards was largely financed with British capital, leading to a close economic relationship between Australian producers and British manufacturers; rural Australia functioned like a traditional colony, producing a staple to supply British industry. But this was also a period, at least in New South Wales, in which individual holdings fell and company ownership increased significantly, especially during the Depression of the 1890s. The squatters' commitment to an ethos of economic individualism, the increase in company ownership, and the introduction of mechanization and contract labour served to harden relations between squatters and the shearers and rouseabouts who formed the rural labour force.

*   *   *

Most of the convicts transported to Australia came from towns and were unused to the hard manual labour of rural work. Yet the free settlers were almost unanimous in agreeing that there were strong advantages in assigning them to farms: in the words of one pastoralist, 'it breaks their old habits … teaches them a way of making an honest living'.[11] In the early nineteenth century most of the farms around Sydney and subsequently most of the pastoral properties on the western side of the Blue Mountains were worked by assigned servants of convict status.

A labour system emerged that depended on complex relations between convicts and their employers. On most properties a task system operated, with servants free to earn extra food and money in the time left over once they had completed their prescribed tasks for the day or week. But although incentives proved more successful than punishment in getting convicts to work, they did not turn them into grateful employees. Observers noted the absence of deference in relations between pastoralists and their workers, most of whom worked as shepherds and hut-keepers, and complained that convict workers were insolent, prone to theft, and always running away. But they also noted that the pastoralists were 'bad masters', who lacked tact and understanding.

Until the 1840s work on most stations was undertaken by a small number of 'permanent' employees. Aside from their normal duties shepherds and hut-keepers also shore the sheep. But once the introduction of fences allowed squatters to reduce the number of 'permanents', they introduced the practice of hiring men on a seasonal basis. These workers, commonly referred to as 'swagmen', formed the core of what Trollope called 'the nomadic tribe', notorious for blowing their end-of-season cheques on drinking sprees and then working as casual labourers, or begging from property to property until the next shearing season.

This restlessness of rural workers, their unwillingness to work for one employer for any length of time, was intensified by the lack of wives and families that might have tied them to a particular place. Colonial discourses

---

[11] Gregory Blaxland to Commissioner Bigge, Bonwick Transcripts, ML.

argued that it was the responsibility of rural women to settle a dangerous and mobile male tribe, but their scarcity meant such an ideology had little impact on the lives of itinerant workers. Moreover, on many farms wives worked in partnership with their husbands, sharing equally in caring for stock, in milking, and in sowing and reaping. On many selections women were even left to manage for themselves while their menfolk sought extra income as miners, shearers, and rouseabouts.

In the 1870s rouseabouts remained restless wanderers; but the social composition of shearers changed. Now they were mostly 'selectors' (small farmers), many of them local, who worked in the shearing sheds in the gap between planting and harvest. As the spread of railway networks and the introduction of bicycles facilitated travel between urban and rural areas, the ranks of shearers were swollen by men from Sydney and Melbourne. However, as pastoralists turned to contractors to provide them with shearers in the early twentieth century, the number of farmers engaged in this seasonal work declined. When they had contracted directly with the pastoralists shearers usually signed up for two or three sheds but under the contract system shearing became a year-round occupation, leaving no room for part-timers with farms to work.

From the mid-1880s, relations between pastoralists and their employees became increasingly marked by conflict. The rabbit plague, which had decreased pasturage and lowered the carrying capacity on many properties, and the low wool prices, which had prevailed for some six years, combined to cut into the profits of the pastoralists. The response of one group of owner-managers was publicly to advertise their intention to lower the rate per hundred sheep shorn. In response, many shearers openly demanded to know why if wages needed to be cut in hard times they were not raised in prosperous seasons. They answered the question by refusing to work in the sheds paying the lower rate and by joining the newly formed Amalgamated Shearers' Union (ASU). Indeed the formation of unions on one side, and an employers' organization in the form of the Pastoralists' Union on the other, was a sign of a widening rift between employers and their workers.

Conflict flared again in 1891–2 as the ASU resolved to concern itself with negotiating agreements between employers and employees, and to prohibit union members shearing alongside non-union labour. The Pastoralists' Union campaigned not only against the closed shop but also in favour of wage-cuts for rouseabouts. Eventually, after a series of strikes, which culminated in pitched battles with the police and the gaoling of the leading

Queensland unionists for conspiracy, the unionists were forced to yield and agree to freedom of contract. But strikes started again in 1894 when, in response to falling wool prices, the pastoralists decided to lower rates both for shearers and shedhands.

The angry events of 1891–2 and 1894 revealed just how bitter relations between pastoralists and their employees had become, especially in the western areas of Queensland and New South Wales, where confrontation and violence were endemic. The unionist shearers protested at the lowering of wages and the hiring of non-union labour by sabotaging shearing machinery and pumps, setting fire to woolsheds and haysheds. So widespread, so bitter was the conflict that the vehicle of pastoralist opinion, *The Australasian Pastoralists' Review*, referred to it as an 'insurrection'.[12] As in 1891 the 1894 strikes failed in their objective; wages remained low, non-union labour continued to be employed. Yet conflict continued to simmer into the new century, for the underlying issues remained unresolved.

The incapacity of pastoralists to understand the expectations and values of their workers, their unwillingness to negotiate with the Australian Workers' Union (AWU), made them more sympathetic to the system of contract shearing and hastened its introduction. Of course, this further reduced personal contact between pastoralists and their workers, because shearers and rouseabouts now negotiated their wages and conditions directly with the contractors. In 1907 the process of determining wages and conditions was removed from the workplace when the Arbitration Commission assumed responsibility for setting rates. The introduction of such a system of mediation brought an end to industrial unrest on a large scale; but it did little to reconcile pastoral employers and their employees. The former usually regarded the rates and conditions prescribed by the commission as too generous, while the latter campaigned to improve them further.

The failure of the strikes of the 1890s not only further alienated pastoralists and workers but also led to the flowering of the notion of mateship among shearers and rouseabouts. The brutal suppression of the strikes strengthened the bonds between the workers, and it convinced them that they could only trust each other. At the same time, they blamed the squatters for not sharing their prosperity, for monopolizing land and capital, denying others an opportunity for upward mobility by acquiring land and thus forcing them into nomadic, wage-earning lives that represented dead ends, not freedom.

---

[12] *Australasian Pastoralists' Review*, 15 September 1894.

Above all, mateship reflected not a culture of optimism but rather one of consolation.

* * *

In the 1860s most colonies passed Selection Acts to allow men with small amounts of capital to establish themselves on Crown lands even when squatters already occupied them. Subsequently, beginning in the 1880s, colonial and state governments replaced selection with closer Settlement Acts. The former had allowed prospective farmers to occupy squatting leases, sometimes in advance of survey. The latter involved the voluntary or compulsory acquisition of large estates, and their division and sale at auction to small-scale proprietors. Closer settlement existed on a smaller scale than selection. Only land that was suitable for agriculture and with access to markets was available under this scheme. Those who proposed the legislation designed to replace large-scale pastoralists with small-scale agriculturalists on the land were driven by two main ideologies. First, supporters of selection in Victoria espoused a language and ideology of agrarianism. For them the progress of 'civilization' required that 'the shepherd should recede before the advance of the husbandman'. In seeking to establish 'a numerous yeoman class upon the soil' they argued for the virtues of a settled, static, rural against an urban, market-oriented society.

However, this vision of an Australian yeomanry did not draw for its inspiration on nostalgia for a lost pre-industrial England. Rather it was influenced by American 'rational agrarians', who sought to create a society based on a morally virtuous and entrepreneurial yeoman class.[13] In contrast, Sir John Robertson and the supporters of the Selection Acts in New South Wales, were primarily concerned with removing the squatters' privileges; and in providing all colonists with the opportunity to acquire land and prosper from it. The language of agrarianism, references to the virtues of a 'yeoman class', were absent from the debates over selection in New South Wales.

Contemporaries were divided in their assessment of how far the Selection Acts succeeded in 'unlocking the land'; and modern historians also still disagree about their effectiveness. In New South Wales, although many prospered

---

[13] *Argus*, 17 December 1861; Crown Lands Commission of Inquiry, Progress Report, Victoria Legislative Assembly, 1878, p. 3.

initially, the vast majority failed in the long run, hampered by a lack of agricultural knowledge and insufficient capital to sustain them through hard times and to improve and enlarge their properties. By 1882 perhaps only one-third of selectors were still on their land. Those who stayed usually did so because they were able to acquire additional acres either legally through the purchase of land belonging to neighbours, or, through 'dummying'—that is, the illegal acquisition of extra land under the Selection Acts in the names of wives and children. In addition, they needed to possess good judgement in acquiring land, choosing only lots that were likely to prove productive and which in any case were located close to markets.

Like the wool industry, farming underwent a rapid process of mechanization after 1850, providing a solution to the rural labour shortage and encouraging large-scale operations. The gold rushes of the fifties, the extension of railways into the hinterlands, beginning in the seventies, the development of disease-resistant wheat strains around the turn of the twentieth century encouraged men with capital to enter the wheat industry—where the risks associated with production were now fewer, while the means now existed to move the product to market. However, the capital required to engage in large-scale mechanized wheat farming was beyond the reach of many selectors with their smallholdings and meagre funds. Rather, they continued to produce foodstuffs for local markets, mostly operating in a barter rather than a cash economy.

In 1843 John Ridley invented a 'stripper', driven through the fields by horses or bullocks, which knocked the heads off the wheat and into a hopper. Although threshing and winnowing were still done by hand in the 1880s, combined harvesters, threshers, and winnowers were beginning to appear, and they became commonplace in the early years of the twentieth century. The result was a dramatic cut in the cost of harvesting as well as in the time it took. By the Great War of 1914 multi-furrowed ploughs drawn by traction machines ploughed wheat fields on large holdings; mechanical devices sowed seed and manure; and combined harvesters completed the task of harvesting and threshing. Now, in some ways, the large wheat farms resembled their sheep-raising counterparts: they had both taken on the characteristics of factories.

Contemporaries, the pastoralists particularly, did not see the selectors as possessing an entrepreneurial ethos. Rather, they described them as belonging to the 'pauper-class', men who had neither the knowledge nor the capital to improve their holdings.[14] Although the majority of selectors sold or surrendered their properties within a few years, others achieved a modest level of prosperity by quickly learning about pastoral, dairying, and agricultural practices, by carefully choosing where to settle, and by their discipline in accumulating capital for the purpose of purchasing more land as well as machinery. Perhaps the precarious circumstances in which many selectors found themselves also forced them into a culture of exploitation. One Victorian labourer claimed the local farmers shared three characteristics: 'exhausting the land, abusing horses and exploiting the labourer'.[15]

And so, three sets of values can be identified among those European Australians who lived and worked on the land: one related to entrepreneurship, which involved a single-minded preoccupation with accumulating wealth as quickly as possible; another to a reluctant self-sufficiency, with aspirations to entrepreneurship; and a third grounded in an opposition to authority, a resentment of the squatters, and (especially from the 1890s) a commitment to mateship.

*   *   *

The squatting leaseholds hindered the establishment and growth of rural towns in nineteenth-century Australia for they acted as barriers to significant population increases. However, the discovery of gold in the 1850s and after, the passage of the Selection Acts, the development of the dairying and wheat industries, the continued expansion in the number of sheep and cattle properties, and the construction of rural railroads resulted in significant rural population growth.

The social hierarchy that developed in towns was sometimes rigid and reflected a degree of antagonism. At the top were the local graziers, many of who in fact had little to do with town affairs but rather found their social and cultural entertainments in the clubs and hotels of the capitals. Next came the professionals—doctors, bank managers, solicitors, clergymen, and school headmasters, as well as business and factory owners. Another level consisted of small businessmen, post office, bank and other office clerks, schoolteachers, policemen, and stock and station agents. And, at the very bottom, were railway and factory workers, shop assistants, labourers, and

[14] Report of the Select Committee on the Present State of the Colony, NSW Legislative Assembly, Votes and Proceedings, 1865–66, Vol. 3, pp. 6–8, 14–15, 72.

[15] William Evans, ed., *Diary of a Welsh Swagman* (Sydney, 1992), p. 70.

artisans. There was little social mingling and while those of modest status sometimes resentfully referred to their 'betters' as 'the umbrella mob', those at the top of the social pyramid retaliated by dismissing those at the base as 'the rabble'.[16]

This small-town middle and professional class became preoccupied with respectability as a means of separating itself from the 'stain' of a convict past, and the masculine culture associated with itinerant workers and the end-of-season drinking spree. In most country towns great care was taken to practise the etiquette associated with respectability and middle-class values. Weddings and funerals were elaborate occasions, and newcomers were carefully scrutinized before they were admitted to membership of polite local society. In rural towns too, those who aspired to respectability joined the campaign for moral reform, in particular supporting the movements for sabbatarianism and temperance. In fast-growing centres like Wagga Wagga in southern NSW the difference between the cultures of the itinerant workers and middle-class townies became increasingly evident. It was a place where large numbers of shearers and rouseabouts stopped to blow their wages on whisky and beer, at least until the ritual of the spree became less common later in the century. But Wagga was also a town where many of the respected and settled citizens belonged to the Sons and Daughters of Temperance.

* * *

There were continuities in this socially complex story, continuities reflected in the plans of Federal and State governments for post-First World War rural Australia that focused almost exclusively on soldier settlement. It was widely accepted that returning servicemen deserved the opportunity to establish themselves as farmers as a reward for their contribution to 'King and Country'. It was also assumed that, because of their wartime experiences, these men were likely to prefer outdoor rather than office life. Many influential Australians also believed that rural Australia remained underpopulated and saw closer settlement as a means of remedying this problem: their aim was to attract not only ex-soldiers to the land but farmers from the British Isles as well. In fact, the state-based schemes were very extensive. By the Second World War, almost 40,000 ex-soldiers had taken up land. At first, there was considerable optimism about these schemes, with

---

[16] *Tamworth Observer*, 1 January 1901, cited in Roger Milliss, *City on the Peel: A History of Tamworth and District, 1818–1976* (Sydney, 1980), p. 113.

politicians predicting a low failure rate. But throughout the 1920s there were regular reports of soldier settlement farmers abandoning their holdings, and by 1933 it was reported that a majority of soldier settlers still farming were insolvent.

Those administering closer settlement policies sometimes blamed the farmers for their failure, arguing that many possessed war-related disabilities, which kept them from their work. But, in the end, they were forced to acknowledge that in fact the failures resulted mostly from misguided policies. A Victorian Royal Commission (1925) concluded that the blocks allocated were too small to be economically viable; and that in any case many of them were unsuitable for agriculture. Perhaps soldier settlement was not the unmitigated disaster that contemporaries and later historians have claimed. After all, as Stephen Garton has argued, by 1939 as many as 20,000 families, or half the original occupants, were still on the land.[17] Still, most of those who took up farms under this scheme expected to be more than subsistence operators. Instead they aspired to the same living standards as city workers, standards that soldier settlement schemes failed to deliver.

During the Second World War the debate over the value and practicality of closer settlement was once again reignited as State and Federal governments proposed to extend soldier settlement schemes to encompass a new generation of returning servicemen. The Federal government insisted that the number of ex-servicemen to be settled was to be determined by the amount of suitable land available, rather than the number of applicants; that the lots provided were to be of sufficient size to farm efficiently; and that only suitable applicants were to be granted access to the proposed scheme. These principles were enshrined in the 1945 War Services Land Settlement Agreement negotiated between the Commonwealth and States.

Altogether, just over 12,000 ex-servicemen were settled on the land under the scheme, a far smaller number than under post-First World War legislation. In most places the short-term failure rate was low; and in Victoria, where almost half of the total number of soldier settlers were located, only 4 per cent left or were removed from their holdings by 1962. And yet the initial successes of these relatively modest projects were not enough to sustain a continued widespread belief in the virtues of a rural economy based on smallholdings. The 1925 Royal Commissioners had insisted that the scheme was not just a business or economic proposition, and should not be evaluated

---

[17] Stephen Garton, *The Cost of War: Australians Return* (Melbourne, 1996), p. 140.

in such terms. But times had changed, and now hard-headed observers were aware that the notion of an idyllic yeomanry was an anachronism, and the choice of farming as a way of life was no longer a realistic proposition. In the interwar period thousands of rural Australians had deserted the bush for city or at least town life, and in doing so had indicated their preference for a living wage rather than a subsistence life. Farming was an economic enterprise and soldier settlers were only likely to succeed if they operated like businessmen, because the alternative was certain failure. After 1945 economists argued with increasing determination that only efficient large holdings could compete in increasingly competitive overseas markets.

And so a cultural ethos that had shaped a vision of Australia's rural and indeed national future for almost one hundred years became more or less irrelevant, as farming came to be understood as just another business. For over one hundred years the notion of a rural Australia, settled by small-scale British agriculturalists, had exerted a powerful influence on the national imagination and shaped land settlement policies. Now it was replaced by an acceptance of economic and environmental reality.

Still, the high prices earned by wool and wheat in the years after the Second World War led to renewed optimism about rural Australia's economic prospects, an optimism that was maintained throughout the 1950s. The deliberate introduction of the myxomatosis virus, which swept through the southern and eastern parts of Australia in that decade, and wiped out as many as 1,000 million rabbits, resulted in an immediate and spectacular increase in the income of woolgrowers. Pasture improvement, based on the introduction of leguminous plants combined with fertilizer, also led to dramatic increases in production and encouraged mixed farming. The pastures now carried more animals per acre while they were also used to grow crops in rotation. The development of new crops like rice and cotton, and the discovery of rich deposits of uranium and iron ore, deepened the belief that rural Australia had 'infinite room for growth'. The diversity of the Australian environment encouraged the belief that the land could be used for a multitude of purposes, including the growing of crops suited to cold, temperate, and tropical climates. Some of the most ambitious agricultural endeavours in this period, most of which proved expensive failures, involved attempts to establish large-scale agricultural operations in the Northern Territory and in the northern regions of Western Australia.

In some rural towns, where the loss of rural population was having a strong impact, reflected in the closing of hotels and chain stores, the cutting of train services, and reductions in the numbers of school, police, and hospital staff, residents expressed concerns and reservations about the future of the local community. Yet despite the drift to the cities and the loss of rural population, many of those who lived in the bush still believed it had a future. 'The Australian Way of Life' did not just represent a suburban creed but it included values reflecting the commitment of rural townsfolk to prosperity, and family-based stable communities. In those towns which grew and prospered, the construction of Olympic-standard pools, bowling and golf clubs, and modern and well-equipped schools was regarded as a sign of progress and modernity. Such a commitment perhaps indicated that for many rural townsfolk the pioneer and bush legends, which stressed that a quintessential Australian character and culture had evolved from the nineteenth-century frontier, were more relevant as foundation myths than as ones encapsulating contemporary twentieth-century aspirations.

By the 1960s and 1970s, however, as it became apparent that the introduction of further irrigation schemes and the application of scientific discoveries and techniques did not necessarily guarantee success in the development of new agricultural projects, and in any case created serious environmental consequences, this optimism was tempered. Academic experts in the field of agricultural policy began to emphasize the need for conservation, the prevention of degradation, and the sustainability of existing crop-bearing land, rather than the expansion of agricultural output. In the light of Britain's application to join the Common Market in 1961, and as a result of the over-production of wheat and wool, they argued that the Australian agricultural and pastoral industries needed to focus on reconstruction and consolidation to meet the challenges of highly competitive international markets. Their assessments of Australia's rural future were qualified and pessimistic for they argued that a system of extensive government subsidies and policies that promoted closer settlement had encouraged inefficiencies in primary industry. In any case, by that era it remained unclear where new markets were to be found, even if the required reform and rationalization of rural industry were accomplished.

Rural Australia's economic ties to the United Kingdom were weakened further with the emergence of new markets in Asia and the Middle East especially, from the late 1970s onwards, markets which economists had not anticipated. A rhetoric of progress and optimism returned to agriculture and pastoralism. Australia was able to enter and compete in these markets not only because of the planting of new crops like cotton, but also because of the development of innovative technologies for planting and harvesting crops, and the use of light planes and helicopters for mustering, all of which acted to reduce costs and labour size. The increase in the value of farm exports by 50 per cent between 1975 and 1985 led to the abandonment of calls for containment and the reappearance of a familiar rhetoric of expansion. Farm lobbyists argued that millions of hectares of arable land awaited cultivation or improvement and that the exploitation of surface water resources represented only a small portion of availability. Despite two extended periods of drought in the past twenty-odd years, the buoyant export market for Australian primary products has made optimists of many rural producers. But the disappearance of large tracts of native woodlands has made pessimists of many scientists. As Rick Farley, a land-use agreement specialist has recently argued, a common care for country may yet unite pastoralists and farmers, Aboriginal leaders, and environmentalists.

In the remote areas of northern Australia conflicts between Europeans and Aborigines continued in the interwar period. As an alternative to their traditional forms of food, which were becoming more and more scarce, Aborigines speared and ate cattle, often to the considerable chagrin of the station managers and owners. The appropriation of Aboriginal women by European men also continued as a source of friction. What exacerbated the level of conflict was the brutal response of the police to alleged Aboriginal depredations. Sometimes the police seemed more intent on punitive expeditions against Aboriginal lawbreakers, expeditions that sometimes ended in their deaths, than in apprehending them for the purpose of a trial by law. In 1928, when Aborigines killed a Northern Territory dingo hunter, the police mounted a retaliatory expedition that resulted in more than thirty officially acknowledged Aboriginal deaths, and many more that were not. By the late 1930s, however, as the authority of the police and the law became more firmly entrenched, both cattle stealing and physical conflicts between Europeans and Aborigines became much less common.

Despite the continued existence of de facto segregation in rural areas, influential Australians became more vocal in their support of integration. They had long supported the assimilation of those of mixed European and Aboriginal parentage and now they also argued in favour of requiring all Aborigines to adopt European ways. Academic experts and government officials argued that the spread of European society meant Aborigines could no longer live like their forefathers, and 'the gates of Eden' were now closed to them. However, a few academics, led by the Sydney anthropologist

A. P. Elkin, argued that Aborigines could only survive if they maintained their communities through adhering to their own languages, rituals, and traditional social organizations. Yet they also needed access to European benefits in the form of education, medical assistance, child endowment, and employment.[18] The blend of western and traditional culture that Elkin proposed was already a reality in some Aboriginal communities.

The Northern Australian Workers' Union lodged an application with the Conciliation and Arbitration Commission in 1964 for equal pay for Aboriginal pastoral workers in the Northern Territory. Although the employers' advocate argued that most Aborigines in the Territory did not work at the rate and level of European employees, the Commission accepted the principle of equal wages. It also deferred implementation until December 1968, on the grounds that its decision might lead to the loss of employment by Aboriginal workers.

The response by Aboriginal pastoral workers to this delay indicated that their concerns were not just with civil and citizenship rights, or with equal pay. At Newcastle Waters and Wave Hill stations, the Aboriginal head stockmen led walk-offs; and in a letter addressed to Federal Parliament the Wave Hill leadership called for the return of 'tribal lands', which had belonged to their people since 'time immemorial'. The Gurindji indicated that they wanted to use their expertise and experience to run their own cattle stations but to do so within the context of Aboriginal law and respect for their country. In 1963 the Yolngu of the Gove Peninsula protested against the mining of land which they had long occupied, by presenting a bark petition to Parliament. Several years later they took their case to court, although Justice Blackburn ruled that as a nomadic people they had no proprietorial title. This decision maintained the traditions of earlier British and colonial jurists who argued that *terra nullius* applied to land occupied by 'savage tribes'.

Aborigines rejected assimilation and demanded land as a means to maintain their cultures and reassert their autonomy. In response both Federal and State governments passed legislation in the 1970s and 1980s designed to provide Aboriginal communities with either freehold or leasehold title land. And the 1992 High Court Mabo decision not only ruled that native title survived the Crown's acquisition, but Justice Brennan argued

---

[18] A. P. Elkin, 'Reaction and Interaction: a Food Gathering People and European Settlement in Australia', *American Anthropologist*, Vol. 43 (1951), pp. 164–86.

for the contemporary irrelevance of doctrines that justified the dispossession of Indigenous peoples—on the grounds that they were 'too low in the scale of social organization to be acknowledged as possessing rights and interests in land'.[19] An argument that had had wide currency not only among jurists, intellectuals, and scientists but also among those who spearheaded the invasion of inland Australia was finally laid to rest. But it also contributed to a rising sense of discontent in rural Australia. Support for the populist One Nation Party, led by Pauline Hanson, which campaigned against gun law reforms, multiculturalism, and Aboriginal rights, was perhaps boosted by the Mabo decision. The strength of One Nation in the bush reflected nostalgia for an older rural Australia, one that privileged Anglo-Celtic culture.

*   *   *

During the nineteenth and early twentieth centuries European Australians had associated the past and future prosperity of the colonies and nation with the prosperity yielded by the 'golden soil' of the inland. The bush offered freedom and opportunity. But after the First World War the better prospects for employment, the improved quality of housing, the almost universal existence of electricity and refrigeration, the introduction of modern industries and advanced form of factory production in the capital cities, all provided powerful inducements for people to move from rural to urban areas. What exacerbated this movement was the fact that to remain internationally competitive the wool, wheat, and cattle industries needed to become increasingly mechanized, which in turn contributed to a loss of employment opportunities and an accelerated depopulation of the wool and wheat belts, in particular. By the end of the Second World War Australians associated a brighter future and higher living standards with life in the city. Once modernization was associated with rural development, now modernity was identified as urban.

In their imaginings and representations of the bush and its peoples, Australians in 1900 broadly conceived of rural Australia as unique—even though from the 1850s onwards a process of cultural incorporation was taking place, a process that accelerated with the introduction of railways and motor cars, radio, cinema, and television. A radical nationalist articulation of the 'typical' Australian, most cogently expressed through the pages of

[19] Richard Bartlett, ed., *The Mabo Decision With Commentary by Richard H. Bartlett and the Full Text of the Decision in Mabo and Others v State of Queensland* (Sydney, 1993), pp. 42, 83.

the *Bulletin* in the 1880s and 1890s, attributed the values associated with mateship, a collectivist morality, adaptability, and egalitarianism to those shearers and rouseabouts who constituted the 'nomadic tribe'.

A more conservative nineteenth-century foundation myth, the pioneer legend, promoted the notion that all of those who first lived and worked on the frontier—squatters, selectors, and itinerant workers—were possessed of a common purpose, that is, to tame the land and guarantee the prosperity of succeeding generations. In contrast with the bush legend, its pioneer counterpart played down the existence of class conflict. Yet in the twentieth century it became a paradox of rural Australia that the development of highly mechanized primary industries, which transformed its economy and society, was accompanied by a deepening rural antagonism towards change.

In the longer perspective of Empire in Australia, here was a telling turn in the narrative. The region that had nurtured radical Australian nationalism in the first century of settlement increasingly became a bastion of Anglo-Celtic conservatism in the twentieth century. The Empire had literally 'gone bush'. The Country Party, which was represented in all seven Australian Parliaments by 1920, remained a socially conservative party, intensely loyal to British culture and the British Crown. When the British government initiated negotiations to join the Common Market in 1961 the leader of the Country Party and Deputy Prime Minister, Jack McEwen, was a vociferous opponent. While he was deeply concerned with the economic consequences of the move, given the high proportion of Australian primary produce sold on British markets, he was also worried about the political and cultural impact. Cutting British and imperial economic ties, he argued, damaged the fundamentals of the political relationship. And when Britain's application to join the Common Market was finally accepted in 1972 McEwen's successor as Country Party leader, Doug Anthony, acknowledged the development as inevitable but took no pride from the fact that Australia was now beyond the old Empire 'on its own'.[20] Significantly, the enduring rural commitment to Britain and Empire extended beyond the political leadership. The Country Women's Association of New South Wales, formed in the 1920s, took and has retained as its motto: 'Honour to God. ... Loyalty to the Throne'.

The continued growth of the capital cities throughout the twentieth and into the twenty-first centuries—a growth stimulated, especially since 1945,

---

[20] Stuart Ward, *Australia and the British Embrace: The Demise of the Imperial Ideal* (Melbourne, 2001), pp. 130–1, 254.

by the arrival of large numbers of immigrants—has served to deepen the divide between rural and urban Australia. Now more than 53 per cent of Australians live in cities with populations in excess of 950,000—whereas in 1906 the nation possessed no urban areas of this size. In 1900 the majority of Australians were native born and of Anglo-Celtic ancestry; but by the mid-1990s overseas born residents from non-English-speaking countries accounted for 18.3 per cent of the country's urban but only 5 per cent of its non-metropolitan population. The multi-ethnic and multicultural nature of urban centres exists in increasingly stark contrast to the Anglo-Celtic culture of rural Australia.

Since the late nineteenth century population decline has characterized many of the country towns included in the wheat and wool belts. Their loss of banks and shops, combined with the poor quality of telephone services and limited educational facilities throughout rural Australia, has convinced many who live in the bush that city people are privileged, and that governments lack an understanding of rural difficulties. In many rural areas employment prospects are limited, and that has sparked a continuing migration of young rural men and women to the cities in search of work.

Importantly, the populations of some non-metropolitan regions have also grown. Towns that have become dormitory suburbs close to the capitals have increased in population, as have the retirement towns and villages along the coasts. Inland regional centres, which have absorbed the population and services from surrounding smaller towns, have also prospered. Tourism and mining, as well as pastoralism and agriculture, have become the backbone of the regional economies, although their interests are not identical. Indeed some commentators now argue that that bush lacks a uniting 'glue', a sense of shared identity and purpose.[21] For while the numbers and proportion of Australians living outside the capitals have increased since the 1970s, this internal migration has not resulted from a renewed commitment to agrarian idealism, a modern push to the bush. Rather the drivers of this major demographic change are the hedonistic attractions associated with coastal sun, surf, and sand. The new Australia of the twenty-first century has turned its back on some of its deepest landed social traditions, leaving behind both its rural ideals and the Empire in which they were nurtured.

---

[21] *The Land*, 1 January 2004.

Select Bibliography

BAIN ATTWOOD and S. G. FOSTER, eds, *Frontier Conflict: The Australian Experience* (Canberra, 2003).

RICHARD BROOME, *Aboriginal Australians: Black Responses to White Dominance 1788–1994*, 2nd edn (Sydney, 1994).

MICHAEL CANNON, *Life in the Country* (Melbourne, 1973).

ANNA CLARK and STUART MACINTYRE, *The History Wars* (Melbourne, 2003).

ROBB LINN, *Battling the Land: 200 Years of Rural Australia* (Sydney, 1999).

ROBERT MANNE, ed., *Whitewash: On Keith Windschuttle's Fabrication of Aboriginal History* (Melbourne, 2003).

STEPHEN H. ROBERTS, *History of Australian Land Settlement, 1788–1920* (Melbourne, 1924).

—— *The Squatting Age in Australia, 1835–1847* (Melbourne, 1935).

RICHARD WATERHOUSE, *The Vision Splendid: A Social and Cultural History of Rural Australia* (Fremantle, 2005).

KEITH WINDSCHUTTLE, *The Fabrication of Aboriginal History. Vol. I: Van Diemen's Land, 1803–1847* (Sydney, 2003).

4

Indigenous Subjects

ANN CURTHOYS

One of the most remarkable stories in modern history is that of the encounter between the Indigenous peoples of Australia and the British Empire—or at least its representatives in the form of officials, soldiers, sailors, missionaries, convicts, and settlers. It is a story that has been told many times and from a range of different vantage points—those of Indigenous peoples, British authorities, the settlers, and the historians from all these groups. Sometimes the Indigenous–British encounter has been viewed as a tragedy and at other times as an adventure; here as a story of catastrophic loss or there as one of immense gain; often as the foundation of a modern nation or alternatively as a story of the death and disappearance of many ancient ones.[1] It is above all the story of land seizure on a massive scale, and of the attempts on all sides to manage its consequences. In the process, Indigenous people became 'subjects' in many senses—British subjects entitled to the protection of British law, a subjected people whose sovereignty was not recognized and whose lands were taken, a favourite subject for European speculation about the nature of man, and a people whose subjectivity or sense of self was both dramatically transformed and yet, in the eyes of authorities, missionaries, and settlers, never transformed enough.

This chapter sets out to understand Indigenous peoples' histories since their contact with Europeans as the product of a three-way relationship: between the Indigenous peoples themselves, the British imperial authorities, and settler interests and societies. It traces these histories from Cook's voyage of 1770, to the present. While the role of Britain clearly declined after the granting of responsible government to the British colonies in Australia between 1856 and 1890, it did not disappear. Even after the Australian

---

[1] See Kevin Blackburn, 'Imagining Aboriginal Nations: Early Nineteenth Century Evangelicals on the Australian Frontier and the "Nation" Concept', *Australian Journal of Politics and History*, Vol. 48, no. 2 (2002), pp. 174–92.

nation was formed in 1901, the Empire and then the Commonwealth continued to influence events in Australia itself. British authorities were appealed to, especially by those unable to achieve the changes they wanted. Indigenous peoples themselves continued to hope the monarch could come to their aid.

In 1788, Indigenous peoples occupied the whole Australian continent. They had done so for around 45,000 years, arriving along the coasts from Africa and through South and South East Asia, reaching Australia long before *Homo sapiens* reached Europe. There was considerable diversity between different peoples—they spoke many different languages and dialects, and each society was multilingual. They differed across the country in their technology (the well-known boomerang and didgeridoo, for example, were not known in parts of the country), their cosmologies, kinship systems, basic foodstuffs, forms of land management, and much else besides.

Yet, for all these differences, some generalizations can be made that hold across the continent, and peoples were often connected to one another through the long-range trading routes which crossed it. The Indigenous peoples were foragers; without domesticable animals the people survived on gathering roots and vegetables, fishing, and hunting kangaroo and other native game. In some areas, fish traps were built and there was occasional plant cultivation and 'fire-stick farming', the skilful ecological deployment of fire. The simplicity of their material technology accompanied a social system so complex that European observers have taken a long time to understand it. Indigenous cosmologies everywhere involved the entwining of landscape, ritual, music, art, and law so that none formed a truly separate domain. While elders held a great deal of authority and power, Indigenous society was segmented into tribes, clans, bands, and families, rather than organized in a hierarchy or by centralized power. Daily life was organized around families and individuals whose strongest relationships were to the land, and through it, to the Dreamtime, and law.

While Cook and the British officials and settlers who followed him saw the Australian Indigenous peoples as extremely simple, living in a 'state of nature', it was in fact their complexity that made them vulnerable to the European invaders. Systems of land ownership were especially complex; rather than living on and owning neat parcels of land, descent groups were custodians of constellations of sacred sites. Landholding and land use were overlapping but distinct phenomena.[2] Land use patterns were intricate, with neighbouring clans foraging and hunting on each other's territory, with special arrangements for travellers and sojourners. These peoples were not 'nomadic' in the sense of wanderers; on the contrary; the land they belonged to was everywhere intricately marked and bounded by sacred sites, the homes of their Dreamtime ancestors, whose spirits lived in the land, rivers, rocks, trees, caves, animals, and plants around them. As Galarrwuy Yunupingu, an Indigenous Australian spokesman, and Hugh Brody, a scholar of Indigenous societies, especially the Inuit, have memorably noted, it is agricultural-commercial peoples who wander, and hunters and gatherers who stay at home.[3] With time to spend on ceremonial life, there was a rich tradition in dancing, storytelling, and rock and bark painting, some of it among the most remarkable that humanity has produced.

Europeans knew little of all this. Towards the end of the seventeenth century, English sea-adventurer William Dampier had encountered Indigenous people on the west coast of Australia, learnt little about them, and regarded them, influentially, as 'the miserablest people in the world'.[4] On reaching Australia's eastern shores in 1770, after his astronomical observations in Tahiti, as instructed, Cook encountered few Indigenous people. Many simply avoided him, watching from the shores, making no contact. Others, such as the Eora in Sydney and the Guugu Yimidhirr in northern Queensland, he did meet to a greater degree, but only in small numbers.[5] They were not interested in trade with Cook and his fellow voyagers. Cook thought them very simple people: technologically backward, with no clothing, very poor types of shelter, and who, most important of all, did not cultivate the land. Importantly for later considerations of British settlement in the region, he noted that they were not warlike, but rather 'a timorous and inoffensive race'.[6] The observations of Joseph Banks, the naturalist on the voyage, supported the view that the Indigenous peoples of eastern Australia would offer little or no resistance to British settlement. He noted their dependence on

---

[2] For a discussion of complex patterns of Indigenous landholding and land use, see Nicolas Peterson and Jeremy Long, *Australian Territorial Organisation: A Band Perspective* (Sydney, 1986).

[3] Hugh Brody, *The Other Side of Eden: Hunters, Farmers, and the Shaping of the World* (New York, 2001); Galarrwuy Yunupingu, Speech to National Press Club, Canberra, 13 February 1997.

[4] William Dampier, *A New Voyage Around the World* [1697], ed. A. Gray (London, 1937), pp. 312–13.

[5] See Nicholas Thomas, *Discoveries: The Voyages of Captain Cook* (London, 2003), p. 361.

[6] J. C. Beaglehole, ed., *The Journals of Captain Cook*, Vol. 1 (Cambridge, 1955), p. 396.

coastal fishing and concluded that further inland the continent was probably uninhabited.[7] When asked at a Committee of Enquiry in 1785 whether land at Botany Bay might be obtained 'by cession or purchase', he said he thought this was impossible, as 'there was nothing we could offer that they would take except provisions and those we wanted ourselves', and suggested that if faced with a settlement of 500 men, they would 'speedily abandon the Country to the New Comers'.[8] The message was clear: neither treaty nor purchase would be necessary.

The British government had instructed Cook not to seize any inhabited land he encountered; he was rather, 'with the consent of the natives to take possession of convenient situations in the country in the name of the king of Great Britain'. In fact, as Alan Atkinson shows in this volume, Cook, without bothering with Indigenous consent, claimed for George III far more than 'convenient situations'. In a ceremony on 22 August 1770, at a place off the tip of Cape York that he aptly named Possession Island, he declared, with imperial hubris, peaceful possession of a whole country of which he knew virtually nothing and had barely seen.

Why was there no idea that this was conquest, to be concluded with either a treaty or purchase? Legal thinking at the time held that colonies were formed either through conquest, or, if the land was uninhabited, settlement. The British did not see the Australian continent as truly inhabited for two reasons. First, as Cook and Banks had assured them, the land was inhabited very thinly. They appear to have shared the view of the world legal authority on the matter, the Swiss Emerich de Vattel, who had argued in 1758 in *The Law of Nations* that a handful of people could not be recognized as having the right to an entire continent; they could not reasonably complain 'if other nations, more industrious and too closely confined, come to take possession of a part of those lands'.[9] Secondly, it

---

[7] J. C. Beaglehole, ed., *The Endeavour Journal of Joseph Banks, 1768–1771*, Vol. 2 (Sydney, 1962), pp. 122–3, quoted in Stuart Banner, 'Why Terra Nullius? Anthropology and Property Law in Early Australia', *Law and History Review*, Vol. 23, no. 1 (2005), p. 2; Alan Frost, *Convicts and Empire: A Naval Question 1776–1811* (Melbourne, 1980), p. 122.

[8] Evidence of Joseph Banks to the Committee of Enquiry into Transportation, 10 May 1785, Public Record Office, HO 107/1, as reproduced in Jonathan King, *'In the Beginning ... ': The Story of the Creation of Australia from the Original Writings* (Melbourne, 1985), pp. 51–62; see also Merete Falck Borch, *Conciliation–Compulsion–Conversion: British Attitudes Towards Indigenous Peoples, 1763–1814* (Amsterdam, 2004), p. 92.

[9] Emerich de Vattel, *The Law of Nations* (1758), ed. Edward D. Ingraham (Philadelphia, 1853), p. 36, as quoted in Banner, 'Why Terra Nullius?', p. 3; Bruce Buchan, 'Subjecting the Natives:

was important to British thinking about property rights in land that the inhabitants did not (apparently) undertake cultivation, a practice Vattel described as an 'obligation imposed upon man by nature', and political theorist John Locke regarded as essential for true possession of land.[10] Thus the British authorities, in deciding to establish a penal settlement in New South Wales, in the 1780s, perhaps saw themselves as simply taking vacant land.[11] We should not imagine them agonizing over their decision; in fact, at this early stage they gave the Indigenous peoples little consideration in their decision to colonize. In so far as they thought about them at all, they saw them as belonging to the past, and the agricultural-commercial British Christians to the future.

Could the British officials who decided on the creation and continuation of the penal settlement at Botany Bay have foreseen the dire consequences for the Indigenous people? Could they have expected the large-scale human destruction and suffering that would ensue? It is impossible to say, yet important to note that the high levels of Indigenous depopulation in North and South America and the Caribbean were well known. Later, as British officials faced the enormity of what colonization was doing, and some realized the only way to save Indigenous lives and communities was to halt colonization itself, the British authorities were always to conclude that this was impossible. Colonization, with its relentless, destructive, logic of displacement and erasure, would continue.[12]

As the First Fleet assembled, Captain Arthur Phillip, the first Governor, was given his instructions. He was to establish the settlement, conciliate the natives, take measures to secure the safety of the officers and convicts, and commence cultivation. In other words, he was to be kind to the Indigenous peoples but not desist from his main task, making real through settlement Britain's possession of the land. The marines, convicts, and free settlers who followed in wave upon wave of settlement from January 1788 onwards, proceeded to take the land as if it were their own, as if it were uninhabited, or as it was later defined in subsequent legal terminology, *terra nullius*,

Aborigines, Property and Possession under Early Colonial Rule', *Social Analysis*, Vol. 45, no. 2 (November 2001), p. 147.

[10] Buchan, 'Subjecting the Natives', p. 146.

[11] Ibid., p. 147. But see Merete Borch, 'Rethinking the Origins of Terra Nullius', *Australian Historical Studies*, Vol. 32, no. 117 (October 2001), pp. 231–2.

[12] See Patrick Wolfe, 'Nation and MiscegeNation: Discursive Continuity in the Post-Mabo Era', *Social Analysis*, Vol. 36 (1994), pp. 93–152.

land belonging to no one.[13] At first this seemed quite easy, as prudent Indigenous people simply waited for the newcomers to leave. There were, in the early stages, moments of cultural exchange that could temporarily suggest that this was not conquest. The bedraggled state of the new arrivals, and the near-starvation conditions of the first two years of the colony, hardly suggested a conventional invasion force. Moreover, Phillip, in pursuance of his orders, handed out presents and ordered his men not to fire unless absolutely necessary. But within months, when the visitors did not leave, Indigenous attacks on officers and convicts began, in an attempt to drive them away. From the beginning, these acts were not to be recognized as indicating the people were defending their land, as the land was not seen as theirs to defend, but rather as criminal acts to be punished and deterred.

The process begun at Port Jackson gradually spread throughout the entire continent. As it became clear the settlers were not going away, and indeed were being continually supplemented by new arrivals, Indigenous peoples reacted in a variety of ways. While we have few direct insights into Indigenous consciousness and ideas, we can gain clues from their actions, and from the accounts of various observers, including missionaries and explorers. A common idea, for a while, was that the newcomers were returned ancestors—who else could they be, and how else could they know the land was there? Yet, as the white men seemed not to know their own relatives, or how to behave, Indigenous peoples everywhere concluded that white people were 'nothing but men'.[14] Once this was clear, one response seems to have been astonishment that white people had strayed so far from their own country that they could no longer care for it.[15]

Henry Reynolds suggests that Indigenous people tolerated visitors easily, so the first arrival of Whites was not of great concern. It was their staying put, and even more, their attempts to drive the people away from their own land, that was the problem. Food sources began to disappear, and ceremonial and religious life, with their care of country, were seriously disrupted. Many conflicts were sparked off by disputes over women; men offered women in

[13] For detailed discussion on this issue, see Henry Reynolds, *The Law of the Land* (Ringwood, Vic., 1987); Michael Connor, *The Invention of Terra Nullius* (Sydney, 2005); and Henry Reynolds, 'A New Historical Landscape? Henry Reynolds Responds to Michael Connor's The Invention of Terra Nullius', *The Monthly*, no. 11 (2006), pp. 50–53.

[14] Henry Reynolds, *The Other Side of the Frontier* (Melbourne, 1982), pp. 26–9.

[15] See Deborah Bird Rose, 'The Saga of Captain Cook: Remembrance and Morality', in Bain Attwood and Fiona Magowan, eds, *Telling Stories: Indigenous History and Memory in Australia and New Zealand* (Sydney, 2001), p. 68.

return for goods that did not come, and then retaliated. Perhaps one of the most important matters, which few Whites understood or reported, was the unwitting desecration of sacred sites, or being forcibly kept away from such sites. With the fundamentals of life—food, access to sacred sites, a nurturing cosmos, an ordered universe—disappearing, it was increasingly clear the invaders must be driven away. Land was essential for livelihood but also for any sense of meaningful life itself.

The attitude of the British officials, convicts, and free settlers also hardened. Some of the officers on the First Fleet had been interested in the Indigenous peoples; virtually unknown to Europeans, they occasioned considerable curiosity. This interest, plus a desire to communicate better with the Aboriginal people, led to the kidnapping first of Arabanoo and then of Bennelong, and placing them within colonial society.[16] It was not long, however, before negative judgements were made and became generally accepted. Watkin Tench remained curious, but even he thought them extremely primitive and of 'fickle, jealous, wavering disposition'.[17] Judge Advocate David Collins thought them as indicative of what all men must have been like before they formed society and acknowledged 'but one authority'.[18] As time went on and settlement spread, negative judgements of Indigenous peoples intensified. They were seen to be ugly, to lack hygiene, to be stupid. They were seen to be especially primitive, possibly the most primitive in the world, with the Tasmanians often seen as the most primitive of all. A popular idea in the eighteenth century, but still evident in the nineteenth, was that all peoples in the world were ranked on a scale, part of the 'great chain of being' commencing with inanimate things and ranging upwards through animals, man himself, heavenly beings, and finally God. On the human part of the chain, the British themselves were at the top, and Australian Aborigines or perhaps the Hottentots at the bottom.

The tragedy of colonization and destruction unfolded. The process was not a simple westward expansion but rather proceeded by the establishment of centres of settlement at various points around the perimeter of the

---

[16] Inga Clendinnen, *Dancing with Strangers* (Melbourne, 2003).

[17] Watkin Tench, *1788: Comprising A Narrative of the Expedition to Botany Bay and A Complete Account of the Settlement at Port Jackson*, edited and introduced by Tim Flannery (Melbourne, 1996), p. 57.

[18] David Collins, *An Account of the English Colony in New South Wales: with remarks on the dispositions, customs, manners, and of the native inhabitants of that country to which are added some particulars of New Zealand* (London, 1798), p. 544, as quoted by Buchan, 'Subjecting the Natives', p. 145.

continent, and fanning inwards from there. A second convict colony was established in 1803, after French interest in Van Diemen's Land, evident in the D'Entrecasteaux Expedition in 1792–3 and the Baudin Expedition in 1801–3, helped prompt the British to assert and secure the island as a British possession. This time, given their experiences at Port Jackson and beyond, they had good reason to expect there would be Indigenous opposition. In fact, the effects of colonization in Tasmania were especially destructive, as recorded by historians from James Bonwick in 1870 to Lyndall Ryan and Henry Reynolds in recent scholarship.[19] As in New South Wales, the British authorities in Van Diemen's Land found themselves in a difficult situation. Given Britain's claiming of the whole of Australia by rights of discovery and settlement, and not by conquest, there could be no acknowledgement of war, and no recognizable enemy. Instead, the laws of the mother country would instantly take effect over the whole country and the Indigenous peoples were to be declared British subjects, subject to and protected by British laws.

The early Governors in both colonies, therefore, set out to show the Indigenous peoples that the rule of law would be applied to them and the white newcomers equally. Phillip in 1789 ordered a white man who had stolen from the Eora to be flogged and arranged for Arabanoo, one of their number, to be present—he was not so much impressed as horrified. Governor Philip Gidley King in June 1802 proclaimed that any injustice to or wanton cruelty against the Aborigines would be punished in accordance with British law.[20] Much later, in 1828, Governor Arthur, in an attempt to impose the rule of law in increasingly violent Van Diemen's Land, displayed on trees a series of boards depicting an Indigenous man being hanged for spearing a white man, and then a white man hanged for spearing an Indigenous man. Yet, as one Governor after another found, imposing the rule of law to govern relations between Black and White proved an impossible ideal. The task was made even more difficult by the fact that the rules of evidence under the British legal system, which required the swearing of an oath to God, were such that Indigenous evidence could not be admitted.

[19] Lyndall Ryan, *The Aboriginal Tasmanians* (Sydney, 1994, first pub. 1981); Reynolds, *Fate of a Free People* (Ringwood, Vic., 1995). For a very different view see Keith Windschuttle, *The Fabrication of Aboriginal History* (Sydney, 2002) and for critiques see Robert Manne, ed., *Whitewash: On Keith Windschuttle's Fabrication of Aboriginal History* (Melbourne, 2003) and Stuart Macintyre with Anna Clark, *The History Wars* (Melbourne, 2003), pp. 161–70.

[20] N. B. J. Plomley, 'Aborigines and Governors', *Bulletin of the Centre for Tasmanian Historical Studies*, Vol. 3, no. 1 (1990–1), pp. 2–3, 6.

Violent conflict, often on a small scale, a killing here, another there, erupted all over the continent, stronger in some places than others. While, in theory, Indigenous attackers were to be brought before the courts and charged with crimes such as theft, assault, or murder, in practice, settlers retaliated against them with force. As settlement went on, authorities and settlers jointly conceived the idea of the 'punitive expedition', the gathering of a group of settlers or soldiers, or both, to answer an Indigenous attack with a bloody reprisal. It is worth remembering that most Governors came from a military or naval background and were used to the exercise of force when deemed necessary. Both Governors Darling and Bourke hoped to curb indiscriminate killing, but each was forced to yield to squatter demands for officially organized expeditions. By the 1830s every Governor had emphasized the necessity for settlers to counter Indigenous resistance through private expeditions, and most had authorized soldier expeditions to assist the progress of settlement. So little were the courts actually used to control the violence that the fiction that there was no invasion, no conquest, and no war was sometimes hard to maintain. Indeed, when Lieutenant Governor George Arthur in Van Diemen's Land, with his own distinguished career in the army behind him, confronted a determined Indigenous uprising in the late 1820s, he gave away the pretence and described it quite openly as war.[21]

Indigenous peoples were to be governed not only through military subjection but also through a process of civilization and Christianization, seen as gifts from the British to the Indigenous peoples. Far from having lost something, the latter now had the opportunity to learn the arts of civilized life, understand and obey British law, and, indeed, to find salvation; they would learn that afflictions borne upon Earth would be rewarded in Heaven. Although British authorities and settlers initially believed that no compensation was due to the Indigenous peoples of Australia for their loss of land (as it had not been theirs to begin with), over time the notion of compensation came to be favoured by the Colonial Office, Governors, and missionaries. It could take a number of forms, such as the provision of schools and missions, or the setting aside of small parcels of land on which they could learn to farm. Governor Lachlan Macquarie was more determined on this aspect of the matter than most. In a dispatch to the Secretary of State, Earl Bathurst, on 8 October 1814, he outlined his project of civilization, to become the basis of assimilation projects thereafter. He proposed a boarding

---

[21] Reynolds, *Fate of a Free People*, p. 66.

school for young Aborigines, which would separate them from their parents and thus the influence of elders, while the adults could be offered a piece of land where they could learn to settle and cultivate.[22] The power of tribal elders would be broken, and Aboriginal people could be taught to be good Christians and useful workers.

All these processes intensified from the late 1820s, when the pace of settlement quickened dramatically. As Bayly writes of the pattern worldwide, the deluge came between 1830 and 1890, when the massive expansion of settler populations led to the large-scale expropriation of native people's land, in Australasia, southern Africa, and North America.[23] Year after year, country by country, the land-taking continued. In Australia, a third new colony was established, this time on the western edge of the continent, marked on 18 June 1829 by Captain James Stirling in his proclamation of settlement giving notice, as was now usual, that crimes committed against the Indigenous population would be prosecuted.[24] In the east and the west, with sheep-farming proving a vast commercial resource, land-hungry squatters and settlers pushed ever outwards from established centres of settlement. As sources of food disappeared, Indigenous reprisals became more frequent, rarely observing the British rules of war—there were few open battles or ordered manoeuvres, and no implicit rules of engagement. The style of warfare they adopted was seen as 'treacherous', 'vengeful', 'ungrateful', and unpredictable, and settler attitudes hardened. Over time, some observers gradually realized that Aboriginal people believed their land had been stolen; as George Augustus Robinson, acting as a conciliator between the government and the Aborigines, put it, the Aborigines of Tasmania 'have a tradition amongst them that white men have usurped their territory'.[25]

With the conflict intensifying and Indigenous depopulation increasingly evident, there were some new concerns in Britain, notably in the Colonial Office. By the 1830s, it seemed that Indigenous peoples would not survive dispossession. The Secretary of State Sir George Murray ordered Governor

[22] Plomley, 'Aborigines and Governors', p. 6.

[23] C. A. Bayly, *The Birth of the Modern World 1780–1914* (London, 2004), p. 7.

[24] Neville Green, 'From Princes to Paupers: The Struggle for Control of Aborigines in Western Australia 1887–1898', *Early Days*, Vol. 11, pt. 4 (1998), p. 448.

[25] N. B. J. Plomley, *Friendly Mission: The Tasmania Journals and Papers of George Augustus Robinson, 1829–1834* (Sydney, 1966), p. 88 (journal entry for 23 November 1829), as quoted in Banner, 'Why Terra Nullius?', p. 10.

Arthur in 1830 to take steps to reduce the violence.[26] A 'reform' Parliament
in 1833 passed an Act abolishing slavery in the British Empire, and the anti-
slavery lobby, now with an excellent intercolonial information network, was
turning its attention to the rapid loss of Aboriginal life in British colonies.
The humanitarians and evangelicals wanted a policy which emphasized
protection, civilization, and Christianization, and they were increasingly
influential in the Colonial Office.[27]

Prompted by events in South Africa, where conflict had broken out
on the eastern Cape frontier between settlers and a coalition of Xhosa
chiefdoms, humanitarians successfully pressed the House of Commons to
establish a Select Committee on Aborigines in 1836, which would investigate
colonial policy across southern Africa, New South Wales, Van Diemen's
Land, New Zealand and the South Sea Islands, and British North America.[28]
The committee was Christian, liberal, and humanitarian, and sought to
protect, civilize, and convert the Indigenous peoples in British colonies.
The evidence it collected on the Australian colonies came from a number
of sources, especially men of religion—Anglican, Quaker, and Presbyterian.[29] The committee's two-volume report, published in 1836–7, argued that
Indigenous peoples were being morally degraded and physically destroyed
through both direct violence and introduced diseases. The effects on Aboriginal people in New South Wales were 'dreadful beyond example, both in the
diminution of their numbers and in their demoralization'.[30] The solution
was Christianization; without it these Indigenous peoples would become
extinct. The committee did not think that colonization should or could be
slowed or stopped, concluding specifically in relation to Van Diemen's Land:
'Whatever may have been the injustice of this encroachment, there is no
reason to suppose that either justice or humanity would now be consulted

[26] A. G. L. Shaw, 'British Policy Towards the Australian Aborigines, 1830–1850', *Australian Historical Studies*, Vol. 25, no. 99 (1992), p. 268.

[27] As discussed extensively in Henry Reynolds, *The Law of the Land*, (Ringwood, Vic., 1987).

[28] Alan Lester, 'British Settler Discourse and the Circuits of Empire', *History Workshop Journal*, no. 54 (2002), p. 26; Zoë Laidlaw, ' "Aunt Anna's Report": The Buxton Women and the Aborigines Select Committee, 1835–37', *Journal of Imperial and Commonwealth History*, Vol. 32, no. 2 (2004), pp. 1–28; Elizabeth Elbourne, 'The Sin of the Settler: The 1835–36 Select Committee on Aborigines and Debates over Virtue and Conquest in the Early Nineteenth Century British White Settler Empire', *Journal of Colonialism and Colonial History*, Vol. 4, no. 3 (2003).

[29] See Shaw, 'British Policy towards the Australian Aborigines, pp. 269–70; Lester, 'British Settler Discourse'; Elbourne, 'The Sin of the Settler'.

[30] Lester, 'British Settler Discourse', p. 27.

by receding from it.' Rather, the committee developed a model of proper British colonization which involved notions of compensation, protection, and civilization.[31]

The plans for the colonization of South Australia occurred at the height of this moment of angst within the British ruling elites of the 1830s. Land rights which had been ignored when New South Wales and Van Diemen's Land were settled had now to be considered seriously. In 1835, the Colonial Office told the South Australian Colonization Commission that unexplored land could not simply be taken, as the Crown needed to be assured that no injustice to the Indigenous occupiers of those lands was involved. The Commission replied, quite correctly, that Indigenous land rights had never been recognized before—land had simply been allocated to the settlers without reference to Aboriginal people.[32] The solution insisted upon by the Colonial Office was to establish a Protector, a colonial official, to watch over the allocation of land, keeping a small portion for the use and benefit of Aborigines, a solution that was also to find favour in New South Wales in the following decade.[33] Yet events in South Australia unfolded much as they did everywhere else. Settlers began to seek government assistance in putting down Indigenous resistance and the Protector had little effect. Punitive expeditions were formed, leading to violent clashes at the Coorong in 1840, Rufus River in 1841, and elsewhere.[34]

The Colonial Office never wavered in its refusal to acknowledge that a war of conquest was occurring, or in its insistence that the rule of law could and should prevail and that Indigenous life could be protected.[35] Secretary of State Glenelg reprimanded Governor Stirling in Western Australia in 1835 for not only authorizing but also participating in a punitive expedition (later known as the Battle of Pinjarra), and reminded him that Indigenous attackers should be apprehended and punished by law.[36] Glenelg reminded Governor Bourke in New South Wales two years later that it was incorrect

---

[31] Clive Turnbull, *Black War: The Extermination of the Tasmanian Aborigines* (Melbourne, 1965, first pub. 1948), p. 241; Lester, 'British Settler Discourse', p. 27.

[32] Banner, 'Why Terra Nullius?', p. 13; Shaw, 'British Policy towards the Australian Aborigines', p. 270.

[33] Shaw, 'British Policy towards the Australian Aborigines, p. 270.   [34] Ibid., p. 281.

[35] Damen Ward, 'A Means and Measure of Civilisation: Colonial Authorities and Indigenous Law in Australasia', *History Compass*, no. 1 (2003), p. 7.

[36] Glenelg to Stirling, 23 July 1835, quoted in Paul Hasluck, *Black Australians: A Survey of Native Policy in Western Australia, 1829–1897* (Melbourne, 1970), p. 50.

to regard the Aborigines 'as Aliens with whom a War can exist, and against whom H. M.'s troops may exercise belligerent right'.[37]

While the Aborigines' Committee's report had been instigated by events in southern Africa, it possibly had its greatest effect in the Australian colonies. In 1838, soon after his arrival in New South Wales and following Colonial Office instructions, Governor Gipps announced that the killing of Aborigines on the frontier was to be construed as murder, and punishable by law. As he put it: 'As human beings partaking in our common nature—as the aboriginal possessors of the soil from which the wealth of the country has been principally derived—and as subjects of the Queen, whose authority extends over every part of New Holland—the natives of the colony have an equal right with the people of European origin to the protection and assistance of the law of England.'[38] Within months of his arrival he ordered the trial of eleven Europeans for the massacre of twenty-eight Aborigines at Myall Creek; after an acquittal and then a second trial, seven of the eleven men were hanged for murder.[39]

Yet Gipps, like his predecessors and contemporaries in other colonies, was unsuccessful in putting an end to frontier violence. He encountered a determined settler majority, led by pastoralists who wanted no impediments to their land acquisition, and supported by many who also regarded Aborigines as their enemies. From their colonial experience, a distinct settler ethos and 'knowledge' of Indigenous peoples and how they should be treated had emerged. This knowledge was not peculiar to the Australian colonies but rather was shared with British settlers in Cape Colony, New Zealand, and elsewhere. The settlers were furious at the way humanitarians, both in England and in the colonies, blamed them for what was happening on the frontiers. They were being portrayed as acquisitive and brutal; the settlers, however, saw themselves as true Britons acting in their own defence. As the *Sydney Morning Herald* put it during the height of debates following the Myall Creek Massacre in 1838, 'The prevailing canting humbug which always attributes the butcherings of savages to European settlers, is almost

---

[37] Buchan, 'Subjecting the Natives', p. 151; Shaw, 'British Policy towards the Australian Aborigines', p. 272.

[38] Proclamation Concerning the Establishment of Commissioners of Crown Land in New South Wales, 21 May 1839, *British Parliamentary Papers: The Aborigines: Australian Colonies, 1844*, pp. 20–1, quoted in Henry Reynolds, *Dispossession: Black Australians and White Invaders* (Sydney, 1989), pp. 188–9.

[39] R. H. W. Reece, *Aborigines and Colonists: Aborigines and Colonial Society in New South Wales in the 1830s and 1840s* (Sydney, 1974), ch. 4.

beyond bearing.'[40] Confronted with these determined pastoralists and their supporters, Gipps could not turn British policy into colonial practice. Nor was the Colonial Office in any position to enforce its policies. By the end of the 1840s, its role had been reduced to the maintenance of the Native Police Force in the remaining frontier areas, an annual blanket distribution, and some minor forms of medical assistance. In effect, the Colonial Office had failed to develop or guarantee policies that offered practical protection to Indigenous peoples.

As the consequences of settlement became evident, observers in Britain and the colonies debated questions of causation and responsibility. Some emphasized the actions of the British and colonial governments, others the convicts and free settlers beyond government control, and yet others the Indigenous peoples themselves. There was a growing idea that the Indigenous people were dying because they had simply given up. The problem was not the actions of the settlers but the Indigenous people's response of hopelessness. This was a not unusual settler response to Indigenous population decline; Brantlinger notes that it was common in extinction discourse worldwide to attribute the disappearance of native peoples to some lack or fault in themselves.[41] With the example of the Tasmanians apparently disappearing by the 1840s, the idea that the Indigenous peoples were doomed to extinction took hold, and most colonial policy makers believed Indigenous people would soon die out. Their own task was to 'smooth the dying pillow' of those of full descent, and to ensure that those of mixed Indigenous–European descent were assimilated into settler society. Indigenous people as a distinct group were to disappear; as one country newspaper put it as early as 1866, 'the barbarous races will melt from the path of the Caucasian, not by a bloody or a brutal series of massacres and poisonings, but by a gradual and beneficial mingling and absorption.'[42]

Historians are confronted with a daunting task in describing and evaluating the devastating impact of colonization on Aboriginal peoples. The widely held nineteenth-century view that the latter were doomed to extinction was a natural corollary to the logic of colonization itself. This assumption that one group of people would necessarily displace another compels us to consider whether Australia's Empire was founded on a fundamentally genocidal

---

[40] Lester, 'British Settler Discourse', p. 39.

[41] Patrick Brantlinger, *Dark Vanishings: Discourse on the Extinction of Primitive Races, 1800–1930* (Ithaca, 2003), p. 2.

[42] *Deniliquin Chronicle*, 17 February 1866.

impulse. In thinking about the terrible context of the Second World War in 1944, Raphaël Lemkin described genocide as having multiple possible causes. One was the destruction of the life world of the invaded by depletion of nourishment leading to malnutrition, disease, and a precipitous decline in birth rates. Another was the destruction of religion and spiritual leadership, and yet another the taking of children so that the next generation would not see themselves as part of the colonized group.[43] All these things happened in the Australian colonies, as so often occurs when an agricultural-commercial society imposes itself on hunter-gatherer peoples. Disease was in many places a major killer. Starting with the early smallpox epidemics, in 1789 and 1829, a string of illnesses were imported against which Indigenous people had little resistance. Diseases common in Europe such as influenza and gastric illnesses were in many cases fatal. Affected by malnutrition and disease, including venereal disease, birth rates declined dramatically before stabilizing and eventually recovering. In a situation where sacred sites were everywhere desecrated and Indigenous people were barred from access, spiritual care for the land and the people was seriously undermined. All this was compounded by the experience of widespread killings on the frontier, often with the express purpose of eliminating the Indigenous presence. Many historians find the term 'genocide' inapplicable in the Australian context on the basis that there was no intent to destroy a people, though some, such as Henry Reynolds and Dirk Moses, agree that Queensland witnessed 'genocidal moments', when the settlers truly did seek to wipe the Indigenous peoples in their way from the face of the earth.[44] Others, such as Tony Barta, argue that what we see in colonial situations like that of the British colonies in Australia is an instance of genocidal relations, in which the primary intent, of taking the land whatever the consequences, overrides all other considerations.[45] Yet others suggest that intent can change over time. As Roger W. Smith argues in general

[43] In *Axis Rule in Occupied Europe* (Washington, 1944), Raphael Lemkin wrote: 'Genocide has two phases: one, destruction of the national pattern of the oppressed group; the other, the imposition of the national pattern of the oppressor. This imposition, in turn, may be made upon the oppressed population which is allowed to remain, or upon the territory alone, after removal of the population and the colonization of the area by the oppressor's own nationals', p. 79.

[44] Henry Reynolds, *An Indelible Stain: The Question of Genocide in Australia's History* (Melbourne, 2001); Dirk Moses, 'An Antipodean Genocide: The Origins of the Genocidal Moment in the Colonization of Australia', *Journal of Genocide Research*, Vol. 2, no. 1 (2000), pp. 89–106.

[45] Tony Barta, 'After the Holocaust: Consciousness of Genocide in Australia', *Australian Journal of Politics and History*, Vol. 31, no.1 (1984), pp. 154–61.

terms: 'Sometimes … genocidal consequences precede any conscious decision to destroy innocent groups to satisfy one's aims. This is most often
the case in the early phase of colonial domination, where through violence,
disease, and relentless pressure Indigenous peoples are pushed towards
extinction.' Smith draws attention to the question of intent *after* the destructive impact of colonization has become apparent. 'With the recognition of
the consequences of one's acts', he argues, 'the issue is changed: to persist is
to intend the death of a people. This pattern of pressure, recognition, and
persistence is typically what happened in the nineteenth century.'[46] While
the question of intent continues to be debated, few dispute the disastrous
consequences of colonization for Indigenous peoples.

Yet population decline and cultural destruction were not the whole story. In those parts of the country where frontier conflict had ended and
Indigenous dispossession was virtually complete, a new set of relationships
between settlers and Indigenous peoples developed. A whole range of social
and economic changes, especially the rapid increase in the size and density
of the British population and the diversification of the colonial economy,
had an enormous impact on Indigenous groups and individuals. Aided
by the expansion of railways and other forms of transport and communication, settlement intensified, with more and larger towns, and more
intensive farming. While Indigenous populations continued to decline in
the face of these pressures, the rate of decline slowed, till at some point it
stopped, and the demographic recovery began. As Bayly puts it on a world
scale, writing of the last two decades of the nineteenth century, the 'final
immolation, ultimately, did not occur … Indigenous peoples, battered and
restricted, began in some cases to learn techniques that made possible their
longer-term survival.'[47] Bayly himself regards the Indigenous Australians as
an exception to this general rule, but in fact they fit very well within it. Many
Indigenous people began to work for Europeans, especially in pastoral work,
in shepherding, sheep washing, shearing, stock riding, and other tasks, but
also in cedar-getting and whaling. In some areas, these forms of support were
supplemented by traditional food-getting such as fishing and collecting eggs
and native honey. Despite loss of land, substantial loss of life, and the destruction of much of their traditional society, the Indigenous Australians still

---

[46] Roger W. Smith, 'Human Destructiveness and Politics: The Twentieth Century as an Age
of Genocide', in I. Wallimann and M. N. Dobkowski, *Genocide and the Modern Age* (New York,
1987), p. 23.

[47] Bayly, *The Birth of the Modern World*, p. 447.

maintained themselves in groups distinct from the European population, with a distinctive identity. British colonial society had become to them all-powerful, and they were now to a large extent economically dependent on it, but it had not absorbed them. The fact of dispossession was a most enduring and bitter element in Indigenous consciousness and orientation to the future and to settler society.

*   *   *

In the mid-1950s, the Australian colonies, with the exception of Western Australia, were granted responsible government, a form of limited self-government which transferred control of internal matters to the colonies themselves, retaining British control over external matters, foreign policy, and defence. Aboriginal policy was one of those matters handed over to the colonists, that is, to those whose interests conflicted most directly with those of Aboriginal people. While this meant a substantial reduction in British influence and interest in Aboriginal affairs, Britain, and especially the Crown, retained some significance for Aboriginal people thereafter. In their continuing loyalty to Britain, the Colonial authorities encouraged Indigenous people to understand the significance of Britain, especially its monarch, much as they had done before Britain left the scene. When Governor Fitzroy announced in 1850 the creation of 'a suitable number of Reserves of moderate extent', Land Commissioners had explained to Indigenous people that Queen Victoria had set aside land for them.[48] Both before and after the granting of responsible government, blankets were distributed to Indigenous people in many country towns on the sovereign's birthday. Indigenous people were involved in royal visits, often to perform a dance or ceremony of some kind at occasions marking a welcome to visiting monarchs, notably in 1867–8, with the visit of Prince Alfred to several colonies. This strategy had an unintended consequence: over time, Indigenous people began to see the Queen as an alternative source of authority, as someone who could help them in their battle with settler governments and peoples, especially in their quest for the return of their land. We know from a range of other imperial and colonial histories how strongly Indigenous and colonized peoples in other regions, such as South Africa, saw the Crown as a possible source of redress for the wrongs they

---

[48] Heather Goodall, *Invasion to Embassy: Land in Aboriginal Politics in New South Wales, 1770–1972* (Sydney, 1996), p. 56.

were suffering at the hands of British settlers and their descendants, and it is clear that Australian Indigenous people had similar understandings.[49]

From the late 1850s, Indigenous peoples began to demand the return of at least some of their land, especially in those areas where they had lost the most. As Heather Goodall has shown, they adopted a variety of strategies to make their case. They might approach the government or the press directly; they sometimes secured a local white figure, such as a policeman or cleric, to convey their demands for them; or they could take direct action by reoccupying and squatting on some of their lands, perhaps building huts and planting crops.[50] In 1859 in Victoria, the Taungerong and Woiwurrung members of the Kulin confederacy in the Goulburn Valley began to petition collectively for the return of some of their land. They first chose land at a culturally significant site, at Acheron, and when driven away by local Whites, settled on another site.[51] Four years later, through the Governor of Victoria, Kulin petitioned Queen Victoria for land at Coranderrk, promising to 'live like white men almost'.[52] Soon afterwards, the Victorian government reserved land for them in their own country, and told them of Queen Victoria's 'interest' in their welfare.[53] With the assistance of a missionary, John Green, they successfully farmed the area through the 1860s and 1870s.

These successful land demands influenced the Yorta Yorta and Pangerang people in the Moira and Ulupna tribes on the other side of the Murray River, in New South Wales, to make similar demands. The people on the privately run Maloga mission sent a petition to the Governor requesting a grant of land on the forest reserve adjoining the mission. Europeans, they said, had taken the land and depleted Indigenous sources of game. 'We feel', they wrote, 'that our old mode of life is not in keeping with the instructions we have received and we are earnestly desirous of settling down to more orderly habits of industry, that we may form homes for our families.'[54] In 1883, after much pressure from Matthews and Sydney-based humanitarians, New South Wales set aside reserves for the purposes of education and employment, and gave the Indigenous people to understand

---

[49] Mark McKenna, *This Country: A Reconciled Republic?* (Sydney, 2004), p. 66.

[50] Goodall, *Invasion to Embassy*, p. 76.

[51] Richard Broome, *Aboriginal Victorians: A History since 1800* (Sydney, 2005), p. 123; Bain Attwood, *Rights for Aborigines* (Sydney, 2003), p. 8.

[52] Broome, *Aboriginal Victorians*, p. 124.   [53] McKenna, *This Country*, p. 67.

[54] Attwood, *Rights for Aborigines*, pp. 28–9.

that these lands were a gift from Queen Victoria.[55] A second petition
for land from Maloga in 1887, addressed also to the Governor, reminded
him of 'the wishes of Her Most Gracious Majesty Queen Victoria'.[56] The
belief that Queen Victoria was personally responsible for these land grants
was to be an important feature in land rights politics in the twentieth
century.

In Western Australia, the story was at once a little different, and yet in the
end depressingly the same. There, where responsible self-government was
not granted until 1890, the British government managed to insert a stronger
protection for Aborigines in the colonial constitution than had been possible
in the other colonies. While still under direct British control, the colony had
established an Aborigines Protection Board in 1886, primarily to regulate
their conditions of employment. Two years later during negotiations over
the Western Australian constitution, in an attempt to secure some protection
for Aborigines, Governor Broome inserted a clause to ensure one per cent
of annual revenue of the colony was spent on Aboriginal protection and
well-being. The Legislative Council reluctantly accepted the clause as the
price for responsible government, but over the next decade, Premier John
Forrest and other members railed in Parliament against these arrangements.
In the course of negotiations with the Colonial Office during the 1890s over
the matter, during which time there was considerable frontier violence and
continuing loss of life through disease and other causes, Forrest expressed
what were by now classic settler views on Aborigines: money was useless
to them, civilization was unwise ('The more civilised a native is, the less
likely he is to stick to constant employment'), and flogging was not a severe
punishment as 'a native is exposed to weather, for he does not wear clothing,
and his skin gets hard and in consequence the cat-o-nine-tails has not
much effect on him'. After consistent pressure from the Western Australian
government, the British authorities gave way, and repealed the relevant
section of the constitution in 1898. Immediately, the budget for the Board
was slashed.[57]

*   *   *

In the debates of the 1890s leading up to the Federation of the six British
colonies into an independent Australian nation, Indigenous policies were

---

[55] Goodall, *Invasion to Embassy*, p. 103.   [56] Attwood, *Rights for Aborigines*, p. 30.
[57] Green, 'From Princes to Paupers', pp. 454–8.

rarely discussed. The notion that Indigenous people were fast disappearing was dominant. In the constitution that emerged from these debates, accepted by Britain in June 1900, the new Commonwealth Parliament attained the right to make laws with respect to the 'people of any race' except the 'aboriginal native race in Australia and the Maori race in New Zealand'; furthermore, these same 'aboriginal natives' were not to be counted in the census. The settler colonies which had developed such harsh policies towards Indigenous peoples were now to be states within a new nation, and to have full control over Aboriginal policy. As democracy was extended for white Australians, for example, by extending the vote to women, it was withheld for many decades from Indigenous peoples. For them, there was a system of totalitarian or near-totalitarian control.

Indigenous peoples seeking land and other rights therefore engaged with state governments; for several decades the new Federal government seemed to have little relevance. Indeed, those seeking change were more likely to seek help from British public opinion and even the British Crown than they were to seek Federal intervention. This was evident first in Western Australia, where direct British authority had only recently ended. An anti-pastoralist campaign, conducted by leaders of the new population which had come to Western Australia during the 1890s gold rushes, was in full swing as the nineteenth century gave way to the twentieth. Liberal and humanitarian in persuasion, they were especially critical of the system of employment, akin to slavery, of Aborigines in the pastoral industry. In the first session of the Commonwealth Parliament in 1901, the Labor member for Coolgardie, Hugh Mahon, denounced pastoralist practices and moved for a Royal Commission. Allegations of 'brutal slavery' appeared in the *London News*, prompting a discreet British request for official comment.[58] In 1904, a Royal Commission enquired into the allegations and into Aboriginal administration generally; the following year, an especially draconian Aborigines Act was passed, increasing government powers of surveillance and control to unprecedented levels.[59]

Appeals to British authorities were evident also in other states. There were further sporadic petitions to the imperial monarch, especially from the growing number of Indigenous activists who began using western

---

[58] Anna Haebich, *For Their Own Good: Aborigines and Government in the Southwest of Western Australia, 1900–1940* (Perth, 1988), pp. 72–3.

[59] The enquiry was the *Royal Commission on the Administration of Aborigines and the Condition of the Natives*; see Green, 'From Princes to Paupers', pp. 454–8.

methods to press their land demands.[60] Jane Duren, an Aboriginal woman from Batemans Bay in New South Wales and a member of the Australian Aboriginal Progressive Association, appealed to King George V in 1926 on the loss of reserve lands.[61] William Cooper, a leading Aboriginal activist in Victoria, petitioned the King in 1933, seeking his intervention to 'prevent the extinction of the Aboriginal race and give better conditions for all'.[62] He was well aware that appealing to British opinion was a good way to put pressure on local authorities, in the late 1930s corresponding with the Anti-Slavery Society and writing a letter to *The Times* in London. Like white Australians, these Indigenous activists took their British subjecthood seriously. Cooper commented that Aborigines were 'his Majesty's subjects and should be considered as much under the safeguard of the Law as any other man and equally entitled to the privileges of British subjects'.[63]

The practice of gaining publicity in the British press as a way of embarrassing Australian governments continued to be a favoured strategy for humanitarians opposed to segregationist and exploitative practices. Mary Bennett, a teacher, writer, and activist, became a leading pro-Aboriginal campaigner in the late 1920s. She was known to readers of the *Manchester Guardian* as 'a champion of the aborigines', and her influential book *The Australian Aboriginal as a Human Being*, published in London in 1930, helped bring Aboriginal demands to the attention of British readers. Bennett was just one of a number of feminist campaigners who took up the cause of Aboriginal rights in the 1920s and 1930s, using the London-based British Commonwealth League (BCL), an organization of women in the Dominions, to do so. The reports of Australian delegates to BCL conferences in London, detailing the treatment of black women as slaves, the removal of children, the proliferation of reserves, and police corruption, were aired in British papers, including the *Daily Mail* in London. The strategy worked to a degree: fear of embarrassment in the eyes of Britain forced some belated government action on the issues.[64]

---

[60] For a discussion of Indigenous petitions in Australia, New Zealand, and North America, see Ravi de Costa, 'Identity, Authority, and the Moral Worlds of Indigenous Petitions', *Comparative Studies in Society and History*, Vol. 48, no. 3 (2006), pp. 669–98.

[61] Attwood, *Rights for Aborigines*, p. 60.

[62] Andrew Markus, 'William Cooper and the 1937 Petition to the King', *Aboriginal History*, Vol. 7, no. 1 (1983), p. 53.

[63] Attwood, *Rights for Aborigines*, p. 61.

[64] Fiona Paisley, *Loving Protection? Australian Feminism and Aboriginal Women's Rights, 1919–1939* (Melbourne, 2000), pp. 11, 113–14.

Two events in 1948 signalled some important changes for Indigenous Australians. One was the passing of the Australian Citizenship Act which established Australians, including Indigenous Australians, for the first time, as Australian citizens; given the continuing allegiance to the British Crown, however, Australians were still regarded as British subjects, a situation which ended only in 1984.[65] This conferral of citizenship, and yet the withholding of many of the rights, such as freedom of movement and, in some states, the vote, enjoyed by other citizens, led many Indigenous activists to demand from this time 'full citizenship'. In doing so, they were assisted by another important event in 1948, the passing of the UN Universal Declaration of Human Rights, signalling a new era worldwide in attention to questions of racial equality. International pressure intensified with the passing in 1957 of International Labour Organization Convention 107 on the employment of Indigenous peoples, and the adoption in 1963 of the UN Declaration on the Elimination of All Forms of Racial Discrimination. Henceforth, governments were urged by the UN to work to eliminate racial discrimination from their society altogether. Senior Australian public servants serving on a committee formed to respond to the changing UN situation, secretly agreed in March 1964 that 'there was an urgent need to remove, as far as practicable, instances of racial discrimination in Australia in order to ensure that Australia's international reputation and influence are not to be seriously endangered'.[66]

Even as the sphere of international surveillance was thus widening, Britain and the British Commonwealth nevertheless remained important for Indigenous campaigners and their supporters. The monarch retained a special importance for Aboriginal people; from 1954 onwards, it became common for them to travel huge distances to perform for five minutes before the Queen or other royal visitors.[67] When Mary Bennett wrote to the Anti-Slavery Society in London in 1955, detailing a range of abuses, the society sent Jessie Street, a well-known Australian then living in London, to Australia to investigate.[68] Doreen Trainor, a member of the Western Australian Original

---

[65] Ann-Mari Jordens, *Redefining Australians: Immigration, Citizenship, and National Identity* (Sydney, 1995), pp. 152–5.

[66] Confidential Report of the Inter-Departmental Committee [Departments of External Affairs, Attorney-Generals, Prime Minister's and Territories] on Racial Discrimination, March 1964, A1838/1, 929/5/6 part 1, National Archives of Australia, as quoted in John Chesterman, 'Defending Australia's Reputation: How Indigenous Australians Won Civil Rights, part II', *Australian Historical Studies*, no. 117 (October 2001), p. 205.

[67] McKenna, *This Country*, p. 64.

[68] Peter Sekuless, *Jessie Street: A Rewarding but Unrewarded Life* (Brisbane, 1978), p. 169.

Australians Progress Association, embarrassed the Australian government mightily when she wrote in 1961 to all Commonwealth Prime Ministers, asking that the 'status, treatment and conditions of the Australian aborigines be put on the agenda of the next Prime Ministers' meeting'.[69] This was at the very time that the Commonwealth Prime Ministers were grappling with the problem of South Africa's continued membership of the Association in the light of its offensive apartheid policies. That a connection was made to the plight of Aboriginal people is indicative of the many ways that the 'winds of change' of decolonization were felt in Australia.[70]

In the end, though, the engagement of Indigenous people with the Australian nation had to be dealt with as a national matter. The campaigns of the 1950s and 1960s culminated in a successful referendum in 1967 to change the Australian constitution, giving the Federal government power in Aboriginal affairs, and for the first time counting Aboriginal people in the national census. In the states, discriminatory legislation was repealed and new legislation outlawing racial discrimination eventually put in its place. Indigenous demands emphasized land rights, autonomy, and sovereignty, as well as the extension of access to the benefits of education, health, and other services, and new leaders like Charles Perkins, Lowitja O'Donohue, Patrick and Mick Dodson, Marcia Langton, Noel Pearson, and Galarrwuy Yunupingu emerged to articulate the necessity for new arrangements and new ways of thinking. Such leaders spoke with a moral authority that was hard to dismiss. For their part, non-Indigenous Australians developed a new form of nationalism which sought new forms of engagement with Australia's Indigenous peoples. Many now felt that the nation had to reconstruct, and indeed redeem, itself though a greater recognition of the Indigenous aspects of Australia's history, culture, and heritage.[71]

A major change in the legal recognition of Indigenous rights came with the landmark High Court judgment, *Mabo v Queensland, no. 2* in 1992, which recognized the existence of Native Title (that is, certain Indigenous rights

[69] Jennifer Clark, ' "Something to Hide": Aborigines and the Department of External Affairs, January 1961–January 1962', *Journal of the Royal Australian Historical Society*, Vol. 82, pt 1, 1997.

[70] Jennifer Clark, ' "The Winds of Change": Aborigines and the International Politics of Race, 1960–1972', *International History Review*, Vol. XX, no. 1 (March 1998), pp. 89–117.

[71] See Anthony Moran, 'As Australia Decolonizes: Indigenizing Settler Nationalism and the Challenges of Settler/Indigenous Relations', *Ethnic and Racial Studies*, Vol. 25, no. 6 (November 2002), pp. 1013–42.

to the occupation and use of land) on Crown Land. This was followed four years later by the *Wik* judgment, which extended that recognition, under certain conditions, to land held under pastoral lease. These two judgments were based in part on the recognition that the British Colonial Office had on a number of occasions recognized native title in the Australian colonies in the 1830s and 1840s, the period when concern about the destruction of Aboriginal peoples in the wake of colonization had been at a peak. While this mid-nineteenth century recognition of native title played little role in settler consciousness, and had since been largely ignored by both governments and legal determinations, it did provide a basis for a very belated legal overturning of the long-standing idea that the Australian continent had been in a legal sense uninhabited at the time of British possession. The judgments were followed throughout the 1990s by legislation and much-agonized public discussion over land rights and indeed Indigenous rights more generally. Alongside them went what was known as a movement for reconciliation, stimulated in part by the government-sponsored Council for Reconciliation, and in part by changed public attitudes. This movement helped keep Indigenous rights and demands in the forefront of public discourse through the 1990s, culminating in the Walk for Aboriginal Reconciliation—known popularly as the Walk Across the Bridge—in Sydney on 28 May 2000, in which up to a quarter of a million people took part, accompanied by many similar events in towns across the country.

In these continuing debates over Indigenous rights and the morality of the nation, the role of Britain faded, but did not entirely disappear. Some Indigenous people did not forget Britain, seeing it sometimes as colonizer, sometimes as potential protector against a settler nation which had great difficulty in divesting itself of harsh acquisitive settler attitudes. On Australia Day, 26 January 1988, activist Burnam Burnam claimed England for Aboriginal people by standing on the beach at Dover and raising the Aboriginal flag, an event widely covered in both the British and Australian media. This theatrical act of inversion was a clever symbolic reminder that an invasion had taken place from one country to another, from one side of the world to another. Another symbolic ceremony, on 27 February 2002, occurred when Adelaide's statue of Queen Victoria was showered with water as a symbolic gesture in the Adelaide Arts Festival's opening ceremony, a day after Queen Elizabeth had left the city. Accompanied by a performance by the Bangarra Dance Theatre, the ceremony was seen as 'an act of healing and cleansing', representing the washing away

of the history of the British Empire and the colonization of Australia.[72]
Yet the British dimension of Australia's history of invasion, settlement,
colonization, dispossession, institutionalization, and exploitation of the
Indigenous peoples of Australia cannot be washed away. It lives on in the
bodies and minds of Australia's population of twenty million, in a myriad
of interactions, policies, identifications, and cultural memories. It is a story
of land hunger and the differences between two forms of society so great
that one almost overwhelmed the other. Yet the Indigenous fightback and
survival against the odds, and the attention paid to it in modern Australia,
are signs that the story of engagement is far from over. The moral, legal,
cultural, and economic aspects of the colonial process are as much under
scrutiny as ever.

Select Bibliography

BAIN ATTWOOD, *Rights for Aborigines* (Sydney, 2003).
RICHARD BROOME, *Aboriginal Australians: Black Responses to White Dominance*
    (Sydney, 2002).
—— *Aboriginal Victorians: A History Since 1800* (Sydney, 2005).
HEATHER GOODALL, *Invasion to Embassy: Land in Aboriginal Politics in New
    South Wales, 1770–1972* (Sydney, 1996).
ANN MCGRATH, *Born in the Cattle* (Sydney, 1987).
MARK MCKENNA, *Looking for Blackfellas' Point: An Australian History of Place*
    (Sydney, 2002).
R. H. W. REECE, *Aborigines and Colonists: Aborigines and Colonial Society in
    New South Wales in the 1830s and 1840s* (Sydney, 1974).
HENRY REYNOLDS, *The Other Side of the Frontier* (Melbourne, 1982).
—— *Frontier* (Sydney, 1987).
CHARLES ROWLEY, *The Destruction of Aboriginal Society* (Melbourne, 1970).
LYNDALL RYAN, *The Aboriginal Tasmanians* (Brisbane, 1981).

---

[72] McKenna, *This Country*, p. 66.

5

Art and the Environment: New Visions from Old

ANNE GRAY

Australia is portrayed as the 'Enchanted Coast', set in a broad expanse of blue sea across the forty-eight panels of Guan Wei's panoramic work entitled *Dow: Island* 2002 (National Gallery of Australia, Canberra). Here is a land beyond the ominous 'Calamity Island', where people are expiring, and 'Trepidation Island', where one group threatens another, and further away than the desirable 'Aspiration Island', onto which people clamber. Australia is a place that people are seeking in their boats across dangerous waters—not any more as Empire builders or colonizers, but as émigrés wanting to live a dream and achieve a better life in a New Society.

Guan Wei (born 1957) is a Chinese-born Australian artist who inevitably looks at Australia from the viewpoint of a recent immigrant, presenting it as an enchanted place, but also guarded by menacing black crows, determined to keep out unwanted refugees. Guan Wei presents this domain using a mixture of artistic approaches—he merges the perspective of European map-makers charting new territory together with the viewpoint of traditional Chinese scroll painters. He evokes a multicultural place where western traditions (of map-making) meet eastern approaches (of art-making), where an understanding of the imperial past converges with an awareness of the present.

This view of Australia and its surrounds is imaginary; and yet the artist powerfully conveys contemporary political attitudes towards 'boat people' and the fate of many refugees searching for a home. He has observed that 'the work is like a big history that includes ancient animals and human migrations and the situation of refugees in the present.'[1] In addition to providing a reflection on contemporary society and Australia's position in the world, Guan Wei also reflects his own response to 'being human in a

---

[1] Guan Wei, 2000, quoted in Deborah Hart, 'Guan Wei: *Efficacy of Medicine* 1995', in Anne Gray, ed., *Australian Art in the National Gallery of Australia* (Canberra, 2002), p. 389.

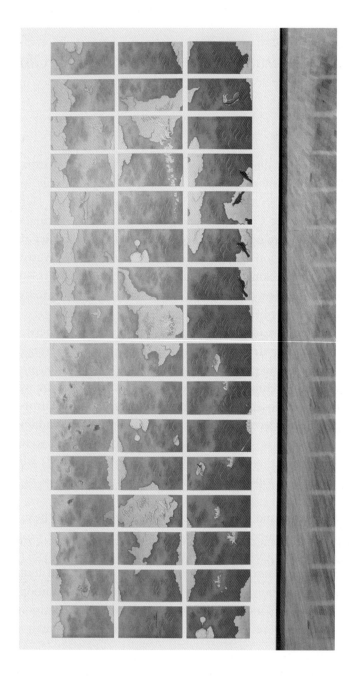

Figure 5.1 Guan Wei, *Dow: Island* (2002). National Gallery of Australia, Canberra, 2003. Courtesy of the artist, Sherman Galleries & Casula Powerhouse Art Centre, Sydney

society of mixed cultures'.[2] He powerfully conveys a new vision of Australia, which goes beyond national borders to evoke cultural coexistence among diverse global cultures.

Here I shall look at some of the ways that artists have portrayed the Australian landscape, and how this reflects both their own relationship to the environment and that of their society. I shall consider how they used European approaches to painting to contribute to the statement they were making, and the ways in which the artists suggested continuity between the new settlement and the 'homeland'. I shall look at the ways in which the artists observed the remarkable scenery of Australia and the activities of the 'pioneers'. I shall also glance at some Indigenous responses to the European invasion. Inevitably, in a subject as large as this, I shall look at a few works of only some of the many artists who have been engaged in this visual exploration of conquest and beyond in a complex historical narrative.

*   *   *

Cartographers charting the territory, and artists on voyages of discovery, were the first to create non-Indigenous views of Australia. During the seventeenth century, mariners employed by the Dutch East India Company discovered 'New Holland' (Australia) as a result of a new sailing route from the Cape of Good Hope through the Indian Ocean to Java, and they made maps charting their discoveries which were later consulted by British mariners.

The artists on Cook's three voyages to the South Pacific (1768–71; 1772–5; 1776–80) did not make many images of the landscape of Australia. The artist of the first voyage, Sydney Parkinson, made many realistic drawings of plants and animals in all their variety, which created great interest and enthusiasm back in Britain, but no landscapes. Cook's second expedition included the artist William Hodges, who produced notable landscape paintings of Tahiti, Easter Island, and New Zealand, but none of Australia. On the third voyage, John Webber's main purpose was to provide drawings of the most memorable incidents, and the costumes, houses, and customs of the people they visited. William Ellis (*c*.1756–85), a natural history draughtsman on

---

[2] Ibid. See also David Williams, 'Guan Wei: Dow Island 2002', in Caroline Turner and Nancy Sever, *Witnessing to Silence: Art and Human Rights* (Canberra, 2003), pp. 48–51, and Deborah Hart, 'Guan Wei: Dow Island 2002', in National Gallery of Australia, *Developing the Collection: Acquisitions 2001–2004* (Canberra, 2004), p. 28.

this voyage, painted the three known views of Australia from these voyages.[3] One of these, *View of Adventure Bay, Van Diemen's Land, New Holland* 1777 (National Library of Australia, Canberra), is a realistically portrayed generic view, showing a varied landscape on one side with trees and water on the other, revealing little of the specifics of the topography or vegetation of the area. It appears to be more of a memento than a scientific record. However, in his use of a generic formula, Ellis conveyed a continuity between the new world and the old, and thereby implied the suitability of this place for settlement.

Cook's purpose on his voyages combined military and scientific objectives—to undertake astronomical observation (the Transit of Venus), to visit unknown lands and people, to collect botanical and zoological specimens, and to search for the mythical southern continent *Terra Australis Incognita*. He charted the east coast of 'New Holland' and New Zealand and claimed them for King George III. Following this, Sir Joseph Banks suggested that Britain might solve its problem of overcrowding in its prisons by transporting convicts to New South Wales, and in 1788 the First Fleet arrived in Botany Bay.

Joseph Lycett (1775–1828) was one of a number of artists to be convicted of forgery and transported to Australia. In 1822, after nine years in New South Wales, Lycett obtained a pardon and returned to Britain, where he made a series of hand-coloured aquatints and etchings, *Views in Australia*, the largest and best known publication of views of New South Wales and Van Diemen's Land (Tasmania) during the early colonial period. In images such as *View on the Macquarie River, Van Diemen's Land, near the fort at Argyle Plains*, c.1824 (National Gallery of Australia) he did not show the hard work required to develop the land or reflect on his experiences as a convict. (Indeed, Lycett never visited Tasmania, and probably based his images of Tasmania on those of another artist.) He portrayed a prosperous landscape which appears to be a mirror to many in Britain and which has been ordered by the European settlers to provide a comfortable existence.

Lycett's views were typical of those of early colonial artists, who often emulated European models of painting. Frequently, what they saw and

---

[3] Bernard Smith, 'The Intellectual and Artistic Framework of the Pacific Exploration in the Eighteenth Century' and Peter Whitehead, 'Natural History Drawing on British Eighteenth Century Expeditions to the Pacific', in William Eisler and Bernard Smith, eds, *Terra Australis: The Furtherest Shore* (Sydney, 1988).

Figure 5.2 Joseph Lycett, *View on the Macquarie River near the Ford, on the Road to Launceston* (c.1824). National Gallery of Australia, Canberra

depicted were what they thought would be considered desirable 'back home'. They showed the results of the colonists' industry through the creation of grazing lands and gardens in a European fashion. In the terms of the analysis put forward by Robert Dixon in 1986 in *The Course of Empire*, they portrayed Australia in the second stage of development: having achieved pastoral and agricultural domestication.[4] In selecting scenes for their images, moreover, artists frequently modified the features of the landscape to comply with conventions of topographic view painting or contemporary British interpretations of the picturesque. In this way they suggested continuity between the new settlement and the 'homeland'. Such images were created essentially for a British market to foster an interest in Australia as a fertile land, and were used to encourage emigration—to a place where one would feel comfortable. In fact, Lycett's images, published in 1825, belied the reality of Australia at that time, when the wool markets had fallen, and when, shortly afterwards, a serious drought threatened the farming industry of early New South Wales.[5]

In another group of works, dated to the 1820s, Lycett depicted the life of Aboriginal people, their land use and ceremonies, as well as their defence of their land against the European invasion (possibly using the work of other artists as a reference). In paintings such as *Aborigines Using Fire to Hunt Kangaroos* (National Library of Australia) he provided an important visual record of the Indigenous people of coastal New South Wales during the early colonial period. He paid tribute to the Indigenous people by making them the focus of his watercolours, in contrast to other colonial artists, such as John Lewin or John Eyre, who depicted the Indigenous people on the edge of their landscapes, as exotic 'extras'. As a convict, and as someone who had no interest in remaining in Australia and occupying land, Lycett was to some extent an outsider in the colonial community, and this may have given him empathy towards the Indigenous people, and helped him understand that they had a way of life worth preserving, a way of life that was being rapidly restricted by European settlement. But if Lycett intended to publish this group of watercolours as he had his *Views in Australia*, this did not eventuate.[6]

[4] Robert Dixon, *The Course of Empire: Neo-Classical Culture in New South Wales, 1788–1860* (Melbourne, 1986).

[5] Janette Hoorn, 'Joseph Lycett: The Pastoral Landscape in Early Colonial Australia', *Art Bulletin of Victoria*, no. 26, pp. 4–14.

[6] Jeanette Hoorn, *The Lycett Album* (Canberra, 1990).

In addition to the Dutch and British expeditions, the French also travelled to the South Pacific. Among these voyages was that of Jules Dumont d'Urville, who visited King George Sound near Albany in Western Australia in October 1826 to undertake scientific research. Louis Auguste de Sainson (1801–87) was the draughtsman employed to record the landscapes and lives and customs of the people they visited as a basis for illustrations for the published account of the expedition. His images show the land as rich and verdant and King George Sound as a desirable place to settle, just as d'Urville had described it. In works such as *Vue d'un etang près la Baie du Roi Georges, Nelle Hollande (A Lake near King George Sound)* 1833 and *View of King George Sound* 1833 (illustrated), he appears to have chosen the most characteristic aspects of the landscape to create an 'artistic' scene rather than a scientific one—a generic view.[7] He depicted a tumultuous sky which seems to be too dramatic to be a true record of the climate and weather, and included an imaginary group of Europeans on a shooting expedition (they carry trophy birds as if they were landed gentry on a rural property in Europe). It all appears to suggest that 'you too could live like this in this country'. In several works he portrayed the Indigenous (Nyoongar) people alongside the Europeans, implying their peaceful coexistence during the course of the expedition (oblivious to the subjections of a future colonial settlement).

The British-born émigré artist John Glover (1767–1849) acknowledged the Indigenous presence in Australia in paintings such as *Mount Wellington and Hobart Town from Kangaroo Point c.*1834. He portrayed Tasmania as a place where western culture existed in harmony with an Indigenous one—at least for a time. He showed Aborigines singing and dancing, fishing and swimming, in an uninhibited fashion, seeming at ease in the natural environment. He contrasted the lives of the Palawa people with those of the Europeans in the settlement on the other side of the River Derwent, with their regimented streets and buildings, hovering tentatively at the base of the mountain and at the edge of the water. He placed these two spheres within a view conveying the mystery and power of the large mass of Mount Wellington. He used artistic licence to transform nature according to his pictorial requirements, changing the profile of Mount Wellington to enhance its height and grandeur and make it a little more like that of the Helvellyn at Ullswater in the Lake District of Britain. Given Glover's adaptation of the Tasmanian topography, it is understandable that a British critic, on viewing

---

[7] Barbara Chapman, *The Colonial Eye* (Perth, 1979), pp. 26–31.

Figure 5.3 Louis de Sainson, *Vue du Port du Roi Georges* (*View of King George Sound*), (1833). National Gallery of Australia, Canberra

Figure 5.4 John Glover, *Mount Wellington and Hobart Town from Kangaroo Point* (1834). National Gallery of Australia, Canberra, and Tasmanian Museum and Art Gallery, Hobart, 2001

works in Glover's 1835 London exhibition, should have seen similarities between his Tasmanian landscapes and views of the Lake District:

The country itself is beautiful and picturesque ... Mountain scenery and the broad expanse of waters bear in many respects a resemblance to the views on the lakes of Cumberland, with the exception of the hills are more lofty, possess more of a primeval aspect.[8]

While Lycett depicted an Australian landscape transformed by pastoral and agricultural domestication—in works such as *Mount Wellington and Hobart Town from Kangaroo Point*—Glover portrayed the Australian landscape largely in its natural state, using distinctly Australian colouring, and including only a hint of future urban development. But he shaped the natural universe through his compositional viewpoint and by changing natural features so that they had a greater likeness to—and continuity with—those of British scenery.[9]

Glover's 'Idyllic Island' quickly became a 'Calamity Island', when George Augustus Robinson, under the auspices of the Colonial government, brought the last of the people of the Big River and Oyster Bay regions from their own land to Hobart, believing it to be in the Aborigines' interest to do so. Ten days after their arrival in Hobart they were shipped to Flinders Island in Bass Strait where they died tragically. It was a shameful moment in Australia's colonial history and in the government's relations with the Indigenous peoples. Glover's placement of the Palawa people on one side of the harbour, and Hobart Town on the other, made a deliberate moral and political point. In some of his later paintings (such as *The Bath of Diana, Van Diemen's Land* 1837), he portrayed an 'Idyllic Island' without the British settlers, imagined scenes showing Indigenous Australians living an untroubled life before the European invasion. This period Glover referred to as 'the gay, happy life the natives led before the White people came here'.[10]

Like Glover, Austrian-born émigré Eugene von Guérard (1811–1901) arrived in Australia as a highly trained artist and with a developed way of looking. He came to appreciate what he found in Australia, and encouraged others to do so as well, but he never entirely lost his European approach.

---

[8] *The Times*, 29 June 1835.

[9] Anne Gray, 'John Glover: *Mount Wellington and Hobart Town from Kangaroo Point*', *Artonview*, no. 29 (Autumn 2002), pp. 18–21; David Hansen, *John Glover and the Colonial Picturesque* (Hobart, 2004).

[10] John Glover to George Augustus Robinson, Mitchell Library, State Library of New South Wales, Robinson Papers, vol. 37, p. 430.

In accordance with his training, he painted with meticulous accuracy, and frequently selected subjects with romantic overtones. As Daniel Thomas has pointed out, von Guérard painted *Ferntree Gully in the Dandenong Ranges* 1857 in a city studio in Melbourne, forty kilometres from the location—based on drawings made on two sketching trips to the area. The painting was considered to be the 'most masterly work' of Victoria's 'greatest landscape painter' and a truthful 'study from nature herself'.[11] It was, as a contemporary critic noted, 'equally valuable as a botanical study', and 'as a depiction of one of the most characteristic features of Australian scenery'.[12] What is more, with his representation of the giant tree ferns clumped closely together with their broad leaves forming a shady glen evoking the 'cool freshness' and the sense of allure of the gully, von Guérard led fellow colonists to appreciate some of the natural scenery of Australia. He created an interest in this particular site, which became a sanctuary that people visited on picnics. Indeed, soon after he painted it, a hotel was established in the neighbourhood.

But the area also suffered the consequences of its popularity when professional fern collectors and excursionists started to remove the ferns. As Tim Bonyhady has noted, for some colonists, the size of Australia's ferns evoked 'a far distant tropical region', while for others, the ferns were 'emblematic of Australia'.[13] Both camps considered ferns to be 'exceedingly romantic'. The businessman Frederick Dalgety purchased the painting and took it with him to London where he exhibited it to considerable praise at the International Exhibition of 1862. Unlike Lycett's views, this painting was not promoted as a record of the achievements of the settlers or as a means to encourage emigration, but rather as a testimony to the remarkable scenery of Australia and the quality of its colonial art. It indicated a move from observing the achievements of Empire to the recognition of an Australian 'homegrown' nature and culture.

* * *

Some thirty years later, in 1895, a critic for the Melbourne *Argus* suggested that 'there can be no doubt that an Australian School of painting is in process

---

[11] Tim Bonyhady, *The Colonial Earth* (Melbourne, 2000); Daniel Thomas, 'Eugene von Guerard: *Ferntree Gully in the Dandenong Ranges* 1857', in Gray, ed., *Australian Art*, p. 53.

[12] Quoted in Tim Bonyhady, *The Colonial Image: Australian Painting 1800–1880* (Sydney, 1987), p. 76.

[13] Bonyhady, *The Colonial Earth*, p. 104.

Figure 5.5 Eugene von Guérard, *Ferntree Gully in the Dandenong Ranges* (1857). National Gallery of Australia, Canberra. Gift of Dr Joseph Brown AO OBE, 1975

of birth.'[14] He was referring to the work of the British-born Tom Roberts (1856–1931), the Australian-born Frederick McCubbin (1855–1917), Arthur Streeton (1867–1943), and their colleagues. His vision of their paintings as forming an Australian school reflected the spirit of the times and a drive for a specifically Australian subject matter from writers as diverse as the Sydney artist Julian Ashton, the Melbourne University professor of moral philosophy Henry Laurie, and the lecturer and entrepreneur Sidney Dickinson.[15] Such ideas were in part a consequence of the non-Indigenous Australians' celebrations in 1888 of 100 years of European settlement (or invasion), and the preparations for Federation in 1901. These events created an increased public interest in Australian history and the natural environment, and fostered a desire to assert a particularly Australian culture. They also demonstrated how successful the imperial 'civilizing' mission had been.

In 1885–6 Roberts painted the townscape, *Allegro con brio: Bourke Street West*, a contemporary view of Melbourne city life. In choosing to paint an urban street scene Roberts selected a subject similar to those painted by a number of artists in Europe in the early 1880s, including Impressionist painters Claude Monet and Camille Pissarro (whose work Roberts may have seen). This shared interest was appropriate in an era when Melbourne's boulevards were compared to those of Paris (although in the 1890s this end of Bourke Street was still an unfashionable one, an area for horse traders and saddlers). It was a time when artists in both Europe and Australia were interested in painting modern life and in giving value to everyday events, as Roberts did in this painting. As its title suggests, *Allegro con brio: Bourke Street West* is a lively composition painted with spirit. Roberts applied the paint rapidly, sketching in the figures quickly, capturing an instantaneous impression. Like Edgar Degas, and contemporary photographers, he cut off buildings and people at the edges to show that this was just a segment of a scene which continues outside the image, just a moment of perception. Roberts portrayed this scene from the balcony of the drapers, Buckley & Nunn, near the post office, accurately recording the particulars of place. He specified the buildings, from the Menzies Hotel at the top of the street

[14] Editorial, *Argus*, 24 August 1895, p. 6.

[15] Julian Ashton, 'Art in Australia and its Possibilities', *Table Talk*, 27 January 1888, p. 3, and 'An Aim for Australian Art', *The Centennial Magazine*, no. 1 (August 1888), pp. 31–2; Henry Laurie, speech to the Victorian Artists' Society, *Table Talk*, 7 June 1889, p. 5; S. Dickinson, 'What Should Australian Artists Paint?', *Australasian Critic*, 1 October 1890, p. 22.

Figure 5.6 Tom Roberts, *Allegro con brio, Bourke Street West* (1885–6). National Gallery of Australia, Canberra, and National Library of Australia, Canberra

to Dunn & Collins booksellers in the foreground. He showed horse-drawn cabs cantering along this busy boom-time street, with others pausing while passengers are set down and picked up; he portrayed some people gathering around a building and others hurrying across the road; and he depicted a group of red-coated soldiers trooping in the opposite direction. He made it appear as if the whole scene would change if the viewer were to glance elsewhere for a moment. He conveyed Melbourne as a modern metropolis, in the model of a European city—one of many that the Empire established around the globe. In Robert Dixon's terms, Roberts showed the colony as having reached the third stage of development, as having become an urban trading centre.[16] In *Allegro con brio: Bourke Street West*, as Humphrey McQueen has noted, Roberts conveyed 'the globalising of the Imperial bourgeoisie'.[17]

Yet Roberts' realization of the light of the midday sun, which blasts the ground and radiates its heat through a sky splotched with puffs of smoke, was distinctly Australian. Unlike Lycett, who used a British model to impress a British public, Roberts adopted a contemporary European approach to give his Australian subject a greater modernity and universality—while portraying particular details of place and capturing a characteristic Australian light. Unlike von Guérard, who depicted some of Australia's more spectacular scenery, Roberts portrayed modern life, yet in doing so he was, like von Guérard, concerned with promoting a national 'homegrown' culture. Extending Dixon's analysis of Empire, this might be regarded as the fourth stage of development of a colony: the development of a self-conscious national artistic expression.

Roberts and his Australian colleagues contributed to the emotional climate around the centennial celebrations through their *succès de scandale*, their *9 by 5 Impression Exhibition* of 1889. These so-called Australian impressionists sought to create 'impressions', to convey the transient moods of nature and the momentary effects of colour and light. They declared in the accompanying catalogue that their aim was to develop 'what we believe will be a great school of painting in Australia'.[18]

[16] Robert Dixon, *The Course of Empire*.

[17] Humphrey McQueen, 'Tom Roberts: *Allegro Con Brio, Bourke Street West c.*1885–86', in Gray, ed., *Australian Art*, p. 78.

[18] Tom Roberts, Charles Conder, and Arthur Streeton, 'Concerning "Impressions" in Painting', letter to the *Argus*, 3 September 1889, p. 7, quoted in Jane Clark, *Golden Summers* (Melbourne, 1985), p. 115.

To some extent this was true, but like the earlier artists, they too used European formulae. In their artistic approach, in painting quickly in the open air, they looked to the *plein air* tradition of France. In their use of small wooden panels, their adoption of poetic and musical titles, as well as in asserting that these 'impressions' were finished, they looked to the subtle, evocative nocturnes of the British-American artist James McNeill Whistler. Charles Conder (1868–1909) in *Herrick's Blossoms c.*1888 (National Gallery of Australia), Roberts in *Going Home c.*1889 (National Gallery of Australia, Canberra), and Streeton in *Impression for 'Golden Summer' c.*1888 (Benalla Art Gallery) conjured up, with a few energetic brushstrokes, atmospheric effects. As noted above, their purpose was not to impress a British (or Australian) public about the development of the colony, but to create a new national art by presenting those 'effects and moods and thoughts of nature' which had impressed them and which they wished to 'impress upon the lovers of their art'. They wanted to 'render faithfully' the multitudinous (and often momentary) sentiments of nature (of Australian nature) in order to make others appreciate these.[19] They took a European approach and used it to open the eyes of Australians to the beauty of the countryside—not to the delights of a specific place (such as a Ferntree Gully), but to individual perceptions such as the softness of a spring morning, the quietness of the last moments of the setting sun, or the brightness of a summer's day.

Australian artists had often depicted subjects that might be found in other places—pastoral landscapes, scenic lake views, fern gullies, and street scenes. Around the turn of the century they sought to portray a subject that they believed would distinguish Australian life from that lived elsewhere: 'a life different from any other country in the world'—the life of the bush.[20] They sought to establish the validity of nationalistic subjects, and to treat them with a seriousness and on the scale of 'history paintings'. They worked in the international tradition of the followers of the late-nineteenth-century French naturalist painter Jules Bastien-Lepage and his ideas of depicting real people and places under natural conditions. Under Lepage's influence they painted naturalistic scenes of labourers, and sought their subject matter close to home. By using this naturalist mode of expression for their 'national subjects' they implied that what they painted was real.

---

[19] Clark, *Golden Summers*, pp. 112–15. Almost all the works were sold within two weeks, suggesting that a good number of those who attended the exhibition appreciated the paintings.

[20] *Sydney Morning Herald*, 21 October 1895, p. 3; quoted in Clark, *Golden Summers*, p. 129.

Roberts painted large-scale heroic images of life on the land with the figure playing a dominant role in works such as *Shearing the Rams* 1888–90 (National Gallery of Victoria). Other Australian painters, photographers, and illustrators had created images of the shearers, but what made Roberts' work different from these previous treatments of the theme was the way in which he painted in oil, working on a grand scale, and presenting his figures as strong, athletic, and skilful, the epitome of masculine labourers.[21] Although others in Australia had treated the subject before Roberts, as Virginia Spate has noted, there are few (if any) European or British precedents in his specific choice of subject.[22] Roberts commented that he wanted to express 'the subdued hum of hard fast working', the feeling of 'being in the bush and feeling the delight and fascination of the great pastoral life and work', and 'the whole lit warm with the reflection of Australian sunlight'.[23] He conveyed an idealized view of happy workers in control of their own output, without any hint of their precarious living or the bitter struggles between them and the landowners which resulted in the shearers' strike of 1890. This was because Roberts was not concerned with particular shearers at a specific moment in time, but with creating a more universal image of the kind of masculine labour which had contributed to the wealth of Australia and the Empire.

McCubbin dramatized the lives of the early settlers and their hardships in a series of large-scale works that began with *Down on his Luck* 1889 (Art Gallery of Western Australia, Perth) and ended with *The Pioneer* 1904 (National Gallery of Victoria). In *The Pioneer* he created a view of three stages in the life of a selector and his wife, from their first arrival in the bush, to their habitation of the land, and ending with their grave. Like McCubbin's other settler images, it was an imaginative reconstruction of a subject from an earlier time. McCubbin portrayed the spirit of the bush: the density of growth and the distinctive silvery greys of the eucalypts. He captured the feel of the Australian vegetation as no artist before had done. He implied that the struggles of such pioneers resulted in the growth of the city visible

---

[21] Leigh Astbury, *City Bushmen: The Heidelberg School and the Rural Mythology* (Melbourne, 1985), pp. 106–13.

[22] Virginia Spate, 'Where the Sun Never Set. Tom Roberts and the British Empire', in Ron Radford, ed., *Tom Roberts* (Adelaide, 1996), p. 76. This essay contains many valuable ideas about Roberts' place in the British Empire.

[23] Tom Roberts, letter to the Editor, *Argus*, Melbourne, 4 July 1890, quoted in Daniel Thomas, 'Tom Roberts: Shearing the rams, 1888–90. The Golden Fleece, 1894', in Radford, *Tom Roberts*, pp. 98–9.

in the distance in the final panel of *The Pioneer*, and that the settlers' development of their own land contributed to the imperial mission of 'civilizing' the bush.[24]

Streeton also depicted pioneers in works such as *The Selector's Hut (Whelan on the Log)* 1890 (National Gallery of Australia). He painted his subject in a palette of strong colours, conveying the glaring light of Australia. He placed his selector beside a characteristic tall slender eucalypt, with the summer wind blowing up the dust on the ground and magpies whirling in the intense blue sky. In addition, as Mary Eagle has pointed out, he portrayed a hardy pioneer who has selected a lonely patch and has been busy clearing the land and making his home in the makeshift hut behind him.[25] Like Roberts' *Bailed Up* 1895, 1927 (Art Gallery of New South Wales, Sydney) and McCubbin's *Down on his Luck* 1889 and *The Pioneer* 1904, it was to some extent an artificial construct. Streeton painted it in the outer suburbs of Melbourne, using Jack Whelan, a tenant farmer on the Eaglemont estate, as his model. When he painted this picture, the speculators, who owned the land and proposed to redevelop it as housing blocks, were far from becoming wealthy: they were having difficulties selling their land because of the financial crash of 1889–90. Most of the contemporary viewers of this work, however, would have accepted the fictional message of this image as suggested by his title, and would have seen Whelan as being like McCubbin's pioneers, as representing one of the many selectors who pegged out their own farms in order to pursue the course of Empire and domesticate the bush.

As Roberts had suggested they should, Roberts, McCubbin, and Streeton painted narrative images of Australian life, a life that was 'different from any other country in the world'; but if that had been all they did, they would have achieved little more than what the newspaper and journal illustrators had already done. Roberts portrayed the appeal of pastoral life and work and warm Australian sunlight, McCubbin conveyed the haunting mystery of the bush, and Streeton captured a brilliant light. It was through this poetic vision of Australian life and landscape that they demonstrated, as the *Age* critic wrote, that 'Australia can produce a strong and beautiful national art of her own'.[26]

[24] Ann Galbally, *Frederick McCubbin* (Melbourne, 1981).

[25] Mary Eagle, *The Oil Paintings of Arthur Streeton in the National Gallery of Australia* (Canberra, 1994), p. 56.

[26] *Age*, 16 August 1906, quoted by Clark, *Golden Summers*, p. 149.

Figure 5.7 Arthur Streeton, *The Selector's Hut (Whelan on the Log)*, (1890). National Gallery of Australia, Canberra

The Australianness of the art of Roberts, McCubbin, and Streeton is not inconsistent with its Britishness. Theirs was a nationalist approach which maintained a loyalty to Australia's British heritage and the Empire—rather than the anti-imperialist, parochial, and isolationist nationalism fostered by some of the *Bulletin* writers and others. We might see *The Selector's Hut* as conveying the feeling of being in the Australian bush because of the painting's dazzling light and bright blue sky, but we understand the 'characteristically Australian' hardships of the selector by reference to another world, that of the cosy English cottages that the selector may have left behind. In reality, the pioneers may not have been so heroic, but these artists were not creating illustrations, they were constructing a mythology for Australia, about how the settlers had survived, lived, and used the land—and in so doing created a national art.

*   *   *

At the turn of the twentieth century Australia was still a group of self-governing colonies. Even when, in 1901, Australia became a Federation it remained a British colony and did not have full power to govern itself. The new Commonwealth of Australia did not have the authority to declare war or peace, and, in 1914, Australia did not declare war on its own behalf—the Empire was at war and so, automatically, were the Dominions. Few Australians at this time, however, would have thought this controversial because most of them, even if born in Australia, would have called Britain (or Ireland) 'home'.[27] As Humphrey McQueen has observed, Roberts and Streeton and many others would have considered it just a matter of emphasis—whether they were Austral-Britons or British-Australians.[28]

In the First World War a number of Australian artists resident in London were appointed Australian official war artists. They travelled to France and painted images of the landscape that had been ravaged by war. In *Villers-Bretonneux* (Art Gallery of New South Wales), the most poignant of his war landscapes, Streeton captured the haunting stillness and early morning beauty of the French terrain, but imposed upon this churned and charred country a disturbing motif: the severed legs of a soldier grotesquely stranded in the field. In this way he contrasted the

[27] Richard White, *Inventing Australia* (Sydney, 1981), pp. 111–12.
[28] Humphrey McQueen, *Tom Roberts* (Sydney, 1996), p. 517.

beauty of nature with the horrors of war. This image, however, is unusual among Streeton's war paintings, which mostly present a timeless country caressed by a soft diffuse light—sometimes presented in the long, narrow format of his Sydney Harbour views. In images such as the watercolour *The Somme from above Corbie* 1918, Streeton conveyed similar feelings to those he expressed to Roberts when describing the French terrain:

below me the steep little gully, all green with upright trees, and the last afternoon light all golden like Australia catches the stems in patches and is diffused among the foliage in [a] most beautiful fashion.[29]

Streeton identified the landscape of France with that of Australia; he loved the Australian landscape, and so too he loved the French countryside. Streeton's lyrical landscapes are images of what the Australians were fighting for—the land that was rapidly being violated by war. The Australian poster *This is what we are fighting for* pointed to the Australian rural harmony in the same way as a British recruiting poster *Your country's call* emphasized the countryside to encourage men to enlist. These posters showed the landscape as a symbol of peace. Streeton did something similar when he identified the French landscape with that of the Australian. Moreover, in seeing the European landscape as resembling that of Australia, he, to some extent, reversed the colonial vision—in which the Australian landscape was shown as resembling that of Britain.

Many of Australia's leading artists were expatriates in London and Paris during the Edwardian era. Many believed, however, that Australia would be the better place to live after the end of the First World War. In 1916, Streeton had suggested to his friend Frederick Delmer, that he felt sure Australia would 'recover much more rapidly than Europe',[30] and in 1924 he wrote to Roberts remarking that:

We feel a little sad at cutting away so to speak from dear old Britain. Britain, the country that's paying for the war—for next 30 years I suppose. She is the Keystone of the world to-day, I think civilization depends upon her more than any other country—the British as a race never know when they are beaten—& then great grit usually wins through.

---

[29] Arthur Streeton to Tom Roberts, 31 July 1918, in Ann Galbally and Anne Gray, *Letters from Smike: The Letters of Arthur Streeton* (Melbourne, 1989), p. 149.

[30] Arthur Streeton to Frederick Delmer, Wandsworth Hospital, London, 26 June 1916, Mitchell Library, State Library of New South Wales, Frederick Sefton Delmer Papers, MSS 4868.

Life here is sunny & comparatively easy—the lovely climate etc, we are personally very well off—But one will miss many stimulating things that exist over in Gt Britain.[31]

When Roberts and Streeton returned to Australia they were welcomed home with celebratory dinners and, on the surface, treated as if they were returning heroes. But although life in Australia was 'sunny and comparatively easy', they missed some of the stimulation of Britain—of living in the heart of the Empire.

In the same year as Streeton told Roberts that he was sad to be leaving 'dear old Britain', the English-educated and one-time Australian jackeroo George Lambert (1873–1930) created a stir in Australia when he first exhibited *The Squatter's Daughter* 1923–4 (National Gallery of Australia), because he had created a new way of looking at the Australian landscape. Like others before him, from Lycett to Streeton, Lambert depicted a rural scene. However, unlike earlier artists such as Streeton, he did not employ an intuitive response to the landscape but adopted the stylized, formalist approach that he had learnt while working in Britain. He gave his painting a quiet harmony, emphasizing the structure of the landscape, showing the trees as still and the squatter's daughter poised in the foreground, with the light of the setting sun permeating the entire scene. In *The Squatter's Daughter* Lambert did not just differ from the earlier artists in his artistic approach, he also suggested a new relationship between the farmer or property owner and their land. Her figure did not need to be strong and athletic because she did not need to work the land—it had become sufficiently bountiful to allow her to enjoy it as a place of recreation. Instead of masculine labourers working for others, Lambert depicted a woman of leisure in command of her terrain; instead of pioneers working the soil he showed a property owner (or his daughter) with only a passing contact with their land; instead of struggle he showed success.

In so doing, Lambert reflected the changes that had taken place in rural life in Australia. The politics and economy of Australia in the 1920s were strongly based on life outside the cities; political power was in the hands of the Nationalist Party and the newly formed, basically conservative Country Party, and half the national income was derived from pastoral and agricultural production. The pastoralists were successful, their yields

---

[31] Arthur Streeton to Tom Roberts, 13 August 1924, in Galbally and Gray, *Letters from Smike*, p. 180.

Figure 5.8 George Lambert, *The Squatter's Daughter* (1923–4). National Gallery of Australia, Canberra. Purchased with the generous assistance of James Fairfax AO and Philip Bacon AM, 1991

profitable, and their relationship with the land more detached than that of the pioneers. Farming was viewed as an ideal way of life, and the bush as a healthy place 'where peace and sanity prevailed'. Paintings like Lambert's *The Squatter's Daughter*, with its view of a lush farming land ordered by the pastoralist to provide a comfortable existence, came to signify these values, to symbolize Australian wholesomeness, as well as productivity and plenty. Lambert used a European model of painting to show the results of Australian industry, and suggested continuity between Australian pastoral landscapes and those of the 'homeland' to show an Australian equality, if not superiority, to the 'mother country'. Such images were a record of achievement, of Australia as an outpost of the Empire that was no longer subservient—Australia had become a nation not just on the cliffs of Gallipoli but also on its own pastures.

Australian-born Margaret Preston (1875–1963) wanted to detach art from storytelling. She did not want to portray a characteristic way of life, capture a particular time, or reveal an Australian light. Rather, she sought to find what was characteristically Australian and thought that if Australian artists looked to Britain and Europe for their approach to art they would become 'copyists'. If Lambert had adopted a European model of painting to suggest continuity, and thence equality or superiority, Preston recommended independence and a rejection of the Empire—at least in her rhetoric. She suggested that artists should take into account the work of Australia's Indigenous people in order to achieve a national style, 'to produce a national Australian culture'.[32] In *Flying over the Shoalhaven River* 1942 (National Gallery of Australia), Preston looked at the scene from above, with clouds passing over the landscape. Her viewpoint may have derived from flying over the land, but it could also have come from her admiration of both Chinese and Aboriginal art. Similarly, her use of opaque browns, whites, and ochres, and her dotted application of paint could be said to be inspired by (or appropriated from) Indigenous bark painting. She believed that their long association with the land had given the Indigenous people a unique way of representing it, but she had no knowledge of the variety of Indigenous cultures and forms of expression. She did not understand the Indigenous peoples' right to possess their own culture, had no interest in Indigenous lore, believing that their 'symbolism' was not a matter for artists, but only for anthropologists. Moreover, she

---

[32] Margaret Preston, *The Orientation of Art in the Post-War Pacific* (Sydney, 1942), pp. 7–9. See also Roger Butler, *The Prints of Margaret Preston* (Canberra, 1987), p. 46.

adopted the traditional European materials of oil paint on canvas, and used a stylized, formalist approach to composition—with the shapes of the mountains and hills reduced to their essential forms and the river simplified into a sinuous rhythmic pattern. Rather than totally rejecting her European background, Preston forged a synthesis between this and what might be considered a newer, more Australian way of representing the landscape in which she incorporated (or appropriated) some aspects of Indigenous Australian art.

*   *   *

In 1942, the year Preston painted *Flying over the Shoalhaven River*, Singapore fell to the Japanese and 15,000 Australians were imprisoned at Changi. Shortly afterwards, the Japanese bombed Darwin and Broome, and Japanese midget submarines entered Sydney harbour. Troops were sent to far-flung places to protect the country. This was the first time since white settlement that Australia itself had been invaded, and Australians became aware of their physical isolation and that they could not rely on Britain to defend their shores. Around this time, a number of artists depicted a contemporary view of inland Australia, a distinctive place, quite different from the landscapes found in Europe.

During the war, in 1944, British-born Russell Drysdale (1912–81) travelled to north-western New South Wales to record the devastating reality of the drought there, one of the worst in Australia's history. In his haunting images of the eroded landscape, such as *The Crucifixion* 1945 (Art Gallery of New South Wales), he conveyed the powerful forces of nature which shaped the land. In his ivory, bone-like tree forms he created 'memento mori'. In depicting these solid sculptural figures, however, Drysdale adopted a similar approach to that of the British artist Henry Moore (whose work Drysdale had seen in London in 1939, and reproduced in magazines in Australia in the 1940s).[33] In works such as *Sofala* [1947], Drysdale painted images of Australian country towns, with buildings framing gaping streets, and 'the heat of a late afternoon, the stifling air, red with dust'.[34] These townscapes were very different from Roberts' *Allegro con brio: Bourke Street West*—instead of Roberts' cosmopolitan image of a busy street, Drysdale presented a scene of quiet calm; instead of Roberts' rapid, impressionistic application,

---

[33] Lou Klepac, *Russell Drysdale* (Sydney, 1983), p. 82.
[34] *Sydney Morning Herald*, 23 January 1948, quoted in Klepac, *Drysdale*, p. 90.

Figure 5.9 Margaret Preston, *Flying over the Shoalhaven River* (1942). National Gallery of Australia, 1983, Canberra. © Margaret Preston. Licensed by VISCOPY, Australia 2007

Drysdale adopted an old-masterly approach to paint. Drysdale reduced the buildings to their essential forms and created a sense of classical order, giving the scene a still, silent, metaphysical atmosphere. He portrayed these Australian towns in a similar fashion to the way the Italian artist Georgio de Chirico painted his imaginary Italian piazzas, capturing the drama of place—an evocative emptiness. In paintings such as *The Drover's Wife* *c.*1945 (National Gallery of Australia), Drysdale created a compassionate image of an outback woman, in all her individuality. Unlike the people in the works of earlier Australian artists, Drysdale's subject is not a man struggling to tame the bush or working up a hard sweat, rather she is a large woman standing in a vast, spare landscape. She has a quiet innocence, a gentle face and eyes, and she seems perfectly at ease in the outback, standing assuredly, with her feet planted firmly on the ground. One of Drysdale's contemporaries suggested that he conveyed 'a difficult and lonely existence, where man constantly battles against the elements',[35] but this is truer for some of the subjects of McCubbin's and Streeton's paintings, than Drysdale's. Although Drysdale's people are often alone, they rarely seem to be lonely; rather, they appear to be in harmony with themselves and their place.

Unlike Lycett, who used a British model to impress a British public, Drysdale shared European approaches to art to convey a new way of seeing and a new understanding of Australian space and Australian people. Yet, the imperial mission remained for some viewers, with a trustee of the Art Gallery of New South Wales voting against the acquisition of one of Drysdale's drought paintings on the grounds that 'if it were seen in England it would be harmful to immigration',[36] and with another viewer writing that 'it will be necessary to prevent [Drysdale's *Woman in a Landscape* 1948 (Art Gallery of South Australia)] appearing in England and Europe, where the effect would certainly defeat the immigration policy'.[37] Drysdale created a new way of looking at the Australian landscape, which was not in terms of topography or about colonization and the settling of the land. Rather, he conveyed a spiritual condition: the timeless forces of nature, the psychic reality of place, and the resilience of humanity.

During the Second World War Australian-born Sidney Nolan (1917–92) was conscripted into the army and served in the Wimmera District of Victoria and discovered the space, heat, and bright light of the landscape in this region. In 1946–7, Nolan painted a series of figurative images based on the theme of the bushranger Ned Kelly (National Gallery of Australia). In choosing to paint this series Nolan selected a characteristically Australian subject, a defiant anti-hero fugitive from the law, of whom Nolan said 'his raids were more in the nature of a protest against society itself', against injustice.[38] (As a recent deserter from the army, Nolan could empathize with such a fugitive.) Nolan was also concerned with the Australian bush and sunlight, commenting that it was 'a story arising out of the bush and

---

[35] Paul Haefliger, *Sydney Morning Herald*, 23 January 1948, p. 2.

[36] Klepac, *Drysdale*, p. 112.

[37] Geoffrey Dutton, *Russell Drysdale* (London, 1964), pp. 73–4.

[38] Elwyn Lynn, *Sidney Nolan—Australia* (Sydney, 1979), p. 66.

ending in the bush'.[39] Like McCubbin in *The Pioneer*, Nolan created an imaginative reconstruction of a story from an earlier time. In doing so, he contributed to a national art—and mythology. In his approach to image-making, however, his source was the work of Henri Rousseau, European folk art, and American primitive art. Moreover, Kelly's black box-like helmet, which has become such a potent symbol, can be related to international abstraction, and particularly to Kasimir Malevich's non-objective paintings composed of bare geometric forms. As Nolan remarked, 'in many ways I was conscious of the fact that the black square had haunted modern art since the First World War … well, since Kasimir Malevich.'[40]

Nolan's Kelly series was not at first appreciated in Australia, and it was not until Jean Cassou, head of the Musée National d'Art Moderne in Paris, claimed that they were 'the work of a true poet and a true painter' and that they made 'a striking contribution to modern art' that the Australian general public began to appreciate them.[41] By 1950, Nolan had made several outback journeys which resulted in images such as *Burke at Cooper's Creek* (National Gallery of Australia), a poignant image of a non-Indigenous Australian's relationship with the harsh land that eventually killed him. Several years later he produced a series of works in which he depicted the heat-hazed countryside and the haunting sense of space of this region. Nolan commented, 'The Australian interior is such a prophetic landscape. At the same time you are aware of its past links with Aborigines and its future links with oil, minerals, uranium. You're in the middle of a past–future situation, the dream within the actuality, and the actuality looks dreamlike.'[42]

At about the same time as Drysdale and Nolan were painting their images of inland Australia, and Margaret Preston was telling non-Indigenous Australians to look to (and take from) Aboriginal art for their inspiration, the Western Aranda–Arrernte artist Albert Namatjira (1902–59) was creating images of central Australia, using a western approach to painting. In watercolours such as *Mount Hermannsburg, Finke River* 1946–51 (National Gallery of Australia), he depicted the ancient mount *Ljalkaindirma* rising from the rolling green pastures on the slopes beneath, untrammelled by

---

[39] Sidney Nolan, quoted in *Australian Artist*, 1–4, July 1948, quoted by Andrew Sayers, 'Kelly's Words, Rousseau and Sunlight', *Sidney Nolan's Ned Kelly* (Canberra, 2002), p. 8.

[40] Lynn, *Nolan*, p. 60.

[41] *Daily Telegraph*, 15 December 1949, quoting Cassou, quoted in Jane Clark, *Sidney Nolan: Landscapes & Legends* (Melbourne, 1987), p. 73.

[42] Sidney Nolan, quoted in Janet Hawley, *Encounters with Australian Artists* (St. Lucia, 1993), p. 177.

European settlers. He scrutinized the effect of the sun on the mount, to convey his deep knowledge of the land and the light and shade that gave it its form at that time of day. He portrayed the beauty of the country of his father and mother, derived from a deeply personal engagement and cultural affiliation with it. At this time, in the 1950s, politicians were still discussing whether the Australian Indigenous peoples were entitled to citizenship, and the applause given to Namatjira and other Arrernte watercolourists who assimilated the European visual tradition was patronizing. Namatjira was, as Galarrwuy Yunupingu has noted, 'painting his country, the land of the Arrernte people. [Namatjira] was demonstrating to the rest of the world the living title held by his people to the lands they had been on for thousands of years ... [and] the Dreamings that had made that country important'.[43] He may have adopted a European approach to painting, but he used this as a vehicle to depict the spirit of his traditional land and to communicate its resonance to non-Indigenous Australians. In doing so he challenged the widespread non-Indigenous Australian view of this terrain as an empty desert and showed it to be a fertile place.[44]

Since European settlement, artists had portrayed pastoral landscapes, fern gullies, and inland Australia using a traditional perspective. In the 1960s Australian-born Fred Williams (1927–82) observed that there was no focal point in the Australian landscape and that this had to be built into the paint. In so doing, he created one of the most original visions of the Australian landscape.[45] He merged a contemporary international interest in abstraction, flat surfaces, and gestural painting with an ongoing interest in figuration. Williams said he was thinking of McCubbin's *The Pioneer* 1904 when he painted *Landscape '69 triptych* 1969 (National Gallery of Australia).[46] But whereas McCubbin depicted a foreground, middle ground, and distance, and showed the earth and sky, Williams created an image that is more closely focused, more intense, more absorbed into the bush. A few strokes of coloured paint suggest the trunks of tall saplings, the cut of a fern,

[43] Galarrwuy Yunupingu, Chairman of the Northern Land Council, quoted in Alison French, *Seeing the Centre: The Art of Albert Namatjira, 1902–1959* (Canberra, 2002), p. 27.

[44] French, *Seeing the Centre*.

[45] Williams' work is represented in the British Museum, the Tate, and the Victoria & Albert Museum in London, the Metropolitan Museum of Art, the Museum of Modern Art in New York, and the Smithsonian Institution, Washington. The Museum of Modern Art held a survey of his work in 1977, and more recently exhibitions have been held in the British Museum (2003–4) and the L. A. Louver Gallery, California (2005).

[46] James Mollison, *A Singular Vision: The Art of Fred Williams* (Canberra, 1989), pp. 139–41.

delicate plants in flower, rocks, and cut logs, the things that someone might notice when sitting immersed in the bush. The liveliness of the sparsely placed gestures against the ethereal grey surface takes us into another realm. Williams' triptych is like a meditation on the bush. In portraying a scene in which the image totally consumes the canvas, and in creating a work in which the painterly gesture dominates, Williams shared an interest with both Monet in his later works and the painters of Japanese screens.[47]

More especially, as in the work of these artists, Williams replaced the ordinary pictorial concepts of up and down, back and front, depth and surface with spatial ambiguity, allowing viewers' consciousnesses to dissolve into visual space. In his assimilation of international modes of expression—both contemporary and historical—Williams placed the Australian visual experience within a globalized world. Yet, Williams' vision of the lack of focal point in the Australian landscape, his understanding of the feel of the saplings, ferns, logs, and delicate plants, was distinctly Australian. He used an international approach to give his Australian subject greater universality, while conveying the spiritual essence of the Australian bush—absolute and enduring.[48]

∗   ∗   ∗

Many Indigenous artists have captured the spiritual significance of the land from their distinct perspective—in a variety of media and artistic approaches. Others have conveyed some of the impacts of European settlement on Indigenous life, culture, and place.

In the bark painting *How World War II Began (through the eyes of the Rembarrnga)* 1990 (National Gallery of Australia), Rembarrnga artist Gela Nga-Mirraitja Fordham presented a moral tale providing a particular perspective of the Second World War. Japanese pearl divers and fishermen who worked the north coast of Australia traded tobacco, rice, sugar, and alcohol in exchange for Indigenous women. In 1941 an Indigenous woman refused the advances of the Japanese divers, a dispute broke out and the Rembarrnga asked the Japanese to leave their land. A little later, on 19 February 1942, the Japanese forces mounted two air raids on Darwin, killing at least 243 people, wounding over 300, and destroying most civil and military facilities in Darwin. The air attacks on Darwin continued until November

---

[47] See Virginia Spate, *Monet & Japan* (Canberra, 2001).
[48] Patrick McCaughey, *Fred Williams* (Sydney, 1980).

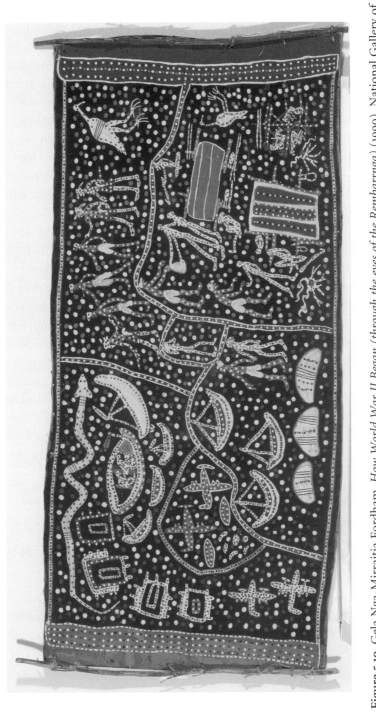

Figure 5.10 Gela Nga-Mirraitja Fordham, *How World War II Began (through the eyes of the Rembarrnga)* (1990). National Gallery of Australia, Canberra, 1990. © Gela Nga-Mirraitja Fordham. Licensed by VISCOPY, Australia 2007

1943, by which time the Japanese had bombed Darwin sixty-four times. The Japanese were preparing to invade Timor and anticipated that air attacks on Darwin would weaken it as a base for a counter-offensive, as well as lower morale in Australia. The Rembarrnga, however, felt that their quarrel with the Japanese divers in 1941 had contributed to the Japanese attack. In *How World War II Began*, Fordham divided his image into sections to tell this story. In the lower right he depicted Indigenous people trading with the Japanese within the setting of traditional camp life, and on the lower left he showed a Japanese man taking an Indigenous woman to his boats. In the centre left he portrayed the Japanese planes and at the top right he presented Japanese men being taken away by police. At the top of the image he drew a version of the Rainbow Serpent as a reminder that the Japanese intruders were on Rembarrnga land.[49] Fordham's painting is a vivid image of outsiders and the invasion of Australia—directly that of the Japanese during the Second World War, and indirectly the European settlers.

Minang–Nyoongar artist Christopher Pease's (b. 1969) *Hunting Party* 2003 was his response to the images of colonial explorers and settlers and their disregard of Indigenous people and their culture. He has quoted and transformed the hand-coloured lithograph of Louis Auguste de Sainson, *Vue d'un etang près la Baie du Roi Georges, Nelle Hollande (A Lake near King George Sound)* 1833 referred to earlier.[50] Pease's work is about Indigenous heritage and identity. He expressed his concern about the environmental devastation of the Nyoongar homelands in the 170 years since d'Urville's expedition—particularly on the wetlands, waterways, and river systems. He conveyed the different way in which Indigenous and European cultures relate to the land and the natural environment. Pease wrote:

The European settlers saw marsh and swampland as useless and of little value (economic and social) … On the other hand, the traditional Nyoongar people knew that the wetlands held a rich and delicately balanced ecosystem. For the Nyoongar people the wetlands also hold spiritual significance through the Wagyl [large serpent], which is the central spirit figure.[51]

In portraying Europeans on an expedition firing their guns at a major ancestral being, the Wagyl, Pease showed the explorers' disregard for the

---

[49] Susan Jenkins, 'How World War II began (through the eyes of the Rembarrnga)', in John McDonald, ed., *Federation: Australian Art and Society 1901–2001* (Canberra, 2001), p. 136.

[50] See pp. 109–10.

[51] Christopher Pease to Brenda Croft, 2004, National Gallery of Australia File.

spiritual beliefs of the Nyoongar people—as well their ignorance of the environmental importance of the wetlands and river systems. In appropriating this European image which was designed to show a European public that King George Sound was a desirable place to settle, Pease has turned the imagery on itself—dramatizing the negative impact of Empire.

* * *

Australian colonial landscapes were initially produced by European artists on voyages of exploration involved in mapping the territory and recording it, then by convicts and settlers from Britain and elsewhere. These artists brought with them European modes of painting and frequently created images to take or send 'home'. By the 1890s, there was a conscious move to foster what was thought of as a 'national school of painting' which sought to portray a subject that the artists believed would distinguish Australian life from that lived elsewhere—an interest which continued in the years immediately following the First World War (although with different imagery).

It is easy to see the development of a non-Indigenous Australian landscape art as being a sponge-like absorption of European standards and techniques foisted onto a new environment and as being condemned by the networks of Empire. To see non-Indigenous Australian culture in this way, however, is to be tunnel-visioned and to fail to consider the painting of landscape elsewhere in the world. John Constable, the nineteenth-century English landscape painter, for instance, looked to the seventeenth century—to French artist Claude Lorraine and Dutch artist Jacob van Ruisdael—in painting landscapes around his home in Dedham. French Impressionist Claude Monet absorbed aspects of the work of the British artist J. M. W. Turner and Japanese printmakers in creating his images of the French landscape. Artists throughout time have looked to their predecessors to find appropriate models and have adapted these for their purpose. And, for all her rhetoric, urging artists to create a national art by taking from the work of Indigenous artists, Margaret Preston, likewise, looked to the structures of well-known European—and Australian—paintings in creating her art.

The forger Joseph Lycett may have made artistic representations of places he had never visited for the enjoyment of people back home, and he may have created illusions about the realities of life in the colony. In doing so, however, he was not so much the forerunner of a culture based on fakery, as working

in a pictorial tradition in which reality is 'moulded' towards a given point
of view. Tom Roberts, Frederick McCubbin, and Arthur Streeton may have
claimed to have observed their subjects with their own eyes, but they too at
times 'faked' their images, painting subjects they had not experienced. When
doing so they were working in a long-standing tradition in which artists
have employed models to construct their scenes. Because they captured an
Australian light and—in some instances—adopted a French 'naturalist'
technique, their images give the appearance of being 'real'. But any idea that
the development of a non-Indigenous Australian art is a gradual progress
towards a more 'authentic' vision of Australia is a myth, because the very
idea of an 'authentic' vision is a construct. A painting—like history—is the
transmission of reality through the perception of an individual. Different
artists choose to emphasize different aspects of the world, using a range of
modes of picture making.

Roberts believed that art is universal and said that 'by making art the
perfect expression of one time and one place, it becomes art for all times
and all places'.[52] Virginia Spate has argued that this was because of Roberts'
faith in the British Empire, and because around the world people saw in
the way he saw.[53] Nonetheless, artists are inevitably part of their own time
and place and, intentionally or unintentionally, this is embodied in their
paintings. Roberts depicted shearing in rural Australia at the turn of the
century and Lambert revealed the leisured relationship towards the land of
the pastoralists in the 1920s. But Roberts' *Shearing the Rams* was not an
illustration of particular shearers at a specific moment and Lambert's *The
Squatter's Daughter* was not a portrait of a particular squatter's daughter
(although some have read it as such). While representing a particular time
and place these artists conveyed more general principles underlying their
subjects.

The process of Empire, of colonization, has taken place through many
different relationships with the land, and these in turn have been expressed
through a multiplicity of visual imagery. It would be a mistake to think
that Australian culture in particular is condemned by the networks of
Empire to fabricate its art out of forms and philosophies borrowed from
elsewhere. Rather, all culture is built upon the art of the past. Australia
is a fortunate 'enchanted' place where its culture has been created by a
blending of the cultures of many people from a range of backgrounds,

---

[52] Roberts, letter to the *Argus*, 4 July 1890.   [53] Spate, 'Where the Sun Never Set', p. 62.

including Australian Indigenous artists. Non-Indigenous artists depicting the Australian landscape have, perhaps inevitably, adopted and modified frameworks used in viewing the landscape elsewhere, synthesizing European, Asian, or Indigenous Australian concepts with their perception of the Australian landscape to create a national art. But in doing so, they have created new visions from old. Together with some remarkable Indigenous artists they have developed a home-grown vision of Australia which is now largely beyond Empire.

Select Bibliography

CHRISTOPHER ALLEN, *Art in Australia: From Colonization to Postmodernism* (London, 1997).

TIM BONYHADY, *The Colonial Earth* (Melbourne, 2000).

JANE CLARK, *Golden Summers* (Melbourne, 1985).

WILLIAM EISLER and BERNARD SMITH, *Terra Australis: The Furtherest Shore* (Sydney, 1988).

ANNE GRAY, ed., *Australian Art in the National Gallery of Australia* (Canberra, 2002).

RON RADFORD, *Australian Colonial Art: 1800–1900* (Adelaide, 1995).

—— *Tom Roberts* (Adelaide, 1996).

ANDREW SAYERS, *Australian Art* (Oxford, 2001).

BERNARD SMITH, *European Vision and the South Pacific* (Melbourne, 1989; first published 1960).

—— with TERRY SMITH, *Australian Painting: 1788–1990* (Melbourne, 1995).

PART II

DYNAMICS: THE INSTRUMENTS OF EMPIRE

6

Empire, State, Nation

JOHN HIRST

Among the Australian people only faint memories now remain of the origins of their polity, which are English not Australian.

When ministers refuse to resign or threaten the independence of the civil service, appeals may be made to Westminster principles, but they do not resonate far. People under forty, if they think at all of the origins of their liberal freedoms, would ascribe them to the UN Declaration of Human Rights rather than to Magna Carta and the Glorious Revolution. Those events used to form part of any historical education in Australia, along with John Hampden and Ship Money, Star Chamber, Charles I losing his head, Judge Jeffreys and the bloody assizes, and the first Reform Bill. And those who did not know these particularities knew at least the slogans of British constitutional liberty: Britons never will be slaves; the Englishman's home is his castle; it's a free country; fair play; I'll have the law on you—which were heard as often in Australia as in Britain.

Robert Menzies (Prime Minister, 1939–41, 1949–66) was not unusual in identifying Australia completely with this British tradition. On his first visit to London (in 1935), he was the keynote speaker at a gathering of the Empire Parliamentary Association. At a time when democracy was in retreat in Europe, and under threat where it survived, he proudly declared in Westminster Hall:

I am confident that our parliamentary system is going to see it through. And why? Because its roots are deeply set in the history and character of the British people. In those countries where it has fallen, a parliament was adopted as the embodiment of an attractive theory. As a fully-grown tree it was carefully transplanted and watered and cared for. And at the first real blast of the storm it fell.

Will our parliaments survive? I believe that they will. The growth of parliament is in truth the growth of the British people; self-government here is no academic theory, but the dynamic power moving through 800 years of national history.[1]

In the early years of his second prime ministership Menzies' great rival was Doctor H. V. Evatt, who led the opposition to Menzies' attempt to ban the Communist Party in 1950–51. As chair of the General Assembly of the United Nations in 1948, Evatt had proclaimed the Declaration of Human Rights, but it was not that document to which he referred in denouncing the Menzies proposal:

This represents a direct frontal attack on all the established principles of British justice … this is one of the most dangerous measures that has ever been submitted to the legislature of an English speaking people. I do not think that a bill of this character would receive a moment's consideration from the mother of parliaments, the British parliament, for in that parliament traditions of political liberty and established justice are always recognised and, are, indeed all powerful.[2]

The points for speakers that the Labor Party produced (for campaigners for a 'No' vote in the referendum to ban the Communist Party in 1951) began in this way: 'The powers being sought by the government constitute a frontal attack on all the established principles of British justice.' And concluded: 'The amendment is contrary to the whole spirit of the Constitution [by which was meant the British constitution]. The amendment involves the sacrifice of Magna Carta and the rule of law.'[3]

It is clear that the Australian people then knew their British history, or the mythological version that sustained British political institutions. The honouring of the British constitution was at the heart of Australian Britishness. The education of Australians in British constitutional liberty came to an abrupt end in the 1960s. Once Britain announced that it was planning to join the European Union (then the Common Market), and hence that it was abandoning leadership of a British world, Australia perforce was moved to shed its British identity. Quite quickly Australia was re-presented as a multicultural society to which all ethnic groups had made and were making their contribution. The British were a suspect ethnic group, since they had been the dominant group in the non-multicultural past. They certainly could not be credited with supplying the central institutions of the polity, for that would explode the claim of equal 'contributions'. This still left

---

[1] *The Times*, 5 July 1935.
[2] *Commonwealth Parliamentary Debates*, Vol. 213, 1951, p. 1213.
[3] *Speakers' Notes*, Issued by the Australian Labor Party, NSW Branch, Trades Hall, Sydney, 1951.

Australians with British institutions; but not the history and myth to explain and sustain them. It was the greater loss since they had no supplanting political myths of their own, which is an enduring legacy of their experience of Empire.

*   *   *

The Australian colonies (except Western Australia) began to govern themselves on Westminster principles in the 1850s. That is, they had a bicameral Parliament and ministers were responsible to the popularly elected lower house. No great struggle was required to achieve self-government, and the new system was inaugurated very smoothly. Australian historians have struggled to make drama out of the 'fight for self-government'. Briefly there was real heat in the fight when, in the late 1840s, the British government attempted to reintroduce a form of convict transportation. This prompted a protest movement across the colonies, with some threats and bluster about independence. But the British policy was driven by one minister, the third Earl Grey, and when he lost office with the defeat of the Whig government (in 1852) the policy was dropped. His successor, Sir John Pakington, gave permission to the colonies to draw up constitutions for self-government. The one open act of defiance of British authority was carried out by gold diggers at Ballarat in 1854. A broadly supported movement against paying the licence fee to dig for gold ended with a couple of hundred men enclosing themselves in a stockade on the Eureka lead, and flying a flag with the stars of the Southern Cross. British troops captured the stockade in a short battle. The republicanism of the rebels who took up arms was not supported by the diggers generally; still less in the colony at large. Independence from Britain had absolutely no point when a new constitution, providing for colonial self-government, was about to be implemented.

Hence, while Australians for the next hundred years knew they were governed on British principles, and indeed may have thought of themselves as living simply under the British constitution, they did not celebrate the coming of self-government. The events of the 1850s that they did remember were the gold rushes, which symbolized new opportunities, sudden wealth, and a hearty egalitarianism.

The reason why the transition to self-government did not mark an era in Australian affairs was that the colonies had been governed so well by the Colonial Office and the British administrators on the spot, the Governors and their officials. This was true both of the ordinary business of government (which was much more expansive than in Britain), and also in preparation for self-government. Unlike the experience of the mother country, parliamentary government in Australia did not displace liberty-threatening tyranny, but a species of enlightened despotism.

Consider at first preparation for self-government. The foundations of an open, liberal society had been laid down under British rule, which explains why the so-called liberals who took power after self-government had so little to do. Usually against the wishes of the putative ruling class of the colonies (the owners of land, sheep, and mercantile wealth), the British administrators in Whitehall and on the spot had been responsible for the following: raising the price of land to provide a fund to pay for the emigration of free working people; the ending of convict transportation (made possible by the above); allowing ex-convicts to enjoy the same legal and political rights as free settlers; granting the Catholic Church the same status and public support as the Protestant churches; the founding of government schools to take children of all denominations; the refusal to allow the squatters of the interior to have any firmer title to their lands than a licence or lease; allowing individual miners rather than companies to dig for the 'royal' mineral gold; refusing to allow the putative ruling class of New South Wales to create a constitution for self-government that was difficult to amend; a disowning in Whitehall of the Governors of South Australia and Tasmania, who had asserted that in the new constitutions upper houses could not be elected.

It is an amazing record of statecraft. Liberal principles were applied to the colonies well in advance of Britain, and sometimes by administrators who opposed them in Britain. The individuals responsible were not always clear-sighted about what they were doing, but among all their decisions none had illiberal consequences. This record has never been properly acknowledged, and is scarcely even hinted at in the histories of Australia, which are too often written on autochthonous principles. Convict origins can easily lead to the assumption that liberal and enlightenment principles played no part in shaping the Australian colonies under British rule—a misapprehension very evident in the history best known outside Australia, Robert Hughes' *The Fatal Shore*.[4]

---

[4] Robert Hughes, *The Fatal Shore: A History of the Transportation of Convicts to Australia, 1787–1868* (London, 1987).

The ordinary business of government began in an extraordinary way. The government was responsible for shipping the subjects it was to govern half way round the globe, and for their safe lodgement in the new world. The government of New South Wales, in the person of the Governor, Captain Arthur Phillip, began its labours in Portsmouth harbour with close attention to the needs of the convicts. In New South Wales Phillip treated convicts as servants of the Crown even when in private employment, which is the status they retained. When convicts had been sent to America, the British government abandoned responsibility for them at the doors of the gaols, whence private contractors carried them to the colonies and disposed of them. There was no convict establishment in America, which makes it easier for modern-day Americans to forget that they received convicts. By assuming responsibility for the convicts, and the survival of the settlement that had been formed to accommodate them, Governor Phillip took on a multitude of tasks and established the tradition of omni-competence in colonial government.

A similar dynamic operated at the convict establishments at Hobart and Brisbane, which became capitals of separate colonies, Tasmania and Queensland. South Australia was founded without convicts; but the responsibility its rulers had accepted for the recruitment and shipping of free labour from Britain under the principles of Wakefield's plan of 'systematic colonisation' had a similar effect. Only at Melbourne, of the colonial capitals, did government follow rather than plan the settlement. Without authorization its first settlers came from Tasmania. For a brief time they governed themselves; but then the Governor of New South Wales, in whose territory the new settlement was located, arrived and appointed a magistrate responsible to himself.

The founding governments of the Australian colonies had the virtues of the British government that created them; they provided a secure world in which all subjects enjoyed protection of their property and liberty. The convicts of course did not have their liberty, but they were deprived of it by the law, which also set the term for their release and protected the property and persons of ex-convicts as if they had always been free.

The early Australian governments were actually better than the British. The government of Pitt the Younger, which sent the convicts to New South Wales, began the process of administrative reform which ended the practice of office under the Crown being considered a form of private property. The new rules operated in Australia from the beginning, so that there were no sinecures; the work could not be done by a deputy; the reward was a fixed salary rather than fees. The Australian colonists had no experience of government as a system of placemen, pensions, fees, and private enrichment. The British officials who ruled under the Governor's control were remarkably efficient and honest.

Government in Australia did not begin with taxation. The funds of the first governments came from the British taxpayer. The constant concern of the Colonial Office was to get the Governor to limit his spending and to raise money by local taxation. It was some time before the colonists in Australia were paying the true cost of their government. For the first hundred years their defence was provided and paid for by the British Navy. Nearly all the funds raised by the colonists could be spent on their own local purposes.

By the self-denying ordinance passed during the American troubles, the British government could not raise money directly in Australia. Britain obtained its benefit from the colonies through the increase of its trade and the returns on the private funds invested in Australia. The Governor's job was to promote the development of the economy, which would enable the colony to pay its way and bring more benefit to Britain. There was a notable harmony between what the British government wanted of the Governors, and what the settlers wanted of the Empire.

Governors and their officials built roads and bridges, improved ports, encouraged exploration, surveyed land for settlement, and provided settlers with their labour force, at first convicts and later free immigrants. In the 1850s, in the last stages of direct British rule, Governor Denison in New South Wales and Governor Hotham in Victoria brought the infant railway system under government control. In South Australia Governor Young championed the development of navigation on the River Murray; he himself having pioneered a voyage up the river; and his government constructed a tramway to carry goods around the treacherous and shallow Murray Mouth. The Governors in all three colonies inaugurated a government telegraph system.

The British government which sent the Governors did none of these things in its own country. The function of government had changed in Australia. It was not primarily to keep order within and defeat enemies without. Rather, it was an etatist instrument to develop the country, and a resource on which settlers could draw to make a success of their own pioneering.

The social character of the government also changed; or rather it did not have a social character. In Britain, government was closely linked to the social order, since it was constituted by the aristocracy and gentry and their connections. In Australia the government was one person, the Governor, who was detached from, and superior to, all groups in the local society. Yet government was much more than the person of the Governor; he embodied the full authority of the British government and was the representative of the Monarch. Government was both more singular and more abstract.

A government that plants a new society will always be different from a government ruling an established order. The particular form taken by the state in Australia reflected the time of its foundation. It was liberal in orientation, because its controllers at Whitehall and on the spot were influenced by the growing authority of liberal ideas in the imperial metropole. The acceptance of responsibility for the well-being of convicts and free migrants came from the new humanitarianism. The commitment to economic advancement, and the means to achieve it, was inspired by the spectacular growth in the British economy. Overall it reflected a new confidence in the capacity of government itself.

Here was a unique 'pattern of government growth', as Oliver MacDonagh might have described it.[5] This had its theorist in Jeremy Bentham, who is sometimes credited with having a large influence in Australia.[6] No doubt Bentham encouraged a more positive role for government; but he himself could scarcely have cast government as a source of so much good unless government had shown itself as a competent instrument. The sailing of the First Fleet to New South Wales—which incidentally Bentham opposed as an affront to his principles of crime and punishment—demonstrated a huge leap in the capacity of the British government. It has been said that no other European power of the time could have attempted it.[7] In Britain the capacity of government was growing at the same time as the notion that government should do less was also strengthening. In Australia the government, cast in a different role, did more without question.

The transition of the Australian colonies to self-government in the mid-1850s was managed as part of the ordinary business of government. The new constitutions were drawn up by the local legislature, the legislative councils,

[5] Oliver MacDonagh, *A Pattern of Government Growth 1800–60: The Passenger Acts and their Enforcement* (London, 1961).

[6] Hugh Collins, 'Political Ideology in Australia: The Distinctiveness of a Benthamite Society', in Stephen R. Graubard, ed., *Australia: The Daedalus Symposium* (Sydney, 1985).

[7] Roger Knight, 'The First Fleet', in John Hardy and Alan Frost, eds, *Studies from Terra Australis to Australia* (Canberra, 1989), pp. 121–36.

two-thirds of whose members were elected and one-third nominated by
the Governor. When, in 1852, the British government indicated that it was
prepared to concede self-government, the councils set to work on their
constitutional task immediately. Elections were not held to take the opinion
of the people. The nominees of the Governor participated in the business
unchallenged. Nothing was done to suggest that the colonists were the source
of authority for the new regime. Only in South Australia was an election
held over constitution-making, after the Governor was caught out for not
revealing the willingness of the British government to accept an elected
upper house.

The draft constitutions were sent to London, and, with minor changes
(the most important concerned the amendment provisions in the New
South Wales document), were accepted by the British government; and
then passed into law as schedules to a British Act of Parliament. They
were put into operation by the imperial Governors, who continued to
play an important part in administration. The Governor in Council, which
was now constituted by the Governor and Cabinet ministers—instead of
the Governor and his officials—was an important organ of government,
giving authority for a myriad of official acts and overseeing and correcting
administration. Government in the Australian colonies had, surprisingly, a
more monarchical cast than in Britain itself—where an individual minister
responsible to the House of Commons became the standard mode of
administration.[8] It was as if the colonists themselves could not provide
sufficient authority to carry on their government.

The more substantial continuity was that the regular business of government remained the same as when Governors fully controlled it: to provide
the infrastructure for the development of the economy. Manhood suffrage
was introduced soon after responsible government, but the style of government remained 'paternal and managerial'.[9] The change was that Parliament
and its wide electorate made it easier for more people to make demands on
the government—for roads, bridges, railways, and local services. If people
wanted something done, they went in a deputation to the minister, escorted
by their local member. If the local member could not get results out of
ministers, he lost his seat at the next election. In the absence of strong
parties, the allocation of public works and services was an important weapon
for ministers trying to maintain majorities.

[8] Paul Finn, *Law and Government in Colonial Australia* (Melbourne, 1987), p. 164.
[9] Ibid., p. 40.

These democratic governments in the colonies, like those run by the Governors, were omni-competent. They ran the school system and the police, which in Britain were the business of local government. Local government in Australia was weak; it was established late and did not cover the whole country. Its chief job was the making of local roads and, in the towns, the collection of rubbish. Where there was no local government, the colonial government did all that was necessary. In most of the countryside of New South Wales there was no local government until 1906. At that date, the State government imposed municipal institutions; previously they were created only if local inhabitants requested them. Many settlers had preferred to get all their services from the centre; and when compulsory incorporation was proposed, they proclaimed the right not to have local government, an Australian innovation in political philosophy.

The colonial governments did all their work without imposing direct taxation. Until late in the nineteenth century there was no income tax and no company tax. The government collected its revenue from taxes that were hardly noticed—duties collected on imported goods—and from the sale of Crown lands—which was not a tax at all. But local government did tax directly; its revenue came from rates collected on land. This was the chief reason why it did so little, and why in many places it did not exist at all. Few wanted to give local government more responsibilities because that would increase direct taxes.

The first government schools were built only if local people raised some of the cost of the building. That gave them some say in the running of the school. But, from the 1870s, the colonial governments, without raising any new taxation, were able to cover the full cost of school building. Local control of education disappeared. Who could quarrel with this when schools were established at no local cost?

This dependence on government, which became a characteristic of the Australian polity, was not a dependence of social deference. The putative ruling class of the colonies, long waiting in the wings, was swept aside in the first years of self-government. In New South Wales, William Wentworth's plan for a local aristocracy was laughed out of court; and after leading the move for self-government Wentworth duly retreated to Britain with other colonial conservatives. They were replaced not by rulers of bourgeois respectability but a distinctly raffish and disreputable collection of politicians, or at least Parliament contained enough members of this sort to earn a bad name. The colonists despised the men who provided them with all their services, which made it possible to accept so much from their hands. 'The government' remained without social character; it was an impersonal force for good.

The business of 'the government' in the colonies was captured well in the novel *Jacob Shumate*, written by Henry Wrixon who had served for a long period in the Victorian Parliament. Soon after Jacob Shumate is elected to Parliament, he is inundated with letters from 'people who had learned to cherish a comprehensive trust in their Government':

The settlers in the Cote Cote Valley wrote to ask when the Government was going to drain their land; or were they to leave the land after the Government had put them on it? The members of the Tum Tum Fox club informed the Member that the Department had sent them down rifles to help destroy the foxes, but where was the ammunition? Did they expect them to kill the foxes without? An indignant parent complained that he did not get the full allowance of sixpence a week per child for bringing his children to school over the limit fixed by law for the allowance—though the road was so bad that he had to put a pair of horses in the trap to carry them. A comparatively poor widow wanted a place for her daughter as a typist, or something respectable, as she could barely make ends meet now with the price of things and the high wage for the house-help.[10]

The characteristics of the Australian state as they were formed under imperial rule were accentuated, rather than abandoned or modified, with self-government. Such a state made little call on citizenship. The citizens had not created the state and were not called on (even as taxpayers) to take a very active part in it; their most characteristic stance was as supplicants for their share of the cornucopia.

But it would be misleading to say these relationships totally defined the colonists' orientation to the state. They were very conscious of being British subjects and the local state, however utilitarian in its daily workings, protected their British rights and liberties and hence their freedom from the state. In this matter the local state was acting as an agent of the parent state, which was the sacred locus and ultimate guarantor of this heritage. It was because they were so certain that their British rights were protected that the Australians expanded the activities of the state so unconcernedly.

*   *   *

In the late-nineteenth century a new state was formed in Australia to bind together the people of the six colonies. The men who carried this project to

---

[10] Henry Wrixon, *Jacob Shumate*, Vol. 1 (London, 1903), pp. 168–9.

completion had high ideals of these colonial people becoming true citizens of the new nation.

In the 1880s, when Federation of the colonies was first seriously discussed, there was great uncertainty about the relationship between the proposed new nation and the Empire. In the colonies, Britain's new interest in Empire was generally welcomed; but it raised the doubt as to whether a new nation would be captured for imperial purposes, or at least prevented from its full realization. In loyalist Victoria there was confidence that the interests of Empire and nation could readily be reconciled; but in New South Wales and Queensland the bounds of national autonomy were projected more vociferously. Such independently minded colonial nationalists found increasing support and gained substantial representation in Parliament.

They did not want immediate 'independence' from Great Britain; but they aspired to a genuine 'home rule', and sooner rather than later. They were generally suspicious of the old imperial embrace. Outside Parliament, overt republicanism was, however, espoused by only a small, if noisy, group of radicals and socialists. Republicanism was more effectively advocated by the Sydney *Bulletin*, the first national weekly, which nurtured a school of strident nationalist literature; and even envisaged a nation outside the Empire.

In 1887, at the first Colonial Conference in London, the colonial Premiers agreed that the colonies would pay a subsidy to offset the cost of the Australian squadron of the Royal Navy. In Victoria the Parliament agreed to the subsidy unanimously. In the New South Wales Parliament the subsidy was passed against concerted opposition, with its supporters giving three cheers for Old England, and its opponents three cheers for Australia. The Queensland Parliament refused to pass the subsidy, and in the election of the same year (1888), the people elected a government of independent colonial nationalists who went under the name of the National Party.

Sir Henry Parkes, Premier of New South Wales and the elder statesman of colonial Australia, watched these movements with dismay. In 1889 he suddenly announced that he was now a firm supporter of Federation, a movement from which he had previously held aloof, and that the colonies must proceed immediately to draft a federal constitution. His aim was to halt the growth of independent nationalism, and to harness it in support of a new nation under the Crown. But he could only attract the independent nationalists if the new nation could have all the power and status proper to its name; and in addition be allowed to have a voice in the Empire's affairs. Simultaneously with his call for Federation, Parkes wrote privately to Lord

Salisbury, then British Prime Minister, urging the creation of an Empire Council which would gradually assume authority for the Empire's defence and foreign affairs.[11]

Parkes was successful in convening a constitutional convention in 1891, which agreed to a federal constitution. However the federal movement came to a halt because Parkes himself could not persuade his own free-trade party to give serious consideration to the draft. The most populous and oldest colony was highly suspicious of Federation because its free-trade principles were likely to be compromised by conjunction with its protectionist neighbours. Federation disappeared from the political agenda as strikes, depression, and bank failures hit the colonies in the early 1890s.

Federation was revived as a democratic crusade in 1893. A conference of federal enthusiasts, meeting at Corowa on the border of New South Wales and Victoria, proposed that a new convention should assemble but elected by the people rather than the parliaments and that the constitution it drafted should be put to the people in a referendum for their approval. This scheme reflected the commitment to complete democracy now being urged by new or radical liberals. Manhood suffrage had been established in the late 1850s, but cautiously and without democratic fanfare. In all colonies except South Australia the property qualifications for the vote had been retained which gave property owners a vote in every electorate where they held property. This plural voting was one of the targets of the new liberals—who were also committed to women's suffrage, the limitation of the power of upper houses, and the regular use of the referendum. It was these new liberals who provided most of the leadership for the federal movement in its final successful stage.

The colonial Parliaments adopted the scheme proposed at Corowa. The people elected a constitutional convention of high quality. All but one of its members were politicians; but without the demagogues, drunks, and roads-and-bridges members they were an impressive group. Part of the inspiration of the leaders of the federal movement was that a federation would carry politics to a new level. A parliament dealing with the life and destinies of a nation would be a grander and nobler institution than the parliaments that haggled over local infrastructure.

The convention met three times in 1897 and 1898. It had to suspend its first sitting because all the Premiers were invited to London for the

[11] John Hirst, *The Sentimental Nation: The Making of the Australian Commonwealth* (Melbourne, 2000), pp. 81–6.

Queen's jubilee celebrations, organized as a great spectacle of Empire by the British Colonial Secretary Joseph Chamberlain. The Premiers were sceptical of Chamberlain's plans for Empire federation, which he unveiled after the festival, but they and their constituents at home were delighted with the prominence that colonial politicians and colonial troops were given in the festivities. Britain's growing interest in the colonies prompted a new enthusiasm for Empire not so that the suspicion of it disappeared but there was no longer fear of entrapment. The independent nationalists withered away; their movement had been prompted more by uncertainty about the relationship between nation and Empire than by a determined anti-British stance. The federal movement of the 1890s, fully under Australian control, indicated that Britain was allowing space for nation-building. The republican movement had disbanded; its radicals had been absorbed into the new Labor Party, which was suspicious of Empire but not opposed to the connection. The *Bulletin* had abandoned its republicanism in 1894.

The constitution was put to the people twice in referendums. At the first referendum in 1898 the four colonies participating voted 'Yes'; but the 'Yes' vote in New South Wales did not reach the required majority set by Parliament. The constitution was then modified by the Premiers to appease New South Wales; and in 1899 put again, this time to five colonies, with Queensland now participating. It was carried in all. Western Australia voted 'Yes' in 1900, just in time to join the union on its inauguration on 1 January 1901.

The referendums were an amazing democratic exercise. The details of a constitution of 128 clauses had to survive popular scrutiny and the crude misrepresentations of its opponents. The United States constitution which presents itself as the work of the people—'We, the people'—was not directly endorsed by them, and had it been put to a popular vote probably would have been defeated. The contemporary historians of the federal movement, Robert Garran and John Quick, who had been activists for the cause, praised the 'high political capacity' of the Australian people:

Never before have a group of self-governing, practically independent communities, without external pressure or foreign complications of any kind, deliberately chosen of their own free will to put aside their provincial jealousies and come together as one people from a simple intellectual and sentimental conviction of the folly of disunion and the advantages of nationhood.[12]

---

[12] *The Annotated Constitution of the Australian Commonwealth* (Sydney, 1901), p. 225.

This was a state founded by its citizens, in a way totally at odds with British notions of sovereignty.

The Commonwealth had its founding myth: 'Ours is not the federation of fear, but the wise, solemn, rational federation of a free people.' These words appeared in one of the guidebooks to the celebrations, which also explained why the new nation should be proud of its achievement of uniting without coercion from within or without: 'Such a federation as ours has only become possible through the advance of intelligence and the development of a higher system of morality than the world ever saw before.'[13] The *Advertiser* in Adelaide adapted President Lincoln's words and put the myth in the form of an epigram: 'The Commonwealth has come from the people by the people to the people.'[14] The poet who won the prize for the best poem celebrating the inauguration wrote:

> Free-born of nations, Virgin white,
> Not won by blood nor ringed with steel,
> Thy throne is on a loftier height,
> Deep-rooted in the Commonweal![15]

The founding myth had virtually been eclipsed before the celebrations were over. The myth-makers had praised the peacefulness of the Federation movement, but in 1899 when blood began to flow in the South African War, the Australian people took a very old-world pride in the deeds of their warriors. The willingness of Australian soldiers to shed their blood turned out to be a more persuasive signifier of nationhood than the construction of a federal constitution in peaceful circumstances. Australians were enthusiasts for the war and the doubters were fewer than in Britain.[16]

So the Commonwealth was inaugurated in Sydney in time of imperial war. The celebrations were organized by the Premier of New South Wales, William Lyne, who had advocated a 'No' vote at both referendums. Imitating Joseph Chamberlain's celebration of the Queen's jubilee, he assembled, with Chamberlain's help, a military display of the Empire to honour Australia's peaceful achievement of nationhood. The Queen's Own Hussars and Imperial Life Guards marched through the streets with troops from India and Australian veterans of the South African War. These were the highlights of the procession.

---

[13] *From Colony to Commonwealth: Being a Brief History of Federation* (Sydney, 1901), pp. 7–8.
[14] *Advertiser*, 2 January 1901.   [15] *Sydney Morning Herald*, 1 January 1901.
[16] See Chapter 12, pp. 291–2.

The first Commonwealth Parliament assembled in Melbourne, the temporary capital, in May 1901. It had been a struggle for the Premiers to secure a royal personage to open it. Queen Victoria had only with great reluctance given permission for her grandson the Duke of York to perform the honours. But a few days after the Commonwealth was inaugurated the old Queen died. The new King, Edward VII, was definitely opposed to his son attending. His mind was changed by a letter from Arthur Balfour, the leader of the government in the House of Commons and the nephew of Lord Salisbury the Prime Minister. 'Surely', Balfour wrote plainly,

It is in the highest interests of the State that he should visually, and so to speak corporeally, associate his family with the final act which brings the new community into being; so that in the eyes of all who see it the chief actor in the ceremony, its central figure, should be the King's heir, and that in the history of this great event the Monarchy of Britain and the Commonwealth of Australia should be inseparably united.[17]

Balfour's reputation as a philosopher-statesman is well deserved. This is exactly what transpired. The *Bulletin* saw it happening and wished it were otherwise; but it was a lone and disreputable voice:

Among the ceremonies which attended the union of a continent and the beginning of a nation there moved a thin, undersized man who has never done anything save to be born, and grow up, and get married, and exist by breathing regularly, and be the son of his father who did the same things. And in the public eye he was, apparently, about three-fourths of the pageant. The men who made the Commonwealth were eclipsed for the time by the man who made nothing of any importance.[18]

The eclipse became perpetual darkness. The organizers of the 100th anniversary of Federation had to run an advertising campaign to familiarize Australians with the name of the leader of the federal movement and their first Prime Minister, Edmund Barton.

Federation had always been envisaged as taking place within the Empire. But in the time it took for Federation to be achieved, enthusiasm for Empire strengthened. The distinctiveness of Australia's mode of nation-building could not compete with the psychic satisfactions that Empire offered. The enthusiasm for the South African War was highly indicative, prefiguring the huge satisfaction Australians were going to draw from the exploits of

[17] Harold Nicholson, *King George the Fifth* (London, 1952), pp. 66–8.
[18] Quoted in Ian Turner, *The Australian Dream* (Melbourne, 1968), p. 256.

their soldiers at Gallipoli in 1915 when, it is claimed, 'the nation was born'. Peaceful constitution-making had not been enough. Those Australians who took their citizenship seriously continued to think of themselves as British citizens; and their constitution was not the Commonwealth of Australia Constitution Act.

*   *   *

The growing enthusiasm for Empire had not deterred the Australian constitution-makers from shaping a constitution befitting a fully self-sufficient nation. Their constitution was to come into force as part of a British Act of Parliament, but they always expected this to be a mere formality: they had drawn up not only a constitution but also those provisions by which the British Parliament would carry their constitution into law. They did not allow for the British government or Parliament revising their handiwork. Every word they had written was simply to be passed into law. This was a very different outlook from that of the designers of the Canadian confederation thirty years before. They had sent broad principles to London and British officials had crafted the British North American Act, which could only be amended by the British Parliament. The Australian document imperiously concluded 'This constitution shall not be altered except in the following manner'—by the Commonwealth Parliament proposing alterations for consideration of the people at referendum.

The constitution took shape at the 1891 convention. Its draftsman was Samuel Griffith, Premier of Queensland and later Chief Justice of Queensland; and then first Chief Justice of the Australian High Court. Griffith displayed in high degree the desire felt by all the federationists—to throw off the demeaning status of 'colonial' and become, instead, citizens of a new nation. Griffith aspired to constitute a self-governing Australian nation—yet one that would remain within an evolving Empire, without being subordinate to Britain. The key remaining link to Britain would be the Crown. Britain would be an equal and an ally, and the people of the settlement Empire would potentially share a common citizenship. This arrangement was not formally achieved until the passage of the Statute of Westminster in 1931. Legally, Griffith could not produce that outcome in the 1890s; but it is what he had in mind as he drew up the constitution.

While the document allowed that Britain could veto Commonwealth legislation (a power thought not likely to be used), it claimed power over external affairs and treaties and British ships in Australian waters; it limited appeals to the Privy Council; it did not explicitly make the new Commonwealth subject to the Colonial Laws Validity Act (1865), which legitimated colonial law-making but subject to the overriding power of the British Parliament. All this survived in the document that went to London in 1899. Griffith had wanted more. In the 1891 draft he provided that the states could not communicate with London except through the Governor-General and that they be given power to alter the office of Governor—their link to the Crown—without Britain's approval. This would ensure that Australia faced the world as a single entity and would never have to bother the British again on constitutional matters. The link to the Crown would be solely a matter for the Commonwealth, and governed by amendment of the constitution. The colonies, as they then were, did not want these restrictions placed on them and they were not retained by the 1897–8 convention.

The officials in the Colonial Office watched the development of the 'separatist' character of the constitution with some dismay. At the first session of the 1897 convention a new, cheeky assertion of independence was added to the opening of the constitution: 'This Act shall bind the Crown.' The officials correctly discerned that the constitution-makers had not taken the existing powers of the colonies and distributed them between states and Commonwealth; rather, they had assumed that all powers were at their disposal, as if British sovereignty did not constrain them. That was certainly Griffith's aspiration having declared at the 1891 convention, 'all prerogatives of the Crown exist in the Governor-General as far as they relate to Australia'—a statement made to support his view that Australia would have the power over war and peace.[19]

The difficulty that the Colonial Office faced was that it knew Australians were very touchy about their right to self-government, and unlikely to accept imperial correction. It decided to work secretly to secure amendments to the draft. At the 1897 colonial conference, held in conjunction with the Queen's jubilee, Chamberlain identified George Reid, free-trade Premier of New South Wales, as the least hostile to his plans for a more united Empire. To him was assigned the Colonial Office critique of the draft constitution so that he might secure amendments when the convention reconvened. The critique included the major objections, and a long list of drafting suggestions designed merely to be helpful. Reid did secure some changes,

---

[19] Roger Joyce, *Samuel Walter Griffith* (St Lucia, 1984), p. 200.

without revealing its inspiration; he passed the critique to Edmund Barton, the leader of the convention and chair of the constitutional committee, who accepted some but rejected most of the drafting suggestions. These changes left most of what the Colonial Office regarded as objectionable still in place; only the reference to treaties had been dropped.

The officials in the Colonial Office were disposed not to carry the dispute further. Chamberlain, however, was not willing to let the over-ambitious Australians redefine the constitution of the Empire. That, after all, was his own project. He brought Barton and four other colonial delegates to London and laid his objections before them. The delegates at first refused to budge on anything, declaring the document awaiting British ratification to be akin to a sacred text. Having been accepted by the whole people at referendum it was beyond their power to agree to its alteration. Chamberlain made clear he was not overawed by the claims of popular sovereignty; and so negotiations did begin. The Australians agreed to drop the offending 'This Act shall bind the Crown' clause—which the British law officers feared might make the external affairs power unlimited. Chamberlain in return dropped his objections over British shipping and the Colonial Laws Validity Act. The impasse came over appeals to the Privy Council, which the constitution allowed in private cases, but not for those concerning the interpretation of the constitution itself. The dispute became public, with Chamberlain appealing over the heads of the delegates to the Chief Justices, Governors, and Premiers of the colonies; and the delegates appealing to any audience in the United Kingdom that would listen to them.

In this case, enthusiasm for Empire in Australia did inhibit the claim to full national status, for Chamberlain was able to collect abundant indications that the colonists saw the limitation on appeals as an act of disloyalty to the Empire in time of war. But the delegates did better than Chamberlain in the imperial heartland. And so a compromise was reached. Constitutional cases that solely concerned the relative powers of the Commonwealth and states would be settled finally in Australia; where they involved other parties and governments anywhere in the Empire, appeals could lie to London. But the new Commonwealth Parliament could change these arrangements so long as the Bill was reserved for the Queen's assent.

Australian national aspirations, as regards constitutional matters, were satisfied by the constitution adopted in 1901. Australians played no part in the demand for formal independence from Britain, which was urged by South Africa, Canada, and Ireland. It did not look for the equality offered in the Balfour Declaration of 1926—that Britain and its Dominions were 'equal in status and in no way subordinate one to another'—and used its influence to ensure that the Declaration avoided the word 'independence'. It regretted the legal embodiment of the new relationship in the Statute of Westminster of 1931, fearing that it would lead to the dissolution of the Empire. Unlike the Dominions that wanted to escape British overlordship, Australia's population was, as it boasted, 99 per cent British; and Britain remained vital in trade and was taken to be crucial for defence. 'Alone Australia is weak', said John Latham the Attorney General, 'as a member of the British Commonwealth Australia is strong'.[20]

The long discussions on the remaking of the Empire were conducted for Australia by National–Country Party Coalition governments. The opposition Labor Party did not hold significantly different views. This is at first surprising because during the war a Labor government had split and lost office over the issue of conscription for the Empire's war in France. After the war the Party's declared policy was to eschew an Empire defence in favour of concentrating on the defence of Australian territory. Yet this lack of enthusiasm for Empire showed itself more in gesture than any serious questioning of the imperial connection.[21] Certainly the Labor Party did not ally itself with the plans of the Irish or the South Africans for the remaking of the Empire. For nearly all the interwar years Labor was in opposition, but its brief period of office (1929–31) coincided with the 1930 Imperial Conference which finally settled the details of the Statute of Westminster. James Scullin, the Labor Prime Minister, kept as his advisers those who had worked for the Nationalist government and he himself echoed their misgivings about the dangers of over-defining the relationship between Britain and the Dominions. Scullin used the occasion to press another matter: the right of a Dominion Prime Minister to give advice on the appointment of the Governor-General. King George V rather reluctantly accepted his recommendation that Isaac Isaacs, a Jewish judge of the High Court, should be Australia's first native-born Governor-General.[22]

[20] W. J. Hudson and M. P. Sharp, *Australian Independence: Colony to Reluctant Kingdom* (Melbourne, 1988), pp. 99–100.

[21] This is the formulation of John Rickard in *Australia: A Cultural History* (London, 1988), p. 203.

[22] L. F. Crisp, 'The Appointment of Sir Isaac Isaacs as Governor-General of Australia 1930: J. H. Scullin's Account of the Buckingham Palace Interviews', *Historical Studies*, Vol. 11, no. 42 (April 1964).

On his return from London Scullin, pressed by the Opposition and the states, supported a move to make the Statute apply to Australia only after it was adopted by the Commonwealth Parliament. The Statute still had not been adopted when the Second World War broke out. Labor took office again in 1941 but was in no hurry to adopt the Statute. In 1942, without fanfare, it did win parliamentary adoption on the narrow grounds that it was necessary to cover wartime legislation regarding merchant shipping and national security.

There is genuine debate among constitutional experts about when Australia became an independent sovereign country. Can it be in 1931, if Australia refused the offer of freedom? But the year of adoption of the Statute (1942), may be too late, since Australia appointed its first overseas ambassadors in 1939. Chief Justice Garfield Barwick of the High Court declared in 1969 that Australia was an independent nation; but he could not pinpoint when this event occurred.[23] Australia is therefore an oddity among the post-colonial nations in that the date of its independence cannot be definitely known. Yet that in no way diminishes Australians' sense that they are now an independent nation and 'people'.

In 1932, a year after the passage of the Statute, Australia's attitude towards Britain momentarily became extremely hostile; but this was prompted by English bowlers aiming at Australian batsmen during the 'Bodyline' Test cricket series.[24] It was in this arena, rather than constitutional formulations, that Australians perhaps most wanted the British to know that they were 'equal in status' and 'in no way subordinate'—and a good deal better. 'Pom bashing' was infinitely satisfying.

The Australian states were excluded from the operation of the Statute of Westminster, that is, formally they remained subordinate to the British Parliament and Monarchy. They sought this position, fearing that an independent Commonwealth might disturb the powers allotted to them under the constitution, even though they were amply protected by the Statute which stipulated that the Commonwealth constitution could only be altered in the way already provided. This meant that the Governors of the states continued to be appointed by the British government, albeit on advice from the Premiers. Some states continued to allow appeals to the Privy Council after the Commonwealth ended them in the 1970s. The connection of the states to Westminster was ended by the passage of the Australia Acts in 1986. Griffith had planned to end it in 1891.

---

[23] Hudson and Sharp, *Australian Independence*, pp. 135–6.
[24] Laurence Le Quesne, *The BodyLine Controversy* (London, 1983). See Chapter 14, pp. 351–3.

Griffith had done his work well—perhaps too well. His constitution did not have to be altered when Australia acquired all the powers of independent nationhood. Since Australians have not had to revisit their constitution to assume their independence, that document still contains what Griffith had to put there in 1891, the power of the British Monarch to veto Commonwealth legislation. That an independent nation leaves this provision unrepealed (to the great puzzlement of the few citizens who read the constitution) is a conclusive demonstration that Australian nationalism has ceased to look for its symbols in constitutional forms.

*   *   *

In 1991 a republican movement of a new sort emerged in Australia.[25] In the 1880s republicanism was associated with socialism and other radical movements for economic and social change; and it found its following among autodidacts from the petit bourgeoisie, and the skilled working class. The movement of the 1990s was initiated in Sydney by the rich and famous, celebrities from the new elite of the world city, totally unlike the old colonial establishments for whom loyalty to the mother country had been an article of faith. These elite republicans had no wider social agenda; they simply wanted to institute an Australian head of state to replace the Governor-General who is formally appointed by the Queen. The republicans felt demeaned by this one surviving connection with the United Kingdom, but they had difficulty in rousing the nation to the passion they felt themselves. The connection is so slight and so unfelt that people cannot be bothered about its removal, even though the majority have lost all the feelings that used to support the British Monarchy. An appeal to get rid of the Governor-General on nationalist grounds was simply bound to fail. When Australians came to vote (compulsorily as is usual) on a republican proposal in 1999, those who identified as Australian in traditional ways were less likely to vote 'Yes' than the new cosmopolitans who think of Australia as a multicultural community.[26]

The republican proposal was designed not to disturb the operations of the Westminster system. So the new president was not to be directly elected

[25] John Hirst, 'Towards the Republic', in Robert Manne, ed., *The Australian Century: Political Struggle in the Building of the Nation* (Melbourne, 1999), ch. 9.

[26] K. Betts, 'The Cosmopolitan Social Agenda and the Referendum on the Republic', *People and Place*, Vol. 7, no. 4 (1999) pp. 32–41.

by the people for fear that the office would acquire a popular mandate that could challenge that of the Prime Minister. Instead, the president was to be nominated by the Prime Minister and then endorsed by a two-thirds vote of both houses of Parliament. Sadly for its republican proponents, the people overwhelmingly wanted to elect the president themselves. They had little understanding or respect for the Westminster system; many of them wanted to elect the president themselves because they had lost faith in the existing system. Now that any deeper understanding of the system had been lost; now that it had ceased to be the embodiment of a particular British genius—it appeared to represent no more than 'politics-as-usual', easily caricatured as scandal, broken promises, and ego-tripping.

The republican proposal was comfortably defeated. For all its patriotic bravado—not least in diverse sporting achievements and a post-colonial strut of hedonistic popular culture—Australia had not yet escaped its imperial past. Empire had gone; yet Australia found itself poorly equipped to shape its new constitutional future in the new century.

Select Bibliography

ALAN ATKINSON, *The Europeans in Australia: A History*, Vol. 1 (Melbourne, 1997).

HUGH V. EMY, *The Politics of Australian Democracy* (Melbourne, 1974).

PAUL FINN, *Law and Government in Colonial Australia* (Melbourne, 1987).

W. K. HANCOCK, *Australia* (London, 1930).

JOHN HIRST, *The Strange Birth of Colonial Democracy: New South Wales 1848–1884* (Sydney, 1988).

—— *The Sentimental Nation: The Making of the Australian Commonwealth* (Melbourne, 2000).

—— *Australia's Democracy: A Short History* (Sydney, 2002).

W. J. HUDSON and M. P. SHARP, *Australian Independence: Colony to Reluctant Kingdom* (Melbourne, 1988).

J. A. LA NAUZE, *The Making of the Australian Constitution* (Melbourne, 1972).

W. G. McMINN, *A Constitutional History of Australia* (Melbourne, 1979).

A. C. V. MELBOURNE, *Early Constitutional Development in Australia*, 2nd edn, (Brisbane, 1963).

STUART WARD, *Australia and the British Embrace: The Demise of the Imperial Ideal* (Melbourne, 2001).

7

Migrations: The Career of British White Australia

ERIC RICHARDS

Fundamental to all the connections between Britain and Australia was their demographic exchange. From its colonial origins, and for over two centuries, several million people from the British Isles were conveyed across the globe. These transoceanic flows were remarkably well controlled and precisely defined in their composition, though the process passed through several transitions.[1] Migration from Britain was the unquestioned assumption in the imperial project of 'peopling Australia'.

In retrospect, it is extraordinary that so remote a settlement could maintain such a homogeneous population composition. This indeed was sustained with single-minded determination until the late 1940s. It resulted in a population conventionally regarded as more British than the British. It was White and almost exclusively British. Australia's adherence to 'Whiteness' was its defining characteristic, the source of minor external friction with much of the rest of the world, even with Britain itself. None of the other great immigrant countries was able to sustain such a degree of homogeneity. At its centre were potent assumptions about race, the snake that slithered its way through Australia's immigration history. Migration was a crucial dimension in the imperial relationship and its consequences survived the other residues of the imperial inheritance.

Australia was the last habitable continent to be grasped by European imperialism. The British regarded it as virtually empty (though there were possibly a million Indigenous people), a *tabula rasa* on which they could conduct exercises in colonial expansion. They determined who came to Australia and how they should live. Even the convict colony of New South Wales—that unsavoury start—was an exercise in control and design.

---

[1] See Eric Richards, 'Migration to Colonial Australia: Paradigms and Disjunctions', in Jan and Leo Lucassen, eds, *Migration, Migration History, History: Old Paradigms and New Perspectives* (Bern, 1997), pp. 151–76.

The first idea was that the convicts would become a self-sufficient society, in the form of a reformed peasantry. Soon there emerged a more market-oriented agrarian society with landowners and labourers, as well as traders and artisans. When the colonies evolved out of convictism another model was introduced which synchronized immigration and land sales, to create a fully balanced society on the English rural pattern. The idea of controlling the shape and composition of Australian life persisted throughout.

The migrations to Australia were achieved in the context of much wider diasporic movements from the British Isles. Throughout the colonial era these migrations were sheltered beneath the protective canopy of the *Pax Britannica*. This gave advantage to the British over other dispersing peoples from Europe and elsewhere. For most of the time there was a sense of demographic complementarity between Britain and Australia, a mutuality of interest which underpinned the entire migrant transaction. It began as a 'simple provincial relationship with Britain'.[2] Australia's ability to call upon transfusions of British people depended on conditions in both places, not merely the commitment to 'White British Australia'. The outer edges of other diasporas, such as those out of Germany, Italy, China, and Japan, in the event, did not reach Australia in numbers large enough to test seriously the prevailing exclusion policy. Nevertheless the fear of such hypothetical inflows recurrently shadowed Australia's immigration regimes.

The assumption that the British Isles could continue to supply all Australia's population requirements proved unrealistic in the 1940s. The eventual disengagement of Australia's population imperatives—first from its British exclusivity and then from its essential 'Whiteness'—was achieved without damage to relations between London and Canberra. In the outcome the demographic relationship between the two countries was altered incrementally and, by the 1990s, reversed. Migration in the post-Imperial decades eventually became less clear-cut than in the great age of migration which, for Australia, lasted until the early 1970s. Nevertheless the legacy of the first 180 years of British migration left an indelible genetic mark on the modern Australian population.

*   *   *

[2] J. M. Powell, *An Historical Geography of Modern Australia: The Restive Fringe* (Cambridge, 1988), p. 336.

Population composition in colonial Australia was controlled by a combination of distance and the special mechanisms for the recruitment of immigrants which were peculiar to Australia. The colonial population was socially engineered from the start. The Australian colonies emerged in a context in which neither slavery nor indenturing were feasible options; instead they were supplied by the last phases of the old convict transportation system. The 162,000 convicts eventually dispatched from Britain were, in the first place, intended to relieve crime and punishment in Britain. They were not, however, a random cross-section of the prison cohorts of the time. They were selected to serve the functional needs of the colonies: the convicts comprised an efficient immigrant intake of 'convict workers'.[3] The relatively small numbers of free immigrants were subjected to a similar degree of selectivity. Thus tradesmen were introduced according to local requirements. More importantly, access to land (providing a lure to any prospective free immigrants) was rigorously restricted to people with a command of capital substantial enough to warrant a free land grant. This created the basis for a severely divided social structure. All other immigration was impractical: the cost of passage was too great, and the possibilities of economic gain too risky, for ordinary migrants who overwhelmingly headed for North America.

Continuity of control was retained despite the decline of the convict system and the termination of free land grants. By the 1830s the Australian colonies transcended their initial function as penitentiaries; now their economic and territorial development required free labour and capital in growing quantities. There was a convergence of metropolitan and colonial sentiment for this shift, but not enough to persuade the British government to finance the export of its people to the other side of the globe. The plan proposed in 1829 by Edward Gibbon Wakefield (and its variants) created a device which effectively employed a tax on land (by way of land sales) to subsidize and control labour migration (by generously assisted passages). This solution yielded a general social return which attracted capital and enterprise. The system depended ultimately on the capacity of Australia to develop its export trades. This became the *sine qua non* of both assisted and unassisted immigration, and of Australia's ability to redirect some of the existing flows of migrants from North American destinations. The diversion of people to Australia was in itself an improbable enterprise which triumphed against the grain of

---

[3] See S. Nicholas and P. R. Shergold, 'Convicts as Workers', in S. Nicholas, ed., *Convict Workers* (Cambridge, 1988), pp. 62–84.

most British emigrant flows. Australia was extremely unusual in expending so large a proportion of its realizable resources on immigration.[4] The costs were shouldered by colonial land buyers who demanded value for money.

Assisting immigrants gave the colonies the power of selection, and no other country exerted such direct influence over its immigrant inflows. With barely any interference from London, the colonies were able to determine the selection, composition, scale, timing, and, most important of all in the long run, the source of their foundation peoples. In part it was designed specifically to counteract the demographic and social defects of the convict population. The Wakefieldian specifications ensured an ideal balance of the sexes, a particular occupational profile, and some monitoring of age, character, and origins. The resultant inflows possessed almost perfect immigrant qualifications—they were young, with few dependants, easily inducted into agricultural and domestic service, balanced between the sexes, occupationally well suited to the colonial economy, and relatively well educated and healthy. Indeed, large numbers of the mid nineteenth-century assisted immigrants were derived from the upper levels of the working populations of the British Isles and, surprisingly, more literate than the home populations.[5]

The control achieved by the assisted system was not total. It failed to replicate among the immigrants the reigning proportions in the home populations, a policy designed to prevent the disproportionate expansion of Catholicism in the colonies. The English, in particular, consistently failed to respond in sufficient numbers to achieve their fractions in the assisted immigrations especially among their womenfolk. Accordingly, from as early as 1840, the Australian colonies diverted their recruitment efforts to Ireland, expressly to compensate for the shortfalls, notably among the female recruitments. The outcome was a substantially larger Irish incoming population than was planned, and this tendency was reinforced by the operation of the nomination schemes which the Irish in Australia took up more vigorously than other immigrant groups. Demographic realities, in effect, prevailed over the original preferences and over recurrent political opposition among colonists.[6]

---

[4] See Eric Richards, 'Migration to the New Worlds: Emigration Systems in the Early Nineteenth Century', *Australian Journal of Politics and History*, Vol. 41 (1995), pp. 391–407.

[5] See Eric Richards, 'An Australian Map of British and Irish Literacy in 1841', *Population Studies*, 53 (November 1999), pp. 345–59.

[6] See John McDonald and Eric Richards, 'The Great Emigration of 1841: Recruitment for New South Wales in British Emigration Fields', *Population Studies*, 51 (November 1997), pp. 337–55.

As the colonies prospered—notwithstanding the imposition of land sales—increasing numbers paid their own passages from Britain and eventually accounted for about half of all immigrants in the nineteenth century. Gold fever in the 1850s brought a much wider spectrum of migrants than before, including a miscellany of British migrants who had not previously regarded Australia as a feasible destination. The hectic intakes of people to the goldfields mocked the idea of controlled immigration. Moreover, employers at large became desperate for labour and resorted to new supplies of emigrants from unconventional sources (including the Highlands of Scotland). Gold attracted a polyglot and motley intake of Europeans and Americans, creating a sudden heterogeneity which colonists tolerated without much concern in the turbulent mobility of that decade. In any case the foreigners were small in number and not concentrated in ethnic solidarities.

A different outcome followed the Chinese goldmining migrants, whose introduction created frictions: they were racially unacceptable, they were indentured, they were overwhelmingly male, they were ghettoized, and they were perceived as a threat to living standards. The Chinese flows into Australia—about 60,000 (with very high return rates)—galvanized opinion among colonists towards a defined 'White Australia policy'. This was the moment when two of the great diasporas of the nineteenth century, the British and the Chinese, converged in Australia, and the exclusion of the latter soon became unambiguous.

The origins of White Australia pre-dated the gold rushes, and were not exclusive to the Australian colonies. Hostility to non-British immigrants was driven by the fear of cheap labour recurrently sought by pastoralists and sugar planters. It was manifested in the 1830s in resistance to plans to introduce Indian and Chinese 'coolies', a system disparaged as a new form of slavery. This argument was heavily reinforced by demands for racial and cultural homogeneity without which, together with high wage regimes, the colonies would not be able to attract working immigrants from Britain. The Colonial Office in London instigated and encouraged exclusion: in 1841 James Stephen, its all-powerful permanent head, declared that Australia should be a land 'where the English race shall be spread from sea to sea unmixed with any lower caste'. Two years later he supported opposition to the introduction of Indian 'coolies' into New South Wales because they would 'debase by their intermixture the noble European race ... [and] introduce caste with all its evils ... bring with them the idolatry and debasing habits of their country … beat down the wages of the poor labouring Europeans … [and] cut off the resource for many of our own distressed people'.[7]

These arguments echoed through all the decades of White Australia. Opposition to non-White immigrants rose in periods of unemployment and at such times even extended to the British immigrant. The economic argument was a powerful motivation but was almost always expressed in racial and cultural language. The policy was never detached from its racial assumptions.

In the 1860s, after the gold rushes, the colonies reverted to their heavy reliance on assisted immigration, which was synchronized with the alternation of good times and recession. All convict transportation was finally ended in 1868 and the Australian colonies competed for migrants with the much larger destinations, overwhelmingly with the United States. The recourse to Irish migrants continued, but the colonies consistently asserted their selection principles and, since they were paying, felt little obligation to consult London. There was no friction with London except when Britain appeared to foist its 'human refuse' on the colonies, or when the colonies recruited too aggressively in districts of labour shortage in Britain. Broadly, the assumption of mutual benefit was unchallenged. The recurrent complaint in the colonies concerned the quality of the recruits.

At the British end there were recurrent anxieties that the conduit of emigration would be blocked. Thus, when the American Civil War threatened to terminate emigration to the United States several commentators urged the British government to foster and protect its other outlets, notably Australia, as substitute destinations for the United States which had always absorbed the vast majority of all British emigrants.[8] Despite such advocacy the British government adamantly refused to intervene in the business of emigration.

The fluctuating transfusions continued until the 1890s. In reality there was no challenge to the homogeneous flows of British people to Australia apart from a few minor streams which trickled from other sources. Since this was a laissez-faire context various minorities indeed reached Australia—a few thousand Germans into South Australia and Queensland, a sprinkling of other Europeans often emigrating to avoid military service or to follow special trades or random connections. Thus a few hundred Italians entered

---

[7] Quoted in Charles Price, *The Great White Walls are Built* (Canberra, 1974), p. 40.
[8] See Herman Merivale, quoted in Eric Richards, *Britannia's Children* (London, 2004), p. 159.

the fishing trades in several places. But they were generally lost in a landscape of Britishness, a few erratics on the Anglophone plain.

The hostility to non-British immigrants was ever ready to erupt publicly. Even in 1906, when the need to encourage immigration had been identified as a national priority, Labor Party delegates from Western Australia asked that a language test be applied to Italian immigrants, 'the object being to secure their deportation, as their presence here was considered a menace to the prosperity of Britishers'.[9] In some respects this xenophobia was imported from Britain itself: the British world was full of hostility to immigrants.[10]

Australia's guiding precept was that Britain was able to satisfy all its immigration needs and that alternative supplies were inferior. That Britain was not able to satisfy all such requirements across the Empire was already crystal clear in other imperial regions: in Natal, in the West Indies, in Fiji, and even in Canada which, by the 1890s, was already diversifying its immigrant supply sources towards Europe, following the massive parallel example of the United States. Specific labour needs even in Australia impelled solutions outside the British stream—the best known cases were the Afghan cameleers, the Japanese pearlfishers, and, most of all, the much greater recourse to Pacific Island labour for the Queensland sugar industry. The last engaged a total of 60,000 islanders, and they eventually became the focus of the racial exclusion campaign that consolidated White Australia.

The debate sprang up fiercely at the time of Federation, when immigration was in retreat and there had been no net immigration for a decade. In 1901 Australia explicitly defined its nationhood in terms of 'Whiteness' within the imperial framework. It set clamps on immigration policy for most of the following century. Thus when Tasmania urgently sought alternative sources of immigrants it looked to attract men from India, but restricted its catchment to retired British officers from the services.[11]

The most famous metaphor depicting Australian immigration was the boa constrictor which takes massive bites of food, slowly digests the meal, and then slumbers again until hungry.[12] Australia awakened from one long sleep

---

[9] See *Argus*, 6 January 1906, quoted in Michele Langfield, *More People Imperative: Immigration to Australia, 1901–39* (Canberra, 1999), p. 185.

[10] See, for example, T. C. Smout, *A Century of the Scottish People, 1830–1950* (London, 1986), pp. 22, 248.

[11] See Ian Pearce and Clare Cowling, *Guide to the Public Records of Tasmania. Section Four. Records Relating to Free Immigration* (Hobart, 1975), p. 19.

[12] See C. H. Wickens, 'Australian Population: Its Nature and Growth', *Economic Record*, 1 (1925), p. 5.

in 1906 when it suddenly became desperate for more people, now conscious
of potential foreign threats and the fact that it had fallen well behind other
immigrant countries.[13] Quickly it generated renewed demands of its demographic relationship with Britain, grasping for immigrants as never before.
The outcome was surprising: Australia was able to command unprecedented inflows of immigrants and reaffirm its essential White Britishness. The
immigrants were generally young, fit, and able-bodied, and disproportion-
ately male too. On the outbreak of the Great War, recently arrived British
immigrants entered the armed forces with greater alacrity than Australian-
born recruits. The great intake of British immigrants before 1914 thus paid a
prompt dividend to the nation, and was a major reaffirmation of Imperial
ties and the defence of Australia.[14]

*   *   *

The Great War blocked the movement of people but also reinforced the
imperative for accelerated immigration after the war to ensure the future
of British White Australia. In Australia there was a determination to return
to the record levels of immigration achieved in 1913, as well as a tenacious
attachment to the idea of rural development—which gave first priority to
Australian and British soldier settlement on the land, and this increasingly
anachronistic assumption was also applied to immigrants in general.[15]

Immigration continued to be regulated and selected on racial criteria,
though other characteristics (such as health, political affiliation, skill, and
literacy) were also employed. Racial discrimination operated in conjunction
with these considerations, but the protection of wage levels was at the
forefront and most insistent in the periods of recession. The argument that
social equilibrium requires a homogeneous immigrant population was a
persistent contender in the public mind.

The post-war international context favoured Australia's agenda. The United States was erecting quotas on immigration; economic crises in Britain
created poor circumstances across the nation, and the European context was fraught. Conditions for recruiting migrants for Australia seemed
propitious—so much so that Canberra was able to persuade the British government, against all precedent, to make indirect payment towards emigrant

---

[13] On the perception of foreign threats at this time see Chapter 10, pp. 242–5.
[14] See Langfield, *More People Imperative*, p. 11.
[15] See Powell, *Historical Geography*, pp. 72–120.

passages to Australia. The Oversea Settlement Committee in 1921 advocated 'a strong policy of State-aided Empire Settlement' and submitted plans for large-scale emigration with British and Dominion assistance. The Committee welcomed the change: 'the policy of *laissez faire,* with its attendant evils, has been abandoned.' Greater care in selection and training was called for, especially 'training farms' and 'training in household work'.[16] A succession of tight (and often ill-tempered) negotiations between the Australian and British governments demonstrated a sea-change in the balance of advantage in the migrant transaction. Australia's hand was strengthened by British recidivism—namely, a return to ideas by which British social and economic problems were to be relieved by Empire emigration.[17] There was wrangling over the terms and the direction of the benefits of migration, and about the responsibility for migrant welfare. There were doubters, including Otto Niemeyer of the British Treasury who remarked (in 1925), 'Emigration is an excellent thing for the uninhabited receiving state, it may be a good thing for the actual emigrant, but it is not so clear that it is for the emitting country.'[18] But there was also a rising chorus of imperial rhetoric trumpeting the notion that Empire trade and migration would provide the glue to hold together the greater entity. Consequently a convergence of Australian and British opinion favoured the expansion of emigration. Mechanisms for recruitment and propaganda were activated, using modern means of advertising to revitalize the flows of emigrants, associated with grandiose development schemes, and urged on by the enthusiasm of Rudyard Kipling and other imperial zealots.

The outcome was positive yet disappointing. British emigration to the Antipodes rose again, but not in numbers sufficient to fulfil Australian expectations; the urge to emigrate was waning; and Australia's reliance on Britain as a source of population was less secure.[19] But this was mainly hidden beneath the severely negative publicity that was generated in the late 1920s regarding the unhappy fate of so many British migrants lured to marginal rural districts in Australia, especially in Victoria.[20] The recriminations against Australia rose to unprecedented levels of public bitterness in the

---

[16] *The Economist,* 11 March 1922, pp. 492–3.

[17] See Michael Roe, *Australia, Britain and Migration, 1915–1940* (Cambridge, 1995).

[18] Ibid., p. 59.

[19] See for example *The Economist,* 24 December 1927, pp. 1142–3.

[20] See R. A. Pepperall, *Emigrant to Australia* (London, 1948); Geoffrey Bolton, *A Fine Country to Starve In* (Nedlands, W.A., 1972).

British press. The insistence on rural settlement (and immigration) as the central requirement of Australian development had become unrealistic. But the Anglo-Australian acrimony was also the result of poor timing and bad luck—the spectacle of large numbers of ill-equipped Britons pioneering on poor Australian land coincided with the catastrophic decline of primary produce prices, drought, and then the Great Depression which struck early and savagely in Australia. It swiftly reversed all immigration, which did not revive again until the end of the 1930s.

In the meantime, the demographic relationship between Britain and Australia was under scrutiny since many of the old assumptions were creaking badly. There were already voices questioning the future of 'the manifest destiny of the British people to spread itself over the wide fields of opportunity', leaving the Dominions exposed to the aspirations of other 'cramped peoples'.[21] If Britain could not supply Australia with migrants then Australia might be forced to look to Europe. Such bleak pessimism was powerfully reinforced by the fear of military danger rising in the East. All this came into ominous focus in the late 1930s.

*   *   *

Demographic pessimism gripped both Britain and Australia in the 1930s and threatened to end migration to the southern continent. These were predictions derived from the declining birth rate evident in both countries from as early as 1900. Some contemporaries declared that emigration from Britain simply exacerbated Britain's own demographic decline.[22] Authoritative commentators declared that the British population had reached its peak (or would soon do so). It was pointed out that, in the 1930s, Britain was the only net immigrant country in the entire Empire.[23] Britain appeared to be running out of people who might emigrate, yet the unity of the Empire could only be maintained with a 'continuous infusion of British blood' which was 'also vital to the interest of British trade'.[24]

The worm seemed to turn, the diaspora had run its course, and the Dominions could no longer count on Britain for their demographic transfusions. The British now told themselves that they must abandon 'the habit

---

[21] Fleetwood Chidell, *Australia—White or 'Yellow'?* (London, 1926), Preface.
[22] See Roe, *Australia, Britain*, pp. 155–6.
[23] *The Economist*, 12 March 1932, p. 570; 2 July 1938, p. 10.
[24] *The Economist*, 28 May 1932, p. 1174.

of regarding emigration as a method of curing British unemployment'.[25] Britain could no longer afford to lose its people. It was an odd doctrine when so many British people were unemployed, though Britain began to emerge from the Great Depression somewhat ahead of most other places (including Australia). These pessimistic diagnoses were not put to any test because Australian immigration was in abeyance. Nevertheless they were early signs of a shift in the demographic balance, a mounting realization that Australia would not be able to rely on Britain for its future population supplies, and should not plan on such an assumption. There were three registers of this evolution.

First, in Britain itself, there was opinion telling Australia that it should begin to think in the way that the United States had been populated, and more significantly, Canada which had absorbed many continental European migrants over the previous half century. In 1938 the Oversea Settlement Board advised the Dominions to seek 'a carefully regulated flow from other countries whose people are of broadly the same stock as ourselves, and who have a similar outlook', such as Scandinavia.[26] Secondly, Australian sensibilities were tested by the flow of Jewish refugees out of Nazi Europe after 1936: the fact that Anglophile Jewry in Australia expressed immediate caution about the entry of European Jews was symptomatic of the wider Australian wariness about non-British immigration.[27] Thirdly, within Australia, there were early signs that some opinion was favouring a more variegated flow of immigrants in the future, even though the initial Australian response to Italian and Jewish immigrants gave little encouragement to radical ideas of immigrant diversification. The general tenor of debate remained muted: as one commentator declared in 1939, 'The Australian prides himself on his high standard of living; he wishes to do nothing that will endanger it. Neither does he wish to bring into being a colour problem such as he sees in South Africa.'[28]

The pessimism of the Depression therefore seemed to bring the grand project to populate Australia to a standstill; and this was redoubled by a parallel debate which questioned the settlement of Australia on an even more general basis. In 1942 W. D. Forsyth's influential *The Myth of Open Spaces* pointed out that most of Australia was uninhabitable and that its

[25] *The Economist*, 29 February 1936, p. 461.   [26] *The Economist*, 2 July 1938, p. 10.

[27] Suzanne D. Rutland, *Edge of the Diaspora*, 2nd edn (Rose Bay, NSW, 1997), pp. 174–201.

[28] See S. J. B. Whybrow and H. E. Edwards, *Europe Overseas: A Survey of Modern Empires* (London, 1939), p. 130.

population requirements would, in future, be very modest and should not be compared with those of nineteenth-century America.[29] Moreover, he argued that Australia's traditional dependence on primary production and exports was increasingly unwise, and he therefore advocated an industrial future for the country. Forsyth chimed in with the notion that Europe was ceasing to be a reliable supplier of migrants: it was the end of the era of mass migration, and Australia would have to come to terms with the structural change in the relations between the Old World and the New.[30] These were all symptoms of Australia's changed place in the world, and important anticipations of a shift in relations with Britain itself.

*   *   *

Post-war planning assumed a return to high levels of unemployment and low labour and migrant demand. A revival of British immigration was expected but planning was largely focused on special recruitments, notably among demobbed military personnel and orphaned children. But a different agenda swiftly emerged which transcended other doubts. This gave highest priority to industrial and demographic expansion almost regardless of costs, but preferably in tandem with imperial sentiment and a re-engagement with 'the British embrace'. Defence and a larger population overrode all other calculations. By 1946 Australia had determined on a momentous expansion of its industrial and demographic resources.

This decisive political commitment turned into a scramble for immigrants. By 1947 it was clear that the pre-war script was half correct: it was not feasible to count on the British for all of Australia's immigrant needs. This became palpable when A. A. Calwell, Minister of Immigration, recruited large numbers of Displaced Persons in post-war continental Europe, and soon extended the migrant net into Europe and eventually into the eastern and southern parts of the old Continent. None of this actually diminished Australia's appeal to Britain; and the imperial dialogue was reactivated. In Britain the surviving zealots of Empire once more cranked up the idea that the British Commonwealth could regain vitality by way of intra-Empire migration and trade, and the channelling of Treasury funds for

[29] W. D. Forsyth, *The Myth of Open Spaces* (Melbourne, 1942), pp. 202–5.

[30] Kingsley Davis, 'The Migration of Human Populations', *Scientific American* (September 1974), pp. 53–65.

subsidized emigration was revived. It was, however, confined to the White Commonwealth, conspicuously Australia, and seemed again to endorse the traditional racial assumptions of Australia's immigration policy.[31] There was also a decisive shift of recruitment towards skilled industrial labour wherever available, a process which had already been quietly anticipated in the late 1930s.[32]

The psychology of emigration in the early post-war years was clouded by nuclear fears. In an atomic war Britain would be a leading target. A recurring strain among imperial supporters insisted that the threat of nuclear war enhanced the urgent need to disperse the British people, and their industries, to Commonwealth locations. As early as 1937, Britain had developed a philosophy of overseas diversification as a contingency against threats to homeland security. Some decentralization of munitions production to Australia actually took place.[33] Australian visitors to London after the war observed a world of shortages, dislocation, and uncertainty, but also new apprehensions of an impending war. Such fears put emigration into a new light.[34] As one observer wrote in 1949: 'At home in England there were now millions looking to the possibility of starting life afresh in some new country, as soon as ships could be found to carry them. In an atomic age, common sense demanded the dispersal of British industry, if this were feasible.'[35]

Anxiety about the nuclear threat therefore revived ideas regarding the vital interdependence between Britain and the Dominions: securing Britain's food supply was critical, but credence was also given to the dispersal of some of Britain's industrial and military infrastructure, and to the relocation of larger numbers of the British people outwards to the Dominions. A British visitor to Australia in 1949 declared: 'Here we've enormous spaces offering a genuine invitation towards dispersal, inside the Commonwealth of Nations. To ignore such an offer seemed imperial folly.' Intensifying atomic anxieties were captured in the words of a British industrialist, Hambleton of Rubery-Owen, setting up new plant in Adelaide:

[31] See Kathleen Paul, *Whitewashing Britain: Race and Citizenship in the Postwar Era* (Ithaca, New York, 1997).

[32] See *The Economist*, 30 January 1937, p. 228.

[33] Michael Foster, 'Modernism, Modernity and "Modernisation": The Culture of Progress in Australia, 1920–1945', Ph. D. thesis, Flinders University, 2003, p. 289, quoting A. T. Ross, *Armed and Ready* (Sydney, 1995), p. 286.

[34] Frank Clune, *Land of Hope and Glory* (Sydney, 1949).

[35] David Esdaile Walker, *We Went to Australia* (London, 1949), p. viii.

There is absolutely not a shadow of doubt that the industrial potentialities of Australia are immense. The problem is surely not so much a matter of saving the English peoples as of preserving the British *race*. We *must* become Empire-minded. This isn't mere sentiment or emotionalism. It is blunt common sense from any point of view and particularly in view of defence.[36]

The essential idea was to create a twentieth-century version of 'Britain beyond the seas'—which was given urgency by opinion polls in Britain showing that many people expected another war within twenty years, which would be fought with atomic weapons. The Dominions would be 'Britain's lungs'.[37] It was a revival of fading notions of an economic and strategic complementarity between the parts of the Commonwealth, and the idea received an enthusiastic reception in Australia as it embarked on its own first concerted industrialization.

Britain's post-war confirmation of its commitment to Commonwealth migration suited Australia to a tee.[38] Recruitment was energetic and sophisticated, helped by the prevailing economic austerity in Britain. Soon, somewhat against expectations and despite shipping shortages, emigrant numbers were again buoyant. The positive differentials in income and prospects between Australia and Britain provided the engine of migration, propaganda was the fuel, and post-war austerity the tailwind.

Reality soon dawned. Though British emigration to Australia picked up, it was insufficient to meet the target of a 2 per cent per annum population growth rate set by Minister Calwell. The inescapable consequence was a rapid widening of the recruitment catchment—towards the 'next-best' White alternative sources in Europe. Calwell orchestrated the radical switch, assisted by bipartisan support, with extraordinary success. Some within the Labor Party were not sorry to dilute the reliance on British sources, thereby following the Canadian example.[39] A social revolution in population composition was engineered with remarkably little disruption or resistance, partly because it was presented as a temporary expedient. The Europeanization of a large part of the Australian immigrant intake became a national priority. It assumed the imperative of rapid population growth and the willingness of the new European immigrants to ensconce themselves in a labour-hungry industrializing economy.

---

36 David Esdaile Walker, pp. 129–30.
37 Roy Lewis, *Shall I Emigrate? A Practical Guide* (London, 1948) pp. 276–7.
38 See *The Economist*, 7 July 1945, p. 10, and 17 August 1946, pp. 241–2.
39 R. T. Appleyard, *British Emigration to Australia* (Canberra, 1964), pp. 32–52.

Another reality was the emerging recognition in Britain that the country was living a contradiction. Britain had entered a period of sustained growth which now absorbed its labour, creating virtually zero unemployment and its own severe manpower shortages. Britain began importing labour—not only from Europe but also from Commonwealth countries (such as the West Indies and India), and was financing some of these labour recruitments. A 'brain drain' also seemed to be threatened by emigration. Hence the British government found itself in the curious situation of paying emigrants to depart (notably to Australia) and simultaneously paying people to migrate to Britain to fill widening gaps in its own workforce. When Prime Minister Harold Macmillan visited Australia in 1958 he was disappointed by the falling number of British immigrants there, and vaguely embarrassed by disillusioned Britons at a migrant camp.[40]

New currents were operating in different directions, and affecting the flow of migrants out of the British Isles. Emigration to the United States, for instance, had virtually ceased. Even the Irish were emigrating less, and now mostly heading for England. As living standards in the United Kingdom rose, the outward flows, at least in net terms, were increasingly insecure and less predictable. In these circumstances, therefore, Australia succeeded, against the odds, to attract substantial numbers of emigrants from the British Isles.[41] Almost half of Australia's greatly increased intake of migrants between 1947 and 1972 still came from the United Kingdom.

In essence, Australia (and, to a lesser degree, some of the other Dominions) had applied artificial respiration to the British diaspora in the third quarter of the twentieth century, breathing life into a fading phenomenon. The interwar Jeremiahs were proved wrong. Yet, impressive though the revival proved to be, it was not enough; and as a consequence Australia followed the experience of the United States and Canada, long delayed, towards the rapid Europeanization of its population. This had been steadfastly resisted for 160 years but, in the event, there were few frictions between London and Canberra, essentially because this transition suited their mutual interests. As early as 1946 *The Economist* had predicted the shift and

---

[40] *Sydney Morning Herald*, 12 February 1958, p. 4. See V. Joan Joynson 'British Assisted Migrants, and Hostels, in the 1950s', in Eric Richards and Jacqueline Templeton, eds, *The Australian Immigrant in the 20th Century* (Canberra, 1998), pp. 106–26.

[41] See R. T. Appleyard, *British Emigration to Australia* (Canberra, 1964), and review of Appleyard in *The Economist*, 4 September 1965, pp. 888–9.

observed that north-west Europe was unlikely to provide many emigrants but that 'American experience shows that, with proper selection, Italians make excellent citizens'.[42] Indeed, in the 1950s, Australia exhausted the northern realms and extended its search into Mediterranean and south-eastern regions of Europe, edging warily into the Middle East, eventually even as far as Turkey.

Against expectation, over three decades of economic and demographic growth, the radically altered immigration programme was politically uncontested and rarely even mentioned in the subsequent political biographies of the day. (The British proportion of Australian immigration fell from 55 per cent in 1961–6 down to 12 per cent in 1980. By 1971 there were fewer British-born in Australia than immigrants born in Europe.) The main manifestation of concern about the decline of Anglo-Australian exchange was the 'Bring out a Briton' Campaign in the late 1950s—the last hurrah of the old demographic dependence.

Australia ceased to rely exclusively on British immigration; there was virtually no pressure in Britain to question the shift, and there was no urgency to augment the number of emigrants leaving the country—on the contrary there were recurrent labour shortages within the British economy itself. Rather than stimulating the outflow to Australia, the British became increasingly wary of, or at best indifferent towards, the outflows. The main political argument concerned the growing absurdity of the British government providing financial assistance to the emigrants, a hangover from the 1920s. Indeed, Britain withdrew from the assistance schemes as soon as it could, and not before inflation had eroded most of the contributions in any case.

*   *   *

Resuscitated over three post-war decades, the demographic transfusions from the British Isles ran down in the 1970s and fewer emigrants arrived in Australia. It was not unambiguously clear whether the demand for, or the supply of, migrants was the critical determinant. Australia terminated its assistance programme, the Calwell agenda. It became a less emigrant-seeking country, a status which coincided with the end of the long boom and the dampening of economic growth. Australia itself dismantled the White

---

[42] *The Economist*, 17 August 1946, p. 242.

Australia policy, eventually by 1973 abolishing all formal discrimination, including the favouring of British immigrants.

The vestiges of racial discrimination had been slow to dissolve under the Liberal–Country Party governments after 1949. Charles Price, the demographer, observed that the apparent reluctance to reform combined with 'its habit of sometimes supporting South Africa, fostered overseas the notion that Australians were a "racist" people almost as bad as the South African Nationalists or the "poor whites" of the southern United States'.[43] The pressure of external opinion against the White Australia policy mounted, especially during the years of decolonization in Africa and Asia. Cabinet Ministers in Australia began to call for the relabelling of the policy because its connotation of racial superiority was false and gave offence. Prime Minister Menzies was increasingly vexed by the intrusion of racial and immigration issues at meetings of Commonwealth Heads of Government. Menzies (and even more vehemently, one of his successors, John Gorton) loathed the way in which he was lectured on the 'principle of racial equality' by newcomer members of the Commonwealth. Menzies and Gorton believed that Australia's immigration policy was perfectly defensible and, in any case, none of their business. Harold Macmillan mollified Menzies with talk about 'the troublesome way the newly independent nations behave', and their 'itch to interfere … with the affairs of the older countries'.[44] But the die was already cast. Australia in the 1960s felt pressure from within and from beyond, and its immigration policy was a growing embarrassment.

The demise of White Australia was therefore urged on, even provoked, by opinion among Commonwealth partners. Australian diplomats and ministers had been badgered about the question for decades and the insistence grew more strident in the 1950s. Britain itself was occasionally embarrassed by White Australia (when, for instance, it affected the selection of migrants within the United Kingdom), but there was little intervention

---

[43] Charles Price, 'Beyond White Australia: The Whitlam Government's Immigration Record', *Round Table*, no. 260, October 1975, p. 371; H. I. London, *Non-White Immigration and the 'White Australia' Policy* (Sydney, 1970), pp. 202–4; David Goldsworthy, ed., *Facing North: A Century of Australian Engagement with Asia. Vol. 1: 1901 to the 1970s* (Melbourne, 2001), pp. 318–23.

[44] Macmillan to Menzies, 8 February 1962, in Ronald Hyam and Wm. Roger Louis, eds, *British Documents on the End of Empire*, Series A, Vol. 4: *The Conservative Government and the End of Empire, 1957–1964*, Part II, Economics, International Relations, and the Commonwealth (London, 2000) p. 662; Ian Hancock, *John Gorton: He Did it His Way* (Sydney, 2002), pp. 185, 304.

against the recruiters. Australia followed its own path, and imperial relations were secondary in the actual demise of the policy. Australia reduced its reliance on the British emigrant supply without any injury to its relations with London. Its eventual renunciation of racial discrimination was greeted with a sigh of relief in the 'home country'.

The disengagement from the White Australia policy was impeded by bureaucratic inertia. When the new head of the Department of Immigration and Ethnic Affairs assumed office in 1980 he discovered his Department still advertising overwhelmingly in Britain and was aghast to hear of 11,000 prospective applicants queuing outside the Australian offices in Manchester. He re-educated his recruitment officers. It meant that, in the post-White Australia regime, 'We had to advertise on a non-discriminatory basis and where the most skilled applicants could be found.' The explicit corollary was that Australia would positively seek migrants in Asia and elsewhere: it was a critical exorcising of White Australia which was also connected with a carefully articulated humanitarian refugee policy.[45]

But there were further changes on the other side of the traditional emigrant exchange. Britain itself, rather belatedly, entered the 'Age of Affluence'. Its own living standards, despite recurrent recession, moved upwards and eventually approached standards long established in Australia. In effect, therefore, the differential between Britain and Australia was eroded—and thus also the *sine qua non* of the eastward migrations. Emigration never ceased; but the flows became less clear-cut, and the movements less unidirectional.[46] The prolonged maintenance of White Australia became entangled with Britain's own migration embarrassments, especially when non-White Britons attempted to emigrate to Australia.[47] When the United Kingdom introduced immigration restrictions the Australian High Commissioner was deluged with complaints from irate Australians being treated as though they no longer possessed special rights in Britain. One exclaimed that he felt 'like an Ancient Roman having to get permission to enter Rome'.[48]

The British remained the largest contributors to Australian immigration into the 1970s; but then fell away precipitously and, by the end of the

---

[45] John Menadue, *Things You Learn Along the Way* (Melbourne, 1999), p. 212.

[46] See *The Economist*, 25 August 1956, p. 622.

[47] See Richards, *Britannia's Children*, pp. 270–1, and Alexander Downer, *Six Prime Ministers* (Melbourne, 1982), pp. 284–6.

[48] Downer, *Six Prime Ministers*, pp. 195–203. See also Geoffrey Bolton, 'Consigning the Cringe', *Australian*, 1–2 July 2000, Supplement, 'Forging a Nation', p. 6.

century, the total number of British-born in Australia declined absolutely. British Australia became a greying, fading fabric, and this tendency helped to reinforce the anxieties of nostalgic conservatives who objected vociferously as Asian immigration rose reciprocally.

Australia had weaned itself off the British blood supply and came to inhabit a more complicated demographic relationship with the rest of the world. Assistance to immigrants had always been a key lever of control and especially facilitated pro-British discrimination. The end of assistance to most migrants was therefore a further decisive retreat from the White British policy. In the longer perspective a structural change had occurred. Australia had reduced its role as a mass immigrant country and Britain had ceased to generate a diaspora. The migration currents between them became much more diverse and ambiguous in the final decades of the old century. These broad directions were not exclusive to Britain or Australia. Thus the people to whom Australia had turned in the 1950s to compensate for the inadequate British flow—the continental Europeans—began, too, to emigrate less reliably.

Two tendencies became visible towards the end of the century which affect-ed the underlying demographic relationship between Britain and Australia. There was the relative decline of Australia as an immigrant nation—not in absolute terms, but as a proportion of the receiving population. In some years in the 1990s Australia received barely more net immigration than it had in 1840–1. Its appetite for immigrants was much diminished by the end of the century—an appetite which was further suppressed by environmentalists' rhetoric which urged a smaller population for the continent in any case. Moreover the reduced vitality of the immigrant agenda was set in a decisively non-discriminatory policy which rendered the British equal with the rest of the world's migrants, at least in the terms set by the Australian government. White British Australia was seen off the premises.

Secondly, the basic requirement of most migration—the income differen-tial between sender and receiver countries—no longer applied consistently. British income levels (magnified by exchange rate movements favourable to the pound) intersected with, and sometimes surpassed, Australian lev-els—so that the basic economic benefit of most migration was eliminated. Consequently the migration exchange reversed, and also the balance sheet of population movements: by 1990 not only was Australia receiving more tourists from Britain than the opposite flow (traditionally much greater), it was also sometimes sending more migrants to Britain than it received from that country.[49] The relationship was inverted. The shift, first away from a British White Australia to a European White Australia, and then hesitatingly towards a non-discriminatory Australia, was a social and demographic revolution; and its management was a substantial national achievement. The fact that it generated so little political disharmony between London and Canberra was the dog that never barked. Indeed, the demographic and economic relationship between the two places had run its course.

Within Australia the demolition of the White Australia policy was achieved with surprisingly little audible opposition, that is until the rise of Asian refugee numbers after the Vietnam War. The decline and termination of the policy occurred in a period in which immigration was increasingly diversified away from the British monopoly. It followed a gradual and incremental path, a succession of small changes in which the rigour of the policy was gradually eased. It was accomplished not so much by stealth as by tentative relaxations which tested and weighed the tolerance of the country to a shift away from the adamantine prohibition of non-White immigration. The regime of labour shortage and the long post-war boom created the best conditions for this form of social experimentation. The shift was traced through the growing acceptance of Italian migrants and prisoners in the Second World War, the entry of 'war-brides' as immigrants, then in the reception of Asian students in the Colombo Plan schemes, and the entry of Commonwealth migrants out of Sri Lanka. The process was much facilitated by the sustained growth of the economy and prevailing high levels of employment until the mid-1970s.

There was a gradual opening of the gates to small categories of alien immigrants which eventually led to the declaration (in 1973) against all forms of racial discrimination. None of this limited the authority of the government to control immigration. To this momentous change in policy there was remarkably little reaction among the British in Australia. There was no significant pressure-group devoted to resisting the shifts in immigration policies, or the ending of White Australia. (In 1991–2 immigrants from southern and eastern Asia accounted for 51 per cent of Australia's immigration.) Even when opposition to Asian immigration emerged in the 1980s, neither British nor European ethnic elements were prominent in the debate. Indeed, the opponents of the alleged 'Asianization of Australia', rather than mobilizing British immigrant opinion, tended instead to invoke

---

[49] See *The Economist* (Asia Pacific edn), 20 April 1991, p. 61.

older models of British Australia as the lost and endangered ideal from which post-imperial Australia had mistakenly departed. There was no direct appeal to the British immigrant as such. The vestiges of British immigration had been seamlessly absorbed into Australian society and exerted little separate or identifiable resistance to the ending of White Australia.

The simple inversion of the 200-year-old imperial demography was complicated by the ambiguity of so much modern international mobility at the start of the new century. Immigration, as permanent settlement, became a relatively small fraction of total movements across borders by the 1990s. Tourism and short-term sojourner movements, refugee allocations, temporary migration, retirement migration, and all other categories, swamped the traditional variety of immigration, even though 'permanent settlement' remained more politically sensitive.

Within this greater complexity of movement, the Australian population simply became less British. And with smaller transfusions of new British immigrants in the last quarter of the century, the proportion of British-born (as indeed of other groups, including the Italians) fell continuously. By 2000 the number of British-born in Australia was sliding fast, while the number of Australian-born in Britain was rising. Among the post-Imperial migrations that linked Australia and Britain indirectly were flows between members of the Commonwealth, sometimes out of disturbed conditions—including migrants from Sri Lanka, South Africa, Zimbabwe, India, and the West Indies—as well as regular and significant inflows from New Zealand.

All this worked to emphasize the change that had been wrought—from the virtual total uniformity and exclusivity of Australian immigration in the days of White British Australia, towards the multifaceted population that had emerged by 2000. It also ran parallel with the later structural transformation in the demographic connections with the traditional people-supplier, the British Isles. By 1960 the British Isles—and more especially Ireland—were exhausting their propensity to emigrate in all directions.

The significance of Australia's post-war call upon the emigrants of the British Isles was that it was able to prolong the British supply for two decades beyond its natural term. The devices it employed—subsidies, exhortation, propaganda, the 'Bring out a Briton' campaign—had prevailed against the tide for a considerable time. Return migration and then the reversal of migration were signals that the essential demographic relationship had reached its end. Australia was left with a legacy of controlling immigration in a world in which migrant flows were quite different. The transformation was achieved with little social turbulence or political upheaval. But this was no guarantee that the scale and composition of immigration would cease to be a latent national anxiety—and in this Australia was in no way exceptional.

By the 1980s the bipartisan concord that had guided Australia immigration policy through its substantial transitions became unhinged. Political parties now made electoral gains by advocating newly discriminatory and restrictive immigration regimes. Thus, despite forty years of successful diversification, it was always possible to ask if Australia could truly cope with larger numbers of non-British immigrants. The snake of discord had remained dormant in Australian immigration policy for four decades after 1945, but at the end of the century it was again released into the community.[50]

Higher levels of unemployment in Australia in the 1980s had set the context, and public apprehension was agitated further by environmentalists' warnings of the dangers of overpopulation, even though Australia's population growth rates had fallen sharply. Images of pathetic boatloads of Asian asylum-seekers arriving off the coast of north-west Australia aroused renewed anxieties, fanned by political persuaders who demanded greater control over informal immigration. The question of control indeed remained paramount. Australia thus determined that it would retain tight authority over the selection of its substantial humanitarian refugee intakes as well as the choice of its economic immigrants (who were increasingly qualified on skill criteria).

With the greater international mobility of humanity in the post-imperial world, the imposition of these levels of control required methods of exclusion which were as severe as Australia had ever witnessed in public policy. They included the increasingly controversial mandatory detention of asylum-seekers, the diversion of boat-people to foreign countries paid to receive them, and the excision of many islands from Australia's official migration zones.

Despite the great changes in immigration engineered in the decades after 1945, post-colonial Australia remained primarily stocked with British genes. British-Australia was no longer replenished from home and the British-born had become a declining minority in a markedly heterogeneous country. As an immigrant from Wolverhampton quietly observed in 1998, 'I'd like some connection still to be with England but ... it's no good saying,

---

[50] See Frank Brennan, *Tampering with Asylum: A Universal Humanitarian Problem* (St Lucia, Qld, 2003).

"This is another England", because it certainly isn't.'[51] Both countries were now wealthy and highly industrialized, both with more diversified populations, and both nervous of uncontrolled immigration from poorer places. The 'simple provincial relationship' between Britain and Australia had ceased long before. Yet, though the demographic transfusions had greatly diminished, the traffic between the two was greater than ever. There had indeed been no rupture. The Britishness of Australia, at least in its demographic foundation, was largely unmoved in the more colourfully variegated society of the new century.[52]

Select Bibliography

FRANK BRENNAN, *Tampering with Asylum: A Universal Humanitarian Problem* (St Lucia, Qld, 2003).

STEPHEN CONSTANTINE, ed., *Emigrants and Empire: British Settlement in the Dominions Between the Wars* (Manchester, 1990).

A. JAMES HAMMERTON and ALISTAIR THOMSON, *Ten Pound Poms: Australia's Invisible Migrants* (Manchester, 2005).

GRAEME HUGO, *Australia's Changing Population: Trends and Implications* (Melbourne, 1986).

JAMES JUPP, *The English in Australia* (Cambridge, 2004).

SIEW-EAN KHOO and PETER MCDONALD, *The Transformation of Australia's Population, 1970–2030* (Sydney, 2003).

JOHN LACK and JACQUELINE TEMPLETON, eds, *Bold Experiment: A Documentary History of Australian Immigration since 1945* (Melbourne, 1995).

CHARLES A. PRICE, *The Great White Walls are Built: Restrictive Immigration to North America and Australasia, 1836–1888* (Canberra, 1974).

ERIC RICHARDS, *Britannia's Children: Emigration from England, Scotland, Wales and Ireland since 1600* (London and New York, 2004).

MICHAEL ROE, *Australia, Britain and Migration, 1915–1940: A Study of Desperate Hopes* (Cambridge, 1995).

GWENDA TAVAN, *The Long, Slow Death of White Australia* (Carlton North, Vic., 2005).

NANCY VIVIANI, ed., *The Abolition of the White Australia Policy: The Immigration Reform Movement Revisited*, Australia–Asia Papers, no. 65 (Brisbane, 1992).

---

[51] Quoted in A. James Hammerton and Alistair Thomson, *Ten Pound Poms* (Manchester, 2005), p. 339.

[52] I wish to thank Dr Robert Fitzsimons for his assistance.

8

Religion and Society

HILARY M. CAREY

Within the archives of the United Society for the Propagation of the Gospel—now held in Rhodes House, Oxford—there is a set of forty lantern slides, one of many produced by church organizations at the height of the imperial age.[1] The slides evoke the great diversity of the Society's work in supporting the missionary thrust of the church in the British Empire at the turn of the twentieth century. Here are churches, mission stations, and peoples drawn from across the globe, together with prayers and hymns. Among the latter, Bishop Heber's popular 'From Greenland's icy mountains' would have been a suitable choice of hymn to open a lantern show in aid of the SPG, even if incongruous for Anglican congregations and potential converts in tropical climates.

The SPG lantern show includes only two images relating to Australia. The first, entitled 'Bush Sunday School', shows a cheerful crowd assembled for the camera beneath eucalyptus trees. The second is a map that delineates the dioceses of Australia and Melanesia, and illustrates the extent of the Anglican presence in the Pacific. Typically, there would be a lecture to accompany a show such as this culminating in a call for donations and volunteers for the mission effort. From the same slide collection there might be another hymn to close. A suitable choice would be Dr Watt's: 'Jesus shall reign where'er the sun | Doth his successive journeys run; | His Kingdom stretch from shore to shore | Till moons shall wax and wane no more.'[2] And finally, almost certainly, there would be a cup of tea.

In the heyday of British imperialism the SPG projected a view of Australia as an isolated rural society in which the major pastoral and mission object was the European settler in the bush. While this was a popular image, it

---

[1] United Society for the Propagation of the Gospel Archives, Box 63, Bodleian Library of Commonwealth and African Studies, Rhodes House, Oxford. (Hereafter USPG Archives.)

[2] Words adapted from Psalm 72 by Isaac Watts (1674–1748), *The Psalms of David* (London, 1718).

was, however, far from complete. For most of Australia's British settlers, not just those on its rural margins, religion was an imperial undertaking that helped them to sustain what has proved to be a remarkably tenacious cultural attachment to Britain. It also allowed the articulation of new colonial and national hierarchies within the formal architecture of Christian denominationalism. Without a securely established church,[3] the interaction of religion and Empire in Britain's Australian colonies was discursive rather than hegemonic, forming an integral part of the 'Ornamentalism' (rather than the 'Orientalism') of British imperialism. But the arrangement was far from absent-minded.[4]

Imperial support for religion in the colonies was supplied in both formal and informal ways; and was probably strongest in three fields of action.[5] In the first place, there was the direct provision of religious services through the appointment and financial support of clergy in the colonies; secondly, there was a range of liberal and humanitarian interventions led by religious leaders at home and abroad to mitigate the perceived evils of Empire such as the dispossession of Indigenous peoples; lastly, there was ideological support by the colonial churches for the imperial ideal. This chapter will consider each of these themes and reflect on the ways in which national Australian institutions, together with the beliefs and habits of religion, ultimately came to emerge in the post-colonial decades following the Second World War. The imperial mode of religious adherence was most significant for members of the Church of England in Australia,[6] the denomination with the largest number of adherents for the greater part of Australia's European history, and so there is more to say about Anglicans than other Australians. However, all Christian denominations and religions were affected in different ways

---

[3] William Blackstone, *Commentaries on the Laws of England* [1765–9], facs. edn, Stanley N. Katz (Chicago, 1979), Vol. 1, p. 106, argued that the common law of England did not extend automatically to British colonies and explicitly excluded laws erected to protect an established church and persecute dissenters.

[4] The cultural force of imperialism was argued by Edward W. Said, *Orientalism* (London, 1978), pp. 76–80; contested by David Cannadine, *Ornamentalism: How the British Saw Their Empire* (London, 2001); and dismissed by Bernard Porter, *The Absent-Minded Imperialists: How the British Really Saw their Empire* (Oxford, 2004). For critique of the omission of religion by Cannadine, see Jane Sampson, 'Are You What You Believe? Some Thoughts on Ornamentalism and Religion', *Journal of Colonialism and Colonial History*, Vol. 3, no. 1 (2002), para. 5.

[5] As suggested by A. N. Porter, 'Empires of the Mind', in P. J. Marshall, ed., *The Cambridge Illustrated History of the British Empire* (Cambridge, 1996), p. 31.

[6] The formal title 'Anglican Church of Australia' was not adopted until 1981.

by the imperial and colonial relationships which have shaped the modern Australian identity.

Religion was essential to the business of Empire, though imperial historians have given most of their attention to the issue of Christian missions to Indigenous people and have not shown much interest in the religious history of the settler Dominions.[7] One advocate for a wider religious interpretation of British imperial expansion has been Linda Colley.[8] In her view, the Protestant identity of Britain was the prime means by which a would-be nation was constructed in the wake of the 1707 Act of Union, which bound Scotland to England and Wales under one Protestant ruler, and a single unified legislative and commercial system. The new British state went on to wage enthusiastic internal and external campaigns against Catholic usurpers, their disloyal supporters in papist enclaves such as Ireland, and also against foreign armies. At the popular level, British history was projected as a kind of melodrama in which Protestants were repeatedly delivered from popery, and specifically from Catholic plots against the person and organs of the state. Even with the defeat of the Jacobites at Culloden in 1745, popular anti-Catholicism continued well into the nineteenth century and beyond. Britons were therefore essentially and not accidentally anti-Catholic. If we accept the Colley thesis (which is by no means uncontested), it was as the heirs to this tradition of Protestant triumphalism that the first convict settlements in Australia were planned and executed in the late eighteenth century.

Protestantism may have been a formative influence on the British identity at home, but the ideal was subjected to particular challenges and distinct limitations in the colonies.[9] Governor Arthur Phillip's official instructions had required him to 'enforce a due observance of religion and good order'[10] in the new settlement. At first only the Church of England received

---

[7] Missions rather than denominations feature in major studies of religion and imperialism: Norman Etherington, ed., *Missions and Empire*, Oxford History of the British Empire Companion Series (Oxford, 2005); A. N. Porter, *Religion Versus Empire?: British Protestant Missionaries and Overseas Expansion, 1700–1914* (Manchester, 2004); Brian Stanley, *The Bible and the Flag: Protestant Missions and British Imperialism in the Nineteenth and Twentieth Centuries* (Leicester, 1990).

[8] Linda Colley, *Britons: Forging the Nation, 1707–1837* (New Haven, 1992), pp. 11–54.

[9] Sources from *Historical Records of Australia* (hereafter *HRA*), and *Historical Records of New South Wales* (hereafter *HRNSW*), and Jean Woolmington, ed., *Religion in Early Australia: The Problem of Church and State* (Sydney, 1976).

[10] *HRA*, ser. 1, vol. i, p. 14; Woolmington, *Religion in Early Australia*, p. 1.

any government support. The Anglican clergy were members of the civil establishment and in 1825 their leading member, Archdeacon T. H. Scott, was given a seat on the expanded Legislative Council and the new Executive Council, with a rank second only to the Governor.[11]

However, Botany Bay's first Anglican chaplains and bishops seem never to have felt entirely secure in asserting rights of precedence and observance which would have been assumed back home. For a brief period, from 1825 to 1829, an effort was made to support the clergy and schools of what was called the 'Established Church of England throughout the Colony' by means of the Church and Schools Corporation. The attempt caused nothing but acrimony and it was hastily abandoned in favour of Governor Richard Bourke's liberal experiment—the 1836 Church Act—which made provision for the four largest denominations on the same terms. The principle was later extended to the other Australian colonies. Drawing on his efforts to advance religious toleration in his native Ireland, Bourke had hopes that his legislation would inspire colonial Christians to be united with government in peace and gratitude, and 'thus there will be secured to the State good subjects and to Society good men'.[12]

Unfortunately, and perhaps inevitably, his hopes were dashed. As costs mounted to pay for the churches, parsonages, and salaries mandated by the Church Act, so did dissenting arguments in favour of purely voluntary aid to religion. The tide of public opinion had early swung against any kind of state funding to religious institutions, even for primary education. Fully reported in the local and British press, the Australian moves were watched with interest, and they came to be reflected elsewhere in the Empire. By 1870, government financial support for religion had been abandoned in Canada and New Zealand as well as the eastern colonies of Australia.[13] Like convictism, religious aid lingered on in Western Australia rather longer than elsewhere; but by 1894 all the Australian colonies had achieved an effective separation of church and state. This was to be one of the features of colonial life that most distinguished it from that of Britain as mother country to the Empire.

[11] Bruce Kaye, ed., *Anglicanism in Australia: A History* (Melbourne, 2002), pp. 7–16. For imperial church governance, see Andrew Porter, 'Religion, Missionary Enthusiasm, and Empire', in Andrew Porter, ed., *The Oxford History of the British Empire. Vol. III: The Nineteenth Century* (Oxford, 1999), pp. 232–5.

[12] Governor Bourke to E. G. Stanley, 30 September 1833, *HRA*, ser. 1, vol. xvii, p. 230; Woolmington, *Religion in Early Australia*, p. 94.

[13] Porter, 'Empires of the Mind', p. 209.

If there ever was an ideal of a unified and assertively Protestant state in Britain, it did not function in the same way in the settler colonies as they developed during the course of the nineteenth century. The political emancipation of Catholics in 1829 followed the pragmatic recognition of the need to accommodate majority Catholic populations in Ireland and Quebec, and this expedited the development of a more inclusive rhetoric uniting Britons of all denominations across the waves. Demographic and social conditions in New South Wales, where there was a Catholic minority ranging from 26 to 30 per cent in census returns throughout the nineteenth century, and articulate and highly ranked advocates for non-Anglican Protestantism, also spurred reform.[14] Both the liberals who influenced policy in the Colonial Office and the officials they appointed in the Australian colonies found that the most practical solution was to press ahead with Catholic emancipation and dissenting advancement with greater speed in the Australian colonies than was possible in the British Isles.

Established airs and graces began to seem like pretension or worse. 'Our Archdeacon is a very high Churchman, but not inimical to the Gospel', wrote the colonial chaplain Samuel Marsden (1765–1838), without apparent irony, yet 'he will not countenance the smallest deviations from the rules of the Established Church.'[15] Over a hundred years later, attachment to establishment Protestantism in Australia was all but gone and in its place there was a tenacious pride of race and faith, the product of colonial imperialism.[16] Even an Australian nationalist such as Bishop Burgman of Goulburn was happy to boast that the Church of England 'has formed the conscience of the British people, she has leavened British traditions and inspired British ideals'.[17]

*   *   *

It was thus a deep paradox of British imperialism that a primary source of national unity, namely Protestant resistance to Catholic insurgency, was transformed in colonial societies into race pride in British humanitarianism.

[14] W. W. Phillips, 'Religion', in Wray Vamplew, ed., *Australians: Historical Statistics* (Sydney, 1987), p. 421.

[15] Samuel Marsden to Lay Secretary, 4 January 1833, Birmingham, University Library, Church Missionary Society Papers, C N/M6, p. 438.

[16] Brian Fletcher, 'Anglicanism and Nationalism in Australia, 1901–1962', *Journal of Religious History*, Vol. 23, no. 2 (1999), pp. 216–19.

[17] E. Burgman, 'The Church and the World Crisis', *Church Standard*, 15 October 1948, cited by Fletcher, 'Anglicanism and Nationalism', p. 218.

This was a source of identity which found ready acceptance in the Australian colonies among people of all denominations, and especially in the key areas where the connections between religion and Empire seem most evident.

It was not until the 1820s, for example, that there is much evident official concern about adequate religious provision being made for Europeans in the settler colonies of the Empire. Nevertheless, the first Australian settlements were not left entirely without the comforts of religion following a long tradition of supplying chaplains to prisons and military establishments. Colonial chaplains were expected to provide Sunday services and celebrate baptisms, marriages, and funerals, the primary rituals of a Christian life. Catholic chaplains were appointed in response to the general belief that Irish Catholic convicts might benefit morally and intellectually from their ministry, and possibly because it seemed inhumane to continue to oblige them to receive compulsory Protestantism as part of their sentences. Governor King reflected a ruling prejudice when stating that 'no description of people are so bigoted to their religion and priests as the lower order of the Irish.' Nevertheless, he gave cautious approval to the provision of Roman Catholic services in the modest hope that 'much good, or at least no harm' might come of it.[18] In the same rather ad hoc way, approval was given, and occasionally taken away, for the services of clergy from other churches, including the Wesleyans, Presbyterians, and Congregationalists, to name the largest denominations.[19]

These accidental arrangements for religious service came systematically to be more unsatisfactory as the population grew, especially after the number of free settlers was encouraged in the wake of the three Bigge Reports issued in 1822 and 1823. Bigge was in favour of giving both funds and encouragement to the better establishment of religion in the colony. An additional impulse toward religious provision was also provided by the passing of the Catholic Emancipation Act of 1829; and the Reform Act of 1832, which broadened the franchise and the perceived need to educate and morally support the British citizenry. Provision for religion in British colonies was regularized.[20] Besides receiving land and money direct from the colonial governments, the Anglican majority was assisted by the two missionary societies, the Society

[18]   Governor King to Lord Hobart, 9 May 1803, *HRNSW*, vol. 5, p. 116; Woolmington, *Religion in Early Australia*, p. 31. More formal Catholic appointments were not made until after Catholic emancipation.

[19]   For the origins and establishment of the major Christian denominations see Ian Breward, *A History of the Australian Churches* (Sydney, 1993), pp. 12–33; Ian Breward, *A History of the Churches in Australasia* (Oxford, 2001), pp. 10–20, 66–82.

[20]   Andrew Porter, 'Religion, Missionary Enthusiasm, and Empire'.

for the Propagation of the Gospel (SPG) and the Society for Promoting Christian Knowledge (SPCK). The SPG provided salaries for chaplains on migrant vessels and made contributions towards the many requests made by colonial bishops for clergy and building projects.

The record of requests to the SPG for support supplies a snapshot of the state of the Anglican Church in Australia in the 1840s, and of the ramshackle arrangements necessary to deal with the expanding communities. From the new colony of Victoria, Bishop Perry of Melbourne optimistically recommended official assistance for service to the thousands of emigrants arriving, while bemoaning that 'the word' was being 'taken out of our hands and badly done' by the Wesleyans. From Adelaide in South Australia, came grim reports. On 20 July 1849 Bishop Short visited Port Lincoln where there had been 'several murders committed by the natives' followed by retaliatory poisoning of the natives with arsenic. Visitation across immense distances uncovered fragile settlements where there might be a chapel, but Sunday was unobserved, there were increasing numbers of 'half-caste' children, and there was an absence of religious observance.[21] Apart from mission work with Aboriginal, Melanesian, and Chinese migrant peoples, the SPG withdrew its support for Australia after 1882, even though funding continued for new dioceses through the Colonial Bishoprics' Fund, established in 1841.

Bishops were essential to the imperial expansion of Anglicanism. In 1847, when three key new Australian dioceses were established (in Melbourne, Adelaide, and Newcastle), there was celebration that the church was rising to meet the imperial challenge. The *Colonial Church Chronicle and Missionary Journal* described the consecration of the Australian bishops as 'the most important chapter in Modern Church History',[22] and published an ode, in nine stirring verses, that expounded the significance of the service in Westminster Abbey:

> Church of the Lord: the spell is melted now
> Which held thee chained and slumbering in thy bower;
> Her signet shines once more upon thy brow,
> His spirit arms thy weakness with strange power;
> And the cold world, dismayed, looks out afar,
> And sees thee harnessed for thy ghostly war.[23]

---

[21] Precis Book for Australia etc, 1847–50, USPG Archives, SPG.X.133. Reports from Bishops of Melbourne (30 March 1848), Adelaide (20 July 1949, 28 May 1850).
[22] *Colonial Church Chronicle*, 1 (1848), p. 12.   [23] Ibid., p. 59.

Although in colonial harness, the Australian bishops did not stay away from Britain for long. Their regular returns, begging for candidates for the colonial ministry and donations of any kind, were reported over the following decades. Like the ping of bellbirds or the warbling of magpies, their visits were ever evocative of the Australian bush, its colonies, and their needs and opportunities. Bishop Nixon of Tasmania asked for pastors to meet the spiritual needs of England's 'convict children', in arguing: 'They have sent us the poison;—will not they send us, too, the only effective antidote?'[24] From Newcastle, north of Sydney, Bishop Tyrrell provided a gripping account of his own adventures in the bush, describing his hard riding and the danger of getting lost in the trackless wilderness.[25] As to inspiring colonial vocations, the Bishop of Brisbane preferred the direct approach in seeking recommendations of 'earnest and judicious Clergymen or candidates for holy orders, men with a sound mind in a sound body, and of a gentle, loving spirit'.[26] The latter plea was no doubt especially heartfelt as the endless bickering and contention of colonial clergy became proverbial. Chaplains were drawn to colonial service because the salary looked attractive compared with a curacy or a poor parish in Britain, and there was the additional promise of adventure on a rural frontier. For a certain number it also provided an escape from indiscretions and incompetences which, all too often, soon became evident to the Australian bishops who received them into their dioceses.

Anglican bishops formed part of the social establishment and they were displayed with their educational attainments, annual salary, and its source in the *Colonial Office List*.[27] In 1862, the Bishop of Sydney, Frederick Barker (Grantham School and Jesus College, Cambridge) received £1,500 pounds from the general colonial revenue, which rose the following year substantially to £2,000. (Bishops dependent on the Colonial Bishoprics' Fund received much less.) However, the handsome salaries are one measure of the value placed on religious office by colonial administrators. One singular feature of the records of colonial establishments in Australia is the inclusion of Roman Catholic clerical appointments—which are otherwise absent from all but the accounts of the former French colony of Mauritius and the island of Trinidad in the West Indies. Some colonial governments went further and, prior to

---

[24] Ibid., p. 117.   [25] *Colonial Church Chronicle*, 10 (1861), pp. 142–4.

[26] *Colonial Church Chronicle*, 7 (1853–54), p. 343.

[27] *Colonial Office List or General Register of the Colonial Dependencies of Great Britain* (London, 1862).

the abolition of state aid, granted stipends to Jewish ministers of religion, though not without some initial resistance. On Jewish emancipation, colonial opinion was generally in advance of both the British Colonial Office and colonial governments.[28] Even once direct aid was abolished, it is important to recognize the very significant provision extended to the churches by way of rate concessions on Christian places of worship, ministers' residences, and church schools. These concessions ensured that the churches retained their prominent positions in the heart of colonial cities and towns in Australia, in close proximity to the organs of government.

Below the higher clergy, a range of other personnel were required in an unceasing flow to build the new churches and nurture the connection with the home institutions. In the absence of state aid, the habit of importing clergy from Britain did not die away. If anything, the perceived and actual need of the Australian churches for clergy trained in the seminaries, universities, and theological training schools of England, Scotland, Wales, and Ireland increased.[29] At the top level, bishops and senior clergy, along with headmasters of the major church schools and university colleges, were almost invariably sought abroad. Before Australian Federation in 1901, it would have been reasonable to assume that all the higher clergy of the Church of England were British-born, the great majority of Catholic clergy were Irish, and that the Presbyterian ministry was overwhelmingly Scottish- or Irish-born.[30]

Among the dissenting Protestant churches, it was more likely that church leaders were Australian-born; however, preachers from Wales and England were especially sought after by Congregationalists and Methodists. In 1880, when their Welsh minister, Thomas Jones, retired, the Collins Street Independent Church in Melbourne was the leading Congregationalist church in one of the wealthiest cities of the Empire. The church's search committee in London approached all the leading Congregationalist preachers in Britain before securing another outstanding Welshman, Llewelyn David Bevan, for

[28] Israel Getzler, *Neither Toleration nor Favour: The Australian Chapter of Jewish Emancipation* (Melbourne, 1970), p. 33. The 1911 census numbered 17,287 Jews who made up less than 5 per cent of the Australian population, a proportion which has remained fairly constant.

[29] Denominational demand for clergy reflected immigration flows, see Walter Phillips, 'Statistics on Religious Affiliation in Australia, 1891–1961', *Australian Historical Statistics*, 4 (1981), pp. 5–15.

[30] Malcolm D. Prentis, *The Scots in Australia: A Study of New South Wales, Victoria and Queensland, 1788–1900* (Sydney, 1983). Table 16 shows that Australian-born candidates ranged from only 6 to 11 per cent of all recruits to the Presbyterian ministry in Australia before 1900.

the post.[31] One of the peripatetic professional elite of the Empire, Bevan had been pastor of Tottenham Court Road Chapel in London, and Brick Chapel, New York, and would continue a national and international ministry from his Melbourne base.

The Catholic Church in Australia formed part of what the colonial episcopacy liked to call the Irish 'spiritual empire', a compensatory discourse which might be called on to justify the drain of the Irish people from their homeland.[32] It drew on the seemingly limitless reserves of mission-minded women and men applying to Irish religious congregations and the missionary seminary of All Hallows, Dublin, supplying not just the leading clerics, but also the priests, sisters, and brothers who staffed Catholic primary and secondary schools, hospitals, and churches throughout the country. A network of Catholic parish and secondary schools was created in Australia in the wake of the abolition of state aid, and it was to Ireland that the Irish-born hierarchy looked to answer the challenge put to them by the education question.[33] In 1915, Irish-born priests and bishops made up at least 70 per cent of all clergy in Australian dioceses.[34] It seemed that Australian-born clergy would never fill the demand, and even Australian foundations such as the Sisters of St Joseph, established in South Australia in 1866 by Mary MacKillop and her English-born confessor, Julian Tenison Woods, sought postulants direct from Ireland.

The initial dependence on British-born clergy was a necessary response to the needs of an expanding migrant population in Australia; but the extent to which such clergy acted to delay the development of distinctive Australian religious traditions is difficult to judge. Scottishness, for example, played a subsidiary role in the definition of Presbyterianism when compared with Englishness in relation to Anglicanism, and this was due at least in part to the dominance of England in the British political union as well as the presence of substantial numbers of Ulster Scots. However, the Irish identity of

[31] Christopher Wood and Marc Askew, *St Michael's Church* (Melbourne, 1992), p. 76–8. Bevan was offered a stipend of £1,450 at a time when the average minister received £300.

[32] Kevin Kenny, 'The Irish in the Empire', in Kevin Kenny, ed., *Ireland and the British Empire*, Oxford History of the British Empire Companion Series (Oxford, 2004), p. 112; E. M. Hogan, *The Irish Missionary Movement: A Historical Survey, 1830–1980* (Dublin 1990), p. 20.

[33] Patrick James O'Farrell, *The Catholic Church and Community: An Australian History*, rev. edn (Sydney, 1985), pp. 138–93.

[34] K. T. Livingstone, *The Emergence of an Australian Catholic Priesthood, 1935–1915* (Sydney, 1977), p. 250.

the Catholic Church was pursued with particular and inventive vigour.[35] In the last decades of the nineteenth century the Australian hierarchy was transformed by the stream of influence exerted from Dublin by the ultra-montanist Paul Cullen who became Ireland's first cardinal in 1867.[36] The first Catholic bishop of Australia, John Bede Polding, was an English Benedictine whose appointment was engineered by the Colonial Office to moderate the Irish character of the Catholic church in the Australian colonies. However, Polding was to become something of an alien in his own church, as Cullen secured Irish bishops in his own image for Australian dioceses. Among this number, the most illustrious was Cullen's nephew and former Secretary, who was to become Cardinal Patrick Francis Moran, third Archbishop of Sydney (1884–1911). In 1900 Moran was at the height of his influence when he hosted the first Australasian Catholic Congress to coincide with the opening of St Mary's Cathedral in Sydney.[37] The Congress Ode exulted in the achievement of the southern church, brought with 'all the might of Rome' to bless her land of exile:

> Australia! sunny Eden of the south,
> The Tir-na-noge of all our old-world dreams,
> The wine of life turns nectar in thy mouth,
> And age grows young by thine elysian fields.[38]

These sentiments reflect the ambitions of the imperial papacy of Pius IX (1846–78) and his successors which Moran celebrated. In Australia, the colonial Catholic church could be imagined not as a minor outpost of the once enslaved Mother Church in Ireland, but as a new Rome, a 'great Spiritual Empire' to rival the political Empire of Britain.[39] The churches supplied the rhetoric of power for both Empire and its spiritual shadow. Irish and Roman imperial influence did not weaken its hold over the Catholic Church in Australia until mitigated by the flood of post-war Catholic migration from European countries outside the British Empire.

*   *   *

[35] H. R. Jackson, *Churches and People in Australia and New Zealand, 1860–1930* (Sydney, 1987), pp. 91–3.

[36] Roman rather than directly Irish dominance of the Australian episcopacy is argued by John N. Molony, *The Roman Mould of the Australian Catholic Church* (Melbourne, 1969).

[37] *Proceedings of the First Australasian Catholic Congress* (Sydney, 1900), p. 643.

[38] Ibid., p. xiv. There is a footnote glossing Tir-na-noge as 'The land of perpetual youth'.

[39] The term is that of Archbishop Roger Vaughan, the English Archbishop of Sydney, cited by O'Farrell, *Catholic Church and Community*, p. 192.

Compared with the impact of colonizing clergy on Australian institutions, the role played by humanitarian lobbyists in Britain was relatively weak. However, this was another area which prompted metropolitan colonizers to turn their gaze south. Humanitarians concerned themselves with the condition of convicts, with the moral situation of free immigrants, especially women, and, in the wake of the abolition of the British slave trade, with the transportation of convicts—another human traffic. However, the most sustained concern was that over the treatment of Australia's Aboriginal people, including their prospect for conversion.[40]

Church missions were small in number so it is difficult to blame them directly for the shattering impact of European occupation on the Aborigines. Some missionary discourse was strongly in favour of British colonization and proposed missions as a providential solution to the problem of the displaced native population. The Australian Church Missionary Society (later merged to form part of the Colonial and Continental Society) had the general object of raising support for religious work in the Australian colonies. Its 1838 meeting in London recommended that missions be established to ensure that the Aborigines did not 'melt away' as the native inhabitants had done in Canada and the United States:

Missionaries only can prevent it. Missionaries, through whom the settlers may be preserved from sinking into habits of oppression and injustice;—Missionaries, through whom the natives may be cultivated and Christianized—may learn the arts of civilized life, and imbibe the lessons of the Gospel. Hottentots, Caffres, North American Indians, and New Zealanders have sufficiently proved that this is not impracticable. Why should we not then repeat the experiment in Australia?[41]

In 1914, the former Australian missionary Herbert Pitts reflected the same pious impracticality when enumerating the 'Call of Empire' together with the 'call of blood', the 'call of the dying', the 'call of conscience', and the 'call of Christ' as constituting the claim of the Aborigines upon the English branch of the Christian church.[42]

Mission societies were considerably more hard-headed when it came to funding and maintaining missionaries in the field. The Wesleyan Methodist Missionary Society (WMMS), the London Missionary Society (LMS), and

---

[40] For a survey history of Australian missions see John W. Harris, *One Blood: 200 Years of Aboriginal Encounter with Christianity: A Story of Hope*, 2nd edn (Sydney, 1994).

[41] *First Report of the Australian Church Missionary Society* (London, n.d. [1838]), p. 2.

[42] Herbert Pitts, *The Australian Aboriginal and the Christian Church* (London, 1914), pp. 130–3.

the Church Missionary Society (CMS) made modest commitments to missions in south-eastern Australia but all had withdrawn by 1844. Western missions had a little more success. In 1836 the Western Australian Missionary Society, organized by Moravian Christians based in Dublin, sent Dr Louis Guistiniani to the Swan River Colony, where he was joined in 1840 by John Smithies of the WMMS who persisted until 1855.[43] None of the missions to the Australian Aborigines succeeded in terms which impressed either the organizers in Britain or the imperial public who devoured mission publications reporting on them. The mission conducted for the LMS by Lancelot Threlkeld was distinguished for its linguistic achievement, but secured no converts.[44] Largely on account of its cost, the LMS dissolved its connection with Threlkeld in 1828 though he continued the mission with assistance from the colonial government. He also acted as a translator for Aboriginal defendants, struggling to represent their interests and using his rhetorical gifts to publicize and denounce atrocities committed against them.[45] After the coastal mission conducted by Threlkeld was entering its final days, the CMS agreed to undertake a mission in association with the colonial government at Wellington Valley in New South Wales where they had the benefit of the buildings attached to an abandoned convict station, and the presence of a detachment of police. Using the language of rights, the CMS reported that the financial support offered by the Colonial Office for the Wellington mission was a small compensation to the people of New Holland for the forcible deprivation of their land, the repayment of a 'debt of justice'.[46]

Making use of the initial reports from missionaries, evangelical humanitarians in Britain in the 1830s and 1840s took up as one of their causes the plight of Aboriginal people in the settler colonies of the Empire.[47] Christian reformers were buoyed by their earlier success in defeating the slave trade and the 'apprenticeship' system, as well as mediation in the New Zealand wars leading to the signing of the Treaty of Waitangi in 1840. The

[43] William McNair and Hilary Rumley, *Pioneer Aboriginal Mission: The Work of Wesleyan Missionary John Smithies in the Swan River Colony, 1840–1855* (Perth, 1981), p. 141.

[44] For Threlkeld's life and published work, see W. Niel Gunson, ed., *Australian Reminiscences and Papers of L.E. Threlkeld*, 2 vols. (Canberra, 1974).

[45] For colonial humanitarians, see Henry Reynolds, *This Whispering in Our Hearts* (Sydney, 1998).

[46] *Proceedings of the Church Missionary Society* (1840–41), p. 93.

[47] Andrew Porter, 'Trusteeship, Anti-Slavery, and Humanitarianism', in Porter, *The Nineteenth Century*, pp. 207–16.

1837 Parliamentary Report of the Select Committee on the Aborigines and the Aborigines' Protection Society which was founded in the same year were intended to moderate the evils of colonization for Aboriginal peoples throughout the Empire.[48] Information on the Aborigines of Australia, the Cape Colony, and Canada was gathered by Thomas Fowell Buxton and his close family staff and included reports by missionaries, ecclesiastics, settlers, and lay sympathizers to the mission cause.[49] The overall situation of the Aborigines in Australia which they revealed to the Select Committee was grave.

Unfortunately, by the time the Select Committee Report was published the influence of the evangelicals, both in London and among the colonists, was on the wane. There was strong resistance to the implementation of its recommendations. The years following its submission to Parliament did not result in the kind of legislative change in support of Aboriginal missions and other benefits for which its authors had hoped. Meetings of the Aborigines' Protection Society, formed with the intention of lobbying for the implementation of the committee's recommendations, were poorly attended.[50] In Australia, the ascendancy of the settlers in the rapid escalation of land appropriation was one undoubted cause of the failure of both missionaries and the Aboriginal Protectors who succeeded them in 1838–9. While humanitarians were initially supportive of the Protectors' succession, it was soon evident that the Protectors had little practical power to resist the expansion of the frontier and the destruction of native people. In Van Diemen's Land, Governor Arthur appointed the Wesleyan layman George Augustus Robinson as 'conciliator' to the Aborigines. Robinson managed to persuade a remnant group to accept exile on Flinders Island in Bass Strait where they rapidly succumbed to the effects of disease, trauma, and poor nutrition. In 1838 Robinson moved to the Port Phillip district but again found that he was powerless to contain the ongoing violence against the native inhabitants. The gloomiest predictions of the humanitarians would seem to have been confirmed.

---

[48] Elizabeth Elbourne, 'The Sin of the Settler: The 1835–36 Select Committee on Aborigines and Debates over Virtue and Conquest in the Early Nineteenth-Century British White Settler Empire', *Journal of Colonialism and Colonial History*, Vol. 4, no. 3 (2003), n. p.; Zoe Laidlaw, 'Aunt Anna's Report: The Buxton Women and the Aborigines Select Committee', *Journal of Imperial and Commonwealth History*, Vol. 32, no. 2 (2004), pp. 1–28.

[49] Rhodes House Oxford, Buxton Papers, MS. Brit. Emp. s. 444, vol. 1, pp. 152–3. (Hereafter Buxton Papers.)

[50] Priscilla Johnston to Anna Gurney, 17 May 1838. Buxton Papers, vol. 1, pp. 148–9.

The imperial phase of missions in the Australian colonies ended with the departure of John Smithies of the WMMS from the Swan River Colony in 1855. Under sympathetic Governors, missions continued to be established by the colonial churches who often employed continental missionaries for the purpose: Moravian missions were established in the Wimmera district of Victoria with the initial patronage of Governor Latrobe; spurred by John Dunmore Lang, the Presbyterian church in New South Wales sent German missionaries to Moreton Bay in Queensland; in Western Australia a Catholic mission was established on a generous government land grant by Spanish Benedictines; German Lutherans in South Australia fostered the first missions to Central Australia. However, the overall efforts were small in scale, and by the end of the nineteenth century most church missions to Aboriginal people were incorporated into the regime of paternal repression inaugurated by the colonial Protection Acts.

It was of more significance for the welfare of the Aborigines that reports of these local missions were not published in the journals of the British missionary societies, and were thus no longer held before the eye of the imperial public. The Aborigines' Protection Society was prescient in predicting that colonial governments were unlikely actively to promote Aboriginal welfare in the absence of external pressure. As the Society Secretary put it: 'The acquisition of self-governing powers by the Australian colonies has increased the difficulties of effective protection of natives by their friends in England.'[51] With the Aborigines removed from the mission landscape of Australia, Indigenous Australians were replaced as objects of missionary interest by European settlers, struggling with isolation and rural hardship in the bush. The Anglo-Catholic Bush Brotherhoods and the Australian Inland Mission, established in 1912 under the direction of John Flynn by the Presbyterian General Assembly and partly funded from a Scottish bequest intended for the aid of Aborigines, were the most significant church ventures ministering to the religious needs of outback Australia.[52] It is this mission landscape, emptied of Aborigines, that is reflected in the visual evidence of the SPG lantern slides of around 1900.

*   *   *

[51] H. R. Fox Bourne, *The Aborigines' Protection Society: Chapters in its History* (London, 1899), p. 22.

[52] Ruth Frappell, 'The Australian Bush Brotherhoods and Their English Origins', *Journal of Ecclesiastical History*, Vol. 47 (1996), pp. 82–97.

Australian Christians were also aware of the need to spread the king-dom of Christ and took active steps to extend the British and Australian spiritual Empire in the Pacific region. This took two major forms. In the first place, Australia, and in particular the colony of New South Wales, was used as a staging post for mission ventures by the major British societies in New Zealand and the other islands of the Pacific. Secondly, Australians were dispatched as trained missionaries to overseas missions that had already been colonized by the British Protestant and, for Catholic missions in the Pacific, French missionary societies. In a third and final phase the Australian churches extended their own missionary outreach to missions in the Pacific, China, and southern Asia. The process has reached maturity with Indigenous Christians from the Pacific and Asia returning to lead parishes and dioceses in the Australian churches. While Australian churches were quick to claim precedence for their work of con-version, almost everywhere native converts from the first missions in the eastern Pacific preceded the agents of the many European societies who proselytized and colonized the area from the beginning of the eighteenth century.

Historians have been divided on the extent to which the Bible followed the flag in the different overseas missionary regions where Australians had some contact. But there seems little doubt that British colonization of the Pacific was initiated by missions under the patronage of succes-sive colonial administrations in New South Wales.[53] Samuel Marsden was the key to these developments. The LMS had dispatched a team of arti-san missionaries to the Society Islands, including Tahiti, in 1796. In 1800, when the missionaries were rebuffed, Marsden offered them sanctuary and patronage in New South Wales and remained the Society's trusted agent after the missionaries returned to Tahiti, which was converted by 1815. He also involved himself with missionaries dispatched by the Wes-leyan Methodists. In 1854, the challenges of maintaining missionaries in so distant a territory prompted the British society to transfer responsibility for missionary work in the Pacific to the newly independent Methodist General Conference of Australasia, Australia's first independent Christian church. In contrast to this Australianization of Protestant missions to the Pacific, Catholic missions, which were no less active in the first half of

---

[53] Ernest Scott, ed., *Cambridge History of the British Empire. Vol. 7: Australia*, 2nd edn (Cambridge, 1988), p. 332.

the nineteenth century, remained under the control of French missionary orders.[54]

For evangelicals, missions were a sign of the vitality of their faith no less than a call from God. For Marsden, the call was to New Zealand. He had been alerted to the capacity of the Maori people of New Zealand through his acquaintance with Ruatara, a Maori seaman whom he befriended on the vessel which brought him from England via Rio de Janiero in 1809.[55] He was instrumental in persuading the CMS to establish a mission to the Maori which began in 1814 at the Bay of Islands. Initially at least, Marsden saw missions as a substitute rather than a cover for British colonization. In 1815, when Ruatara died, he wrote to the Secretary of the CMS that the young Maori had been well aware of the danger posed by Europeans based in New South Wales, suspecting 'our object was to deprive the New Zealanders of their country and that as soon as we had gained any footing over there we should pour into New Zealand an armed force and take the country to ourselves'.[56]

The south-west Pacific, including the lands known since the 1830s as Melanesia and which include New Guinea, the Solomon Islands, New Hebrides, and Fiji, was proselytized rather later than Polynesia. The Catholic Vicariate Apostolic of Melanesia was erected in 1844, but was controlled by French Marist Fathers. Protestant missions began in 1850, led by Bishop Selwyn of New Zealand who saw the potential of the region. He was inspired by the first synod of Australasian bishops which met in Sydney in 1850 to form the Australian Board of Missions for Australian natives and the islands of the west Pacific. Selwyn was aware that native converts from Polynesia were already playing a leading role in the work of conversion when he founded the Melanesian Mission which became one of the best known of all Protestant mission projects in the Pacific.[57]

Throughout the second half of the nineteenth century, Australians expanded their engagement with the missionary fields of the Pacific in tune with the rise of a more independent colonial nationalism.[58] Australian Methodists

---

[54] Ralph Wiltgen, *The Founding of the Roman Catholic Church in Oceania, 1825 to 1850* (Canberra, 1979).

[55] A. T. Yarwood, *Samuel Marsden: The Great Survivor* (Melbourne, 1977), p. 124.

[56] John Rawson Elder, ed., *The Letters and Journals of Samuel Marsden, 1765–1838* (Dunedin, 1932), p. 141.

[57] David Hilliard, *God's Gentlemen: A History of the Melanesian Mission, 1849–1942* (Brisbane, 1978), p. xii.

[58] David Hilliard, 'Oceania', in *Encyclopedia of Missions and Missionaries*, ed. Jonathan Bonk (New York, 2007), pp. 299–305.

were the most active at first and had founded three missions in Melanesia by 1902. A mission in what is now Vanuata was begun by Presbyterians from Nova Scotia and Scotland but, in a typical shift of responsibility southward, it was taken over by New Zealand and Australia. Tensions between Anglo-Catholic and Protestant styles of churchmanship, as well as social and national divisions between colonial and metropolitan Britons, were significant in some of these missions. The death of the first Anglican bishop of Melanesia, J. C. Patteson was a spur to mission engagement by Australian Anglicans who founded a mission in Papua in 1891. The Anglican mission in Papua recruited lay missionaries and artisans from Australia although its English leadership were graduates of the major universities and high churchmen.[59] Australian anxieties about their place in the Empire were thus played out in Australia's own aspirational Empire.

Australian missionaries in New Guinea and elsewhere in the Pacific were drawn into debates about the most suitable path for development in the region. As in other imperial frontiers, missionaries were expected to be the voice of conscience in disputing economic exploitation by European settlers and traders. Anglican mission literature extolled the virtue of the Papuans,[60] virtues which were transmuted during the Second World War to images of the 'fuzzy wuzzy angel' who succoured Australian servicemen on the Kokoda track. In this way, Australian missionaries in the Pacific led the way both for the extension of national territorial aspirations and for the Christian aspirations of civilization and conversion. In the twentieth century, many Australian missionaries went beyond the Pacific to the major mission fields of India and China. Australian women played a particularly significant role in the 'faith mission' to inland China, as Ian Welch has been active in demonstrating.[61] The Seventh-Day Adventists have a long history in the region, but since the Second World War, and since Australia's own decolonization of its Pacific territory of New Guinea in 1975, they have been joined by other conservative Protestants, including Jehovah's Witnesses, Assemblies of God, and other Pentecostals. While many of these communities have their origins in the United States, the proximity of Australia and New Zealand ensures that

[59] David Wetherell, *Reluctant Mission: The Anglican Church in Papua New Guinea, 1891–1942* (Brisbane, 1977), p. 73.

[60] Ibid., pp. 296–300.

[61] Ian Welch, 'Nellie, Topsy and Annie: Australian Anglican Martyrs, Fujian Province, China, 1 August 1895', *Proceedings of the First Biennial TransTasman Conference on Australian and New Zealanders in Christian Missions* <http://rspas.anu.edu.au/pah/TransTasman/papers.php> (accessed 26 August 2006).

many of the missionaries continue to draw personnel and funding from this region, sustaining an Empire of Australian evangelicalism long after other forms of colonial power have withered away.

*   *   *

Religion had an important role to play in the struggle over imperial, British, and Australian national identities. By the 1870s, colonial governments in Australia were constitutionally largely independent from Britain; and the same could be said for the Christian denominations. However, the absence of legal bonds did not lead to the collapse of attachment to Britain. Indeed, for leading Anglicans, love of Britain was an article of faith, in some cases almost literally. After attending the Lambeth conference of 1958 in London, Bishop Hilliard wrote: 'The sojourn in the enchanted island did me a tremendous amount of good, as I knew it would, for England is my second religion.'[62] A third-generation Australian of modest origins, Hilliard also believed that there was no conflict between his loyalty to Australia and his love of Britain, a sentiment he submitted to verse:

> But when my warm tribute to England I bring
> I would not that any should misunderstand;
> I love not Australia the less when I sing
> Of the splendour and charm of her dear mother-land.[63]

Such ardour was perhaps typical only within the Anglican colonial communion, though Wesleyans could be just as proud to be British; but Hilliard's sentiments endured. During the second royal visit in 1963, the Presbyterian Prime Minister, Robert Menzies, made the monarch blush when he illustrated the emotions of the ordinary Australian who merely glimpsed her royal progress by quoting the Elizabethan poet Thomas Ford (d. 1648): 'I did but see her passing by, and yet I love her till I die.'[64] Such courtly notions seemed

---

[62] On England, Hilliard to Fisher, 21 March 1956, Lambeth Palace Library, Fisher Papers, vol. 165, fol. 106, cited by Fletcher, 'Anglicanism and Nationalism', p. 217. For cricket, also a 'second religion', see Janet West, *Innings of Grace: A Life of Bishop W. G. Hilliard* (Sydney, 1987), p. 76.

[63] 'The Beauty of England', in *What Shall I Render to the Lord and other Verses* (1959), cited in West, *Innings of Grace*, p. 135. See also David Hilliard, 'The Ties That Used to Bind: A Fresh Look at the History of Australian Anglicanism', *Pacifica*, Vol. 11, no. 3 (1988), pp. 265–80.

[64] A. W. Martin, *Robert Menzies: A Life, Vol. 2. 1944–1978* (Melbourne, 1993), p. 455. The quotation (not identified by Menzies) comes from the lyric 'There is a lady sweet and kind' in Ford's *Musicke of sundrie kindes* (1607), bk. 1.

neither excessive nor unpatriotic to many Australians in the context of the cult of monarchy nurtured by the post-colonial churches.

The Federation of the Australian colonies in 1901 marked the formal achievement of nationhood by Australia. Leading churchmen rhetorically embraced it as an opportunity to further the wider cause of British unity, though not without some sectarian shuffling for precedence on the Commonwealth stage.[65] Federation encouraged the Presbyterians, Congregationalists, and Methodists in their own efforts towards church union in Australia, efforts not fully rewarded until later in the century.[66] Henry Hutchinson Montgomery, Anglican bishop of Tasmania, believed that Federation was a 'deeply religious question' that would inspire Australians to seek a wider, and more spiritual union leading ultimately to Federation 'with our own race everywhere'.[67] The political union in Australia was but a reflection of the 'free Federation of Churches' that characterized the relations of the Anglican Communion which crossed all borders. Montgomery gave up his See in 1901 in order to take up the position of the Secretary of the Society for the Propagation of the Gospel, a position tantamount to that of 'Archbishop of Greater Britain' with a commitment to the development of an imperial church.[68] Such aspirations were felt widely by other Australian church leaders. Church support for British imperialism both in Britain itself and in the colonies was, however, always qualified. It did not extend to jingoistic excess, or even to endorsement of institutions such as Empire Day, which prelates such as Archbishop Donaldson of Brisbane considered no better than a contrived attempt to instil a patriotism with which he did not wish to associate himself or his church.[69] For Presbyterians, there had always been a Calvinist distaste for ritual and symbols, including those of national adherence, and a greater appetite for independence from the state.[70]

---

[65] Richard George Ely, *Unto God and Caesar: Religious Issues in the Emerging Commonwealth, 1891–1906* (Melbourne, 1976), pp. 129–30.

[66] The Uniting Church of Australia, comprising the Methodist, Congregationalist, and most Presbyterian churches, was inaugurated on 22 June 1977.

[67] Hobart *Mercury*, 27 May 1898, p. 3, cited by R. S. M. Withycombe, 'Australian Anglicans and Imperial Identity, 1900–1914', *Journal of Religious History*, Vol. 25, no. 3 (2001), p. 288.

[68] Steven Maughan, 'An Archbishop for Greater Britain: Bishop Montgomery, Missionary Imperialism and the SPG, 1897–1915', in D. O' Connor, ed., *Three Centuries of Mission: The United Society for the Propagation of the Gospel 1701–2000* (London, 2000), pp. 358–70.

[69] Ruth Frappell, 'Imperial Fervour and Anglican Loyalty 1901–1929', in Bruce Kaye, ed., *Anglicanism in Australia: A History* (Melbourne, 2002), p. 94.

[70] Prentis, *The Scots in Australia*, Table 16: National Origins of Recruits for the Presbyterian Ministry 1823–1900.

Significantly, however, Methodists vied with Anglicans in their avowal of imperial citizenship and loyalty to Britain.[71]

The high point of Christian patriotism in Australia was felt during and immediately after the First World War, though the churches had earlier given fervent support to Australian participation in the South African War.[72] Clergy from all denominations volunteered to serve as chaplains, with evangelical Protestants showing especial enthusiasm for military service. Imperial demonstrations were linked, sometimes explicitly, to expectations that the crisis might encourage renewed religious commitment. Differing denominational postures of loyalty mattered little in the early stages of the war, when enlistment was brisk. However, one of the bitterest political disputes in Australian history was fought on the issue of conscription.[73] The lines of the conflict cannot be neatly drawn along religious lines, but, in general, Catholics identified with the Australian Labor Party and the union movement which opposed conscription, whereas middle-class Protestants identified with conservative Empire loyalists who supported it. The leader of the anti-conscription forces was the Irish-born Catholic Archbishop of Melbourne, Daniel Mannix (1864–1963). At the outset of the war, Mannix was contemptuous of attempts to accuse Catholics of disloyalty for continuing to press their claims to state support for education: 'The Catholic schools—all of them, apparently—have been singled out as breeding grounds of disloyalty. Probably the nuns have not been enlisting in sufficient numbers.'[74] Radicalized by his exile from Ireland, Mannix was stunned by the British response to the Irish rebellion of Easter 1916 into support for the rebels, something withheld by the Catholic hierarchy in Ireland. Simultaneously, Mannix decided to intervene in the Australian anti-conscription campaign, the only Catholic Bishop in Australia to do so, leading to a polarization of the issue along politico-religious lines. While Protestant church leaders had seen the war as a call to Empire and race, Mannix dismissed the conflict as a trade war which Catholics could choose, or choose not, to support. When the conscription referenda were defeated, Prime Minister Billy Hughes, who

---

[71] Don Wright and Eric Clancy, *The Methodists: A History of Methodism in New South Wales* (Sydney, 1993), pp. 130–1.

[72] Robert Linder, *The Long Tragedy: Australian Evangelical Christians and the Great War, 1914–1918* (Adelaide, 2000); Michael McKernan, *Australian Churches at War* (Sydney, 1980).

[73] O'Farrell, *Catholic Church and Community*, pp. 334–46.

[74] *Advocate*, 24 July 1915, cited by Colm Kiernan, *Daniel Mannix and Ireland* (Dublin, 1984), p. 86.

had led the 'Yes' campaign, branded Mannix a friend of Germany, and a deadly enemy of Australia.[75]

A close analysis of the outcome of the two referendum campaigns of 1916–17 reveals that Mannix failed to consolidate the Catholic vote, and that many conservative Christians were unmoved by the hectoring tactics of the Prime Minister.[76] Australians voted against conscription, but they also turned away from the Protestant identity which Linda Colley saw as inextricably linked to the eighteenth-century establishment of the British nation.[77] The bitter descent of Ireland into civil war simultaneously crushed the identification of Catholic Australians with the Irish cause. A new Australian identity was being formed.

After the war, and after the construction of the war memorials which remembered the dead and praised the war effort, the nexus with Britain began to be loosened. Anzac Day became the most significant focus of Australian nationalism in the aftermath of the war, and the churches again played their part in developing the new tradition. The Church of England had inherited the role of unofficial bearer of the national faith, and this was reflected in part by the significant role given to Anglican forms of worship devised for Anzac Day following the initiative of Dublin-born Canon David John Garland.[78] Anzac Day services could be held in cemeteries or beside war memorials which were sited on common ground, establishing new sacred spaces in the Australian landscape.[79] Catholic servicemen were, nevertheless, not permitted to attend by the hierarchy. Only in the Anzac Day march did comrades of all denominations commemorate the war dead collectively. It is likely that the over-eagerness of most churches to support the war despite the human cost was one factor in hastening the coming secularization of Australian society, even while private religious practice remained strong.

The Second World War again saw the churches offer their support to the national effort, but they did so with more circumspection than in

---

[75] Ibid., p. 117.

[76] Alan D. Gilbert, 'Protestants, Catholics and Loyalty: An Aspect of the Conscription Controversies, 1916–17', *Politics*, Vol. 6, no. 1 (1971), pp. 15–25.

[77] Colley, *Britons*, p. 53.

[78] John A. Moses, 'Canon David John Garland and the Anzac Tradition', *St Mark's Review*, Vol. 54 (1993). Idem, 'Anglicanism and Anzac Observance. The Essential Contribution of Canon David John Garland', *Pacifica*, Vol. 19 (February 2006), pp. 58–77.

[79] K. S. Inglis, *Sacred Places: War Memorials in the Australian Landscape* (Melbourne, 1998), p. 136.

1914–18. Post-war migration was responsible for making a more decisive break with Britain. Although the new settlers came in large numbers from Britain, the churches were better able to respond to their pastoral needs from local resources. Throughout the 1950s, church membership and vocations to the ministry and religious life remained high in Australia until the challenges of the 1960s saw decline in all Christian denominations.[80] Nevertheless, the rise of national religious movements independent of the home churches in Britain was slow, reflecting the conservative role of the churches in preserving traditional forms of cultural adherence. The Church of England began the painful process of detachment from its informal position as the national church of Australia. But it was not until the 1970s that a significant proportion of the Anglican episcopate was drawn from the locally born and trained clergy.[81] Catholics were also brought with reluctance to abandon their dependence on Ireland. The first Australian-born archbishop, Norman Gilroy of Sydney, was appointed a cardinal in 1946 and eschewed the Irishism of his predecessors, though not their deference to Rome.

'Australianness' was not something actively embraced by any Australian church until at least the 1960s. Change came gradually, encouraged by the ecumenical movement culminating in the formation of the Australian Council for the World Council of Churches. The 1977 founding of the Uniting Church from the merger of Methodists, Congregationalists, and the majority of Presbyterians led naturally to a decline in emphasis on the ethnicities of the constituent denominations and a renewed interest in a distinctly Australian identity for the new church.[82] Indeed, the Uniting Church has made strong claims to be the first 'Australian' church and has embraced Australian forms of worship while often leading the way in moves towards reconciliation with Aboriginal Australians. Prospects for a permanent reconciliation appear to have diminished in recent times, but not the committed engagement of the churches.

*   *   *

[80] David Hilliard, 'God in the Suburbs: The Religious Culture of Australian Cities in the 1950s', *Australian Historical Studies*, 97 (1991), pp. 399–419; idem, 'The Religious Crisis of the 1960s', *Journal of Religious History*, Vol. 21 (1997), pp. 209–27.

[81] B. H. Fletcher, 'Anglicanism and National Identity in Australia since 1962', *Journal of Religious History*, Vol. 25, no. 3 (2001), pp. 324–45.

[82] Brian Fletcher, 'Australian Anglicanism and Australian History', *Kenneth Cable Inaugural Lecture. Australian College of Theology Occasional Paper No. 3* (Sydney, 2004).

Having contributed significantly to historical debates about Australia's place in the world, the churches became increasingly marginal in the last decades of the twentieth century. Secularization of the wider society was hastened by revelations about the historical abuse of women and children in the care of church organizations, and possibly also by press coverage of church resistance to the ordination of women and gay clergy. Despite such social trends, churches which represented a conservative moral order have grown stronger in census returns on religious affiliation than the mainline denominations and increased their political influence under the administrations of Prime Minister John Howard.[83] Christian churches benefited in other ways from the negotiations which they conducted with Aboriginal people for the handing over of former mission sites and the renunciation of the paternalism of earlier times.[84] One mark of this has been the emergence of Aboriginal Christian movements, and syncretist rituals in former mission territories, notably the vibrant Aboriginal Pentecostal movement in north-western Australia.[85] Catholics celebrated the first national Aboriginal mass in Melbourne at the time of the Eucharistic Congress in 1973. Indigenous elements of this liturgy such as the initial 'smoking' ceremony were adopted for other large public events, such as Pope John Paul II's mass in honour of the beatification of Mary MacKillop in 1995. New currents in Aboriginal Christianity have merged with the broader social movement initiated by the Keating Labor government with the establishment of the Council for Aboriginal Reconciliation in 1991 to create what appears to be a distinctive post-colonial religious consciousness in Australia. Reconciliation now includes a cycle of rituals such as the commemoration of sorry days, the formal delivery of apologies, and processions (such as the bridge walks) which were conducted in most Australian cities in 2001.

However, the break with British denominationalism may be more apparent than real. In the last decades of the twentieth century, the historian Peter Read has noted that many Australians of his class and education had lost confidence in their ability to claim ownership or belonging in Australia. It is only with reluctance that he begins to use the once popular colonial term 'native-born' to refer to himself, an Australian who has come to a sense of

---

[83] Marion Maddox, *God under Howard: The Rise of the Religious Right in Australian Politics* (Sydney, 2005).

[84] Roger C. Thompson, *Religion in Australia: A History*, 2nd edn (Melbourne, 2002), pp. 127–31.

[85] Heather McDonald, *Blood, Bones and Spirit: Aboriginal Christianity in an East Kimberley Town* (Melbourne, 2001).

national identity drawing on both Black and White traditions.[86] Although the embrace of the Aboriginal cause and culture mark a new departure in national religious consciousness in Australia, it is useful to recall that such concerns are not entirely new. Indeed, the religious identity of Australians would appear to continue to harmonize with themes from the imperial past.

Select Bibliography

IAN BREWARD, *A History of the Australian Churches* (Sydney, 1993).

—— *A History of the Churches in Australasia* (Oxford, 2001).

HILARY M. CAREY, *Believing in Australia: A Cultural History of Religions* (Sydney, 1996).

B. H. FLETCHER, 'Anglicanism and Nationalism in Australia, 1901–1962', *Journal of Religious History*, Vol. 23, no. 2 (1999), pp. 215–33.

JOHN W. HARRIS, *One Blood: 200 Years of Aboriginal Encounter with Christianity: A Story of Hope*, 2nd edn (Sydney, 1994).

DAVID HILLIARD, *God's Gentlemen: A History of the Melanesian Mission, 1849–1942* (Brisbane, 1978).

—— 'The Ties That Used to Bind: A Fresh Look at the History of Australian Anglicanism', *Pacifica*, Vol. 11, no. 3 (1988), pp. 265–80.

H. R. JACKSON, *Churches and People in Australia and New Zealand, 1860–1930* (Sydney, 1987).

BRUCE KAYE, ed., *Anglicanism in Australia: A History* (Melbourne, 2002).

PATRICK JAMES O'FARRELL, *The Catholic Church and Community: An Australian History*, rev. edn (Sydney, 1985).

STUART PIGGIN, *Evangelical Christianity in Australia: Spirit, Word and World* (Melbourne, 1996).

MALCOLM D. PRENTIS, *The Scots in Australia: A Study of New South Wales, Victoria and Queensland, 1788–1900* (Sydney, 1983).

ROWAN STRONG, *Anglicanism and the British Empire, c.1700–1850* (Oxford, 2007).

ROGER C. THOMPSON, *Religion in Australia: A History*, 2nd edn (Melbourne, 2002).

DAVID WETHERELL, *Reluctant Mission: The Anglican Church in Papua New Guinea, 1891–1942* (Brisbane, 1977).

JEAN WOOLMINGTON, ed., *Religion in Early Australia: The Problem of Church and State* (Sydney, 1976).

---

[86] Peter Read, *Belonging: Australians, Place and Aboriginal Ownership* (Melbourne, 2000), pp. 4, 222.

9

Money: Trade, Investment, and Economic Nationalism

GEOFFREY BOLTON

Once upon a time, the story began, there was a pioneering community originating in an outcast convict colony, which in less than a hundred years took possession of a continent and its offshore islands, and turned them into an economic success. The Australasian colonies were not only prolific suppliers of wool and minerals for industrialized Britain and Europe, but they also provided their workers with one of the highest living standards in the world. But instead of proclaiming their republican independence at the dawn of the twentieth century, Australia and New Zealand remained tied to Mother England's apron strings. Their young men were sent to sacrifice their lives defending Britain's interests in European wars, but when war came to the Pacific the British deserted them. Despite all this, even at the start of the twenty-first century Australians were slow to cast off their colonial status to assume their true role as an Asia-oriented, multicultural potential republic. As the then Prime Minister, Paul Keating, put it in an effective but superficial speech in 1992, Australian conservatives remained enmeshed in a 'forelock-tugging' relationship with the Mother Country.[1]

More than sixty years ago Brian Fitzpatrick put forward an explanation of Australia's failure to develop a strong and authentic sense of nationalism.[2] Building on the insights of Hobson and Lenin, he argued that Britain was overwhelmingly Australia's major source of overseas investment. The maintenance of the British Empire in Australia required the collaboration

[1] Stephen Alomes, *A Nation at Last?: The Changing Character of Australian Nationalism* (North Ryde, 1988); N. D. McLachlan, *Waiting for the Revolution: A History of Australian Nationalism* (Melbourne, 1989); *Commonwealth Parliamentary Debates* (House of Representatives), 27 February 1992, pp. 372–3.

[2] Brian Fitzpatrick, *British Imperialism in Australia 1783–1833* (London, 1939); *The British Empire in Australia: An Economic History 1834–1939* (Melbourne, 1941); Brian Fitzpatrick and E. L. Wheelwright, *The Highest Bidder* (Melbourne, 1965).

of a comprador class of local businessmen. Hence Australian nationalism became associated with radical and working-class politics, fortified by the large minority of Irish-Australians, whereas the conservatives could be identified with a mindless Anglophilia. In these circumstances Australia failed for a long time to develop a distinctive national culture and remained dominated by British models.

The reality was a good deal subtler and more complex. Historians have failed to agree on the motives for the settlement of New South Wales in 1788, but none has suggested that Britain's primary motive was financial investment. For the convict colony's first three decades the military commissariat was Britain's main source of funding for the colony. Whaling and sealing provided the Australian colonies with their first major staple for export income, but much of the potential gain from this source was taken by American competition, and by the mid-nineteenth century indiscriminate slaughter brought the traffic to a low ebb. Private investment was meagre. The Bank of New South Wales, established in 1817, was capitalized by local investors. Its stabilizing influence may have played a part in attracting a trickle of free emigration and capital from Britain in the 1820s. Noel Butlin has observed that much of the colonial prosperity of that period 'was dependent on the British government subsidising the colonies, supplying youthful populations with substantial skills, and, after 1825, encouraging considerable private investment in Australia'.[3]

Many of the early investors at that time were land companies hoping to turn a profit from the large-scale development of cheap domains. Most originated outside London. The pioneer, the Australian Company of Leith and Edinburgh (1822–33), hoped to draw its profits from shipping, trade, and loans, and its Aberdeen-based successors, the Scottish Australian Investment Company and the North British Australasian Company, looked to land acquisition and loans. West of England cloth manufacturers backed the Van Diemen's Land Company founded in 1824. Only the Australian Agricultural Company, also launched in 1824, was London-based, surviving to the present day because its local managers exchanged their original grant in New South Wales for better country lying in the path of pastoral expansion northward.[4] During the next decade, parties of speculators, some influenced by the

[3] N. G. Butlin, 'Australian National Accounts', in Wray Vamplew, ed., *Australians: Historical Statistics* (Sydney, 1987), p. 127.

[4] D. S. Macmillan, *Scotland and Australia 1788–1850: Emigration, Commerce, and Investment* (Oxford, 1967); A. L. Meston, *The Van Diemen's Land Company, 1825–1842* (Launceston, 1958).

colonizing theories of Edward Gibbon Wakefield, formed companies to bring emigrants and capital to the founding of new Australasian colonies. Of these the most successful were the South Australian Company, dominated by George Fife Angas (1836), and the New Zealand Company (1840). Angas was also prominent in the establishment of new British-based banks to serve the Australian colonies. Nine such banks were established between 1835 and 1863 confining their operations to Australia and New Zealand and choosing to operate internationally through correspondent banking networks.[5]

From the 1830s, wool came to the fore as the major export commodity. Cheap land, affordable labour and transport costs, and a reputation for quality commended the Australian clip to Yorkshire woolbuyers. Australian wool production stood in 1850 at a little under 19 million kilogrammes, rising by 1880 to just over 160 million, about half of it from New South Wales. By that year the value of recorded wool exports stood at £14.3 million. Wool was to constitute Australia's major export to Britain for more than a century, except for two decades after 1851 when it was overtaken by the discovery of gold in New South Wales and Victoria.[6]

Control of the export trade fell during the nineteenth century into the hands of specialist middlemen, mostly of Scottish origin. F. G. Dalgety (1817–94), starting from a Melbourne base, 'realized, earlier than most, the greater strength of a business with its London headquarters closely co-operating with colonial branches'.[7] Living in England after 1859 he oversaw a firm which, by 1880, shipped 70,000 bales annually, about 7 per cent of the entire Australasian clip. In Sydney, Thomas Mort (1816–78) was the first to conduct regular wool auctions, and in later life experimented with the export of refrigerated meat. After his death his firm merged with its main competitor to form Goldsborough, Mort & Co. in 1888.[8] Elder, Smith & Co. was an Adelaide firm evolving from several smaller businesses in 1863. Incorporated in 1882 with a capital of £200,000, the company established a London office the next year. It has been estimated that between 1866 and 1884 about 10 per cent of British long-term capital invested in the pastoral

[5] D. T. Merrett, 'Paradise Lost: British Banks in Australia', in G. Jones, ed., *Banks as Multinationals* (Reading, 1990); 'Global Reach by Australian Banks, 1830–1960', *Business History*, Vol. 37, no. 3 (1995), p. 70.

[6] See the essays in W. K. Hancock and A. Barnard, eds, *The Simple Fleece* (Melbourne, 1963).

[7] R. M. Hartwell, 'Frederick Gonnerman Dalgety, 1817–94', in *Australian Dictionary of Biography* (Carlton, 1972), Vol. 4, p. 4.

[8] A. Barnard, *Visions and Profits: Studies in the Business Career of Thomas Sutcliffe Mort* (Carlton, 1961).

industry was handled and controlled by these pastoral companies. Their dominance survived a shift in marketing practices; in 1880 less than a third of wool sales for the export market were conducted within Australia, but by 1920 the proportion was to rise to 93 per cent, with Western Australia last to change.[9]

After 1851, gold stimulated a massive increase in immigration, as well as an inflow of British capital for financial, mining, and trading interests, although the British government did little to encourage investment or migration beyond granting self-government to all the colonies except Western Australia during the 1850s. It was Victoria that in 1858 took the initiative by floating a government loan for public works on the London Stock Exchange. Until that time, North America, and especially the United States, had been a major outlet for British capital investment, but between 1861 and 1865 the American Civil War cast a dampener on such enterprise. Subsequently the United States went in for a systematic policy of repatriating foreign loans in favour of domestic capital. This encouraged the swing of British interest towards Australia and New Zealand, although South America proved a strong counter-attraction until the Barings crash of 1890.[10]

Resuming after a slump in 1867, British investment in Australia and New Zealand grew steadily for the next quarter of a century. Communication improved after steamship companies such as the P&O and Orient Lines took advantage of the opening of the Suez Canal in 1869, with the colonies competing for regular services. From the 1870s the major shipping companies plying to Australia formed a cartel, the 'Conference', stabilizing freight rates and schedules but provoking complaint among Australian exporters.[11] Britain was linked by telegraph to the south-eastern Australian colonies in 1872 and to Western Australia in 1877. The pace accelerated after 1877 when the British government, persuaded by the New Zealand financier-politician Sir Julius Vogel (1835–99), passed the Colonial Stock Act recognizing colonial government bonds as securities on British stock exchanges. While the Crown Agents continued to handle loans for the less populous Australian colonies,

---

[9] Simon Ville, 'The Relocation of the International Market for Australian Wool', *Australian Economic History Review* (hereafter *AEHR*), Vol. 45, no. 1 (2005), pp. 73–95.

[10] Donald Denoon, *Settler Capitalism: The Dynamics of Dependent Development in the Southern Hemisphere* (Oxford, 1983).

[11] Competition between colonies is illustrated in Stephanie Jones, 'The Decline of British Maritime Enterprise in Australia: The Example of the Australian United Steam Navigation Company, 1887–1961', *Business History*, Vol. 27, no. 1 (1985), p. 59. For the 'Conference' see J. Bach, *A Maritime History of Australia* (Melbourne, 1976), chs. vii–viii.

the government of New South Wales entrusted the negotiation of loans to the Bank of England in 1884, and Queensland followed suit in 1885. Victoria in 1886 went to the London and Westminster Bank, followed in 1890 by Western Australia and Tasmania. Most of the colonies appointed Agents-General, usually seasoned politicians, to negotiate this borrowing as well as to supervise immigration and dispense hospitality to visitors from their home colony.[12]

It has been estimated that during the 1880s Australia was probably the leading field for British investment. Borrowing by Australian colonial governments, which as late as 1873 stood at only £400,000, rose to £10.8 million in 1879 and to £51.4 million for the period 1883–6. In the same four years, private borrowing accounted for £30.1 million. Railways absorbed around three-fifths of public investment and perhaps more; it has been calculated that in Queensland they accounted for 72 per cent of public investment between 1860 and 1915.[13] Most government railway investment went into rural districts where lines of dubious profitability were built to satisfy local politicians. Colonial Premiers such as Queensland's Sir Thomas McIlwraith and London speculators sought to span Australia with transcontinental lines built by private enterprise on the land grant principle, following North American examples, but none of these schemes came to fruition except in Western Australia, and there the results were discouraging. As Noel Butlin has shown, much capital was absorbed in residential building, especially between 1881 and 1888 when this sector represented more than £65 million in new capital formation. Senior British public figures such as Lord Carnarvon (Colonial Secretary 1874–8) and Lord Rosebery (Prime Minister 1894–5) invested in urban real estate in Sydney, Melbourne, and even Darwin, almost always making a loss.[14]

This surge in investment during the 1880s did nothing to inhibit Australia's national aspirations. On the contrary this was a period when senior judicial and political figures spoke of the inevitability of an Australian republic, when Queensland's McIlwraith defied Gladstone and raised the flag in Papua New Guinea, and when the young Alfred Deakin attacked the great Lord Salisbury to his face for his neglect of Australian interests in the South

[12] A. R. Hall, *The London Capital Market and Australia, 1870–1914* (Canberra, 1963), chs. iv and v.

[13] J. Laverty, 'The Queensland Economy 1860–1915' in D. Murphy, R. B. Joyce, and C. Hughes, eds, *Prelude to Power: The Rise of the Labor Party in Queensland, 1885–1915* (St Lucia, 1978), p. 31.

[14] N. G. Butlin, *Investment in Australian Economic Development 1861–1900* (Cambridge, 1964) ch. 4. Evidence for Lord Rosebery's investments will be found in the Mentmore Papers, Buckinghamshire County Record Office, Aylesbury.

Pacific. Unfortunately the financial credibility of the Australian colonies was coming under strain, first through the overexposure of the Charters Towers goldfields in 1886–8, and then by the excesses of the Melbourne property boom. Alarm bells rang in 1890, when the London firm of Baring Brothers came to disaster over South American investments, exposing the weakness of the tender system which until then had characterized much overseas borrowing. In that year, Donald Denoon has written:

the Australasian colonies had accumulated greater debts per head than anywhere else in the world. The *Bankers' Magazine*, torn between awe and alarm, calculated that the Australasian colonies had public debts of over £50 per head, Queensland leading the field with nearly £70, followed by New Zealand with £63. By comparison the British public debt per head was a mere £18, the Cape's was £16, and Canada's a frivolous £12.[15]

Allan Hall contends that, even so, there was no real risk that British investment would be withheld from Australia, but in 1891 several financial writers expressed concern that the public works on which the Australian colonies spent their loan money did not generate enough income to cover the cost of interest. Two or three of the Australian colonies for the first time experienced difficulty in raising loans on the London market.[16] Defiantly McIlwraith, then Treasurer of Queensland, denounced the Bank of England for failing to support a loan, and withdrew his statement only when the Bank threatened to have no further dealings with Queensland. At Charters Towers, when British investors tried to compensate for their overcapitalization by cutting wages, the miners responded by supporting a vigorous, if short-lived, republican movement.[17]

Then came the crisis of nerve which led to the bank crashes of 1893, and the pattern of behaviour between Australian borrowers and British investors seems to have shifted significantly:

Recurrently from the 1880s to the 1930s received opinion in the City of London saw Australia not as uncreditworthy, but as unnecessarily lengthening its credit

---

[15] Denoon, *Settler Capitalism*, p. 52.

[16] A. R. Hall, *London Capital Market*; see also Hall, *The Export of Capital from Britain 1870–1914* (London, 1968). But note the strictures of John Fortescue, 'The Seamy Side of Australia', *Nineteenth Century*, Vol. 39 (1891), pp. 229–36 and *The Economist*, Vol. 49 (1891), pp. 1393–4.

[17] Mark McKenna, *The Captive Republic: A History of Republicanism in Australia* (Melbourne, 2001); G. C. Bolton, *A Thousand Miles Away: A History of North Queensland to 1920* (Canberra, 1963), ch. 9; A. L. Lougheed, 'British Company Formation and the Queensland Mining Industry', *Business History*, Vol. 25, no. 1 (1983), p. 76.

risks by wayward extravagance; it was felt that working class political leaders were inherently unsound and their financial conduct untrustworthy.[18]

In this environment the firm of Robert Nivison and Company began its rise to an unrivalled pre-eminence as specialist brokers for colonial, and especially Australian, share issues. Its role has been too much neglected by historians.[19] Quitting the London and Westminster Bank to operate independently, Nivison developed a technique for raising colonial government loans through underwriting syndicates instead of relying on the process of tender. Winning a reputation for probity, Nivison soon built up a virtual monopoly in floating Australian government loans. Queensland took its business to the firm as early as 1893, and between 1900 and 1906 the rest of the Australian colonies (or states as they became at Federation in 1901) followed. The importance of a trusted contact in London was especially marked at a period when the Australian pastoral industry remained depressed by drought. The Western Australian goldfields, the one bright spot on the Australian horizon, were tainted by the scandalous promotions of such entrepreneurs as Whitaker Wright and Horatio Bottomley, and were at best risky; of sixty mining companies listed in 1894, representing an investment of probably £18 million, only one-fifth survived by 1900.[20] It took time for the pundits to enthuse about investment in Australia. In 1902 *The Economist* declared: 'Australia will never find its true place until borrowing from abroad absolutely stops.'[21]

These strictures should be placed in context. The Australian colonies were not the only members of the British Empire—Newfoundland and Natal were others—to stumble into financial imprudence. There was a long-standing belief in London that combinations of several colonies were a much stronger prospect for investment than small self-governing units on their own. As Secretary of State for Colonies, Joseph Chamberlain gave encouragement to the Australian Federation movement of the 1890s. When the Australian delegates visited London in 1900 to advise on the passage of

---

[18] R. P. T. Davenport-Hines, 'Lord Glendyne', in R. T. Appleyard and C. B. Schedvin, eds, *Australian Financiers: Biographical Essays* (Melbourne, 1988), pp. 202–3.

[19] Exceptions are Davenport-Hines, 'Lord Glendyne'; R. S. Gilbert, 'London Financial Intermediaries and Australian Overseas Borrowing, 1900–29', *AEHR*, Vol. 11, no. 1 (1971), pp. 39–47.

[20] J. W. McCarty, 'British Investment in Western Australian Gold Mining, 1894–1914', *University Studies in History*, Vol. 4, no. 1 (1961–2).

[21] *The Economist*, Vol. 60 (1902), p. 849.

the legislation creating the federated Commonwealth, their major dispute with Chamberlain lay with the right of appeal from Australian courts to the judicial committee of the Privy Council; and it emerged that the British government was perfectly willing to allow a considerable degree of Australian autonomy over constitutional appeals provided that commercial and civil cases might still be referred to the ultimate authority of the Privy Council. This safeguarded the interests of British investors against the vagaries of colonial jurisprudence.[22]

Some found the Federal government a disappointment. It would be a long time, wrote a columnist in *The Economist*, before the bad impression created by the first twelve months of the Commonwealth government would be effaced. The Australians, in his view, had given offence to the French over the New Hebrides and to the Japanese by their immigration policy, as well as abusing the British for 'reluctance to unquestionably champion Australia's so-called rights and aspirations'.[23] He was referring, be it remembered, to that first Commonwealth Parliament which has usually figured in Australian history books as an example of nation-building achievement, and to a ministry dominated by such archetypes of bourgeois liberalism as Barton, Deakin, and Forrest. So two stereotypes came into being which were to bedevil Anglo-Australian relations for many years: one, the image of Australian politicians as irresponsible mediocrities, foolish if not corrupt; the other, the image of a pampered working class on whose excessive wages the capital of British investors would be squandered.

Even when the Australian economy improved after the ending of the drought in 1903, the Australian State governments still had occasional difficulty in raising funds on the London market. Butlin calculated that the drought of 1902 was followed by a substantial outflow of capital from Australia until reversed in 1912.[24] It has been conjectured that nervous investors saw the growing strength of the Australian Labor Party as a menace to public credit. Australian politicians tended to blame the restrictive practices of a 'ring' of London stockbrokers and bankers. This theory gained some currency in 1908 when the South Australian Treasurer, A. H. Peake, invited the firm of Elder, Smith & Co. to arrange the conversion of a South Australian loan through Lloyds Bank instead of going through the usual

[22] J. A. La Nauze, *The Making of the Australian Constitution* (Carlton, 1972), pp. 248–69.

[23] *The Economist*, Vol. 60 (1902), p. 190.

[24] N. G. Butlin, *Australian Domestic Product, Investment and Foreign Borrowing 1861 to 1938/39* (Cambridge, 1962), ch. xix.

channels. Nivison & Co. refused to broker the transaction, the London Stock Exchange condemned it, the Agent-General for South Australia resigned in protest, and Lloyds Bank quit. It was an instructive lesson for the future.[25]

For their part, some British interests were concerned about Australia's role as a trading partner. In the decade 1887–96 Britain had regularly provided 70 per cent of Australia's imports, with a further 11–12 per cent coming from other British possessions. By 1902–6 the British share was down to 58 per cent, though the figure from elsewhere in the Empire had increased slightly. The main competition came from the protectionist economies of the United States and Germany. Some British industries, such as the manufacturers of wire, maintained their foothold in the Australian market by product diversification; others were slow to respond.[26] As a destination for Australian exports Britain's share of the market had also fallen: from an average of 72 per cent in 1887–96 to 46 per cent in 1902–6. France, Germany, the United States, and Belgium meanwhile all increased their share of Australia's exports. British shipping also was yielding ground to foreign competitors. At the Colonial Conference of 1907 Australia's Sir William Lyne said: 'Twenty years ago as you looked over the vast expanse of Sydney harbour you saw the British flag flying at nearly every masthead. Shortly before I left last month … nearly half the shipping in Sydney harbour … was foreign.' He estimated that of 7.4 million tons of shipping entering and leaving Australian waters in 1906 less than 2 million had come direct from or gone to the United Kingdom.[27]

Remedial measures were attempted. In 1905 the United Kingdom's Board of Trade dispatched a commissioner to Australia to investigate the conditions and prospects of British trade, and in December 1908 the Board appointed a permanent commissioner to advise British manufacturers of Australian requirements and opportunities.[28] Meanwhile the Deakin government's tariff legislation of 1907–8, although primarily intended to protect Australian industries, introduced preference on a number of items imported from Britain or the British Empire. Between 1910 and 1914, despite the

[25] Davenport-Hines, 'Lord Glendyne', pp. 200–1; Gilbert, *London Financial Intermediaries*, p. 42.

[26] L. R. Fisher and A. Smith, 'International Competition in Australia's Wire Market, 1880–1914', *Business History*, Vol. 22, no. 1 (1980), pp. 71–86.

[27] *Colonial Conference, 1907* (Cd 3523), pp. 328–9, quoted in Bach, *Maritime History*, p. 144.

[28] *Official Year Book of the Commonwealth of Australia*, No. 5, 1912, pp. 630–49.

ascendancy of Labor in the Commonwealth and most State Parliaments, British investment and immigration increased significantly, partly attracted by policies of agricultural expansion. Following the Imperial Conference of 1911 a royal commission (1913–17) was appointed to report on the state of trade between Britain and its Dominions, but it was overtaken by the outbreak of the First World War.

Half a century earlier Sir Charles Dilke had doubted whether the colonies would come to Britain's aid over a crisis in Serbia or Luxemburg, but the events of 1914–18 proved him wrong. The Anzacs who lost their lives at Gallipoli or the Western Front were honoured in Britain as in Australia. But because Australia, in circumstances of spectacular acrimony, declined to follow the British example in introducing conscription, some saw Australia as falling short of the admirable British model.[29] This may have coloured Anglo-Australian financial relations during the next twenty years; but the immediate commercial result of the war was to draw Britain and Australia closer. If war made shipping lanes hazardous between Australia and the United Kingdom it also eliminated German competition. Some British firms, such as the explosives firm Nobels, established Australian subsidiaries which benefited from tariff protection.[30] In 1916 agreement was reached on a scheme under which Britain acquired the entire Australian wool clip at an agreed price. 'In the absence of one document containing specific details of the agreement … ', writes its historian, 'it relied on the mutual interpretation and goodwill of men on opposite sides of the world who had never met but who were vested with the responsibility of carrying out their side of the bargain. It was truly a gentlemen's agreement.'[31] It was a remarkable example of Anglo-Australian cooperation.

Wartime experience suggested the desirability of price stabilization through orderly marketing. With peace, the problem arose of disposing of unshipped wool held in Australia on behalf of the British government. Late in 1920 Australian woolgrowers and the British government formed an officially backed company, the British Australian Wool Realization Association Limited (BAWRA). Although it succeeded in managing an orderly

---

[29] See, for example, the articles from the Melbourne correspondent of *The Round Table*, in L. L. Robson, ed., *Australian Commentaries: Select Articles from the Round Table* (Carlton, 1975), pp. 73–88.

[30] P. Richardson, 'Nobels and the Australian Mining Industry', *Business History*, Vol. 26, no. 2 (1984), pp. 156–69.

[31] Christopher Fyfe, *Gentlemen's Agreements: Australian Wartime Wool Appraisements* (Dalkeith, W.A., 1996), p. 13.

transition to peacetime marketing, BAWRA could not persuade woolbrokers and growers to agree to a long-term central organization to control the offering and sale of wool and went into liquidation in 1926. Although prices on the auction market fluctuated considerably during the remainder of the 1920s and the 1930s, Britain continued to dominate the market, taking 30–40 per cent of greasy wool exports in each year of the 1930s.[32] From 1918 until 1930 net capital inflow into Australia, mainly from British sources, reached unprecedented heights, totalling £455 million, of which more than two-thirds was government borrowing. Some of this investment followed from a revived interest in the settlement of British migrants in rural Australia. During the 1920s British manufacturers losing ground in foreign markets renewed their attention to exports to Australia. The establishment of the Empire Marketing Board in Britain in 1926 with funding to support industrial research within the British Empire was linked with the foundation in the same year of Australia's Commonwealth Scientific and Industrial Research institute (CSIR, later CSIRO).[33]

Not that the London capital market was an easy touch. In an illuminating study of Queensland loans policy from 1920 to 1924 Tom Cochrane has shown how a Labor Premier, Edward Theodore, failed to raise finance in London for his ambitious developmental schemes because his government had raised rents on pastoral leases and was in the process of abolishing the nominee (and conservative) Legislative Council. Advising the Colonial Office the Conservative politician Sir Arthur Stanley argued against intervention by Whitehall to overrule Queensland's legislation because Australian voters would react against British political interference and allow Theodore to 'escape from the very difficult position in which he finds himself'. Instead, wrote Stanley, 'a mere veto of measures when passed will not be nearly so effective as the cutting off of supplies.'[34] Unable to raise capital in London, Theodore was eventually forced to borrow inadequate amounts at high rates of interest in New York. Having learnt his lesson he bowed to pressure and eventually became a capitalist himself.[35]

---

[32] Ibid., pp. 109–19.

[33] C. B. Schedvin, *Shaping Science and Industry* (Sydney, 1987) pp. 8–18; Kosmas Tsokhas, *People or Money? Empire Settlement and British Emigration to Australia, 1919–1939* (Canberra, 1990); *Making a Nation State: Identity, Economic Nationalism and Sexuality in Australian History* (Carlton, 2001).

[34] T. Cochrane, *Blockade: The Queensland Loans Affair 1920–1924* (St Lucia, Qld, 1989), pp. 9, 138.

[35] Ross Fitzgerald, *Red Ted* (St Lucia, Qld, 1995).

Politicians less radical than the Theodore of 1920 often thought themselves pitted against the London 'ring' in attempts to negotiate easier terms. The aged Sir William McKell informed an interviewer that he regarded as his toughest political battle a visit to London in 1926 to renegotiate New South Wales loans without an interest rise.[36] When I read this I was reminded of my own meeting with Sir James Connolly, a former Agent-General for Western Australia, who was prouder of a similar achievement than of any of the social welfare measures that he had piloted on to the Western Australian statute book. Stanley Bruce as Prime Minister (1923–9) strengthened Australia's hand by centralizing borrowing on the Federal government and setting up the Commonwealth Loan Council, at first on a voluntary basis (1923) but later as a statutory body (1927). This improved on, and to some extent superseded, the informal role of Nivison & Co. in bringing order to the loan market, but came too late to cushion the effects of the Great Depression of 1929 on the Australian economy.

It did not help that the 1920s saw the rise to influence of Sir Otto Niemeyer, that product of Balliol College who, having beaten John Maynard Keynes for top place in the Civil Service examinations, became the controller of finance at the Treasury in 1922 while still under forty, and then moved in 1927 to the Bank of England. More than anyone else, Niemeyer was responsible for Churchill's contentious decision to return to the gold standard in 1925, as a result of which the Bank of England temporarily suspended the availability of overseas loans. The Australian voluntary loan council responded by authorizing state governments to raise loans on the New York market, with the active support of Nivisons.[37] Niemeyer's attitude towards Australia was consistently hostile and belittling. One of his memoranda was headed: 'Arrival of Australia as a Mendicant (or as a burglar).'[38] Some within Australia echoed Niemeyer's conviction that British investors were subsidizing excessive wages and living standards for Australian workers, and predicted disaster.

The smash came with the Great Depression of 1929. With a sharp fall in overseas export prices and a massive increase in unemployment, Australia's Commonwealth and state governments were hard pressed to pay interest on the borrowing of the 1920s, and could raise no more loans on the London

---

[36] Chris Cunneen, *William John McKell* (Sydney, 2000), p. 85.

[37] Gilbert, *London Financial Intermediaries*, p. 44.

[38] Michael Roe, *Australia, Britain and Migration 1915–1940: A Study of Desperate Hopes* (Cambridge, 1995), p. 52.

money market. The Australian Federal government agreed that the Bank of England should send an expert to enquire into the financial outlook and advise on measures for restoring Australia's credit. That expert was Niemeyer, backed by Professor Theodore Gregory of the London School of Economics. Not without relish they prescribed harsh medicine. Australian governments must cut their expenditure, including social services, and reduce wages. It is easy to believe the story that when the Speaker of the House of Representatives asked Niemeyer if he was finding his visit satisfactory, the banker replied: 'That depends on whether you do as you're told.'[39] This was the kind of attitude that led radical historians of the 1930s, such as Fitzpatrick, to read Australian history in terms of the dominance of British capital, and to see the financier as the enemy of Australian nationalism. In 1931, after input from leading Australian economists, the Commonwealth and State governments adopted a modified version of Niemeyer's recommendations, the Premiers' Plan.[40]

John Thomas Lang, Labor Premier of New South Wales from October 1930 to May 1932, argued for the suspension of interest payments to the British bondholders and the reduction of interest on Australian government borrowings to 3 per cent. When he announced that New South Wales would not pay interest due in London in April 1931 the Commonwealth government was obliged to uphold Australia's credit by meeting the debt. A year followed in which Lang's posturing populism was offset by a grudging conformity to Federal deflationary policies, but in April 1932 the Commonwealth government moved against New South Wales, using new powers to enforce the payment of state debts. Next month the State Governor dismissed Lang, who was soundly defeated at the ensuing elections. His overthrow was not due, as he claimed, to 'the secret money power', but London sources were undisguisedly relieved at his loss of office.[41] A residual nervousness nevertheless made it difficult for Stanley Bruce, now Australian High Commissioner in London, to negotiate the conversion of Australian loans to a lower interest rate in 1932–3. Bruce thought it one of his hardest-won victories.

[39] Bernard Attard, 'The Bank of England and the Niemeyer Mission 1921–1930', *AEHR*, Vol. 32 (1992), pp. 66–83.

[40] Simon Ville, 'Niemeyer, Scullin and the Australian Economists', *AEHR*, Vol. 44 (2004), pp. 143–60.

[41] Bede Nairn, *'The Big Fella': Jack Lang and the Australian Labor Party 1891–1949* (Carlton, 1986); H. Radi and P. Spearritt, eds, *Jack Lang* (Sydney, 1977); for Lang's own version see *Why I Fight* (Sydney, 1934).

Meanwhile the pressures of the world economic crisis led Britain to espouse the cause of Empire free trade thirty years after Joseph Chamberlain had first proclaimed its merits. The Ottawa conference of 1932 set the scene for preferential tariff agreements between members of the British Commonwealth. During the 1920s the British proportion of Australia's export trade had slipped somewhat, falling to less than half the total. France took more than 10 per cent during the 1920s but fell away with the onset of the Depression; the United States showed a similar pattern after an increase in tariffs in 1930; Germany and Belgium were also trading partners, though not on a large or consistent scale. After Ottawa the British share of Australia's export trade rose once more to over 50 per cent, peaking at £78.7 million in 1938. Wool accounted for between one-third and one-half of the total. Of other pastoral products hides, skins, and tallow were of greater importance than mutton or beef. British firms such as Bovril and Vesteys preferred to import chilled meat from their holdings in South America than to draw frozen beef from their underdeveloped properties in northern Australia. Wheat ranked second among Australia's exports to Britain, though world grain prices were low for most of the 1930s. Mining ran a poor third, although the revival of the Western Australian goldfields following improved prices in the 1930s stimulated a useful input of British capital.[42]

In general, Australia still fulfilled its traditional role as a supplier of primary produce to the United Kingdom, in turn providing a faithful market for British manufactures. However, after 1923 the British contribution to Australia's total imports was always less than 50 per cent. Although the British-aligned firms of Shell and Anglo-Persian (later BP) accounted for just over half the petrol consumed by motor vehicles, the United States provided most of the rest, fuelling the tractors working Australian farms and the kerosene (paraffin oil) providing heat and light for many homesteads.[43] In 1927 imports from the United States accounted for more than one-quarter of the Australian total, and although the American share of the market fell away until the Second World War it had recovered to 15 per cent by the late 1930s. Japan took more than 10 per cent of Australia's exports between 1931 and 1936, but in the latter year the Australian government, against the

[42] R. T. Appleyard and M. Davies, 'Financiers of Western Australia's Goldfields', in Appleyard and Schedvin, eds, *Australian Financiers*, pp. 160–89.

[43] D. F. Dixon, 'Competition in the Australian Petrol Market During the Inter-War Period', *AEHR*, Vol. 16, no. 2 (1976), pp. 110–27.

wishes of the pastoral lobby, imposed a trade diversion policy in favour of Britain which penalized and offended Japan. It was Australia and not Britain that between 1936 and 1939 subsidized the P&O subsidiary the Eastern and Australian Steamship Company, enabling it to withstand Japanese competition in Australian waters. In a period of renewed international tension the British connection was paramount.[44] Nevertheless at the same time successive Australian governments were countering over-reliance on the fluctuations of primary produce markets by fostering industrialization behind tariff protection, thus providing a source of future competition for British exporters. During the 1930s the number of Australians employed in manufacturing rose to 500,000, an increase of 20 per cent.

The Second World War weakened Britain's pre-eminence for Australian trade and finance, although a number of bulk-purchasing agreements helped the mother country to feed and clothe its citizens. Once again Australia set up a central Wool Committee to monitor the sale of the entire clip to the United Kingdom, receiving in return generous terms from the British. Like the BAWRA agreement of the 1914–18 war this marked a high point of Anglo-Australian economic cooperation facilitated by a common culture. In Fyfe's words, the deal was 'accomplished without any official written documentation, not even a handshake'.[45] Although trade between the two countries was hindered by enemy action, Australia's imports from Britain increased significantly during the war, reaching a peak of £82.2 million in 1943. Even this figure was outstripped by the massive quantities of American goods arriving under the Lend–Lease agreement and defence requirements. In the three years 1943–5 American goods valued at over £300 million reached Australia. It was an omen for the future.

Melanie Beresford and Prue Kerr have argued that the 1940s represent a turning point for Australian capitalism. Pushed by its need for American aid, they say, Britain was obliged to consent to the Bretton Woods agreement of 1944 setting up those instruments of United States financial hegemony, the International Monetary Fund and the World Bank. The Chifley Labor government showed 'a remarkable display of cynicism' in selling the scheme to the Australian public, despite the forebodings of populists within its

---

[44] J. Shepherd, *Australia's Interests and Policies in the Far East* (New York, 1940), ch. 3; Kosmas Tsokhas, 'The Eastern and Australian Steamship Company and the Shipping Dispute between Australia and Japan, 1936–39', *Business History*, Vol. 34, no. 2 (1992), pp. 50–68.

[45] Fyfe, *Gentlemen's Agreements*, p. 367; S. J. Butlin and C. B. Schedvin, *The Australian Economy 1942–1945* (Canberra, 1980).

ranks.[46] This analysis has been challenged, to my mind persuasively, by David Lee. He shows that, far from yielding to American dominance, the Chifley government between 1945 and 1949 went to considerable lengths to maintain sterling reserves, shore up the British economy, and risk unpopularity with the electorate by resisting wage increases and maintaining rationing of imports.[47] On the other hand the Chifley government turned a deaf ear to British hopes of resurrecting the old complementarity of an Australia providing a sure market for British manufactures in return for wool, wheat, and minerals. Instead, by supporting new manufacturing industries protected by tariffs, and especially by backing the plans of General Motors for the mass production of Holden cars, Australia looked to supplant Britain in its own home market.[48]

No doubt the Chifley government was motivated in part by sympathy for the Attlee Labour government in Britain, but even more it was concerned to uphold Britain as a counterbalance to an over-mighty United States. It was the Menzies government (1949–66) that abolished petrol rationing despite its possible effect on dollar reserves; a risk survived because of good fortune in the timing of the post-war wool boom. Despite its Anglophile rhetoric the Menzies government's policies in a number of important aspects such as Pacific security, defence procurement, and overseas borrowing favoured an American alignment at the expense of British interests. Nevertheless throughout the Menzies period Britain continued to be Australia's major trading partner and provider of investment overseas and Australia's biggest source of migrants. An agreement of 1947 initiated the 'ten pound migrant' scheme under which British emigrants who paid that modest sum and agreed to stay for at least two years were given passages to settle in Australia. Nearly half a million applicants took advantage of the scheme before its termination in 1971, constituting the biggest single source of 'new Australians' with about 44 per cent of all Australia's immigrants during that period.[49] The trading arrangements that had sustained the United Kingdom during the 1939–45

[46] M. Beresford and P. Kerr, 'A Turning Point for Australian Capitalism 1942–1952', in E. L. Wheelwright and K. Buckley, eds, *Essays in the Political Economy of Australian Capitalism*, Vol. 4 (Sydney, 1980), pp. 148–71.

[47] David Lee, *Search for Security: The Political Economy of Australia's Postwar Foreign and Defence Policy* (St Leonards, 1995).

[48] G. Zappola, 'The Decline of Complementarity: Australia and the Sterling Area', *AEHR*, Vol. 34 (1994), pp. 1–5.

[49] R. T. Appleyard, *British Emigration to Australia* (Canberra, 1964); *The Ten Pound Immigrants* (London, 1988).

war were maintained long into the post-war years; in 1950, for example, the British Ministry of Food entered into a fifteen-year agreement guaranteeing Australia an assured market for its beef at a price no lower than its present level.[50]

After the end of rationing in Britain in 1954 both Britain and Australia began to find their preferential arrangements restrictive as they sought to expand and diversify their markets. Geography suggested that Australia might look more to East and South Asia and Britain towards Europe, although Britain's reactions were lukewarm during the negotiations leading to the establishment of the European Economic Community in March 1957.[51] Throughout the 1950s and 1960s Australia's Minister for Trade was the redoubtable (Sir) John McEwen, leader of the Country Party which was the junior partner in the conservative coalition government. As a young politician McEwen had seen the ill effects of the 1936 Trade Diversion Policy on woolgrowers and had listened to arguments that Australian primary producers were disadvantaged by the bulk-purchasing agreements of wartime. It was also clear that technological change and the stimulus of wartime had brought Britain nearer to agricultural self-sufficiency than at any time since the late eighteenth century; the third quarter of the twentieth century was to be a golden age for British farming. It behoved Australia to diversify its markets for primary produce.

In 1956 Australia sought a renegotiation of its commercial agreements with Britain, keeping its existing preferential treatment in Britain while gaining greater flexibility to seek trade benefits elsewhere; but the trade agreement signed in November 1956 did not significantly dismantle the existing arrangements. Both parties nevertheless were edging towards regional alignments that might in time supersede imperial preference. Australia signed a trade agreement with Japan in 1957 and began to find an increasing market for wheat in Communist China. Britain entered the rather ineffectual European Free Trade Agreement in 1959. At the end of the 1950s, however, Britain was still Australia's major source of trade and provided around 60 per cent of overseas private investment. Between 1956 and 1961 Australia was responsible for more than 58 per cent of all Commonwealth borrowings in the London market, and held £470 million in sterling reserves.[52]

---

[50] J. G. Crawford, *Australian Trade Policy 1942–1966: A Documentary History* (Canberra, 1968).
[51] H. G. Gelber, *Australia, Britain and the EEC, 1961 to 1963* (Melbourne, 1966).
[52] Ibid., pp. 58–9.

In the opinion of a qualified observer, Lord Carrington, British High Commissioner to Australia 1958–61, not enough was done to build on this pre-eminence: 'The British had the ball at their feet and threw the game away.' British business, Carrington discovered, 'was inclined to take the Australian market for granted. Some British enterprises had done very well, but British manufacturers seldom bothered to take Australian customers' needs into account'.[53] If this was the result of overfamiliarity, so was Australia's trust in the British connection. When Britain decided to seek admission to the European Economic Community in 1961 the Australian government expressed shock and dismay; Menzies allegedly remarked that in British eyes Australia no longer counted for a row of beans. Australia's protests, though strongly reinforced by New Zealand and Canada, were without effect. A respite came only when, after months of negotiation, General de Gaulle decided in January 1963 to veto Britain's entry into the Common Market.[54]

This episode cured Australian complacency about the British connection, and in economic terms it served to highlight trends which were already advancing. Between 1950/1 and 1962/3 Australian purchases from Britain dropped from 48 per cent to 30 per cent of an increased import total, and exports to Britain went down from 33 per cent to 18.6 per cent in the same period. Following the treaty of 1957 Japan was gaining ground as an Australian trading partner. Together with the United States, Japan also came forward as a major source of investment during Australia's 1960s mineral boom based on a massive increase in iron ore and coal exports. With apt symbolism, 1966, the year of Menzies' retirement, was also the year that the British government under Harold Wilson responded to a series of financial crises by ruling that preference in overseas investment should be given to underdeveloped countries rather than mature economies such as Australia. Renewed pressure on sterling during 1967 following an international oil crisis led to a 14 per cent devaluation. Under these financial constraints, although the Vietnam War was arousing fear of China's intentions, Britain decided on the withdrawal of its armed forces from South East Asia.[55]

[53] P. Carrington, *Reflect on Things Past: The Memoirs of Lord Carrington* (London, 1988), p. 134.

[54] Stuart Ward, *Australia and the British Embrace: The Demise of the Imperial Ideal* (Melbourne, 2001); J. G. Crawford, 'Britain, Australia and the Common Market', *Australian Outlook,* Vol. 15, no. 3 (1961), p. 221.

[55] John Darwin, *Britain and Decolonisation: The Retreat from Empire in the Postwar World* (London, 1988); Carl Bridge, ed., *Munich to Vietnam: Australia's Relations with Britain and the*

Australia's Prime Minister, John Gorton, was 'appalled and dismayed'. This policy, he said, would reduce Britain 'to a status a little less than Italy and a little more than Sweden'. The British government persisted, and relations with Australia cooled. Roy Jenkins, Britain's Chancellor of the Exchequer, found reason to fear 'a massive, immediate, and for us crippling switch of Australian sterling into gold or dollars. Not much kith and kin politics about that'.[56] The Gorton government talked the language of economic nationalism and reducing dependence on foreign investors. It was hardly surprising that in 1971 Britain negotiated itself into the European Economic Community without much compunction for Australian or New Zealand interests, and from then on the divergence between Britain and Australia quickened. Britain imposed restrictions on Australian passport holders in 1971, and Australia retaliated three years later with a visa requirement for Britons. Assisted immigration to Australia from Britain was scaled down in 1971 and terminated in 1974, thus ending the period when about half of Australia's migrants were of British origin. The Whitlam government (1972–5) began the lengthy process of dismantling Privy Council appeals and other relics of the colonial relationship.[57] Among its least fortunate initiatives was an attempt in 1974–5 to tap investment from Arab sources enriched by the oil crisis of the previous year through an unorthodox intermediary. The fiasco of the 'Khemlani affair' not only hastened Whitlam's downfall but also ended Australia's flirtation with economic nationalism. Overseas investment, having dwindled sharply during the Whitlam years, would resume under his successors after 1975, but its sources would be the old firms: Britain, but increasingly the United States and Japan.

In 1978 and 1979 Britain was still the nation contributing the largest single input of investment into Australia, but subsequently its share of Australian investment and trade fell inexorably. Paul Kelly has argued that imperial protection had been a major pillar of the Australian settlement during the first three-quarters of the twentieth century, and its withdrawal may have been a major factor in stimulating the deregulation since 1983 of the

United States since the 1930s (Carlton, 1991); Philip Ziegler, *Wilson: The Authorised Life* (London, 1993), chs. xiii and xvi; Andrea Benvenuti, ' "Layin' low and sayin' nuffin": Australia's policy towards Britain's second bid to join the European Economic Community, 1966–67', *Australian Economic History Review*, Vol. 46 (2006), pp. 155–75.

[56] *Age*, 21 July 1971, quoted by Bruce Grant, *The Crisis of Loyalty: A Study of Australian Foreign Policy* (Sydney, 1972), p. 14; Roy Jenkins, *Roy Jenkins in Australia* (Sydney, 1974).

[57] G. C. Bolton, 'The United Kingdom', in W. J. Hudson, ed., *Australia in World Affairs, 1971–1975* (Sydney, 1980), pp. 209–30.

Australian economy under the Hawke, Keating, and Howard governments.[58] But the myth of Britain as the major arena of business enterprise was still powerful enough during the 1980s to entice Australian-based entrepreneurs such as Alan Bond and John Elliott to overreach themselves by attempting to thrust into British companies.[59]

If their forays did not outlast the slump of 1987, a more substantial legacy remained. In 1992 a survey by Dun and Bradstreet showed that Australians owned 1,039 companies in Britain, ranking fifth among foreign countries owning British companies. It was not a one-way traffic, as the early 1990s saw something of a revival in British enterprise in Australia. In 1992 British Airways spent $665 million on acquiring a 25 per cent stake in Qantas; the Arena GSM consortium, controlled by British-based Vodafone, won the right to run Australia's third mobile telephone licence; and, in its biggest offshore deal, British Telecom won a ten-year contract to run the New South Wales government's communications network. By the beginning of the twenty-first century Britain stood sixth among Australia's trading partners and was a comparatively minor, but not insignificant, source of investment. Perhaps it would be reasonable to argue that the old springs of Anglo-Australian economic interdependence were losing themselves in the wider sea of globalization.

Yet the referendum of 1999 showed that Australia was not yet ready to cut its ties with the British monarchy and to heed the trumpets of republicanism. Although this was the result of divisions within the republican movement, it may be doubted whether the ebb and flow of Australian nationalism has much been affected by changing patterns in British trade and investment. Conservative knights have flouted British interests, Labor governments have treated them with solicitude—sometimes; and sometimes the reverse has been true. Australia's relationship with Britain has sometimes been brought into public debate as a by-product of Australian party political manoeuvres, but these have little to do with the actual historical record. Undoubtedly, British trade and investment have played a pre-eminent role in Australian economic development, and the chapter has not yet closed. This role was often facilitated by a shared culture, which gave rise to occasional misunderstandings and recriminations whenever either party placed self-interest ahead of the implied obligations of the imperial family. But there is

---

[58] Paul Kelly, *The End of Certainty: The Story of the 1980s* (St Leonards, 1992).

[59] Trevor Sykes, *The Bold Riders* (St Leonards, 1994), pp. 216–20.

little to suggest that these periodic difficulties fostered the emergence of a separatist Australian national sentiment.

Select Bibliography

R. T. APPLEYARD and C. B. SCHEDVIN, eds, *Australian Financiers: Bio-graphical Essays* (Melbourne, 1988).

MELANIE BERESFORD and PRUE KERR, 'A Turning Point for Australian Capitalism 1942–1952', in E. L. Wheelwright and K. Buckley, eds, *Essays in the Political Economy of Australian Capitalism*, Vol. 4 (Sydney, 1980), pp. 148–71.

N. G. BUTLIN, *Investment in Australian Economic Development 1861–1900* (Cambridge, 1964).

J. G. CRAWFORD, *Australian Trade Policy 1942–1966: A Documentary History* (Canberra, 1968).

DONALD DENOON, *Settler Capitalism: The Dynamics of Dependent Development in the Southern Hemisphere* (Oxford, 1983).

BRIAN FITZPATRICK, *British Imperialism in Australia 1783–1833* (London, 1939).

—— *The British Empire in Australia: An Economic History 1834–1939* (Melbourne, 1941).

A. R. HALL, *The London Capital Market and Australia, 1870–1914* (Canberra, 1963).

PAUL KELLY, *The End of Certainty: The Story of the 1980s* (St Leonards, 1992).

DAVID LEE, *Search for Security: The Political Economy of Australia's Postwar Foreign and Defence Policy* (St Leonards, 1995).

C. B. SCHEDVIN, *Australia and the Great Depression: A Study of Economic Development and Policy in the 1920s and 1930s* (Sydney, 1970).

KOSMAS TSOKHAS, *Making a Nation State: Identity, Economic Nationalism and Sexuality in Australian History* (Carlton, 2001).

SIMON VILLE, 'Niemeyer, Scullin and the Australian Economists', *Australian Economic History Review*, Vol. 44, (2004), pp. 143–60.

STUART WARD, *Australia and the British Embrace: The Demise of the Imperial Ideal* (Carlton South, 2001).

10

Security: Defending Australia's Empire

STUART WARD

Every day on Sydney Harbour, thousands of commuters, day-trippers, and pleasure craft sail past one of Australia's most imposing relics of Empire. The squat, sandstone-clad Martello tower of Fort Denison, with its views of the Opera House and Harbour Bridge, has become in recent years a popular tourist destination, and an exclusive setting for weddings, corporate functions, and New Year's Eve parties. But for all its status as a Sydney landmark, few who sail by ever pause to consider its significance. As one of the last fortifications of its kind ever built in the British Empire (and one whose structure and purpose had become obsolete by the time of its completion in 1857), Fort Denison staged no glorious scenes of military derring-do, no defining historical moment that might have etched its importance into the national consciousness. Its major selling point as a tourist attraction is precisely its lack of military engagement, which has enabled it to survive as one of the world's finest examples of the Martello fortress design. As a monument to Australia's imperial past, however, it remains impregnable to contemporary scrutiny—apparently untouched by the mythologizing power of historical experience.

Yet both the original purpose of Fort Denison and the circumstances surrounding its construction speak volumes about the problem of defending Australia's Empire. Constructed in the mid-1850s under the governorship of William Denison, the Fort was the direct outcome of one of Australia's first invasion scares. The occasion was the Crimean War—a conflict in which colonial sympathies were almost unanimously in support of Britain's struggle against imperial Russia. And it was these very sympathies that brought the question of the defence of the colonies to the fore. Shortly after news of the outbreak of hostilities reached Sydney, a public meeting was convened in York Street to express the colony's determination 'to maintain to the utmost of their ability ... the security of this portion of her Majesty's empire'. Speech after speech by 'the most respectable inhabitants of the city' pointed anxiously to the vulnerability of the Australian colonies.[1] Although the war was being waged in the remote waters of the Black Sea, Russia was also a Pacific power that might conceivably raise trouble closer to home—either for the purpose of stripping the colony of valuable assets, or merely for the sake of striking a morale-boosting blow against the British. It was with these fears in mind that one speaker complained of 'the failure of every scheme which had been propounded in by-gone years for the defence of the harbour', leaving the colony 'open to every assault'. Major Thomas Mitchell was supremely confident that Britain would triumph in the Crimea, but added wryly that in the meantime he 'should not like to have his house knocked about his ears'. The colonial politician John Darvall summed up the prevailing anxiety: 'Situated as this colony [is] in such a crisis', Australians had 'all to lose' should Russia prevail.

Of the dozen or so speakers who addressed the meeting, only one had the temerity to suggest that it was precisely the colony's wholesale support of Britain in the Crimea that lent credibility to talk of a Russian naval bombardment. The prominent Australian republican John Dunmore Lang protested that 'we [are] an isolated colony, and not in any way mixed up in the disputes pending between the mother country and Russia'. He ridiculed the 'virtual declaration of war on the part of this puny colony against the whole Russian Empire', and urged his fellow colonists to reconsider a course that might transform the tranquil Pacific into 'a scene of bloodshed and turmoil such as was hardly surpassed in the annals of the Old World'. While he had every admiration and sympathy for the British people, and a 'genuine attachment to her Majesty and the British nation', he felt bound to recognize the 'sheer absurdity and impotence' of a defenceless colony going out of its way to provoke one of the most powerful nations in the world. For Lang, it was Australia's vulnerable strategic outlook that applied the brake to his imperial ardour. He impressed upon his audience his grave doubts 'whether Britain now would be able in times of war to defend all her numerous colonies'. Indeed he regarded this prospect as 'physically impossible'.

Thus began one of the most enduring debates in Australian history. How was Australia's tenuous hold on a remote British outpost to be secured against external threats? For the overwhelming majority of those present at the 1854 meeting, it was unswerving adherence to the Empire's cause, wherever it may

[1] The following account is taken from the exhaustive summary of proceedings reported in the *Sydney Morning Herald* on 23 May 1854. See also Mark McKenna, *The Captive Republic: A History of Republicanism in Australia, 1788–1996* (Cambridge, 1996), pp. 86–9.

be, that offered the best guarantee of the defence of Australia. In the words of James Norton, solicitor and Leichhardt estate-holder, it was the cultivation of mutual affection and 'enthusiasm' between the colonies and the Mother Country that provided the one and only 'safeguard against the attacks of the enemy'. Lang's attempt to argue the contrary view was vigorously shouted down—indeed at one point he almost had to abandon his speech amid the general tumult. As with later advocates of this view, his isolationism was condemned as the reckless ravings of a man whose loyalties seemed clearly compromised. Yet even the most ardent loyalists were prone to nagging doubts about the security guarantee afforded by the British fleet, and urged the necessity of making local provisions for the defence of the colony.

Denison himself, arriving in Sydney a few months after the Crimean outbreak, expressed his astonishment at 'the panic which led people in these colonies to insist upon fortifying themselves against the Russians'. But he recognized the woeful defences of the harbour, and could not rule out the prospect that he might be awoken one morning by 'a 32lb. shot crashing through the walls of my house'. He therefore set about the construction of Fort Denison—one of the first fully manned and operational fortifications in Australia—partly as a political measure to quieten the locals, and partly as insurance for the future against what he considered the more credible threats in the Pacific posed by the Americans and the French.[2] Significantly, however, in reaching this solution he appealed to the Colonial Office to pay greater heed in future to the peculiar anxieties of the Australian colonists. He suggested that it would bind the colonies 'more cordially to the Mother Country', and avoid the confusion and misunderstanding of the Crimean panic, if greater stress could be laid on 'the community of interest between the Mother Country and the Colony which renders the defence of the latter a matter of importance to the former'.[3]

Here lay the nub of the problem. Few doubted the existence of a deep-rooted community of language, culture, and constitutional principles that bound the Australian colonies to Britain—indeed, even Lang himself affirmed it. But when it came to the 'community of interest', colonial Australians were inclined to see their own, distinctive problems as an under-populated, under-resourced, and largely defenceless outpost in what seemed

---

[2] William Denison to Roderick Murchison, 21 May 1855, quoted in A. B. Shaw, *Fort Denison, Sydney Harbour* (Sydney, undated), p. 7.

[3] William Dinison, official dispatch dated 10 April 1856, Mitchell Library, Sydney, Denison Correspondence, FM3/795.

to them a remote and potentially volatile part of the world. While the defence of Australia might indeed be a 'matter of importance' to British interests, it would never assume the same critical importance as it had for the colonists themselves. Denison's emphasis on the 'community of interest' between Australia and Britain was to remain a core assumption of Australian defence thinking for more than a century, but this would always be understood in terms of the peculiar needs of 'Australia's Empire'. And to that extent it held out the potential for endless misunderstanding. Fort Denison thus stands not only as a reminder of Australia's instinctive identification with an imperial cause, but also as a remnant of settler-colonial anxieties about the promise of imperial defence.

In the early colonial period, episodes like the Crimean War 'panic' were relatively few and far between. For the most part, it was Australia's isolation from the affairs of Europe that afforded the best guarantee of the colonies' physical security. With the conclusion of the war in 1856, the spectre of naval bombardment subsided quickly and the public 'tended to lapse into their old apathy'.[4] In 1858, the *Sydney Morning Herald* poured scorn on the 'fools' who 'can now laugh at fears they no longer feel', while the task of securing the colonies against external attack remained unresolved.[5]

Yet within a decade or so this situation began to change, and the search for some durable means of holding potential adversaries in the region at bay was begun in earnest. Mounting political tensions in Europe and the ensuing 'scramble' for Empire among the great powers coincided with the withdrawal of the British garrisons from Australia in 1870. This came at the end of a period of extended debate in Britain about the financing of British troop deployments in self-governing colonies. In the words of one 1862 House of Commons resolution: 'Colonies exercising the rights of self-government ought to undertake the main responsibility of providing for their own internal order and security, and ought to assist in their own external defence.'[6]

These developments raised obvious questions about the defence of the colonies against any extension of European rivalries into Pacific waters. The defeat of France by Prussia in 1870 was interpreted as a sign of the inevitable

---

[4] Roger C. Thompson, *Australian Imperialism in the Pacific: The Expansionist Era, 1820–1920* (Melbourne, 1980), p. 22.

[5] *Sydney Morning Herald*, 12 December 1856.

[6] Quoted in Peter Burroughs, 'Defence and Imperial Disunity', in Andrew Porter, ed., *The Oxford History of the British Empire. Vol. III: The Nineteenth Century* (Oxford, 1999), p. 328.

escalation of conflict between the peoples of Europe. The *Sydney Morning Herald* proclaimed the arrival of a new 'epoch in which the war of the races has clearly begun', with immediate repercussions for the Australian colonies: 'The course of events is tending to destroy the security which Australians hitherto found in isolation ... Space and distance have lost their old meaning. The great net of international rivalry catches the whole world in its sweep.'[7] Two years later, the completion of the telegraph link to London brought an even greater immediacy to the distant conflagrations of the Old World. In anticipation of the telegraphic revolution, Archibald Michie entertained his fellow-colonists with a future vision when 'millions of British citizens may any morning be mustered by the wires for defence of any part' of the Empire.[8]

The expansion of European empires into the Pacific was a cause of genuine concern in Australia and New Zealand, serving both to magnify as well as to refine imperial sensibilities, and prompting the colonial governments to promote a programme of expansionism of their own. It was in July 1870 that the colonial Premiers, meeting in Melbourne, first gave collective voice to their Pacific ambitions, calling on the British government to annex the Fiji islands. But in the following decade they went on to extend their wish-list to include New Guinea, the New Hebrides, and the Solomon Islands among others. In an adaptation of American practice, they dubbed this an 'Australasian Monroe Doctrine for the Pacific', designed to deny European rivals any foothold in the Pacific from which they might threaten the Australian or New Zealand coastline. In the words of Victorian Premier James Service, the policy was based on 'no lust of territory or expectation of the immediate settlement of the islands of the Pacific'. Rather, the objective was the more limited one of keeping 'the English people in these distant lands as far removed as possible from the dangers arising out of European complications'.[9] There are indications that Queensland, at least, had ulterior motives relating to the Pacific Island labour trade.[10] But it remains significant

[7] Quoted in Neville Meaney, ed., *Under New Heavens: Cultural Transmission and the Making of Australia* (Melbourne, 1989), p. 398.

[8] K. S. Inglis, 'The Imperial Connection: Telegraphic Communication Between England and Australia, 1872–1902', in A. F. Madden and W. H. Morris-Jones, eds, *Australia and Britain: Studies in a Changing Relationship* (Sydney, 1980), p. 34; K. T. Livingstone, *The Wired Nation Continent: The Communications Revolution and Federating Australia* (Melbourne, 1996).

[9] Quoted in Neville Meaney, *The Search for Security in the Pacific, 1901–1914* (Sydney, 1976), pp. 16–17.

[10] Clive Moore, 'Queensland's annexation of New Guinea in 1883', *Royal Historical Society of Queensland Journal*, Vol. 12, no. 1 (1984), pp. 26–54.

that, even here, security imperatives seemed so impelling as to provide an ideal pretext for more commercially minded activities. Australia's imperial ambitions in the Pacific—or 'sub-imperialism' as Roger C. Thompson has termed it—flowed logically out of a perceived strategic vulnerability.[11]

The British authorities in no way shared the colonists' desire to add these widely scattered Pacific islands to an already unwieldy and burdensome Empire. Even the more imperially minded Disraeli government blanched at the idea of occupying New Guinea, particularly when it emerged that the Australian colonies had no intention of contributing to the cost. Disraeli's rejection of colonial demands underlined a fundamental dilemma: the Australian colonies were committed to an imperial strategy as a means of securing their interests in the Pacific, but the ultimate arbiter of imperial policy—the British government—could not be relied upon to accord those interests a high priority. On the contrary, seen from Britain, the colonists' demands seemed overblown, their fears unfounded, and their interests secondary. The colonial governments were thus confronted with the contradictions in William Denison's key premise—that an imperial 'community of interest' would provide the foundation of colonial defence. In affirming their mutual commitment to Empire, the British and colonial governments were not necessarily speaking the same language.

In 1883 the Queensland government sought to resolve this innate dilemma by taking matters into its own hands. In response to press rumours about an impending German annexation of New Guinea, Premier Thomas McIlwraith moved unilaterally to claim the eastern half of the island on behalf of the British Empire. In a hastily improvised ceremony, the Union Jack was hoisted over Port Moresby and a toast proposed 'to the latest gem added to the British Crown'.[12] The British Crown, for its part, was only informed of this new acquisition after the fact, much to the irritation of the Colonial Office. Despite the support of all the other colonies for Queensland's action, the Colonial Secretary, Lord Derby, refused to endorse this pre-emptive strike, and demanded a complete withdrawal. He dismissed as groundless Queensland's suspicions of Germany, and recorded his incredulity when a delegation of Australian Agents-General visited him in June 1883:

[They] came to me with a gigantic scheme of annexation, including not only New Guinea, but the New Hebrides, Samoa & in fact all the South Pacific within about

---

[11] Thompson, *Australian Imperialism in the Pacific*, p. 1.
[12] Quoted in Moore, 'Queensland's Annexation', p. 28.

1000 to 1500 miles from the Australian coast. They were very much in earnest, said this was a turning pointing in the fortunes of Australia, the danger was imminent, any foreign settlement established near them would be their ruin. I asked them more than once why or how? but could get no answer. I tried a little mild sarcasm, asking them whether they did not want a whole planet to themselves … but I found the matter too serious for joking: they could not think themselves safe in a country as big as Europe if Italy or Germany had a harbour within three of four days steaming of their shores.[13]

Derby made little effort to conceal his view that Australian defence anxieties were as irrational as they were self-indulgent. In response, the colonial Premiers at a meeting in Sydney expressed their indignation at Britain's indifference to their collective security needs. They resolved 'that further acquisition of dominion in the Pacific, south of the Equator, by any Foreign Power, would be highly detrimental to the safety and well-being of the British possessions in Australasia, and injurious to the interests of the Empire'.[14] And on this occasion they undertook to pay a share of the cost of securing the Pacific against unwanted European rivals.

In this they assumed the convergence of imperial and Australasian interests, but again they were to be disappointed. Gladstone's ministry was engaged in difficult negotiations with France and Germany over British involvement in Egypt and the Mediterranean, and from this perspective the Queensland government's actions were regarded as an unnecessary impediment to the 'interests of the Empire'. The colonial governments, for their part, were equally incredulous when the British later conceded the north-east portion of New Guinea to Germany in 1886, in return for Germany's recognition of Britain's claim to the south-east portion. Although the Queensland government acquired a share in the administration of the new territory, the entire deal ran counter to their original aims in annexing the island—to keep the Germans out, not welcome them in. James Service voiced his 'boundless' exasperation: 'I protest in the name of the present and future of Australia. If England does not yet save us from the danger and disgrace, as far at least as New Guinea is concerned, the bitterness of feeling

---

[13] Diary entry, 28 June 1883, quoted in Graeme Powell, 'A Diarist in the Cabinet: Lord Derby and the Australian Colonies, 1882–85', *Australian Journal of Politics and History*, Vol. 51, no. 4 (2005), pp. 489–90.

[14] Quoted in Neville Meaney, ed., *Australia and the World: A Documentary History from the 1870s to the 1970s* (Melbourne, 1985), pp. 60–1, 63.

towards her will not die out in this generation.'[15] It was intolerable, he wrote to the Governor of Victoria, that Australia should have to 'stand by and see territories, the possession of which she regards as essential to her safety and well being, pass to another power'.[16]

The problem of reconciling Australian security concerns with wider imperial strategy was to have a number of significant repercussions in Australia. In particular, it prompted the colonies to look to their own defences. From 1870, with the departure of the British garrisons, the colonial governments recognized the inadequacy of part-time voluntary militias, and gradually began to introduce paid, permanent forces that might be better subject to military discipline. The late 1870s and 1880s were also a busy period for the erection of fortifications, with new batteries built to defend Sydney, Melbourne, Hobart, Brisbane, Adelaide, Newcastle, Wollongong, and Townsville. On the advice of British military experts Sir William Jervois and Peter Scratchley, these fortifications were designed to defend against coastal attacks and were conceived, not as a substitute for the protection of the Royal Navy, but rather a means of holding out against seaborne raids while help was on its way. These developments, marked as they were by considerable increases in defence expenditure, were not, however, part of a continent-wide plan or even of an integrated policy within each colony.

It was for this reason that security concerns were among the earliest impulses towards the Federation of the Australian colonies. One of the forerunners of Federation, the ill-fated Federal Council of Australasia, had been set up in 1883 as a direct response to the British government's rejection of Queensland's New Guinea adventure. The Council was given jurisdiction over 'the relations of Australasia with the islands of the Pacific', so that the imperial authorities might understand that the colonies spoke with one voice on Pacific matters. Later in the decade, a report on the scant defences of the Australian colonies by Major General J. Bevan Edwards became the catalyst for the Federation debates of the 1890s. Henry Parkes took the Edwards report as his point of departure in his celebrated 'Tenterfield Speech' of October 1889, in which he called for a Federal constitution in order to 'preserve the security and integrity' of the colonies. Indeed, he referred to no other argument for Federation whatsoever.[17]

---

[15] Quoted in Thompson, *Australian Imperialism in the Pacific*, p. 92.
[16] *The Age*, 25 December 1884 in Meaney, *Australia and the World*, p. 68.
[17] W. G. McMinn, *Nationalism and Federalism in Australia* (Melbourne, 1994), pp. 106, 132–3.

From the late 1880s, Australian security anxieties were shifting towards what Parkes termed a 'new awakening Asia'. China became the new focus of invasion fears, not because of any studied appraisal of Chinese designs on Australia, but because of the assumed tenets of natural law. Thus Francis Adams, an intellectual and social commentator, writing in the radical journal *Boomerang*, could cast his mind back a thousand years to the disappearance of the Hindu civilization of Borobudur in Java—'Aryans as well as we are'—and draw the obvious lessons of history: 'The Asiatic ... must either conquer or be conquered by, must either wipe out or be wiped out by the Aryan and the European.'[18] These views were given academic respectability by Charles Henry Pearson's highly influential *National Life and Character* in 1893, which predicted that the Chinese 'will sooner or later overflow their borders and spread over new territory, and submerge weaker races'. Australia's proximity to these dangers seemed self-evident. 'We will wake', Pearson warned, 'to find ourselves elbowed and hustled, and perhaps even thrust aside.'[19] While these views were subjected to vigorous criticism and dispute, the disagreement was more over whether the Chinese could, rather than would, seal the fate of White British Australia. It was a question of means rather than ambition—the former was open to question, the latter generally taken for granted. Henry Parkes believed that the most likely means available to the Chinese was the insidious, cumulative movements of population. At the Federation Convention of 1891, he declared that when the day of reckoning with China arrived, 'it will not be by the bombardment of one of our rich cities' but by 'stealthily effecting a lodgement in some thinly-peopled portion of the country, where it would take immense loss of life and immense loss of wealth to dislodge the invader. I think that the new form of warfare from which we may suffer is almost certain to take that form.'[20]

These perceived dangers arising out of Asia emerged at a time when an imperial civic culture was taking root in Australia. While adherence to British institutions and values, and an inevitable affection for the 'home' country, had long permeated public life in the colonies, it was only during the late-Victorian atmosphere of looming crisis that colonial identities became securely anchored within a pan-British ethnic framework. It was in this

---

[18] Quoted in David Walker, *Anxious Nation* (St Lucia, 1999), pp. 40–1.

[19] Charles Henry Pearson, *National Life and Character: A Forecast* (London, 1894), pp. 41, 90.

[20] Henry Parkes, 13 March 1891, *National Australasian Convention Debates* (Sydney, 1891), p. 316.

era that the imperial federation movement took hold, the civic worship of Queen Victoria acquired overt imperial trappings, Empire Day was adopted, and volunteers were recruited to serve an imperial cause in the Sudan and later South Africa. A. B. Patterson's refrain that 'those who fight the British Isles, must fight the British race' might not have stirred the passions of earlier generations of volunteer militia. But given the prevailing ideological context of the inevitability of racial struggle, the cause of the British peoples all over the world necessarily became Australia's cause. Thus, George Cathcart Craig, in advocating the *Federal Defence of Australasia* in 1897, could dedicate his volume 'to those noble sons of the British race at Home or in the Colonies, true to kith and kin, and who glory in the name of Anglo-Australian'.[21] Even those groupings who did not necessarily 'glory' in the achievements of the British race could be nonetheless reconciled to that vision by the imperatives of imperial defence. The Irish-Australian social reformer Edward O'Sullivan, for example, advocated the unity of the 'Anglo-Celtic race', proclaiming in 1895: 'What does it matter what reforms we attempt to make, or what progress we make in social legislation or in other respects, if, after all, we are liable to a sudden attack by an overwhelming force, which may beat down all those reforms, and throw us back in the race of progress?'[22]

This is not to say that the emergent race patriotism was simply an emotional response to the needs of physical and material security. The idea of a 'greater British' nation was as much a response to the wider processes of rapid modernization that brought forth, across the whole western world, new types of community allegiances and loyalties that were couched in the language and ideology of nationalism. This was a concept of 'the people' that appeared, in various guises, in all parts of the British settler Empire, from which it can be inferred that its Australian variant emerged independently of any specific threat to Australian security. Indeed it may well be the case that the widely perceived dangers to Australia were themselves construed out of a 'Greater British' habit of mind. As often as not, it was the latent British sensibilities of Australian colonists that determined how external threats were identified and understood *as threatening*. Looked at dispassionately, French occupation of the New Hebrides need not have concerned Australians any more than the contemporaneous American seizure of Hawaii (or the later US occupation of the Philippines). That one stirred colonial anxieties

---

[21] George Cathcart Craig, *The Federal Defence of Australasia* (Sydney, 1897), p. 2.

[22] Quoted in Craig Wilcox, *For Hearths and Homes: Citizen Soldiering in Australia, 1854–1945* (Sydney, 1998), p. 22.

while the other seemed vaguely reassuring was, in itself, an expression of the colonists fundamental identification with an imperial and racialized world view (with the Americans—not for the last time—standing in as 'Anglo-Saxon' cousins).[23] Nonetheless, the fact that Anglo-Saxon racialism was far more pronounced and absolute in Australia than in Canada or indeed Great Britain itself can in large part be put down to the perceived sense of strategic vulnerability that came with being one of the most far-flung of Britain's imperial outposts.

Fashioning a defence policy that might live up to these expectations of racial unity was to become the source of countless disagreements with Britain in the first sixty years of a federated Australia. The British government proved to be no more concerned about an Asian threat to Australia than it had been about German and French ambitions in the Pacific. The Japanese victory over Russia in the Battle of Tsushima in May 1905 underlined Japan's emerging naval strength in the region. Within weeks of the victory, Australian Prime Minister Alfred Deakin voiced his concerns publicly: 'As a fact, Japan is the nearest of all the great foreign naval nations to Australia. Japan at her headquarters is, so to speak, next door, while the Mother Country is many streets away, and connected by long lines of communications.'[24] Again, this statement emphasized how different the Empire looked when viewed from Australia. It also underlined how Australia's security anxieties were clearly shifting from China to Japan. The British response, however, was to renew the Anglo-Japanese Alliance a few months later, so as to enable them to withdraw their capital ships from the Pacific and meet the rapidly escalating naval competition from Germany in European waters. For the Australian government, the idea of leaving the protection of imperial territories in East Asia to the Japanese fleet seemed almost perverse. This implicit downgrading of the Pacific in Britain's global strategy caused Australians—reluctantly—to question the reliability of the Royal Navy.

It was a renowned Australian imperialist, F. W. Eggleston, who first elucidated the 'two ocean dilemma' in a 1912 essay. The build-up of naval rivalry between Britain and Germany, he argued, had raised an acute dilemma for imperial and Australian security interests. He surmised that should Germany and Japan join forces at some point, Britain

---

[23] See, for example, *The Age*, 21 November 1892; 25 June 1897. The American annexation was grudgingly welcomed as a check against the Japanese gaining a crucial foothold in the Pacific.

[24] *The Herald* (Melbourne), 12 June 1905.

would be forced to jettison all of its obligations in the Pacific in order to meet the threat at home. Although himself an advocate of imperial federation, Eggleston was forced to conclude: 'Hitherto Australians have relied upon England alone for the conduct of policy, and willingly; for they conceived the interests of both parts of the Empire to be the same. Now that we find that the defence of Australia depends upon an entirely different set of problems from those which face England the Australian point of view is inclined to change.' This was a remarkably prescient critique of the 'community of interest' doctrine. In an echo of John Dunmore Lang, Eggleston concluded: 'Can any nation depend for its defence upon a foreign policy conducted by statesmen responsible to another nation?'[25]

Unlike Lang, however, Eggleston had no separatist inclinations. His passionate belief in 'the unity of the British race and its mission of civilization to the world' helped to shape his view of the Asia-Pacific region as inherently alien and menacing.[26] Yet it was precisely the unique challenges of living in these un-British surroundings that prompted him to view Australia in a different light, setting it apart from the British of Britain. In other words, Eggleston distinguished between his Australian and British loyalties, not in terms of distinctive ethnic or cultural criteria, but in terms of the realities of divergent interests. This same logic prompted Alfred Deakin, pre-empting Eggleston by a few months, to pronounce in the House of Representatives: 'Australia, in spite of herself, is being forced into a foreign policy of her own because foreign interests and risks surround us on every side. A Pacific policy we must have.'[27] Deakin's words were quite deliberate and deserve careful attention. In spite of a perceived British civic and cultural ethos which united the Australians and the British as one people, the realities of divergent security concerns compelled him to fashion a national defence and foreign policy.

At this time, Australian defence strategy was concerned as much with policy as with the means to implement it. Neither Eggleston nor Deakin envisaged an entirely self-sufficient Australian defence force that alone might compensate for Britain's preoccupation with the gathering crisis in Europe. Instead, Deakin turned to Australia's 'Anglo-Saxon cousins' for support. In 1908 he invited President Theodore Roosevelt to allow America's 'Great

---

[25] Warren G. Osmond, *Frederic Eggleston: An Intellectual in Australian Politics* (Sydney, 1985), pp. 60, 63.

[26] See Chapter 15, pp. 375–6.   [27] Quoted in Meaney, *Under New Heavens*, p. 407.

White Fleet' to visit Australia during its world tour. The overwhelming warmth and enthusiasm with which the Americans were greeted went far beyond good neighbourly relations. In the words of one of the many popular verses penned for the occasion, the expectation was that America would join forces with their British brethren against the Asian menace:

> Not heedless of your high descent,
> The grand old Anglo-Saxon race,
> To check with stern unflinching mace
> The swarming, hungry Orient.[28]

The following year (and in a similar vein), Deakin first floated the idea of a Pacific pact which would extend the United States' Monroe Doctrine to the Pacific.

Nonetheless, the chief priority of the Australian government lay in the formulation of an imperial defence policy that would safeguard Australia against the threat of Japan. When the Admiralty at the 1909 Imperial Defence Conference put forward the idea of an imperial Pacific fleet composed of Australian, Canadian, and British squadrons, the Australians responded immediately and enthusiastically by contributing to the common cause. The British proposal came at a time when the government was contemplating the establishment of an Australian Navy, and raised the difficult question of how far an Australian fleet should be subject to the control of the British Admiralty. As the Minister for Defence, Joseph Cook, told Parliament in 1909, 'We must remember, first of all, that Australia is part of the Empire, and that within our means we must recognise both our Imperial and local responsibilities ... it is our duty to add to the fleet strength of the Empire.'[29] At the same time, however, it was assumed that in fulfilling this duty, Australia was also claiming a greater say in the deployment of the combined 'strength of the Empire'. And this implied clear limits to Australian compliance in British strategic planning. When, for example, in 1914 the British requested that the Australian fleet be moved to Europe from the Pacific (where, it was intimated, it was not needed), in order to counter the looming German threat, the Australian government refused. Cook insisted that Australia 'could not rely upon the Japanese treaty alone

---

[28] F. J. Burnell in the *Sydney Morning Herald*, 21 August 1908.
[29] Quoted in Peter Dennis, et al., eds, *The Oxford Companion to Australian Military History* (Oxford, 1995), p. 517.

for the peace of the Pacific'. Australians, he said, 'had their white Australia policy and they must at all cost defend it'.[30] Again, this betrayed a lack of trust in the underlying assumptions of imperial defence, and a residual fear that Australia might indeed be forced to rely on its own devices in the Pacific.

The onset of the First World War brought Australia and Japan together as wartime allies, with Japanese battle cruisers helping to escort the first contingent of the Australian Imperial Force to Europe. But Australian suspicions of Japanese ambitions in the Pacific remained. Labor leader Andrew Fisher's instinctive pledge of 'our last man and our last shilling' to the imperial war effort was carefully qualified five days later by a (now largely forgotten) elucidation of Australian priorities—namely to 'provide first for our own defence, and then, if there was anything to spare, offer it as a tribute to the Mother County'.[31] Ultimately Fisher was to contribute far more than loose change, but it is significant that in the early stages of the war he grappled rhetorically with two rival conceptions of defence policy—one which viewed imperial and Australian defence imperatives as virtually synonymous ('our interests and our very existence are bound up with those of the empire') and another which saw them as part of a carefully graded set of potentially conflicting priorities.

Australian suspicions of Japanese ambitions in the Pacific resurfaced during the conscription referenda of 1916 and 1917, when both the 'yes' and 'no' campaigns appealed to the danger that Japan might suddenly take advantage of the strategic situation and turn belligerent.[32] But it was at the Paris Peace Conference in 1919 that Australian anxieties about Japan came sharply back into focus. Here, Prime Minister Billy Hughes fought 'root and branch' (in the words of a Japanese delegate) to prevent the insertion of a racial equality provision in the League of Nations covenant. The mere fact of Australia's participation in the Conference—independently of Britain—signalled that Hughes had taken on board the message of Deakin and Eggleston: British diplomacy could not be relied upon to secure Australia's strategic objectives in the Pacific. This was borne out by Hughes' trenchant opposition to anything that smacked of a concession to the Japanese. He rejected a series of compromise formulae put forward

---

[30] Quoted in Neville Meaney, *Towards a New Vision: Australia and Japan Through 100 Years* (Sydney, 1999), p. 68.

[31] *The Argus*, 5 August 1914.   [32] On the conscription debate see Chapter 8, pp. 206–7.

by the Japanese which would have been acceptable to other delegations, including the British and South African. On the subject of Australia's annexation of German colonial possessions in New Guinea he was equally stubborn. Armed with a map of the world centred on Australia, he sought to demonstrate to the Conference that 'if there were at the very door of Australia a potential or actual enemy [read Japan] Australia could not feel safe'.[33] For Hughes, the imperative of preserving a British Australia—'more British than the people of Great Britain' as he put it—was absolute. He would sooner 'walk into the Seine—or the Folies-Bergère—with my clothes off' than give way on principles that secured the very foundation of White British Australia.[34]

The post-war settlement failed to allay Australian fears about potential Japanese aggression. Throughout the interwar years, Australian defence planning became increasingly dependent on the so-called Singapore strategy, in which the security of British interests in Asia and the Pacific were to be guaranteed by the construction of an imposing naval base in Singapore. The Singapore base served as a kind of talisman, reassuring Australians that something large and impregnable would guard the sea lanes between Australia and Japan. The precise details of how Singapore would keep Australia free from foreign aggression were never fully worked out, and were even disputed by some military experts. Indeed, Prime Minister S. M. Bruce made the extraordinary remark at the 1923 Imperial Conference: 'While I am not quite as clear as I should like to be as to how the protection of Singapore is to be assured, I am clear on this point, that apparently it can be done.'[35] Bruce's observation combined the complacent certainty that came with membership of the world's most powerful naval Empire, with the perennial doubts about the capacity of that Empire to accommodate a variety of divergent material interests.

The real question mark over the Singapore strategy was the 'two ocean' dilemma. In theory, the base could be reinforced by a British fleet within six weeks of any sign of trouble. But would a fleet be dispatched at all if Britain were entangled at the same time in Europe or the Mediterranean? This

[33] W. J. Hudson, *Billy Hughes in Paris: The Birth of Australian Diplomacy* (Melbourne, 1978), p. 20.

[34] Hughes was eventually forced to give in on the principle of 'annexing' New Guinea for Australia, having to settle instead for Woodrow Wilson's concept of a League of Nations 'mandate'. Peter Spartalis, *The Diplomatic Battles of Billy Hughes* (Sydney, 1983), p. 175.

[35] Quoted in Jeffrey Grey, *A Military History of Australia* (Cambridge, 1999), p. 23.

question became increasingly pressing in the 1930s, with the rearmament of Germany and the emergent imperialism of the Japanese. The Lyons government repeatedly put the question to the British government, and invariably received the same assurances. During a 1934 visit to Australia, Britain's senior civil servant, Sir Maurice Hankey, responded to Australian misgivings with the familiar community of interest theme. 'It was not likely', he said, 'that Britain was going to let her vast interests in the Far East go by default.'[36] In a report to the Australian government his assurance was even more absolute: 'Even in the very extreme case of simultaneous trouble in Europe and the Far East', he reasoned, Britain's naval strength was 'sufficient to enable a numerically superior battle fleet to be sent to the Far East and yet leave a small margin of strength in both theatres.' In reality, Hankey could never have backed this statement up. As he was well aware at the time, the British service chiefs were at loggerheads with the National government of Ramsay MacDonald over Britain's thinly stretched naval defences, and the paltry sums being spent on rearmament. In a confidential dispatch to Stanley Baldwin, Hankey warned that any admission that Britain could not 'assert sea power in the Pacific' would be 'absolutely shattering' in Australia, adding: 'No greater blow could be dealt to the unity of the Empire.'[37]

Not everyone in Australia took British assurances at face value. The Army chiefs in particular questioned the logic of the Singapore strategy, pointing out that 'what for Britain is merely the acceptance of a risk means for Australia the facing of imminent disaster. Australia, with her various interests, is part of the stake, and is therefore not in a position to take a detached view of the question.'[38] The Chief of the General Staff, Colonel J. D. Lavarack, was even blunter: 'There is very little better reason for following British advice on local defence than there would be for following Australian advice on the defence of London.'[39] In rejecting Hankey's views, one member of the Australian Staff Corps, Major H. C. H. Robertson, quoted an alternative British assessment by Admiral Sir Richard Webb: 'To imagine that we are going to uncover the heart of Empire and send our fleet thousands of miles

[36] Quoted in Eric Andrews, *The Department of Defence: The Australian Centenary History of Defence, Vol. V* (Oxford, 2001), p. 82.

[37] Eric Andrews, *The Writing on the Wall: The British Commonwealth and Aggression in the East, 1931–35* (Sydney, 1987), pp. 161, 164.

[38] Ibid., p. 128.

[39] John McCarthy, *Australia and Imperial Defence 1918–39: A Study in Air and Sea Power* (St Lucia, 1976), p. 59.

into the Pacific with only one base, Singapore ... is to write us down as something more than fools.'[40]

Yet this is more or less what both parties continued to assume as war loomed. British assurances about Singapore continued to be reaffirmed (and relied upon) even after the declaration of war on Germany, with Winston Churchill cabling Prime Minister Robert Menzies in August 1940: 'If however contrary to prudence and self-interest Japan set about invading Australia or New Zealand on a large scale, I have explicit authority of Cabinet to assure you that we should then cut our losses in the Mediterranean and proceed to your aid sacrificing every interest except only the defence position of this island on which all else depends.'[41] Churchill's proviso: 'if contrary to prudence and self-interest', revealed the fundamental divergence of perspective. Seen from half a world away, and in the midst of a major European crisis, a direct Japanese military threat to Australia seemed as improbable as it was insignificant.

The Japanese attack on Pearl Harbour in December 1941 was to alter the position dramatically. The events which culminated in the fall of Singapore on 15 February 1942 have generated an often heated debate in Australia over the years—from Prime Minister John Curtin's charge of an 'inexcusable betrayal', to Paul Keating's widely publicized parliamentary tirade some fifty years later against the British effort at Singapore.[42] With the passage of time, Singapore has acquired its own mythological status as the definitive crisis that 'really put the acid test on all the implied privileges of unlimited protection'.[43] In many respects, the poor British showing at Singapore, and the subsequent 'cable battle' between Curtin and Churchill over the recall of Australian troops from the Mediterranean in order to defend their own country, was the realization of John Dunmore Lang's century-old predictions about the 'physical impossibility' of covering all bases of Empire at once. The speed with which the Japanese proceeded from Singapore to the bombing of Darwin (only four days later) seemed to confirm the allegation that Britain's abandonment of Singapore was tantamount to

[40] Andrews, *Writing on the Wall*, p. 173.

[41] Quoted in John McCarthy, 'The "Great Betrayal" Reconsidered: An Australian Perspective', *Australian Journal of International Affairs*, Vol. 48, no. 1 (May 1944), p. 62.

[42] Keating, *Commonwealth Parliamentary Debates*, Representatives, Vol. 182, 27 February 1992, p. 374. See Chapter 12, pp. 303–4.

[43] This was how former NSW Premier Jack Lang put it in the 1960s, quoted in James Curran, *The Power of Speech: Australian Prime Ministers Defining the National Image* (Melbourne, 2004), p. 199.

sacrificing Australia. The Australian troops who were eventually diverted to New Guinea in August 1942 to fight the Japanese on the Kokoda Track were to live out the worst nightmares of generations of Australian doomsayers.

Yet for all this, the Singapore crisis had only a limited impact on Australia's identification with Empire and Britishness. Curtin's December 1941 proclamation that 'Australia looks to America, free of any pangs as to our traditional links or kinship with the United Kingdom' was by far the most frank admission by an Australian Prime Minister of the severe limitations of the imperial community of interest. But a call to arms for a new Australian nationalism in the face of an obsolescent Britishness it clearly was not. To the extent that it was understood as such it was greeted by 'immediate and emphatic' protest.[44] The Returned Servicemen's League issued a spirited rebuttal of Curtin's statement: 'In case there should be the slightest vestige of doubt where the RSL stands, let it be stated that the RSL is British, and aggressively so.'[45] The opposition parties were equally quick to respond, reminding Curtin that 'Australia is nearly 100 per cent British and will not stand for the kind of talk we are getting.'[46] Such was the furore that Curtin was forced to issue a subsequent press statement to clarify that he 'did not mean that Australia regarded itself as anything but an integral part of the British Empire. No part of the British Commonwealth is more steadfast in its devotion to the British way of life and to British institutions than Australia.'[47]

Nor did the abject failure of the Singapore strategy sound the death knell of imperial defence. Despite Curtin's determination to 'look to America' at the time of the Japanese advance towards Australia, both the Curtin and Chifley governments sought to revive the imperial defence ideal at war's end. For the Labor governments of the 1940s, the experience of British capitulation in the Pacific War had revealed, not the obsolescence of imperial defence cooperation, but the pressing need to bolster it, and to give it such a substantive character that it would not fail again. This was to be achieved by insisting on greater Australian involvement in imperial defence planning, thereby ensuring that Australia's problems and perspective would not be so easily brushed aside. Curtin's belief that Australia's voice in the world

---

[44] K. H. Bailey, 'Attitude to Britain', *Round Table*, Vol. 32, no. 127 (June 1942), pp. 419–21.

[45] *British and Proud of It*, 1942, reprinted in John Arnold et al., *Out of Empire: The British Dominion of Australia* (Melbourne, 1993), p. 73.

[46] *Sydney Morning Herald*, 30 December 1941.

[47] Bailey, 'Attitude to Britain', p. 421; *Age*, 30 December 1941.

was 'more impressive as a member of a family than it could ever be … as a separate and distinct entity', went hand in hand with the Labor government's imperial defence strategy.[48] It formed the basis of his proposal at the 1944 Commonwealth Prime Ministers' Conference for the establishment of an imperial secretariat to allow for 'full and continuous consultation' among Commonwealth countries and to strengthen 'the noble ties that unite us'.[49] His External Affairs Minister, H. V. Evatt, was equally preoccupied with using Australia's standing in the Empire to gain greater influence over strategic planning in the region—or as Evatt himself put it, to establish Australia as a 'trustee of British civilisation in the Pacific'.[50] Like Deakin, Eggleston, and Hughes before them, the Labor leaders of the 1940s believed that 'British countries' owed each other an instinctive pledge of mutual assistance in the face of security threats. Equally, the experience of direct attack at the hands of the Japanese suggested that their distinctive security concerns might go unheeded without vigorous Australian advocacy in the councils of Empire. This resulted in periodic clashes between the British and Australian Labour governments, as well as between senior bureaucrats in Australian government departments over the best way of asserting Australia's influence.[51]

A heightened awareness of the importance of the United States to the security of the Pacific was a further consequence of Australia's wartime experience. The obvious decline in British power in the post-war years led successive governments to pursue a formal American defence guarantee as a vital new plank in Australian security policy. This objective became increasingly urgent with the escalation of Cold War rivalries, in which the century-old fears of Russian power in the Pacific resurfaced in a new, ideological guise. The Maoist revolution in China brought the traditional fear of Asia into this same frame of reference, fuelling growing concerns at all levels of government about the likelihood of a third world war.[52]

---

[48] See Curtin's speech of 28 February 1945, quoted in David Day, *Reluctant Nation: Australia and the Allied Defeat of Japan, 1942–45* (Oxford, 1992), p. 310.

[49] Speech by Prime Minister Curtin in the House of Representatives, 17 July 1944, in Meaney, *Australia and the World*, p. 505.

[50] Neville Meaney, 'Australia, the Great Powers and the Coming of the Cold War', *Australian Journal of Politics and History*, Vol. 38, no. 3 (1992), pp. 316–33, 323.

[51] See David Lee, 'Britain and Australia's Defence Policy, 1945–49', *War and Society*, Vol. 13, no. 1 (May 1995), pp. 61–80. See also Christopher Waters, *The Empire Fractures: Anglo-Australian Conflict in the 1940s* (Melbourne, 1995).

[52] David Lowe, *Menzies and the Great World Struggle: Australia's Cold War, 1948–54* (Sydney, 1999).

Significantly, with the outbreak of the Korean War in June 1950, the Liberal–Country Party Coalition government of Robert Menzies announced its offer of military support before the position of the British government had been made public. Although Menzies' Cabinet was aware that Britain intended to commit its own ground troops, it was nonetheless considered useful from the point of view of relations with the United States that Australia was seen to make its own commitment to the Cold War in Asia independently of Britain.[53]

It was in this new post-war context (more so than Curtin's wartime rhetoric of 1942) that Australia entered into the ANZUS Treaty with the United States in 1951. ANZUS was no simple substitute of one 'dependent' relationship for another as it is often portrayed.[54] The Menzies government would have happily welcomed Britain as a full member of ANZUS, but was blocked by American concerns that the pact should not appear to underwrite Britain's colonial possessions in the region.[55] It was suggested at the time—by, among others, Labor leader H. V. Evatt—that for Australia to enter into such an arrangement with the United States was 'un-British'. But this view was shouted down in a media chorus led by the *Age* in Melbourne: 'Mr Menzies expresses the general view of this country when he dismisses as unfounded the suggestion that the Treaty entails a drawing away from Great Britain.'[56] What the ANZUS pact did signify was an acknowledgement that Britain alone could no longer fulfil Australia's security needs in the region. As the chief Australian negotiator of the treaty, External Affairs Minister Percy Spender conceded that Australia 'has a much greater stake in [the] Pacific than has the United Kingdom ... we have to live in the Pacific—our headquarters are in the Pacific'.[57]

Yet precisely because the terms of the American alliance had to be written down, ANZUS was never an adequate substitute for the unwritten, instinctive, familial assumptions that characterized the British defence guarantee. And for this reason the regional defence partnership with Britain

---

[53] Ibid., p. 63. See also Robert O'Neill, *Australia in the Korean War, 1950–53. Vol. 1: Strategy and Diplomacy* (Canberra, 1981), pp. 62–76.

[54] See David McLean, 'From British Colony to American Satellite: Australia and the USA During the Cold War', *Australian Journal of Politics and History*, Vol. 52, no. 1 (2006), pp. 66–7.

[55] See R. G. Casey diary entries of 17 July 1951, 14 July and 3 August 1952, in T. B. Millar, ed., *Australian Foreign Minister* (London, 1972).

[56] *Age*, 16 October 1952; see also *Sydney Morning Herald*, 15 October 1952.

[57] Quoted in McLean, 'From British Colony ...', p. 71.

would continue for a further two decades. This was borne out by Australia's participation alongside British forces in the 'Malayan Emergency' (1948–60), the Menzies government's support of Britain during the Suez crisis in 1956 (in the face of American opposition), the provision of Australian facilities for British nuclear testing throughout the 1950s, and Australia's military contribution to the 'Confrontation' dispute with Indonesia in the mid-1960s. Across the whole history of imperial relations, this was the era in which Australia and Britain cooperated most closely in regional defence.[58]

For a brief period during the Vietnam War, the American alliance seemed to have eclipsed Australia's erstwhile devotion to Empire and Britishness. The visit to Australia of President Lyndon Johnson in November 1966 brought forth the kind of rhetoric that had once been reserved for the Mother Country. Prime Minister Harold Holt's 'All the Way with LBJ' seemed vaguely analogous with the enthusiasm of earlier generations for 'the British Empire, right or wrong'. Even the British High Commissioner in Canberra at the time of Johnson's visit felt that Britain had been unceremoniously nudged aside in Australia's affections. As he complained to his superiors in London, 'in the middle of this Viet-Nam-oriented Australian–American love-feast, the representative of the British Government was decidedly the skeleton at the barbecue'.[59] Yet this situation barely outlived Holt himself. Within two years, Johnson's successor, Richard Nixon, coming to terms with America's defeat in the Vietnam War, issued a carefully worded warning to his regional allies—known as the 'Guam doctrine'—that in future they should expect to assume the lion's share of responsibility for their own defence. There could be no clearer indication of the transience of the special attention showered on Australia by the United States during the Johnson–Holt era. It was the immediate, short-term political exigencies of the Vietnam conflict that had brought the two countries so closely together. And ironically, it was partly the fact that the British had chosen to stay out of Vietnam that prompted Johnson to value so highly the moral and material support of the Australian government.

[58] P. G. Edwards with G. Pemberton, *Crises and Commitments: The Politics and Diplomacy of Australia's Involvement in Southeast Asian Conflicts, 1948–1965* (Sydney, 1992); Wayne Reynolds, *Australia's Bid for the Atomic Bomb* (Melbourne, 2000).

[59] Jeppe Kristensen, 'In Essence Still a British Country: Britain's Withdrawal from East of Suez', *Australian Journal of Politics and History*, Vol. 51, no. 1 (March 2005), pp. 40–52, 43.

Australia's ongoing search for security in the post-imperial era has been marked, above all, by the sheer absence of an alternative to Britain and Empire as the primary anchor of regional defence. By the end of the 1960s, not only had the Americans decided to disengage from mainland South East Asia, but the British, too, had indicated emphatically that they were abandoning the last vestiges of Empire in the region. One of the clearest indications of Britain's diminishing sense of obligation to Australia was the 1961 decision to seek membership of the European Economic Community—a move which, although initially unsuccessful, became emblematic of a more general narrowing of Britain's horizons. This was later followed by the Wilson government's determination to withdraw its military presence from 'East of Suez' in 1967. Both decisions were a watershed, marking the limits of Britain's sense of obligation to underwrite Australia's economic and military security.

In Australia, these final acts of imperial retreat brought forth some gloomy musings about Australia's prospects for survival in the medium to long term. Although the experience of Britain's failed EEC negotiations had served notice on the Australian government about Britain's future intentions, the subsequent withdrawal of troops from South East Asia nonetheless provided the last in a long line of Australian disappointments. Newspapers in Melbourne and Sydney reacted to the news with headlines that were almost apocalyptic in tone. 'Waken to our peril' was the verdict of the *Melbourne Herald*, while in Sydney the *Daily Mirror* wrote of a 'Far East Death Warrant'.[60] The loudest and most emotional reaction came from Australia's High Commissioner in London, Alexander Downer (Snr), who complained that 'many prominent people here are now in a mood to use every weapon to justify their desertion of the Old Commonwealth'.[61] Harold Holt was more resigned, frankly admitting in 1967: 'When I was a young man the Royal Navy safe-guarded the Commonwealth and the safety of this country of ours. We took it for granted. Now this is no longer so.'[62] Henceforth, no one would assume that Australia's defence was Britain's problem.

But this left a whole series of question marks over the future of Australian defence policy. In December 1968 the *Sydney Morning Herald* accused the

---

[60] *Melbourne Herald* and *Daily Mirror*, 19 July 1967, quoted ibid., p. 46.

[61] Quoted in David Goldsworthy, *Losing the Blanket: Australia and the End of Britain's Empire* (Melbourne, 2002), p. 167.

[62] Quoted in Jeppe Kristensen, 'In Essence Still a British Country', p. 48.

government of 'defence dither' in its failure 'to make the central decision on which all the others depend ... Are we to maintain a forward defence posture or not?'[63] The tradition of 'forward defence' had long been predicated on following the lead of 'great and powerful friends', but it seemed unclear where Australia's defence priorities should lie in the post-imperial world. In August 1969, External Affairs Minister Gordon Freeth told Parliament that 'old patterns' were breaking up in Australia's region and new ones emerging, and that henceforth 'Australia has to be watchful, but need not panic whenever a Russian appears'.[64] This implied that the old Crimean bogey was finally being laid to rest, but it offered no alternative basis for Australian defence policy. As the *Australian* bluntly put it several months later: 'We have no defence philosophy because we seem uncertain of what we are supposed to be defending.'[65] This was a prime example of the sense of disorientation that the end of Empire brought in its train. Just as the certainties of Empire and Britishness had once ordered Australia's strategic landscape, helping to distinguish between friend and foe, so too the unravelling of the British Empire threw Australian defence calculations into disarray. One of the immediate consequences of this new situation was the institutional merger of the separate service departments into a single Department of Defence in November 1973. The rationale behind the new Department was the need to develop new defence doctrines to deal with the dramatic transformation in Australia's strategic outlook. Although the identification of potential threats remained an exercise fraught with uncertainty, there was no question as to where the primary responsibility for Australian defence now lay. Henceforth, the goal of 'self-reliance' became the ubiquitous catchphrase of Australian defence policy.[66]

The demise of the British defence guarantee also presaged the idea of Australia's strategic 'engagement with Asia'. Just as the Japanese Trade Treaty of 1957 was an acknowledgement that imperial trade preferences could no longer secure Australia's economic viability, so, too, moves towards closer diplomatic relations with China and South East Asia from the 1970s

---

[63] *Sydney Morning Herald*, 11 December 1968.

[64] Quoted in Anthony Burke, *In Fear of Security: Australia's Invasion Anxiety* (Sydney, 2001), p. 131.

[65] *Australian*, 18 November 1969.

[66] Andrews, *Department of Defence*, pp. 198–200. On the theme of 'self-reliance' see Australian Defence White Paper, *Australia's Changing Strategic Circumstances*, November 1976, p. 10; The self-reliance theme was finally given some policy substance a decade later in the Hawke government's Defence White Paper, 'The Defence of Australia', March 1987.

were designed to establish a new, post-imperial footing for Australia's regional security. This was nothing short of a revolution in Australian strategic and defence thinking, signalling an attempt to embrace those very countries that had long loomed so menacingly in the imperial imagination. The culmination of these steps was the Hawke government's Asia-Pacific Economic Cooperation initiative in the late 1980s, and Paul Keating's Security Treaty with President Suharto's Indonesia in 1995. The Keating government's 1994 Defence White Paper made explicit the extent of the conceptual shift: 'Just as a sense of community has emerged in relation to economic interests in Asia and the Pacific...so too a sense of shared strategic and security interests is emerging.'[67] In theory, at least, the Australian 'community of interest' had been recast in a regional mould.

The transition from 'Empire to Asia' has by no means been smooth, however, and government policy has not always been in step with public opinion. Moreover, the imperative of Asian engagement has sometimes been difficult to reconcile with inherited notions of liberal democracy, human rights, and the rule of law—a dilemma that came to the fore over Australia's defiance of the Indonesian government in East Timor in 1999 (events which led to Indonesia's abrogation of the 1995 Treaty). Australia's historical baggage as a loyal British outpost has undoubtedly hindered attempts to include Australia more fully in the regional strategic dialogue. As Alison Broinowski observes, 'when *excluding* Australia is in their interests, Asian opinion leaders represent Australians as white, Western, British, American stooges who are anti-Asian and lack history and culture'.[68]

Equally, some of Australia's imperial habits of mind have been a long time dying. At a time when both Labor and the conservative parties persist with the idea of sending service personnel abroad for the ostensible purpose of bolstering security at home, it is worth considering whether these measures represent the final reflexive twitchings of a long-deceased imperial instinct. Australia's 'historic partnerships' are repeatedly invoked as the primary rationale for military involvement abroad, despite the erosion of the historical and material foundations of those partnerships in recent decades. John Howard's close relations with George W. Bush were reminiscent

---

[67] Department of Defence, *Defending Australia*, Defence White Paper 1994 (Canberra, 1994), p. 3.

[68] Alison Broinowski, *About Face: Asian Accounts of Australia* (Melbourne, 2003), p. 229.

of those between Johnson and Holt in the Vietnam era, as was his conviction
that Australia's security needs in the face of new global terror networks were
best served by achieving the closest possible partnership with the United
States. Howard's Foreign Minister, Alexander Downer, seemed to suggest
that maintaining the American alliance was, in itself, sufficient reason for
sending troops to Iraq in 2003. 'It wasn't a time in our history to have a great
and historic breach with the United States,' he said. 'If we were to walk away
from the American alliance it would leave us as a country very vulnerable and
very open.'[69] This view was bitterly contested by those who contended that
Australia's unstinting support for Bush's 'war on terror' only served to make
Australia more vulnerable to terrorist attack. As with John Dunmore Lang
in 1854, however, this view was generally pushed to the margins of political
debate, which in itself suggests that some of the fundamental contours and
alignments of Australia's defence debate remain rooted in the imperial past.

This is by no means the only surviving legacy of Empire. Anxiety about
the Pacific has also resurfaced in recent years—so much so that Australian
politicians, defence strategists, and journalists now routinely refer to an
'arc of instability' stretching from the Indonesian provinces of Aceh and
Irian Jaya to Papua New Guinea, Bougainville, Vanuatu, and Fiji. The
presence of Australian police and service personnel in Timor, Papua New
Guinea, and the Solomon Islands is a new departure based on an old
premise. Alexander Downer's claim that 'if we don't fix up the Solomon
Islands, nobody will be able to', represents both a continuation of age-old
assumptions about the inherent dangers of Australia's geography, and a
new-found awareness that no distant power can be relied upon to hold these
perceived dangers at bay.[70] Although the context has altered dramatically,
Australia is still grappling with the imperial dilemma of how best to deploy
its limited defence capacity—whether as part of a global combined effort
of 'like-minded' countries, or as a more localized, self-reliant force geared
towards regional stability. The relatively minimal Australian contribution to
recent wars in Afghanistan and Iraq, compared with the massive investments
of money and personnel in Timor, New Guinea, the Solomons, and Fiji,
suggests that the balance has tipped decisively towards the latter. But
this—together with the 'triumphalism' that has accompanied some of

[69] Quoted in Robert Garran, *True Believer: John Howard, George Bush and the American
Alliance* (Sydney, 2004), p. 161.

[70] Nick Squires, 'Australia Enters Island War Zone', *Sun Herald*, 29 June 2003.

these activities—suggests that 'Australia's Empire' could be acquiring new meanings out of old.[71]

For the best part of a century, colonial and Federal Australian governments pursued the aim of security within the Empire from the standpoint of a set of contradictory assumptions. On the one hand, in order to allay the security anxieties of a vulnerable people, the Empire acquired the status of a stable, timeless, and above all, permanent fixture in the Australian strategic imagination. An ingrained expectation that Britain would respond selflessly whenever Australians felt threatened, served to perpetuate an often complacent reliance on imperial protection well into the twentieth century. Yet William Denison's imperial 'community of interest' remained an ambiguous and, at times, shaky concept. As the fort that bears his name gives testimony, unswerving faith in imperial certainties coexisted with residual anxieties about the fragile edifice of the British world. Australian governments from the colonial era right down to the 1960s remained prone to nagging doubts about the capacity, or even the resolve, of the British government to make good the promise of Empire. Robert Menzies' 1962 plea to Harold Macmillan (quoting Proverbs 22:28): 'Remove not the ancient landmark', encapsulated the fine line between the Australian conception of Empire as both eternal truth and ultimate deception. Menzies' biblical reference implied a religious faith in the verities of imperial protection. Yet the very suggestion that these verities might be 'removed' betrayed his underlying doubts about the enduring quality of the imperial link. While the rhetoric of Empire held that Australia's interests were ultimately indistinguishable from those of the British world as a whole, the realities of Australia's regional problems and aspirations progressively undermined the mutuality of the imperial ideal. The imperative of loyalty and the prospect of betrayal thus provided the axis around which Australia's Empire revolved.

Select Bibliography

JOAN BEAUMONT, ed., *Australia's War, 1939–1945* (Sydney, 1996).

CARL BRIDGE, ed., *From Munich to Vietnam* (Melbourne, 1989).

ANTHONY BURKE, *In Fear of Security: Australia's Invasion Anxiety* (Sydney, 2001).

---

[71] On the media 'triumphalism' over Australia's role in the INTERFET exercise in East Timor see Richard Woolcott, *The Hot Seat* (Sydney, 2003), p. 168; Rawdon Dalrymple, *Continental Drift: Australia's Search for a Regional Identity* (Aldershot, 2003).

DAVID DAY, *The Great Betrayal: Australia and the Onset of the Pacific War, 1939–42* (Sydney, 1988).

P. G. EDWARDS with G. PEMBERTON, *Crises and Commitments: The Politics and Diplomacy of Australia's Involvement in Southeast Asian Conflicts, 1948–1965* (Sydney, 1992).

DAVID GOLDSWORTHY, *Losing the Blanket: Australia and the End of Britain's Empire* (Melbourne, 2002).

JEFFREY GREY, *A Military History of Australia* (Cambridge, 1999).

JOHN MCCARTHY, *Australia and Imperial Defence 1918–39: A Study in Air and Sea Power* (St Lucia, 1976).

NEVILLE MEANEY, *The Search for Security in the Pacific, 1901–1914* (Sydney, 1976).

—— ed., *Australia and the World: A Documentary History from the 1870s to the 1970s* (Melbourne, 1985).

ROGER C. THOMPSON, *Australian Imperialism in the Pacific: The Expansionist Era, 1820–1920* (Melbourne, 1980).

DAVID WALKER, *Anxious Nation* (St Lucia, 1999).

PART III

CULTURES: THE CONCEPTION OF EMPIRE

11

Monarchy: From Reverence to Indifference

MARK MCKENNA

On 4 June 1788, King George III's 50th birthday, the colony of New South Wales was barely five months old. Captain Lieutenant Watkin Tench, the First Fleet's most polished literary stylist, had celebrated his 30th birthday only a few weeks earlier. Winter had closed in on the fledgling settlement at Sydney Cove. As Tench looked around him at the small community of 1,000 men and women now eking out a living 12,000 miles from home—'this forlorn and distant circle'—he wrote of his utter delight at the 'hours of festivity' occasioned by his King's birthday. Sydney's Aboriginal people—the Eora—watched as the newcomers performed one of their most ancient rituals. At first light, the ships of war in the harbour fired a twenty-one gun salute, repeated at noon, and throughout the day innumerable loyal toasts were drunk to the King's health. So often did the colonists raise their glasses, one Aborigine thought that the name of their drink must be 'King'. In the years to come, royal titles would be bestowed on Aboriginal elders across Australia in the form of nameplates, the irony of their dispossession in the name of the Crown all the more palpable.

The first birthdays of the British Monarch to be celebrated on Australian soil were a precursor of those to come. Grog was dispensed, holidays and royal pardons granted, the colony's first plays were performed, the governing classes feasted, and bonfires were lit in the evening. The King's birthday became Australia's first national day. Into what Tench described as 'the dreariness and dejection' of this exiled fleck of Empire came the 'exhilarating effect' of ritual and theatre, and through its well-lubricated practice, the misty-eyed memories of home. From the beginning, the Monarchy in Australia was performed into being.[1]

---

[1] L. F. Fitzhardinge, ed., *Sydney's First Four Years: A Narrative of the Expedition to Botany Bay and a Complete Account of the Settlement at Port Jackson 1788–1791, Captain Watkin Tench* (Sydney, 1979), pp. 60, 152; Ken Inglis, *The Australian Colonists* (Melbourne. 1974), p. 65.

In the Australian colonies, distance from Britain would exaggerate affection and loyalty in the same way as it would exaggerate fear and anxiety. Colonization was a magnifier. It threw everything into sharp relief. As Tench and many others discovered, the question of what it meant to be British suddenly seemed all the more pressing in a far away colony. Like the lost Europeans rescued in the bush by Aboriginal people, who sang their songs at night to remember their English language, colonists in indigenous Australia had an urgent need to tell the stories that reminded them of their cultural identity. After all, the very essence of the colonial project—the acquisitive eye, the departure from home, the journey out-wards, and the subsequent invasion and conquest of other lands—was an expansionist mission that begged the definition of purpose and identity. To leave Britain was to know Britain. And Britishness, in all its self-confident assertion, was defined as much (if not more) from the outside as from within.

At the heart of Australian colonial narratives of belonging to 'the British race' was the Monarchy—all the larger somehow because of its physical absence. In *Australian Colonists*, Ken Inglis tells the story of a Presbyterian minister travelling alone in the bush in the mid-nineteenth century, racked 'by the feeling of separation and exile'. After travelling for days he stumbled upon the first sign of 'civilization'—a lonely hut inscribed with the letters 'V.R.'. As he recalled in his journal: 'It seemed as if distance had been suddenly obliterated; I felt that I was still a member of the British family—and a subject of the British Queen, whom she was caring for even at these ends of the earth, and would defend against all deadly.'[2]

As was so often the case, Monarchy in the colonial setting was an act of imaginative recreation. Australia had no royal court, no ladies in waiting, no mistresses of the robes, and no palaces and estates reserved for the exclusive use of one family. But it did possess the idea of Monarchy; Monarchy as the pinnacle of racial identity and the righteousness of Empire, Monarchy as the symbol of virtue and justice, the source of appeal against arbitrary rule, and the cultural guardian angel for the exiled colonial. Even in death, remembering the Monarch could be a source of comfort. In 1861, the ill-fated journey of the explorers Burke and Wills was drawing to its tragic conclusion on the banks of Cooper's Creek in South Australia. With only weeks to live, and at a time when they were barely strong enough to do anything other

---

[2] Inglis, *The Australian Colonists*, p. 69.

than collect and pound nardoo for their daily survival, Wills still found the reserve to honour his Queen. On the morning of 24 May, he wrote in his journal that he had decided 'to celebrate the Queen's birthday by fetching from Nardoo Creek what is now to us the staff of life'. For the colonist, to 'celebrate' the Monarch was to reaffirm one's right to belong on foreign soil.[3]

Monarchy's mark on the Australian landscape and *mentalité* is indelible. Like the ubiquitous portrait of the reigning Monarch that once adorned the foyers and meeting rooms of so many public and private institutions in Australia, the Crown looms large in the history of every stump and street corner. Even the place names of Australia's Antarctic territory reveal something of its historical relationship with the British royal family. The map shows names such as 'King George V Land' and 'Princess Mary Land'. And not far from 'Mount Menzies', as if scripted for historical alignment, lie 'Princess Elizabeth Land' and 'Prince Charles Mountains'. Superficially at least, there seems little doubt that Australia is indeed Crown land. In the rituals of exploration and the law, government and religion, in countless levees, balls, regattas, parades, and public celebrations, in the awarding of imperial honours, and in the unveiling of innumerable statues and memorial plaques, the Australian people celebrated and defined themselves through Monarchy. And they did so long before the first member of the British royal family to visit Australia, Prince Alfred, arrived before adoring crowds in 1867.

In the twentieth century, as visiting royals came with increasing frequency, almost every major national event was presided over by royalty. The inauguration of Australia's Federal Parliament in Melbourne in 1901, the opening of Parliament House in the capital Canberra in 1927, the opening of the Melbourne Olympic Games in 1956, Sydney Opera House in 1973, the High Court in 1980, and finally, Canberra's new Parliament House in 1988. The frequency of the royal visit in the late twentieth century (there were six tours between 1788 and 1954 and there have been more than fifty since then), has created a rich oral history surrounding the Monarchy in Australia. For many Australians, of course, memories of their fleeting contact with royalty are nothing less than an affirmation of the virtues of Australia's British heritage and traditional values. Since 1788 only Anzac Day

---

[3] Journal of William John Wills, Friday May 24 1861, in Kathleen Fitzpatrick, ed., *Australian Explorers* (Oxford, 1959), p. 369.

has brought enthusiastic crowds onto the streets in comparable numbers. No other figurehead has managed to embody the Australian nation in the same way as royalty, especially Queen Elizabeth II in 1954, certainly no Governor General or Prime Minister, except perhaps for fleeting moments. From any historical perspective—cultural, political, or social—it is impossible to deny Monarchy's pivotal role in the formation of Australian identities. Whether it be the history of local community organizations such as the Country Women's Association (CWA), the emergence of state and regional identities, the motivating force for military engagement, or the origin and maintenance of national identity up until the 1960s, the Monarchy is crucial to our understanding.

Despite the centrality of Monarchy to any history of Australia, there is a yawning gap in the historiography. To date, no one has attempted a history of Monarchy in Australia, largely because, as Peter Spearritt remarked in 1993, the Monarchy was for so long 'part of 'the natural order of things', it needed no explanation.[4] Since Australian history emerged as a distinct field of historical enquiry in the 1950s, the Monarchy has been treated with a mixture of condescension and bemusement, more often pilloried than understood. For the generation of historians active between the 1950s and 1970s (many of whom were left-leaning), the most pressing reason to write history was to discover what was unique about Australian society. In this nationalist framework, allegiance to Monarchy (which was British and therefore 'foreign'), was frequently depicted as an example of psychological or cultural dependence, one that denied the aspirations of Australian nationalism. The only scholarly discipline to acknowledge Monarchy's importance was law, which focused primarily on explaining the changing role of the Crown in the evolution of Australia's legal and political institutions. At the same time, conservative intellectuals in Australia failed to explore the history of the very traditions they sought to maintain, the Monarchy being merely one example of this phenomenon. Perhaps they could still hear Walter Bagehot's advice ringing in their ears—do not 'let daylight in upon magic'. The result of the conservative silence and the left's dismissal of Monarchy as silly and contemptible have been to leave a vast terrain of Australian cultural history unexplored. It is only now that historians in Australia have begun to follow in the footsteps of historians in

---

[4] Peter Spearritt, 'Australians and the Monarchy', in Annette Shiell and Peter Spearritt, eds, *Australians and the Monarchy* (Melbourne, 1993), p. 6.

Britain, particularly those such as David Cannadine and Vernon Bogdanor, and treat Monarchy seriously.[5]

While many of the traditions of Monarchy frequently described as having been in existence since 'time immemorial' were invented in the Victorian era, the mass appeal of Monarchy cannot be understood by limiting the agency of the very people who sustained it. To think of traditions being 'invented' risks overstating conspiratorial manipulation on the part of the ruling classes, as if allegiance to Monarchy, for example, was the mere result of imperial propaganda, designed solely to exert social control. Popular monarchism in the British Empire during the nineteenth and twentieth centuries was created and sustained by 'British people' and Indigenous subjects in all their diversity, particularly in the dialogue between imperial authorities and colonies. In 1867, during the visit of Prince Alfred to Melbourne, an *Age* editorial remarked that 'those who took so much trouble [to welcome Prince Alfred] seemed to enjoy the result of their exertions, as much, if not more, than the recipient.' The majority of ordinary people were clearly benefiting. The spectacle of Empire was of their making too. The Monarchy was a vehicle through which the people of Australia expressed their unity, a means through which they celebrated their individual and community identity, a means through which they made the Empire in their own image. They were much more than passive recipients of the Empire's 'Prince of the blood'.[6]

In April 1866, almost two years before Alfred arrived, 'tens of thousands' of people gathered in Sydney's Hyde Park to attend the unveiling of a statue of Prince Albert Saxe-Coburg-Gotha, Queen Victoria's husband, who had died at the age of 42 in December 1861. The public response foreshadowed many of the functions Monarchy would later serve during royal tours. When the Governor, Sir John Young, rose to address the crowd, most of whom could not hear a word he said, yet remained dutifully silent, he told them the statue was the expression of the 'free unbiased voice of the people'. After the statue was unveiled, the choirs sang the German anthem, 'Des Deutschen Vaterland' before the crowd roared three cheers for the Queen. The German-born Albert had been canonized the son of two empires—the British Empire and the German colonial empire fast approaching. The day

---

[5] Historical research on Monarchy in Australia is limited but the most crucial work, including Cannadine and Bogdanor, is listed in the Select Bibliography at the end of this chapter.

[6] *Age*, 26 November 1867. 'Prince of the blood' is an expression used in the *Times* editorial, 14 January 1868.

before, the *Sydney Morning Herald* editorial declared that the Australian colonies could 'never regard the Germans as aliens ... the loss of the Queen has been the loss of thousands of her subjects'. The following day, feasting on the image of the crowd's loyalty, the same editorial proclaimed the scene triumphantly: 'here were multitudes of people in a country only recently inhabited, met to celebrate the highest example of human virtue'. In this event, one of the first mass demonstrations of public feeling for Monarchy on Australian soil, it is possible to see the sources of its appeal in the century to come.

Albert's greatest service to the people of New South Wales was to die. In death, he provided a personal symbol—reified and idealized—through which the colonists could express their unity as a British people, a need desperately felt in a distant colony. In the Sydney of 1866, the Monarch embodied the idea of the nation and the nation that mourned Albert's death was both imperial and colonial, demonstrating how loyalty to a benign Monarch fostered the development of a dual nationalism. Official speakers at the unveiling ceremony persisted with the illusion that the British Empire would, like the universe, continue to expand indefinitely, until the globe was coloured pink and peopled by millions of the British race. When they spoke of their allegiance to Monarchy, their language betrayed the connection between imperialism and militarism. Crowds 'fell in line' and people 'advanced' under orders as soldiers might do. To walk in the line of allegiance to the imperial Monarch was to prepare to walk in the line of war. From another perspective, every commemoration and celebration of Monarchy was a symbolic reclaiming of the Australian continent. As the *Herald* editorial reminded its readers, the continent was 'only recently inhabited'. This myth was repeated fifteen years later in the official souvenir of the visit of Princes Edward and George to Queensland in 1881. The Princes, it was claimed, had visited a country that was 'just emerging from Aboriginal savagery ... [where] all was waste and barbarous ... [these] colonies have no history'. In the late twentieth century, many of Queen Elizabeth II's speeches in Australia recalled the British 'occupation' of the continent and the creation of a 'civilization' in what had previously been 'wilderness'. In 1954, NSW Labor Premier Cahill likened the arrival of Queen Elizabeth II at Farm Cove to that of Governor Arthur Philip in 1788. Until the late twentieth century, every arrival of royalty on Australian soil was a reassertion of British conquest and settlement, a forgetting of the Aboriginal occupation of the continent, in which Aboriginal people were reduced to decorative adornment or viewed as curiosities destined for the museum, and history conveniently began again. With the arrival of the phenomenon of the royal tour in 1867, all of these functions of Monarchy were magnified several times over.[7]

Prince Alfred's tour of the Australian and New Zealand colonies in 1867–9 occurred at a pivotal moment in the relationship between the people and their sovereign. Vernan Bogdanor has described the 'massive emotional significance' acquired by Victoria and her family during the late nineteenth century. Linda Colley, meanwhile, has drawn attention to the increasingly patriotic and nationalistic mass celebration of the Monarchy which had begun earlier in the century during the latter half of George III's reign, and was not seen again until late in Victoria's reign. With the growth of imperialism and a 'new age of popular government', the Monarch became the key symbolic arsenal of British expansion, the personal link between the colonies and the mother country. After the withdrawal of British troops from Australia in 1870, the Colonial Office recognized the potential value of extending imperial honours to the colonies. 'Loyalty to the throne and to a common nationality' was now 'the principle bond of union for many colonies'. As the British world expanded, members of the royal family needed to be seen in the colonies in the same way as the Monarch needed to be seen in various parts of Britain. If it were necessary to visit the realms of Scotland and Wales, it would be necessary to visit far-flung realms such as New Zealand and Australia. This was acknowledged by Queen Victoria, within Whitehall, and by colonial governments. In June 1867, for example, Victoria instructed her son Prince Alfred to visit South America, the Cape Colony, China, India, Australia, and New Zealand. The royal tour, together with telegraphic press coverage (after October 1872), of coronations, royal weddings, births, funerals, romances, and fashion, became the building blocks of an Empire of common feeling.[8]

---

[7] On the unveiling of Prince Albert's statue, see *Sydney Morning Herald*, 23 & 24 April 1866; see also the speech of Mr. David Buchanan in the Legislature of NSW, February 1862 (Mitchell Library, Pamphlet); and Reverend James Carter, *Reflections on the Death of HRH Prince Albert, A Sermon Preached at St. Mark's Picton on the death of HRH Prince Albert, Sunday morning March 2 1862* (Sydney, 1862). For allusions to 1788 see Queen Elizabeth's speech at Canberra Jubilee celebrations, 12 March 1963 in *Canberra Times*, 13 March 1963 and Cahill in *Charles and Diana in Australia* (Herald Weekly Times, 1983), p. 85.

[8] Vernon Bogdanor, *The Monarchy and the Constitution* (Oxford, 1995), pp. 36–40; Linda Colley, *Britons: Forging the Nation* (London, Pimlico edition 2003), pp. 210, 230, 235–6. On Victoria also see Margaret Homans, *Royal Representations: Queen Victoria and British Culture*

Colonial loyalty, uncritical as it often was, differed sharply from the loyalty to the Monarch at home, fluctuating far less, especially because of its removal from domestic political culture in Britain. The criticism Victoria suffered at home, for example, over her marriage to the German Albert and her reclusive lifestyle after his death, did not surface with any intensity in colonial Australia. As the *Age* remarked as late as 1886, Australians often behaved as if the Monarchy should be exempt from criticism, even competing with one another in their loyal overtures. Thus, in 1868, the Australian colonies tried desperately to outdo one another in their displays of loyalty to Prince Alfred. For *The Times*, this pointed to the legitimacy of the Empire's further expansion and the need for *Lebensraum*:

These are not favoured colonies, protected plantations, commercial monopolies, but simply gatherings of British subjects, quietly and peaceably elbowed out of this island, and making the best of their case by looking for elbow-room elsewhere.[9]

In Australia, little 'elbow room' could be found for Prince Alfred. During his six-month tour, he visited every Australian colony except Western Australia. In the words of Melbourne QC A. C. Michie, the Prince was 'taken into affectionate custody' by the entire population. At times, Alfred was treated as a 'live curiosity', a circus act 'after the fashion of Barnum'. As the mother of one NSW politician wrote from country NSW, 'I feel intensely loyal, a live Prince went past Tomago this afternoon.' In country Victoria, during a tour of the goldfields, on a day when the temperature soared above 100 degrees Fahrenheit, a crowd of 100,000 people greeted Alfred in Ballarat. The 1954 tour of Queen Elizabeth and Prince Philip, the first visit of a reigning British Monarch to Australia, is conventionally remembered as the 'high point of royal adulation in Australia', thanks largely to the way in which film dominates contemporary historical memory.[10] But the tour of

1837–1876 (Chicago, 1998), p. xx; P. W. Pike, *The Royal Presence in Australia 1867–1986* (Adelaide 1986), p. 1. On the withdrawal of British troops in 1870 see Colonial Office dispatches, Honours: Minutes and Memoranda, Co448/1A 1858–1868, 'Candidates for Honours' 31 March 1864. W. Stafford quoted by Bowen, Governor of New Zealand, in a dispatch dated 4 September 1870, National Library of Australia.

   [9] *The Times*, editorial, 14 January 1868. Disraeli quoted in Mark McKenna, *The Captive Republic: A History of Republicanism in Australia* (Cambridge, 1996), p. 117; *Age*, 14 December 1886.

   [10] Pike, *The Royal Presence in Australia*, pp. 1–12; *Age*, 14 September 1867; a 'live prince' in A. W. Martin, *Henry Parkes* (Melbourne, 1980), p. 234; Also see A. C. Michie QC, *Loyalty*

Alfred in 1867–8 and that of Edward, Prince of Wales, in 1920, both deserve equal billing. In an age before air travel and electronic communication, both Alfred ('the sailor Prince') and Edward ('the digger Prince') conducted more extensive and gruelling tours. In 1920, Edward visited 110 cities and towns across Australia in the space of three months. In early 1868, the *Age* spoke of the people of Melbourne as giving the appearance of being 'drunk with loyalty'. The *Adelaide Advertiser* even suggested the Australian colonies federate under the leadership of Prince Alfred, while a pamphlet published on the same theme proposed that Australia separate from Britain as an independent constitutional Monarchy with Alfred as King.[11] By far the most significant event during the tour, however, was the attempted assassination of Alfred in Sydney. In stark contrast to the prevailing tone of fanatic loyalty, the shooting of Alfred by the alleged Fenian conspirator Irishman Henry James O'Farrell sent the colonies into paroxysms of hysteria.

At Clontarf beach, after lunch on 12 March, Alfred was on his way to view a display of spear throwing by a group of Aborigines. O'Farrell forced his way through the crowd to within six feet of the Prince and fired. Alfred fell to the ground exclaiming 'Good God, my back is broken'. Before he could turn the gun on others, O'Farrell was grabbed by a group of men close by. The Prince was carried back to his tent in considerable pain, with doctors soon discovering that the bullet had narrowly missed the royal spine and lodged just below the surface of the abdomen. Meanwhile, O'Farrell was being attended to by the mob. The crowd shouted, 'Lynch him!', 'String him up!', and by the time the police managed to get hold of him, half his clothes had been torn off, his body was covered in bruises, and his face was badly swollen from repeated beating and kicking. If not for the efforts of the republican John Dunmore Lang and other official guests, O'Farrell would have been dismembered. The Prince was brought immediately by steamer back to Sydney and then on to Government House. Thousands kept vigil outside newspaper offices until midnight hoping for news of his condition. Within a few weeks, he made a

---

Royalty and the Prince's Visits, a lecture delivered at the Princess Theatre, Melbourne, 12 July 1869 (Melbourne, 1869), p. 6.

11 K. Fewster, 'Politics, pageantry and purpose—the 1920 tour of Australia by the Prince of Wales', *Labour History*, Vol. 38 (May 1980), p. 59; *Age*, 25 November 1867; *Adelaide Advertiser* quoted in Pike, *The Royal Presence in Australia*, p. 2; *A Proposal for the Confederation of the Australian Colonies with Prince Alfred, Duke of Edinburgh, as King of Australia, By a Colonist* (Sydney and Melbourne, 1867), pp. 4–5.

complete recovery, cancelled his planned visit to New Zealand, and sailed home.[12]

In the weeks following the shooting, colonial embarrassment and 'royal rage' was acute. As the *Sydney Morning Herald* exclaimed, 'we now feel that the crime of this man ... will associate this country with his name, and before all nations'. Public 'indignation' meetings sprang up spontaneously throughout the colonies, speakers straining to find the words for such 'foul disgrace', such 'revolting crime', 'one recalling the treacherous deeds of the dark ages'. O'Farrell had provided Australia with the first in a long line of 'un-Australian' acts, although, as time passed, it would no longer be necessary to attempt to assassinate a British royal to earn the epithet. In Sydney, 20,000 people made their way to Hyde Park in 'concentrated wrath', Protestants and Catholics alike (protestations of Catholic loyalty to the 'most gracious sovereign' being made in a climate of extreme pressure). The streets 'seethed' with anger. O'Farrell's act also inspired a flowering of Australian verse. In his poem 'Australia Vindex', the poet Henry Kendall imagined a young female Australia reeking revenge on O'Farrell:

> I will set my right hand on thy neck
> And my foot on thy body, nor bate,
> Till thy mane shall become as a wreck
> And a byword for hisses and hate!

In NSW Parliament, the colony's two leading politicians, Premier James Martin and Henry Parkes, found a way to transform public outrage into legislation, securing the passage of the Treason Felony Act in order to protect the colony from what they claimed was a Fenian 'conspiracy against the British Crown'. The Act provided for the 'suppression and punishment of seditious practices' such as 'any attempts at deposing the Queen, establishing a republic' and 'factiously refusing to drink the Queen's health'. The British government later refused royal assent for the bill. Owing largely to Parkes' efforts to prove that O'Farrell belonged to a Fenian network, O'Farrell was hanged on 21 April, barely six weeks after the assassination attempt. He insisted he had acted alone and denied the allegations till the end. No evidence was ever found to support Parkes' claims. When Prince Alfred suggested his assailant be spared, Parkes and Martin responded tersely that they 'did not think that His Royal Highness should interfere in the administration of our laws'. Here was a wonderful irony. Australian

---

[12] *Sydney Morning Herald*, 13 March 1868.

liberals staking out their legislative independence only because British royalty dared to suggest they temper their passion for extreme loyalty to the throne.[13]

The colonial response to the assassination attempt prefigured that of governments and the conservative press to republican activity in the late nineteenth and early twentieth centuries. While the political context varied, one thing remained consistent: public displays of disloyalty to the throne and the British Empire would not be tolerated. They were met with the predictable loyalty rally: a mass display of public fealty to the Monarch choreographed by the colonial authorities. In 1886, when one member of the Victorian Legislative Assembly, A. S. Bailes, dared to suggest that an Australian republic was imminent, he was challenged to a sword duel by a colleague and forced to make a public apology. Later, a public meeting was called to denounce him and declare his electorate's true feelings of loyalty to the Crown. In 1887, after republicans hijacked two public meetings in Sydney called to devise methods for celebrating Queen Victoria's Jubilee, Henry Parkes again led the loyalty crusade. On 15 June, at the appropriate venue—Prince Alfred Park—the public gathered to 'tread disloyalty into the dust'. Enforced by police, troops, and hired thugs, the rally represented, in the words of one of the colony's leading politicians, George Dibbs, 'loyalty gone mad'.

Later, as the colonies debated the prospect of Federation 'under the Crown', any serious suggestion of republican independence was considered to be out of order. After Federation, in the early years of the twentieth century, supporters of Irish separatism and communism who displayed open disloyalty to the throne and Empire were charged with treason, a charge that would continue to be levelled against republican MPs in Australia as late as the 1990s.[14] While such a long-standing and consistent pattern of state-orchestrated loyalty indicates the depth of attachment to the

[13] Kendall's poem can be found in W. H. B. Yarrington, ed., *Prince Alfred's Wreath: A Collection of Australian Poems* (Sydney, 1868), p. 14. For details of the O'Farrell affair see *Sydney Morning Herald*, 13–20 March 1868; Mark McKenna, *The Captive Republic: A History of Republicanism in Australia 1788–1996* (Cambridge, 1996), pp. 112–15; Allan Martin, *Henry Parkes* (Melbourne, 1980) pp. 232–40.

[14] Details of the loyalty rallies in the late nineteenth century can be found in Mark McKenna, *The Captive Republic*, pp. 130–1, 136–50, 197–8, 211–13. In 1921, the shredding of the Union Jack at a Labor Council meeting in Sydney resulted in yet another loyalty rally where thousands gathered to denounce communism and reaffirm their allegiance to throne and Empire. See, e.g., Mark McKenna and Wayne Hudson, *Australian Republicanism: A Reader* (Melbourne, 2003),

Empire in Australia, it also displays a profound psychological anxiety. The mere thought of Australia being independent of Britain and finding itself alone was enough to motivate the public shaming of those who displayed the slightest hint of disloyalty. There was also a deeply embedded fear that the British Monarch and government might perceive Australia as disloyal. At times, Australia seemed to cling so tenaciously to the ideal of a British community that it pointed to a pathological insecurity in the body politic. Without the link to an 'ancient civilization', with its ritual and splendour, its might and race pride, many Australian politicians seemed terrified at the prospect of finding intrinsic worth within their own society. The fear of isolation was not only geographic and strategic (be it defence or economic isolation), it was also cultural and spiritual.

Still, the depiction of Australian society as being uniformly loyal until the 1960s is flawed. The celebration of Empire Day (1905–54), for example, never succeeded in the manner the authorities intended, remaining a day for the conservative Protestant establishment to express its loyalty to Crown and Empire. Not celebrated in Catholic schools between the wars, and fractured further by the conscription crisis during the First World War, Irish separatism in the 1920s, and opposition from sections of the trade union movement in the 1930s, Empire Day always struggled to be seen as a truly national celebration. The existence of strong and widespread republican opposition to Monarchy, especially within the labour movement in pre-Federation Australia, also pointed to the limits of Monarchy's appeal. Post-Federation, Labor leaders soon saw that the Monarchy posed no threat to their agenda of social and political reform. Until 1991, when the Labor Party's federal conference in Hobart passed a half-hearted motion to work towards the declaration of an Australian republic on 1 January 2001, Labor did not oppose the Monarchy. What it did oppose was any attempt to import class distinctions through the granting of imperial honours and awards. The long-held belief that the acceptance of imperial honours was fundamentally opposed to Australian national sentiment always remained within the Party. In 1929, the Scullin Labor government was the first to recommend the cessation of imperial honours.

Monarchical allegiance was another matter. Because Monarchy remained largely detached from its aristocratic base in Australia, and was not aligned

pp. 153–63. On republican MPs being charged with treason see NSW Legislative Council, Parliamentary Debates 7 May 1992, pp. 34–8.

with the interests of one particular class, it was easier for Labor to embrace monarchical loyalty. It is certainly true that on some occasions the Party's attitude to the throne was pragmatic, as in 1945 when Prime Minister John Curtin, keen to shore up the traditional relationship between Australia and the United Kingdom after the Second World War, appointed the Duke of Gloucester as Governor General. But the mythology created by Prime Minister Paul Keating in the 1990s—that of a republican Labor Party constantly battling conservative parties bent on displays of embarrassing fealty to the Crown—is simply inaccurate. In both major political parties, loyalty to the throne was complex and layered and it frequently transcended party-political divisions. Just as Curtin's successor, Ben Chifley, described Monarchy as a 'handy constitutional fiction', Labor's leader throughout the 1950s, Bert Evatt, opposed republican India's remaining in the Commonwealth and seemed just as enamoured of the young Queen Elizabeth in 1954 as Prime Minister Robert Menzies. Also keen to display his loyalist credentials was NSW Labor Premier J. J. Cahill. Cahill was presented to the Queen more than thirty times during the tour, earning the sobriquet 'I'll see you again Cahill' from a slightly more sceptical media. Equally, Harold Holt saw Monarchy far less earnestly than Menzies, whom he would ultimately succeed as Prime Minister in 1966. In Holt's 1953 'Coronation diary' he sounds more like an upper class Barry Mackenzie (stuffing his coat pockets with cut sandwiches 'for the long session ahead of us at the Abbey') and eager to use the Coronation festivities to strut his own sartorial elegance (in full evening dress Holt wrote that he 'felt like some Minister from a middle European principality attending a wedding').[15]

How, then, was the perception of a uniform, undifferentiated, loyal Australian Dominion perpetuated? The press coverage and official literature from Australia's most significant royal tours—Prince Alfred in 1867–8, the Duke and Duchess of Cornwall and York in 1901, Edward, Prince of Wales in 1920, the Duke and Duchess of York in 1927, Queen Elizabeth II and Prince Philip in 1954, and the Queen Mother in 1958—would deaden the sensitivities of the most forgiving historian. Not because it portrays a people

---

[15] S. Firth and J. Hoorn, 'From Empire Day to Cracker Night', in J. Arnold, P. Spearritt, and D. Walker, eds, *Out of Empire: The British Dominion of Australia* (Melbourne, 1993), pp. 127–47. On imperial honours see Michael Maton, *Imperial Honours and Awards to Australians 1901–1992* (self published, 1997), p. 26; Ged Martin, *A Bunyip Aristocracy* (Sydney, 1986), p. 189. Also see *Charles and Diana in Australia* (Herald Weekly Times, 1983), p. 85 for Cahill. On Evatt see Frank Bongiorno in Select Bibliography and for Holt see his 'Coronation Diary' held in the National Archives of Australia in Canberra (hereafter NAA) M2608, 3.

worshipping the Monarchy, but because the language is so repetitious and superficial. Such were the sympathies of the *Age* correspondent, marooned in Sandhurst in 1867:

I wonder if the Melbourne public have got as tired of reading reports of up-country demonstrations in honour of HRH Prince Alfred as I have of writing about them ... I have exhausted all my powers of description, and yet ... I am sitting down to describe over again a scene I have witnessed, with very slight variations, any day this last three weeks ... and in doing so make what I write readable ... I have prowled the streets of this dusty town for hours in search of an idea and I haven't found one myself, what's worse I haven't found a man with one which was worth stealing.[16]

The descriptive language used in the media coverage of royal tours is an obstacle to understanding popular monarchism. This includes the ubiquitous newspaper supplements devoted to coronations, royal weddings, and funerals with biographical features bearing headlines such as ' His Majesty's Humanity', 'An Excellent Shot', 'A Little Englander', a 'Sense of Tact', and 'His Majesty as Cricketer'. The coverage is reliably fawning and hyperbole is the order of the day. The language used by reporters varies little over the years. Descriptions of crowds lead easily to images of an uncomplicated and uniform mass emotion—the 'sea of humanity', the 'swollen streams', the 'cheering multitudes', and the 'countless thousands'. Articles lapse into descriptions of spectacle and panorama replete with the standard tropes of journalistic coverage—the 'radiant' smile, the 'frenzied' loyalty, the curtains that part as royalty arrives ('and then she is gone'), and the ubiquitous 'glimpse', which is in fact a gawk, a lingering voyeuristic gaze. Such coverage usually includes the public speeches of the royal visitor. The royal speech is reminiscent of an absent parent ('my, how you've grown'), with its predictable comments on 'your wonderful development and progress'. In sum, this language tends to disguise the many reasons people may have had for joining the celebrations during royal tours, the novelty of public celebration, the chance to be part of a crowd, and the opportunity to join friends in the sheer delight of public spectacle. The royal tour provided the provincial society the chance, for a brief moment, to play the metropolis, to become 'a city radiant with light', and to construct its own historical narrative.[17]

---

[16] *Age*, 19 November 1867.

[17] *The Evening News*, 23 June 1911; speeches of Queen Elizabeth II in Australia 1954–1992, National Library of Australia, MS 9174.

There were many reasons for attending royal welcomes and functions. On a hot summer's day in November 1867, a crowd of 70,000 waited in great anticipation at Melbourne's Botanic Gardens for Prince Alfred to host a public banquet. When news broke that Alfred would not be attending, decorum was lost. There was a mad rush on the wine. 'Many men were seen scampering across the paddock with several bottles under their arms.' Tables were rushed, food grabbed, beer barrels emptied, and at one point in a desperate effort to retain some semblance of order, bread was thrown to the crowd. Men and boys rolled about on the grass drunk and gorged with food, their clothes sprayed with red wine, challenging passers-by to fight. As the *Age* remarked, it was a 'disgusting bauch'. 'Ninety nine out of a hundred went to witness a great novelty, just as they would have gone to see a horse race or a balloon go up.'[18]

On other occasions, the appearance of Empire solidarity was not what it seemed. As was customary, shopkeepers in Bathurst, west of Sydney, were instructed to close during the celebrations for the coronation of George V in June 1911. When several shopkeepers decided to stay open, members of the ultra-loyalist British Empire League pressured them to close down. In 1920, many Labor Party and trade union branches resolved that they would take no official part in the tour of the Prince of Wales.[19] Another forgotten aspect of the loyalty displayed during royal visits is the irony and playfulness with which many people passed their time. Those who waited were not all under the spell of royalty. One woman, tired of waiting for the Prince of Wales at Randwick Racecourse in 1920, quipped that the young Prince had turned Australia into 'a nation of waiters'. A few days earlier, when Edward arrived in Sydney to a grand welcome parade, two donkeys, standing on a vacant block in Pitt Street, were commandeered by a group of diggers. Then followed a scene which foreshadowed one of the more memorable moments in Peter Weir's 1980 film *Gallipoli*, in which the character played by Mel Gibson (mock monocle over squinted eye) rides a mule down a back lane in Cairo, sending up English officers as he passes them by. Mounting the donkeys, the diggers proceeded to ride them round the corner into George Street, intending to 'escort the Royal carriage'. The crowd roared with laughter, before police stopped the diggers and forced them to dismount. Incidents like this point to the danger in interpreting the theatrical display

---

[18] *Age*, 25, 27, and 30 November 1867.
[19] *Daily Telegraph*, 23 June 1911; K. Fewster, *Politics Pageantry and Purpose*, pp. 63–6.

of Monarchy as a form of social control. As David M. Craig has suggested, to
view the Monarchy simply as imperial propaganda 'effaces' its complexity,
as well as that of its subjects.[20]

Buried in the official coverage of the royal tour is the view from the other
side—that of the royal visitor—the person who must endure hundreds of
formal welcomes and declarations of loyalty to the point of falling ill with
exhaustion. Organized down to the last detail, royal tours resemble overseas
package tours for the infirm tourist. One obligation of royalty on tour (or
anytime for that matter) is to avoid public spontaneity, which is why the
tedium of their role sometimes rises to the surface. In 1920, after heavy
rain, the Prince of Wales' train derailed in Western Australia and the royal
carriage tipped over. The Prince emerged from the carriage waving a cocktail
mixer in the air. 'At last', he exclaimed, 'I have done something that was
not in the official programme.' During a royal tour in 2000, there was more
than flippancy in Prince Philip's remark in Wagga, in western NSW, when
he referred to himself as 'the world's leading plaque unveiler'.[21] The burden
of royalty, like the royal gossip and pap that has long been the stock in trade
of the tabloids, with its highly gendered language—female royalty inspiring
a particular brand of feverish adulation and voyeurism from 'hysterical'
women—is not unique to the history of Monarchy in Australia. Other
aspects, however, reveal a struggle on the part of the Australian people to
remake the Monarchy in their own image, to Australianize the Monarchy,
often with comic effect. In early 1959, Brian O'Leary, Assistant Managing
Director of Hills Hoist Australia, wrote to the South Australian Premier,
Thomas Playford:

Having been genuinely impressed with the good will resulting from the visits of
their majesties the Queen and Queen Mother, the executives of our company feel
prompted to demonstrate their loyalty and patriotism by presenting each ... with
a Hills Rotary Hoist. Being unique to our country, we trust the Hills Hoist will
serve as a pleasant reminder to the Regal ladies of the many happy times it was
our pleasure to enjoy with them.

In case the Queen and the Queen Mother were unfamiliar with the laundry
practices of Australian suburbia, photos of Hills Hoist washing lines were
attached to the letter for their perusal. This would surely convince them

---

[20] *Daily Telegraph*, 21 June 1920; *Evening News*, 16 June 1920; David M. Craig, 'The Crowned
Republic? Monarchy and Anti-Monarchy in Britain, 1760–1901', *The Historical Journal*, 1 (2003),
p. 172.

[21] Pike, *The Royal Presence in Australia*, p. 33; *Sydney Morning Herald*, 22 March 2000.

to accept. Robert George, Governor of South Australia, passed news of the offer on to Governor General William Slim. This was, said George, 'rather an unusual offering! I believe these hoists are not available in other countries. It is possible one would be useful to the Palace and Clarence House.' Slim wrote in the margin of George's letter, 'I think this is nonsense'. The Palace, which always refused gifts from private companies, declined the offer, and the royal ladies lost their chance to grace the backyard of Buckingham Palace with a Hills Hoist.[22]

In other areas, such as race, Australians succeeded in casting the Monarchy in their own image. Against a background of xenophobia and racial anxiety, crystallized after Federation in the form of the White Australia policy, the Monarch was more often seen as a symbol of 'racial purity' in Australia. As the Prince of Wales told Prime Minster Billy Hughes in 1920, he had come to understand that the Australian people were 'determined that this nation shall be pure of race'. Standing next to royalty was a chance for Australia's political class to bask in race pride. But their florid declarations of loyalty always ignored the allegiance of Chinese-Australians, Jewish-Australians, and Australia's Indigenous people. Ironically, many of these Australians, like Sydney's Rabbi Einfeld at the time of the coronation of George V in 1911, saw Monarchy as a symbol of 'freedom from all forms of racial and sectarian prejudice'. In the late nineteenth century, when anti-Chinese racism was at its height in Australia, the Chinese community publicly expressed their loyalty to the throne. The Chinese address to Prince Alfred at Castlemaine in 1867 was remarkable for both its fealty and its poetic grace. The address welcomed 'Great England's lesser lord' and thanked the 'reigning dynasty of England' for permitting Chinese merchants to trade in Australia and beyond. The language of the address was touching:

All the people skip for joy at [the Prince's] presence … and [they] love you as the Kaum Hong tree, which shaded Choo Kong, the brother of the Emperor Moon, when he stayed his horse to rest during his tour of inspection of the Empire. Following in your track, sweet rains fall, making no noise.[23]

The Monarchy could be employed as both the symbol of racial superiority and the protector of racial equality—a sovereign for all seasons. When

---

[22] National Archives of Australia, A2880 (6963319) includes the letter from Brian O'Leary to Thomas Playford, 13 February 1959, and the letter from George to Slim, 5 March 1959.

[23] Prince of Wales quoted later in *Sydney Morning Herald*, 9 May 1927, supplement, p. 4. Einfeld in *Daily Telegraph*, 23 June 1911. Chinese address in *Age*, 18 December 1867.

Australian politicians welcomed royalty, they never claimed to speak on behalf of both Aboriginal and non-Aboriginal people, unlike in New Zealand, where Prime Ministers always welcomed visiting royals on behalf of both Maori and Pakeha. In the wake of the first substantial wave of non-British immigration after 1945, Australian governments made clear their intention to instil monarchical allegiance in new European immigrants so that they might become born-again Australians. In Australia, perhaps more than any other commonwealth country, to be British was to be White, or at least White at heart. Perhaps this is one reason why the Monarchy, for so long the lodestar of Australia's dream of racial purity, came to be seen as increasingly 'foreign' as the White Australia policy collapsed in the 1960s and the long silence over Australia's Aboriginal history was shattered.[24]

The British Monarchy has never lost its foreignness on Australian soil. From the first moment of contact with the Australian environment, royalty moved through the landscape cocooned in little Britain, shielded at every point from the dust, flies, mosquitos, and the terror of Australia's 'vast open spaces'. Whenever the royal car drove on Australia's dirt roads, it travelled first in line, covering the loyal subjects of the Antipodes trailing behind in a cloud of dust. In 1954, the Australian government, following recommendations made in a CSIRO report, ordered the spraying of public buildings with DDT, in order to ensure that the royal couple would not be pestered by bushflies. In the Northern Territory, the government was concerned that the Queen's white skin would be 'marked' by mosquito bites. More spraying was recommended. The royal party were also warned to be 'dentally fit' in preparation for top-end cuisine. As late as 1977 RAAF helicopters were 'filled with aerial spraying to keep bushflies away from royal visitors' in Canberra. Occasionally, the protective shield was penetrated, as in the welcome parade for Queen Elizabeth II in 1954 at Adelaide, when a speck of red dust lodged in the Queen's eye and she required medical attention. And what's in a speck of dust?[25]

Set against the harshness of Australia's environment, British royalty appeared fragile, other worldly, and incompatible, an impression accentuated

[24] New Zealand Prime Minister M. J. Savage, in *Daily Telegraph*, 13 May 1937, supplement, p. 3; Walsh in *Sydney Morning Herald*, 24 November 1948. On 17 April 1953, the Federal government sent a circular memorandum to the Directors of all Immigration Centres encouraging them to organize coronation celebrations; see NAA, A445/1.

[25] NAA, A9708/1 Royal Visit 1954, Fly and Mosquito Control; Kate Cumming, *Royalty and Australian Society: Records Relating to the British Monarchy held in Canberra* (Canberra, 1998), p. 148; *Sun Herald*, 6 March 1977; Pike, *The Royal Presence in Australia*, p. 71.

by the glacial like crispness of the visitors' formal attire, which seemed impervious to heat, dust, and wind. Photographs of Prince Charles and Princess Diana, taken during the couple's visit to Uluru in 1983, and published in glossy spreads in the *Women's Weekly*, retain a disturbing, almost ghostly quality. Charles, standing in an off-white short sleeved safari suit, its colour exaggerated by the glowing red backdrop of the rock, and Diana, in a perfectly pressed long white dress (white leather purse draped over her shoulder), appear like cardboard cut-outs, strange visitors from a far away world. In the 1980s, as 'the red centre' emerged as Australia's 'heartland', the link to an 'ancient' past was no longer Britain or her Monarchy but Aboriginal country. By the time Australians began at last to acknowledge the Indigenous history of their land, the Monarchy had already become peripheral. It was easier to see it as an echo of old allegiances, a reminder of the dream of an imperial family of British peoples that had disappeared in the space of one generation. In 1954, when 9 million Australians welcomed the newly crowned Queen Elizabeth II, it seemed unthinkable that this would be the final display of mass enthusiasm for royalty in Australia. In a prophetic transaction, the Daimler automobiles used to transport Queen Elizabeth and Prince Philip in 1954, and the Queen Mother in 1958, were sold to a Rockhampton undertaker in 1960.[26]

During the 1963 royal tour, only nine years after the national embrace of Elizabeth II in 1954, politicians and journalists would remark on the rapid change that had taken place. Crowds were becoming less reverent and less numerous, Britain had launched the first of several attempts to join the EEC, and the politics of the new social movements were led by a new generation of intellectuals who no longer saw the Monarchy as an appropriate symbol for an independent and modern Australia. A new nationalism was swiftly supplanting the old narratives of Empire loyalty. Survey data revealed a steady decline in support for the Monarchy from the 1960s, with the first poll to show a majority of Australians (57 per cent) supporting a republic in 1992. Changing attitudes were also reflected within the Monarchy itself. As early as 1960, Prince Philip wrote to Robert Menzies, telling him that the age of long formal tours such as the 1954 extravaganza were over. With the ease of jet air travel, British royalty would now visit Australia more frequently and for shorter periods. What had once been rare would soon become common,

---

[26] Photographs in *Charles and Diana in Australia* (Herald Weekly Times, 1983); *Charles and Diana '83 Historic Australian Tour* (Canberra, 1983). Daimlers in *Sydney Morning Herald*, 3 February 1960.

while the old formality of earlier royal tours would be dropped in favour of more relaxed and people-friendly itineraries. Philip, always one for the bon mot, led by example, surprising journalists in Melbourne in 1967 when he suggested Australia should dispense with the Monarchy and become a republic if it felt it was getting no 'value' from the Monarchy. The increased media intrusion into the private lives of royalty brought greater intimacy at the same time as it dissolved the aura of royalty. The children of Elizabeth and Philip became the prey of the international paparazzi, a profession bent on letting a particularly harsh daylight in upon royal magic.[27]

In Australian television, newspapers, and magazines of the 1960s and 1970s, a flowering of Australian satire, not seen since the late nineteenth century, had enormous fun at royalty's expense. Barry Humphries' Dame Edna Everage offered advice to the Australian housewife on what to do if the Queen 'popped in for a cuppa'. Aside from swapping her 'multi-coloured rollers and stained chenille brunch coat for an elegant coiffure and a crisp Crimplene', Dame Edna suggested handing 'hubby' 10 dollars and hustling him out the back door so he could go down to the neighbourhood bistro and 'discuss republicanism'. Humphries' affectionate satire appeared in *Woman's Day*, sharing the page with the more traditional royal tour articles in 1977, a reminder that satire was not necessarily undermining Monarchy, but had simply found a cultural space to coexist with more conservative values. From the 1960s, the tone and style of the media's coverage of royalty varied enormously depending on which member of the royal family was featured. Coverage of the Queen was always respectful and dignified. When it came to Anne and Charles, however, the language of journalists reflected a desire to modernize and democratize the Monarchy. In 1970, when Princess Anne visited Townsville, she was described as the 'swinging 19 year old Princess'. At James Cook University, she 'got with it' among thirty undergraduates. In Sydney, Anne complained about 'that bloody wind'. The new openness was characteristic of the Monarchy's infinite capacity for adaptability and reinvention. As Brisbane's *Courier Mail* put it in 1970: 'Republic? Heck-No! The new Royal ideas suit 1970 Australians. They are in tune with people, irrespective of national background. And isn't that what the Monarchy is

[27] Philip in *Age*, 3 March 1967. His letter to Menzies appears in Cumming, *Royalty and Australian Society*, p. 161. Poll in *Sydney Morning Herald*, 29 February 1992. For examples of new nationalism in the 1960s see Donald Horne, *The Lucky Country* (Ringwood, 1964) and Geoffrey Dutton, ed., *Australia and the Monarchy* (Melbourne, 1966). Also see Stuart Ward, *Australia and the British Embrace: The Demise of the Imperial Ideal* (Melbourne, 2001).

all about now—to be a unifying agent in a mixed up world?' In a similar fashion, when Charles visited Australia in the early 1990s, he travelled not on a private plane but on 'the people's airline'. Sydney's *Daily Telegraph Mirror* reported that Charles was 'slumming it on a Qantas Boeing 747'. 'Other passengers', said the *Telegraph*, 'might see [Charles] waiting in line for a toilet ... they might see him walking around in fluffy, grey sockettes, which are complimentary in all Qantas amenities packs ... [or] making small talk over drinks, nuts, and Japanese crackers in the Qantas first class lounge'. The Monarchy was being asked to perform its age-old trick, to be both ordinary and extraordinary. And despite the shattering of much of its earlier mystique, it continued to retain a unique allure for many Australians, one largely independent of the republic debate and one that transcended mere celebrity. Like children's bedtime stories of fairy princesses, magnificent castles, and royalty in gilded coaches, Monarchy dredges up ancient dreams, seducing many into believing the most astounding fiction of all—that a human being should be worshipped for no other reason than birth alone.[28] The rapturous reception given to Princess Mary of Denmark in early 2005 was certainly explained by her Australian origin. But it also demonstrated that Australians had little problem with the institution of Monarchy when it was not connected with their Constitution.

While it is true that there has been a move away from the restrained and reverential media coverage of royalty found in the early twentieth century, the trend is not always symptomatic of a desire for change. For every shift away from the Monarchy there are always countervailing tendencies. There was no significant movement for an Australian republic until the 1990s. Just how unaccustomed Australians were to open talk of their independence in the presence of the Monarch could be seen in February 1992. Labor Prime Minister Paul Keating, in a short speech of welcome before the Queen, spoke of Australia's 'necessarily independent' outlook in the south-east Asian region. A widespread public debate ensued concerning the propriety of Keating's remarks. In response, the Leader of the Opposition, Dr John Hewson, accused Keating of not having 'learned respect at school'. Similar comments were made when Keating's wife, Annita, failed to curtsy when meeting the Queen. Shortly afterwards, Keating provoked even more controversy by placing a guiding hand behind the Queen's back at an official function. For

---

[28] Humphries in *Woman's Day*, 14 March 1977. Report on Charles in *Daily Telegraph Mirror*, 20 January 1994. *Courier Mail* editorial, 13 April 1970. Report on Anne in *Courier Mail*, 21 April 1970.

this sleight of hand, he was crowned the 'Lizard of Oz' by the Fleet Street press. Some years later, Keating offered his own perspective on 'the touching scandal':

I did but touch her as she passed by ... I rather liked the Queen. I think she liked me. She always used to sit me next to her on the Britannia. We used to have a yarn about the silver on the table. I'd tell her a few jokes. She said to Robert Fellowes, her private secretary, 'I think the Prime Minister is trying to get off with my silver'. I said to her, 'The papers think I'm trying to get off with you'.[29]

Australia's late leaving from the Monarchy was entirely consistent with its history. While South Africa had ended imperial honours as early as 1925, and Canada in 1919, Australia's conservative politicians continued to queue eagerly for peerages and imperial honours until the 1970s. The very thought of these men sitting in the House of Lords contained an element of farce in excess of anything Dame Edna might have realized on stage. In 1972, so many requests for imperial honours were made by Australian governments that the British government sent the list back and asked for it to be culled. Even when the Whitlam Labor government introduced an Australian honours system in 1975, the Fraser government reinstated imperial honours in 1976. Only in 1992, did all State and Federal governments finally resolve to cease making imperial awards. In 2006, Australia remains the only Commonwealth country to continue to issue Queen's birthday stamps.[30] Meanwhile, the last vestiges of popular monarchism have been played out in the republic debate.

In 1992, Australians for Constitutional Monarchy (ACM) was launched in Sydney. The group formed in direct response to the Australian Republican Movement (ARM), founded in 1991. The scene at Sydney Town Hall was nostalgic and strangely moving. The movement's founders—Justice Michael Kirby being the key figure—stood on a platform as the Australian national anthem was sung. The vanguard had deliberately chosen to avoid singing God Save the Queen, lest they be depicted as outmoded conservatives longing

---

[29] For one example of countervailing tendencies see the pro-monarchy editorial in *Sydney Morning Herald*, 7 March 1977. Keating in *Sydney Morning Herald*, 29 March 2000. Also see McKenna, *The Captive Republic*, pp. 248–53.

[30] On the conservatives' longing for imperial honours see *Age*, 4 June 2005; also Martin, *A Bunyip Aristocracy*, p. 186; Whitlam in Commonwealth of Australia, *Parliamentary Debates*, House of Representatives, 15 April 1975, p. 1581; Fraser ibid., 1 June 1976, p. 2702. Details on stamps in *Golden Jubilee of Queen Elizabeth II, 2nd February–5th May 2002*, An Exhibition to honour the 50th anniversary of the accession to the throne, National Philatelic Club (Melbourne, 2002).

for another era. As the meeting was about to close, one man at the rear began to sing the old song with gusto. Before long, everyone in the hall was singing in unison—'God Save our Gracious Queen'—and the old glory days of the British Empire were reborn. By the end of the decade, when the republic—framed as 'minimalist' with a President appointed by a two-thirds majority of Federal Parliament—was put to referendum in 1999, the ACM had deserted the Monarchy, preferring instead to fight behind the banner 'Let the People Have their Say'. Having begun as defenders of a hereditary head of state in 1992, they aligned themselves successfully with supporters of a directly elected President in order to win the referendum. Since the late 1990s, in an effort to counter the republican movement's argument for an Australian head of state, many of Australia's leading monarchists have claimed that the Governor General, not the Queen, is Australia's head of state. The most prominent example is Sir David Smith, a former secretary to the Governor General and member of ACM. Smith has insisted that the term 'head of state' is of little use 'in Australia's constitutional debate', having been 'introduced by republicans'. Such claims contradict not only the historical record, but the reality of Australia's constitution, which explicitly refers to the Governor General as 'Her Majesty's representative in the Commonwealth'. Moreover, the term 'head of state' is not a republican invention. In 1992, the founding charter of ACM referred to Queen Elizabeth as 'the head of state'. Thirty years earlier, Governor General Sir Paul Hasluck maintained that 'a head of state' was 'an essential and integral part of modern national government'. Hasluck, a former conservative politician and no republican, also made it quite clear that 'the Queen of Australia as head of state fits in with both the principles and practices of [Australia's] form of government'—a constitutional Monarchy. The fact that many Australian monarchists no longer see Elizabeth II as head of state has left the Queen without a meaningful role. The British Monarchy has become Australia's constitutional Tower of Pisa.[31]

Australia no longer sees itself as one of the Queen's 'realms', as it is still described today on the royal family's official website. As John Hirst remarked in 1991, the Monarchy has lost its civic personality in Australia and yet it lingers, long after its resonance has departed. The symbolic emptiness of the Monarchy is actually the end point in the story of its success. Always benign,

---

[31] Sir David Smith, *Head of State* (Sydney, 2005), p. 14; *Leadership Beyond Politics: Australians for Constitutional Monarchy, Charter for Defence of the Australian Constitution* (Sydney, 1992); Sir Paul Hasluck, *The Office of Governor General: William Queale Lecture 1972* (Adelaide, 1972), pp. 2–3.

never an obstacle to Australia's independence, the Monarchy has performed a gradual disappearing act since Australia was settled in 1788. From the 1830s, the relationship between London and the colonies facilitated representative democracy and greater autonomy. As the colonies became self-governing and the new Federation emerged, the monarchical link provided the gloss of continuity, acting as the symbolic trustee of the people's right to freedom from arbitrary rule (also for Aboriginal people) and a shared focus of allegiance for all. No step towards Australian independence, including the recent push for a republic, has ever been opposed by the Crown.

Given the Monarchy's success in presiding over peaceful and incremental political change—independence by osmosis rather than declaration—it is hardly surprising that modern republicans are not anti-monarchical. Republicans oppose the Monarch's foreignness more than they reject Monarchy per se. Their programme of minimal political change, with its emphasis on protecting 'the current system', reflects the British constitutionalist tradition that has long characterized the common sense of Australian politics. Since the movement's inception in 1991, republicans have focused almost exclusively on the nationality of the head of state at the expense of wider constitutional reform. Australian republicanism embraces patriotic reform—an Australian President—before democratic reform or the need for constitutional recognition of Indigenous Australians. As Australians prepared to vote in the republic referendum in 1999, Aboriginal leaders were in London, visiting Queen Elizabeth II. Disappointed at the failure of Australian governments to address injustice, they petitioned the Monarch, in a now long-established tradition of protest. The irony was palpable. Aboriginal leaders were seeking an audience with the very figure republicans wished to remove from the Australian constitution. Their presence in London was a telling reminder of the failure of the republican movement to address Indigenous concerns in its platform.

Turning towards the future, it is clear that the retreat of Monarchy from Australia's civic culture raises several dilemmas, rarely contemplated. As the old stories of British Empire and Commonwealth unity have subsided, Australia has been left without a popular narrative of nationhood. In the sphere of politics, nothing of similar emotional resonance has been found to replace Monarchy. Anzac Day, now stripped of its imperial origins and reinvented as an exclusively Australian story of national awakening, has become Australia's dominant national myth. If Australian republicans remain silent on wider constitutional reform, Australia will remain a nation defined by a military myth and sporting prowess—a nation without a founding political moment, save the pointless disaster of Gallipoli in 1915.

The declining resonance of Monarchy has also altered the alignment of executive power in Australian federal politics. The changing role of the office of Governor General is a case in point. In the words of one of Australia's leading constitutional lawyers, Professor George Winterton, the office of Governor General has 'undergone greater transformation since federation than any other constitutional institution'. For most of the period following Federation in 1901, the Governor General was seen as the embodiment of the British connection in Australia. From being the representative of the imperial government in the first decades of the twentieth century, the office mutated to 'virtual invisibility' in the years between 1926 and 1969 before an intense moment of controversy in 1975, when Governor General Sir John Kerr dismissed Labor Prime Minister Gough Whitlam. Kerr did not seek counsel from his Monarch, a failure to consult which allegedly disappointed the Queen. After Kerr, the office returned to a period of 'quiescence' until 1996, when the Labor government appointee Sir William Deane achieved an 'unprecedented positive community profile'. Since Deane's departure in 2001, there has been considerable evidence of growing 'public concern' over the lack of community involvement in the process of appointing the Governor General (currently appointed by the Prime Minister). As Winterton explains, this concern reflects the Australian public's preference for a republic with a popularly elected President.

During Robert Menzies' time as Prime Minister (1949–66), the Crown hovered above the office of Prime Minister, commanding enormous symbolic importance. Now that the Crown has receded as a binding source of civic and national identity, and the office of Governor General has played an increasingly minor role in symbolic politics over the last decade (existing very much in the shadow of the PM), there is no symbolic power beyond that of the Prime Minister. There is, in fact, nothing 'beyond politics'. In the wake of international terrorism, former Prime Minister John Howard became Australia's chief 'commander', Anzac impresario (and mourner). On one occasion, at a welcome-home parade held in Sydney in 2003 for troops returning from Iraq, Howard usurped the role of the Governor General by taking the royal salute. As the British Monarchy has waned, and the symbolic repertoire of Australian politics has been choreographed increasingly from the corridors of Prime Minister and Cabinet, the office of the Australian

Prime Minister has become more Presidential. The absence of an Australian head of state capable of doing what Monarchy once did—'penetrating the spirit of the country and touching all inhabitants'—has created a symbolic vacuum. There is a clear need for a national leader who can speak from a non-partisan perspective, someone who can provide the Australian people with moral and national leadership beyond the sphere of partisan politics.

After Queen Elizabeth II's tour to Australia in 2000, the *Sydney Morning Herald* observed that the Queen's visit was 'suffused with a sense of transition, as of an image fading'.[32] Faded as the image may be, there is little sign of an image of equal depth and resonance rising to claim its place.

Select Bibliography

JOHN ARNOLD, PETER SPEARRITT, and DAVID WALKER, eds, *Out of Empire: The British Dominion of Australia* (Melbourne, 1993).

ALAN ATKINSON, *The Muddle-Headed Republic* (Melbourne, 1993).

VERNON BOGDANOR, *The Monarchy and the Constitution* (Oxford, 1995).

FRANK BONGIORNO, ' "Commonwealthmen and Republicans": Dr H. V. Evatt, the Monarchy and India', *Australian Journal of Politics and History*, 1 (2000), pp. 33–50.

DAVID CANNADINE, 'The Context Performance and Meaning of Ritual: The British Monarchy and the Invention of Tradition, c.1820–1977', in E. Hobsbawm and T. Ranger, eds, *The Invention of Tradition* (Cambridge, 1983), pp. 101–64.

JANE CONNORS, 'The 1954 Royal Tour of Australia', *Australian Historical Studies*, Vol. 25 (April 1993), pp. 371–84.

DAVID GOODMAN and JEANETTE HOORN, eds, *Vox Republicae: Feminism and the Republic* (Melbourne, 1996).

---

[32] Memories of the ACM launch in 1992 are my own. On the 'civic personality' of the Monarchy in contemporary Australia see John Hirst, 'The Conservative Case for an Australian Republic', *Quadrant*, September 1991, pp. 9–11; Alan Atkinson, *The Muddle-Headed Republic* (Oxford, 1993), p. 7. On the changing role of the Governor General in Australia see George Winterton, *The Evolving Role of the Governor General*, available at <http://www.republic.org.au>. For the Queen's alleged displeasure with Kerr in 1975, see Sir Michael Heseltine being interviewed in the first episode ('Child of Empire') in Paul Kelly's *100 Years: The Australian Story* (ABC Documentary, 2001). Much of the final sections of this essay draws together threads from my recent work, specifically: *Australian Republicanism; This Country: A Reconciled Republic* (Sydney, 2004); and 'Howard's Warrior's', in R. Gaita, ed., *Why the War Was Wrong* (Melbourne, 2003), pp. 167–200. Final quote on the Queen's tour in 2000 in *Sydney Morning Herald*, 3 April 2000.

GARETH GRAINGER and KERRY JONES, *The Australian Constitutional Monarchy* (Sydney, 1994).

W. J. HUDSON and M. P. SHARP, *Australian Independence: Colony to Reluctant Kingdom* (Melbourne, 1988).

DOUGLAS PIKE, *The Royal Presence in Australia 1867–1986* (Adelaide, 1986).

GEORGE WINTERTON, *Monarchy to Republic: Australian Republican Government* (Oxford, 1986).

12

War and Commemoration: 'The Responsibility of Empire'

JOY DAMOUSI

On Anzac Day 2003, Rebecca Fortescue, one of the thousands of modern day pilgrims to venture to Gallipoli, described the scene at the site of Australia's legendary First World War battle. Arriving at Lone Pine, she observed how 'there were bodies everywhere and if you could imagine everyone wearing khaki, that was a haunting flash of what the battle field might have looked like.' As everyone joined in a rousing rendition of 'I am Australian', and a round of 'cheers and applause' for the veterans of any war present, 'a lot of people lost it and started crying.' This service, she reflected, was better than the official Dawn Service, 'because we could tailor it to the Australian perspective and not be so diplomatic to Turkey. It was much more emotional and everyone joined in'.[1] This ritual, and the emotional sentiment that is attached to it, encapsulates an increasingly popular form of war commemoration undertaken by Australians in the twenty-first century. It continues the tradition of pilgrimage to war sites and captures the contemporary response of youth to remembering war.

There have of course been many different types of war commemoration since the beginning of the last century, but one of the ways in which contemporary participants have differed from their earlier counterparts has been in the increasing absence of any acknowledgement of Empire in their remembrances. Empire is no longer considered central to Australia's war story; nor does it figure in how Australia's involvement in war is remembered. This silence surrounding Empire mirrors Australia's shifting relationship to the Monarch and to Britain, for as the ties to Empire loosened, Empire's meaning and place within commemorative war practices underwent a

---

[1] Rebecca Fortescue, Journal Entry, 24 April 2003, Gallipoli, <http://www.nma.gov.au/exhibitions/community/anzac_pilgrims/anzac_memories/rebecca_fortescue>.

dramatic change. In the present day, a message from the Queen at public events has been the extent of any semblance of 'Empire'.

This chapter considers the Australian experience of a succession of imperial wars, tracing the gradual shifts in Australian commemorative practices of war in the past century. Commemorations are ever changing and contested: each generation defines them to suit the needs and interests of the contemporary moment. Commemoration and memory of war provides one of the most compelling case studies that captures the shifting paradoxes, contradictions, and inherent tensions of the place of Empire and 'the imperial' in Australian history. The South African War and the two major world wars were fought in the name of Empire but different meanings were attached to Empire at these different times. Collective memory is malleable, diverse, and contradictory; the place of the Empire in commemoration offers a challenge to exploring why some rituals, symbols, and identifications persist and why others have disappeared over time.

The wars amplified the paradox of loyalty—at once to nation and Empire. Societies sustain various public memories and commemorations at the same time. Initially, the commemoration of the First World War as a celebration of the heroic feats of the sons of Empire coexisted with that of the mythology of Anzac and the Australian character. But while the collective memory of imperial war defined an imagined community of Britishness, the significance of the local, Australian contribution gradually expanded to overshadow the narrative of Empire. Even though there were subtle signs of this shift early, the peculiar 'double loyalty' endured during the interwar years. It was progressively undermined during the post-Second World War era with the shift of alliance to another Empire—that of the United States. Although there are never unanimous decisions about how to commemorate war, public memory was soon characterized in ways that would render Britain increasingly marginal.

The commemoration of war continues to define notions of Australian identity. Anzac Day—the 25th of April—has enjoyed a robust revival and the yearly pilgrimages have become immensely popular among the young. Ideas of Empire are not foremost in their minds, however—it is the universal and generic qualities of heroism, courage, comradeship, and loyalty they celebrate. In its current configuration, war has been commemorated by the current generation of Australians with scant understanding of the historical forces that gave rise to it. In appropriating the war story for understanding Australian identity and 'character' without understanding the role of Empire, the history of power, politics, and war has subsequently been lost.

*   *   *

Australia's involvement in imperial wars has its origins in the pre-Federation era. Australian colonists were recruited to fight in the New Zealand Wars against the Maori in the 1840s and again in the 1860s, and a New South Wales contingent was raised in 1885 to join the British force sent to the Sudan to avenge the death of General Gordon. Neither occasion, however, provided the stuff of national legend. Although the New Zealand campaigns were to furnish Australia's first monument to an imperial war (in Hobart in 1850), they did not provide the basis for any meaningful martial tradition. The 'Australian' contribution to the conflict was insufficiently discernible, and, in any case, many of the volunteers remained in New Zealand to claim their bounty in the form of confiscated Maori lands. Nor was the circle of violence, massacres, and reprisals between settlers and Australia's own Indigenous people incorporated into the pantheon of imperial exploits. There is virtually no commemorative culture of Australia's frontier wars because they were deemed not to have happened. The deaths and sacrifices of the Indigenous population were not understood in martial terms, and an awkward, deafening silence served gradually to erase these local wars of Empire. Only recently have monuments to Indigenous–settler conflict been erected—such as the memorial walk at the site of the Myall Creek massacre in New South Wales—and historians have begun to include frontier conflict in their studies of commemoration.[2]

The Sudan expedition, by contrast, was unambiguously located within the imperial-martial tradition, and occasioned high hopes that the New South Wales contingent might bring home eternal glory and renown to the Australian colonies. That this proved not to be the case was due to the contingent's 'misfortune' in arriving too late to join the battle. The commanding officer, Colonel John Richardson, consoled his troops on their return to Sydney that, 'It was not our fault that we did not reap for the credit of the Colony a larger share of glory.' This did not dispel the feeling among the Contingent, and colonial society at large that, in the words of one volunteer, 'too many of us had come back.' An undertone of public mockery and ridicule greeted

---

[2] K. S. Inglis, *Sacred Places: War Memorials in the Australian Landscape* (Melbourne, 1998), p. 24. On frontier conflict in Australia see Chapters 1–4 in this volume.

the returning 'veterans', although most of this was directed at the 'jingo' politicians who had committed the colony to war in the first place. Apart from a few obscure wall plaques in Sydney churches, the only substantial memorial marking this episode was the statue of General Gordon, raised by public subscription in Melbourne in June 1889. The memorial made no mention of Australia's 'contribution', and revealed mixed feelings about Australia's duty to respond to the Empire call. While the Melbourne *Argus* could hail the statue as tangible proof that 'the people of this colony are not provincial, but are of the Imperial race', *The Bulletin* in Sydney was less enthused. 'The martial figure of General Gordon,' proclaimed a lead article in March 1889, 'built in a burst of hysterics by old women of both sexes in Melbourne, will be sold for old metal when the raving crank of Khartoum is estimated at his true value as a bloodthirsty fanatic.' The derogatory reference to 'old women' points to the way in which commemoration carried highly gendered overtones. A celebration of imperial masculinity has been a constant theme in the remembrance of war and imperial adventures.[3]

But it was the involvement of Australians in the South African War at the turn of the century that threw into sharp relief the tensions in allegiance between the imperial and the colonial. For those who were supportive of the war, it provided Australians with the sense that they were embedded within Empire and an important part of the imperial endeavour.[4] The war began over a year before the Australian states federated in 1901, and it was therefore the governments of the Australian colonies which volunteered their support and dispatched their contingents when the call came from Britain. The number of men who travelled to South Africa was 16,378—only 518 of whom perished. Yet as K. S. Inglis observes, before the wholesale slaughter of the Great War, this seemed a large number of casualties to contemporaries.[5]

Those who supported the war did so on the basis that Britain was fighting to protect her colonial citizens. Discussion about Australian involvement also sharpened debate about the role and meaning of the Empire and Australia's obligations within it. To supporters, the British were fighting in defence of 'civilization', against Afrikaner domination and the threat of a despotic,

---

[3] K. S. Inglis, *The Rehearsal: Australians at War in the Sudan 1885* (Sydney, 1985), pp. 132, 135, 139–40, 154–6.

[4] John Rickard, *Australia: A Cultural History* (London, 1988), pp. 113–14.

[5] K. S. Inglis, 'Preface', in L. M. Field, *The Forgotten War: Australian Involvement in the South African Conflict of 1899–1902* (Melbourne, 1979), p. v.

archaic culture.[6] In some circles, the war was considered necessary and just. Imperialism for these supporters meant 'the spreading of civilization, the progress of humanity, the march of enlightenment'.[7] The South African War was therefore a test for Australia whose 'manifest destiny' was to defend, protect, and support 'the most exalted traditions of the British race'.[8] The modern-day notion that the war was fought for someone else's cause was alien, as Australia was seen to be part of the family of nations within the British Empire.[9]

Although it appeared that there was an enthusiastic embrace of the expedition to the South African War in the public expressions of patriotism, indications of quiet resistance were apparent. Some radical nationalists opposed the war, while others such as Labor supporters queried why Australians should be part of a war which they had no say in shaping.[10] In Sydney, *The Bulletin* condemned the dispatch of Australian troops from the outset, declaring at the end of 1899: 'So wholly without concern for Australia is the Transvaal war—seeing that Britain is in no need whatever of assistance to crush a foe so very small—that even if the war were being made on just grounds instead of being a war of plunder and imperial aggrandizement, we would have no excuse for embarking on it.'[11] However, it is undeniable that the involvement in the South African War elicited the support of most Australians. Empire Day was the symbolic gesture of this connection. It was officially recognized in 1905 on 24 May and aimed to promote an imperial citizenship.[12]

The South African War has often been described as the 'forgotten war', overshadowed by the events of the Great War, but there were efforts made to remember Australia's contribution to the Empire and its imperial connection by honouring those who served in it. As K. S. Inglis has meticulously documented in his influential work *Sacred Places*, monuments were built across the nation to commemorate the South African War. The sacrifice to Empire is writ large both figuratively and symbolically on these memorials and is central to contemporary understandings of Australia's contribution to the war.[13]

---

[6] Barbara Penny, 'The Australian Debate on the Boer War', *Historical Studies*, Vol. 14, no. 56 (April 1971), p. 527.

[7] Penny, 'The Australian Debate', p. 529.

[8] Quoted in Penny, 'The Australian Debate', p. 531.   [9] Inglis, *Sacred Places*, p. 47.

[10] Rickard, *Australia*, p. 114.

[11] Quoted in Sylvia Lawson, *The Archibald Paradox: A Strange Case of Authorship* (Ringwood, 1983), p. 210.

[12] Rickard, *Australia*, p. 115.   [13] Inglis, *Sacred Places*, pp. 46–7.

The discussions surrounding the nature of these commemorations highlighted prevailing ideas about Australia's involvement in this war and how it should be remembered. Ten years after the end of the war, the South African Soldiers' Association in Victoria announced its intention to erect a suitable monument to honour their sacrifice; plans were made to commemorate the 228 Victorian soldiers who died. Such a memorial, it was hoped, would 'commemorate not only Victoria's dead, but also Victoria's assumption of the responsibility of empire'.[14]

By 1911, there were certainly issues of national, and not only imperial, pride that were associated with the monument. Such a memorial was seen by J. B. S. Williamson as a 'national memorial ... to the rising generations; a nation's pride and a nation's gratitude'.[15] But patriotism to the Empire continued to be central. In November 1911, the *Argus* editorialized on the need to celebrate this imperial spirit. Australia's involvement in the South African War underlined 'the fact that membership of the Empire involves duties as well as privileges, and the sacrifices so gladly made by the daughter nations in their desire to help the motherland did more to quicken the Imperial spirit and impress the world ... than ... a century of lip service in times of peace'. Civic pride and civic honour were involved 'in making whatever monument is decided upon adequate to the occasion and worthy of themselves'.[16] What was to be remembered in erecting such a monument was the enduring relationship between war, manliness, and Empire: not only the bravery and sacrifice of soldiers, but also Australia's willing assistance to the Empire and the imperial brotherhood. 'We as a race, spread though we are in every corner of the world, are prepared to stand and fall together.'[17]

The coming of the First World War overshadowed these plans to honour the dead in the earlier war. Victorian ideals about masculinity, honour, and loyalty were tested on a grander scale in the Great War. The heroic contribution to the imperial cause—in the colossal and titanic battles which were glorified through accounts such as those by the war correspondent C. E. W. Bean—provided the context for the Anzac myth. The casualties of 60,000 were 120 times the number that perished in South Africa. As Craig Wilcox has eloquently put it: 'By the end of the Great War, Australia's South African experience seemed decidedly trivial.'[18] He reflects that, after 1918,

---

[14] *Argus*, 12 May 1911.   [15] *Argus*, 24 May 1911.   [16] *Argus*, 2 November 1911.

[17] *Argus*, 3 November 1911.

[18] Craig Wilcox, *Australia's Boer War: The War in South Africa, 1899–1902* (Melbourne, 2002), p. 361.

the South African War became a metaphor for 'anything old or antiquated'; three state memorials were erected after 1918, compared with the 1500 to the new war. When the Australian War Memorial opened in the nation's capital, Canberra, in 1941, it gave no recognition to any conflict before 1914. The small number of memoirs and reminiscences which reflected on the loss of men in South Africa would soon rapidly be subsumed by the flood of reminiscences of the Great War.[19] For a time, efforts were made to commemorate the earlier war as part of the Anzac tradition, but it was difficult to reconcile the older imperial patriotism of the South African War veterans with the idea that April 1915 represented a new beginning for a new nation.[20] Nevertheless, the institutions which were formalized by the South African War, such as Empire Day, continued to stress the unity of Empire by race.

All previous meanings and understandings of Empire, of nation and of 'home' were transformed by the First World War. It at once consolidated the emergence of a nation and the changing place and meaning of Empire within the Australian imagination. The call to arms to support the cause of Empire was embraced with enthusiasm by Australians, best remembered by Labor leader Andrew Fisher's pledge to defend the British cause to 'our last man and our last shilling'. Before the end of 1914, 50,000 men had enlisted.[21] The excitement was shared by most men of enlistment age, who saw war at that time as an exhilarating adventure, and by women, who were proud to make their contribution to the Empire by willingly giving their sons, brothers, and their husbands. The new recruits were dubbed the 'Australian Imperial Force' (AIF), conveying the sense that Australia's destiny was intertwined with that of the Empire. The war provided the context which created the Anzac myth and, subsequently, the annual public holiday which celebrates Australia's first entry into the war at Gallipoli on 25 April 1915.

What distinguished the commemoration of the Gallipoli landings from earlier imperial adventures in South Africa and the Sudan was not merely the scale of the conflict and the extent of the casualties, although this is obviously significant. Even before the outbreak of war, there was a sense of inevitability about Australia's impending baptism of fire. C. E. W Bean, whose Gallipoli dispatches and other war writings were instrumental in popularizing the Anzac legend, had for several years prior to the war prophesied the military glory that awaited the Australian bushman. In his 1910 travelogue *On the Wool Track*, he referred to the peculiar qualities of the Australian

[19] Craig Wilcox, p. 361.   [20] Ibid., p. 362.   [21] Rickard, *Australia*, p. 118.

bush in providing 'the raw material for soldiers'.[22] The bushman's unique endurance and determination in fighting bushfires, he claimed, would one day serve him equally well on the battlefield: 'Short of putting a man up and running a piece of iron through him, there is probably nothing more like real warfare in the world.'[23] He would later make this same comparison in eulogizing the achievement of the AIF at Gallipoli. 'The Australian of the bush is frequently called upon to fight bush-fires,' he observed, 'and fighting bush-fires, more than any other human experience, resembles the fighting of a pitched battle'.[24] For Bean, the peculiar adaptability of the bushman to wartime service was not merely an Australian national trait, but a tribute to the fact that 'Australia is as purely British as the people of Great Britain—perhaps more so.'[25] He described the unique qualities of the bushman as inherently British qualities, but qualities which only really came to the fore under Australia's harsh outback conditions: 'That extraordinary versatility, the capacity to do anything ... obviously exists pre-eminently in the British race. But it does not come out till the race gets to places like Australia, where it has to.'[26] Five years before the first shots were fired at Gallipoli, then, Bean had formed a clear vision of Australian soldiers displaying the superior martial qualities of the British race-warrior, fine-tuned by bitter experience on the Australian frontier.

This same sense of expectation—of an impending military triumph waiting to happen—was in evidence from the moment war was declared on 4 August 1914. Australia's first wartime military manoeuvre—the dispatch of a regiment from Townsville to Thursday Island to secure the Torres Strait on 8 August—was hailed by the local paper as a day to 'be remembered in the history of Australia as that on which the first contingent of her new citizen forces was sent forth on active service conditions'.[27] Three months later, the sinking of the German Cruiser *Emden* off the Cocos Keeling Islands provided another contender for a national day of remembrance. The *Sydney Morning Herald* proclaimed: 'Monday, November 9, 1914, is a date that will be remembered with pride by the people of Australia for all time. Australians, indeed, are likely to grow prouder of it as time goes on ... it was our first sea fight; and on that day a new Australia was born ... [it] has brought home to us

---

22 C. E. W. Bean, *On the Wool Track* (New York, 1910), p. 138.   23 Ibid., p. 134.

24 C. E. W. Bean, *The Story of ANZAC* (Sydney, 1933), p. 46.

25 Bean, *On the Wool Track*, p. 139.   26 Ibid., pp. 146–7.

27 *North Queensland Register*, cited in Craig Wilcox, *For Hearths and Homes: Citizen Soldiering in Australia, 1854–1945* (Sydney, 1998), p. 75.

the responsibilities as well as the glories of nationhood.'[28] At almost the same time, and at the opposite end of the country in Western Australia, the *Albany Advertiser* rejoiced in the departure (from Albany) of the convoy carrying the first AIF to Europe on 31 October. 'Such a sight has certainly never been seen before in Australia, and no man or woman breathing today will probably live to witness another spectacle in any way approaching it in magnificence.'[29] Yet none of these dates or events were to become markers of national achievement for future generations. Like the South African War before them, they were to be eclipsed by the landings at Gallipoli on 25 April 1915, a conflict whose scale, significance, and duration—if not the military outcome—seemed to provide the necessary raw material for annual commemoration. But what the false dawns of 1914 do indicate is that it was the timing of Gallipoli that was at least as important as the material achievements of the Anzac troops. The imperative of establishing Australia's martial credentials—and thereby cementing the place of a new nation in the networks of Empire—loomed large in the rhetoric and reportage of the Gallipoli landings. As Richard White so eloquently puts it: 'With the landing of Gallipoli in April 1915, the ready-made myth was given a name, a time and a place.'[30]

Bean's emphasis on the Australian embodiment of imperial or 'British' race qualities, also points to one of the key dilemmas of Australia's experience and commemoration of the First World War. The reality of military disaster at Anzac Cove fuelled an anti-British sentiment, for the belief that the catastrophe at Gallipoli was a failure of British strategy soon gained currency.[31] Despite this, Gallipoli did not dent the view, or cloud the sentiment, that Australia remained a part of the Empire. 'Britain' emerges in Australia's story as not only the cause for which Australians fought, but also the yardstick against which Australians measured the distinctiveness of their own wartime achievements. The anti-British strain in the conventional Gallipoli narrative has received greater emphasis from the post-imperial generation of historians—so much so that it is often the experience of disillusionment with Britain that is seen to underpin the wartime birth of a national consciousness.[32] As E. M. Andrews argued in 1993, the experience

---

[28] *Sydney Morning Herald*, 14 November 1914.   [29] *Albany Advertiser*, 21 November 1914.

[30] Richard White, *Inventing Australia: Images and Identity, 1688–1980* (Sydney, 1981), p. 128.

[31] Rickard, *Australia*, p. 118.

[32] See for example Bill Gammage, *The Broken Years: Australian Soldiers in the Great War* (Canberra, 1974); Gavin Souter, *Lion and Kangaroo: The Initiation of Australia, 1901–1919*, (Sydney, 1976).

of fighting alongside the English 'led many soldiers to see Australia with new eyes and consider her apart from Britain'.[33]

It is important, though, to distinguish between a natural resentment of the perceived bungling of the British officer corps (also prevalent among the lower ranks of British regiments) and a complete renunciation of the imperial tie. This distinction was personified by Australia's wartime leader Billy Hughes, who, while losing no opportunity to berate his British counterparts about the conduct of the war, and holding little trust in the capacity of British leaders to prosecute the war in accordance with Australia's material interests, could nonetheless adopt Bean's imperial race rhetoric with unrivalled fervour. Visiting Britain in the midst of the conflict he spoke of the 'cradle of our race' whose 'glorious traditions stretch back into the grey dawn of time'.[34] Hughes could insist on the imperative of conscripting Australia's youth to the Empire's cause (to the point of fighting and losing two referenda on the subject), while remaining deeply sceptical about the effectiveness of the Imperial War Cabinet.[35] Despite his disillusionment with Lloyd George, Hughes could boast, in placing the Treaty of Versailles before the Australian Parliament, that Australians 'were more British than the people of Great Britain'.[36]

What had shifted from 1915 was a more pronounced sense of nationhood which supplemented rather than supplanted a connection to the British Empire. In the fifteen years after Gallipoli, Anzac and the First World War meant not only defending the values of Empire—crucial as these continued to be—but the commemorations also included a celebration of qualities attached to Australian soldiers. 'To the mass of people', reported the *Sydney Morning Herald*, 'the name of Anzac stands, and should only stand, for heroism, sacrifice, and faithfulness unto death.' It is not the 'blunders or misdirected courage, the splendid failure, the magnificent withdrawal' that should be remembered but the 'great cause and those who suffered for it'.[37] This dual loyalty to nation and Empire reflects John Rickard's observation that 'myth-building engendered by the Great War did not weaken ties with Britain, it only made them more complex.'[38] The war not only provided the

---

[33] E. M. Andrews, *The Anzac Illusion: Anglo-Australian Relations during World War I* (Cambridge, 1993), p. 217.

[34] W. M. Hughes, *'The Day'—and after: War Speeches* (London, 1916), p. 60.

[35] On the conscription crisis see Chapter 8 in this volume, pp. 206–7.

[36] *Commonwealth Parliamentary Debates*, 10 September 1919.

[37] *Sydney Morning Herald*, 25 April 1930.   [38] Rickard, *Australia*, p. 135.

foundations of a national myth, but contributed a whole new vocabulary to Australia's commemorative culture; the Dardanelles, the Somme, Pozières, Passchendaele, Villers-Bretonneux, St Quentin, Birdwood, Monash, and Simpson were to become household words.

During the interwar years, commemoration most commonly took place in public centres, with long sombre processions of returned men, but these were not the only practices which remembered those who had perished in the war. There were other types of remembrance that evolved over time, which included Armistice Day with its two minutes' silence, the giving of poppies, the laying of wreaths at significant sites such as local memorials, and religious gatherings at churches and at local branches of the Returned Sailors and Soldiers Imperial League of Australia (RSSILA). These provided an opportunity for families, and in particular, women, to grieve publicly for their lost men. The maternal sacrifice of giving their sons, however, could never be elevated into the national glory of commemoration as the ultimate sacrifice of their sons occupied centre stage. At both a local and national level, commemorations evolved around the celebration of the qualities of the heroism of men in war. This did not, however, extend to the recognition of the war service of Aboriginal soldiers, which remained unacknowledged.[39]

The symbols and regalia of Empire continued to occupy centre stage in public events and Australians predominately maintained a dual loyalty to Australia and Empire. During commemorative occasions in the interwar years, the Australian connection to Empire was often manifest in messages from the King and Queen and the presence of British Royalty on public occasions that consolidated this relationship. On Anzac Day in 1925, the Governor General made this connection explicit: 'The tender messages of sympathy from the King and the Queen and the Prince of Wales remind us that we are enfolded in the warm sympathy of the British race throughout the whole Empire.'[40] This sentiment was expressed in the context of the achievements also of the Australian people and nation. Indeed, it was the contribution to the wider imperial cause that seemed to make these national achievements worth celebrating. Thus, *The Age* could write in April 1926 that Australia emerged 'into the full bloom of nationhood' at Gallipoli, while affirming that 'its men had proved themselves worthy of the

---

[39] Robert A. Hall, *The Black Diggers: Aborigines and Torres Strait Islanders in the Second World War* (Canberra, 1997), p. 1.

[40] *Argus*, 27 April 1927.

highest traditions of the British race.'[41] The two minutes' silence was also a significant way in which the commemorative moment bonded Australia to the Empire. On Armistice Day in 1930 it was noted that 'silence for two minutes in memory of those who lost their lives will be observed in British and Allied countries throughout the world.'[42]

But by the 1930s, the next generation had emerged who did not remember the war, and commemorative occasions were not always saturated with the rhetoric of Empire. Editorializing Anzac Day twenty years after Gallipoli, the *Argus* believed that for the generation 'of young men and women, grown to manhood and womanhood since 1915', and who 'does not know war as a living, terrible experience', it was 'fitting that they should look to the future boldly, strengthened in their optimism by the story of Anzac, which is first a symbol of endurance, fortitude, and high courage'. It declared that pride of race was a virtue; 'it toughens the national fibre'. But the message was also explicitly anti-war: 'The story of Anzac is also a warning—a cry out of the past that men should never again be called upon to make the sacrifice of all that life offers upon the sombre altar of war.' While the world moved on, and there were opportunities to remember, there 'is no need to adorn or to romanticise their achievements ... They do not ask the young to glorify war ... All they hope is that the spirit which made Anzac Day possible may be rekindled in other causes and other crises.'[43]

The connection and loyalty to Empire remained, however, ever-present throughout these years. In his autobiography, the political analyst and cultural commentator Donald Horne remembers how allegiance to Empire was a central part of his schooling. He recalls how, during the 1930s, as 'well as being Australians we were also British, the first-class citizens of the Empire, and at school this was what we were most taught to admire'. One of the themes of the history curriculum was the growth of the Empire, where they studied how the 'Imperial Dominions Joined the Mother Country in Fighting For Freedom'. On Empire Day, patriotic speeches were delivered as well as songs sung such as 'Rule Britannia', 'Three Cheers for the Red, White and Blue', and 'Advance Australia Fair'.[44]

---

[41] Quoted in Ewan Morris, 'The Anzac Legend', in Peter Dennis, Jeffrey Grey, Ewan Morris, and Robin Prior, eds, *The Oxford Companion to Australian Military History* (Melbourne, 1995), p. 45.

[42] *Argus*, 11 November 1930.   [43] *Argus*, 25 April 1935.

[44] Donald Horne, *The Education of Young Donald* (Sydney, 1967), p. 61.

At the same time, war commemoration also had a national appeal which celebrated the qualities of Australian soldiers and, by implication, the Australian nation. This was especially the case with the twentieth anniversary of Gallipoli in 1935. On this occasion, huge parades wove through the streets of capital cities and local towns.[45] The reunions were well documented as men from various brigades and units would come together for a celebration, which usually meant many of them would be drunk—an aspect of their celebration which was later to be the subject of vitriolic criticism by subsequent generations.[46] Different types of commemoration—local, individual, and collective—evolved during the interwar years—not all of which focused on Empire.[47]

On a more individual basis, grief and loss of sons and husbands was often channelled through the rhetoric of imperial sacrifice. For mothers in particular, wartime grief became explicable and manageable through the notion of the 'sacrificial mother'. Motherhood had been given an elevated status and encapsulated the essence of feminine sacrifice in war. The giving of their sons for the imperial cause—in some families like that of Mrs Clara Nitchie who had six sons on active service at once—was celebrated and eulogized in the press where their sacrifices were described in patriotic terms. But even the most patriotic mothers were ambivalent about the extent of their imperial duty and uneasy about how far their responsibility to the war effort stretched. Ellen Derham supported her son Alfred when he enlisted. Although she was thankful he was not a coward and would do his duty, she insisted, 'I want no Victoria Cross—I want my son.' When her second son, Frank, enlisted there was pride that her sons were 'of so much use to their country', but also tears and sadness. The elevated status of the sacrificial mother was, however, short lived. It did not survive commemorative practices in the future, as any notion of wartime sacrifice was overshadowed by the ultimate sacrifice.[48]

At the government level, militarism and Empire were drawn together overtly in displays of military strength and power. In 1935, it was reported that '[t]here was admiration for senior officers, splendidly equipped and mounted on magnificent chargers, and for the many bands equipped in brilliant new uniforms.' At a congregation after the main march, 4,000 returned soldiers,

---

[45] *Argus*, 25 April 1935; 26 April 1935.   [46] *Argus*, 25 April 1935.

[47] *Argus*, 26 April 1935.

[48] See Joy Damousi, *The Labour of Loss: Mourning, Memory and Wartime Bereavement in Australia* (Cambridge, 1999), pp. 32–4.

nurses, and relatives of the men who fought in the war gathered at the Exhibition Buildings. Many of those who spoke were in military uniform: the Governor wore military uniform—at his first Australian commemoration of Anzac Day—as did the Anglican Archbishop, who wore the uniform of an army chaplain. The occasion was strewn with military regalia and colours. Huntingfield, the Governor, noted that the achievements of the various regiments illustrated how the 'world would have these deeds for ever as examples of the gallantry of the British race'. In Sydney, the Reverend Rumble announced from the pulpit that it was not necessarily wrong to participate in war and the Church did not automatically condemn it. 'War could be just and necessary. It was lawful only if the cause was just and if it was the only means by which an injustice could be remedied ... God permitted war because mankind had deserved it.' Others were more critical of this military culture. Anzac Day was often a commemorative day to reflect on the purpose of war in general. The head of the prestigious Ivanhoe Grammar School, the Reverend S. L. Buckley, said that war 'was a horrible, foul, and terrible business ... Not all the deeds of gallantry and sacrifice that occurred during a war could alter that fact. No returned soldier having seen what he had seen would hope for a moment for another war'. In other schools, the Empire was lauded and values of 'loyalty and race', freedom, service, and devotion were exalted as exemplary values. The sacrifices of Gallipoli were made so that the freedom which was expected under the British flag could be preserved.[49]

In 1939, on the eve of another war, Empire and nationhood were not necessarily seen in contradictory terms. Prime Minister R. G. Menzies, a devotee of the Monarchy and an imperial admirer, reflected these sentiments when he declared war on Germany 'as a result' of the British declaration: he was unable to separate the aspirations of Australia from those of Britain. The outbreak of the Second World War invited comparisons between the two world wars. On Anzac Day in 1940 the *Sydney Morning Herald* reproduced C. E. W. Bean's account of Gallipoli. Ever loyal to both Australia and the British Empire, Bean encapsulated the dual commitment of his generation, lauding the values, qualities, and heroism of the Australian warrior within the wider conquests of the British Empire.[50] The idea of a new generation of soldiers carrying the mantle of the Anzacs was a typical recruiting technique in the early stages of the war.[51] It appeared prominently in Charles

---

[49] *Argus*, 26 April 1935.   [50] *Sydney Morning Herald*, 25 April 1940.
[51] See Joan Beaumont, *Australia's War, 1939–45* (Sydney, 1996) p. xxii.

Chauvel's 1940 war film *Forty Thousand Horsemen* depicting the exploits of the Australian Light Horse in Palestine. The film's opening titles declared:

> ... with pride, their own sons are saying today:
> The torch you threw to us we caught
> And now our hands will hold it high
> Its glorious light will never die.[52]

As these examples clearly show, the culture of remembrance that had grown out of the First World War helped to determine popular understandings of the Second. This sense of continuity was clearly conveyed in the decision to name the new force the 'Second AIF'. And in many ways, the early phase of the war did seem to follow a familiar pattern. As in 1915, Australian troops were dispatched to imperial theatres of war in the Mediterranean. And as at Gallipoli, those dispatched to defend Greece and the island of Crete were to suffer heavy losses before being evacuated. Menzies visited London in 1941 and, like Hughes before him, found himself in profound disagreement with his British counterparts over the conduct of the war. Yet the language and rhetoric of Empire continued to shape his public pronouncements, particularly in his widely publicized addresses to the British public. As *The Times* commented on his departure, Menzies had 'made it unmistakably plain to the world that Australia is with us to the last'.[53]

The notion of the 'Empire's call' was reiterated in 1940 in public addresses and commemorative ceremonies. The Empire occupied a place in the formal proceedings in telegrams from the King and the Queen, delivered by the Governor General: 'Once again the peoples of the Empire have received the call to take up arms in defence of justice and freedom, and all who have answered it may find a noble inspiration in the deeds of those whom we commemorate to-day.'[54] The launch of the Australian War Memorial in 1941 helped to strengthen these connections. Its vision was to present Australia emerging on the world stage, through its connections to the British Empire. But it also attempted to commemorate Australian service and sacrifice and to assist a generation to grieve for its war victims.[55]

---

[52] Quoted in Stuart Ward, 'A War Memorial in Celluloid: The Gallipoli Legend in Australian Cinema', in Jenny MacLeod, ed., *Gallipoli: Making History* (London, 2004), p. 64.

[53] 5 May 1941, quoted in A. W. Martin, *Robert Menzies: A Life. Vol. 1, 1894–1943* (Melbourne, 1993), p. 355.

[54] *Sydney Morning Herald*, 25 April 1940.

[55] Michael McKernan, *Here is Their Spirit: A History of the Australian War Memorial 1917–1990* (St Lucia, 1991), p. xiv.

The fall of Singapore in February 1942, however, represented an entirely new departure for Australians, precipitating a different set of meanings that would be attached to Empire and war.[56] The Japanese advance of 1941–2 brought the war into Australia's hemisphere, and thereby altered conventional Australian perceptions of war as a duty performed on far-flung imperial battlefields. Moreover, the failure of Winston Churchill's War Cabinet to reinforce the Singapore base, despite repeated assurances to the contrary, introduced an element of ambivalence into the commemorative rhetoric of imperial loyalty. For some, Britain's failure was explained away by the exigencies of war and the impossible logistics of fighting Germany and Japan simultaneously.

But the 'Great Betrayal' of February 1942 undoubtedly became the source of what John Ramsden has termed the 'bundle of irreconcilable paradoxes' that typified post-war memories of war, Empire, and Winston Churchill in particular.[57] On the one hand, Churchill was hailed in Australia as the saviour of the war effort, who led his people through the Blitz and defied Hitler against the odds. This view was manifest in countless official memorials, statues, street signs, and other symbolic tributes to the wartime leader, and the repeated (but ultimately futile) attempts to persuade him to visit Australia.[58] Yet running counter to this was an alternative, unofficial undercurrent of resentment and dissent. Carl Bridge has described how, growing up in the 1950s, 'few Australians were not told the moral tale' of Britain's and Churchill's abandonment of Australia.[59] In this view, Churchill was portrayed as the architect of the bungled Gallipoli campaign, and the arch-villain of Singapore, who disingenuously secured the assistance of Australian troops in the Mediterranean, only to refuse requests for their return in Australia's hour of need. That Churchill was also said to have denigrated Australians as a race descended from 'bad stock' only served to underline his malign intent. This was a view that would later find expression in the television drama of David Williamson, works of history by David Day and others, and the Prime Ministerial rhetoric of Paul Keating, who, on the fiftieth anniversary of Singapore, expressed an enduring resentment against

[56] On the military and security implications of the defeat at Singapore, see Chapter 10 in this volume.

[57] John Ramsden, *Man of the Century: Winston Churchill and his Legend Since 1945* (London, 2002), p. 436.

[58] See ibid., chapter 10.

[59] Carl Bridge, 'Poland to Pearl Harbour', in Bridge, ed., *Munich to Vietnam* (Melbourne, 1991), pp. 38–9.

'a country which decided not to defend the Malayan peninsula, not to worry about Singapore and not to give us our troops back to keep ourselves free from Japanese domination'. That such a widely popularized counter-myth could coexist with more conventional accounts of Churchill's unrivalled genius, is testament not only to the enduring emotional appeal of Britishness in Australia, but also to the capacity of new realities subtly to undermine the tenets of imperial loyalty.

The vital role played by the United States in the Second World War also posed a challenge to the traditional nexus of Empire and nation in Australian war commemoration. Australia's obvious reliance on America in turning back the Japanese advance during the Battle of the Coral Sea in May 1942, and the charismatic wartime presence of General Douglas Macarthur in Australia, suggested a shift in Australia's allegiances and loyalties. Prime Minister John Curtin seemed to make this explicit in his widely publicized statement on the eve of the Fall of Singapore: 'Without any inhibitions of any kind, I make it clear that Australia looks to America, free of any pangs as to our traditional links or kinship with the United Kingdom.'[60] The reality, however, was more complex, and this raised inevitable difficulties when it came to commemorating Australia's wartime partnership with the Americans. In 1946, the first annual 'Coral Sea Week' festivities were staged as a token of Australia's gratitude (and a thinly disguised reminder to the Americans of what was expected of them in any future Pacific conflict). A more permanent monument was the Australian–American War memorial, opened in Canberra in 1954. On these occasions, the underlying tensions with the imperial commemorative tradition were generally diffused by reassuring reminders that Britain also fought alongside America. Significantly, Queen Elizabeth II was chosen to open the new memorial in Canberra during her royal tour. On this occasion Menzies was at pains to stress that this memorial did not diminish Australia's ongoing commitment to the British Commonwealth. 'Our nation is British in blood, tradition and sentiment,' he declared.

Throughout the 1950s, Australians continued to celebrate British royalty and culturally identify themselves as a part of the Commonwealth of British nations which was reinforced by the royal tour of 1954.[61] But with the decline of Britain as a world power and the move increasingly towards the United States, culturally, politically, and economically, the ties to Britain began to

---

[60] *Melbourne Herald*, 27 December 1941.   [61] Rickard, *Australia*, p. 207.

loosen. Australia's military commitment to the American-led Korean war in 1950, and the signing of the Australian and New Zealand regional pact (ANZUS) with the United States in 1951, signalled a diplomatic shift from Britain to America.[62]

The 'post-war, baby boomer' generation was also beginning to be more critical of the loyalties of their forebears. In his play *The One Day of the Year*, Alan Seymour documents this shift. Katharine Brisbane described the play as 'a turning point in the post-war movement away from British gentility towards examination of the knotty working-class roots of Australian life'.[63] It dramatized the generational conflict between father and son about the Anzac myth; it denounced war and was critical of the ways in which an earlier generation had given war legitimacy through the ritualizing process.

At the same time as the first production of the play was being performed, in 1960, there was further criticism in an article published in the University of Sydney student newspaper *Honi Soit*. The author condemned Anzac Day as the 'annual ritual of national narcissism', and 'a protracted sentimentalising of a brutal, unlovely phenomenon'. The focus on the dead revealed 'a neurotic morbidity that was the mark of an unbalanced personality'. Anzac Day perpetuated the fallacy that war was 'an ennobling activity'. The grief that was shown on Anzac Day was simply 'a bonanza of emotionalism, hypocrisy and alcohol'. Apart from providing beer and poker machines, 'it had outgrown its purpose'. The counter-attack on these radical views was swift and immediate. The Chancellor of the University, Sir Charles Blackburn, 'deplored the article', describing it as 'perverted and disloyal'. Brigadier Fewtrell of the RSSILA said that the students were ill informed, and were ignorant of the work the RSSILA 'was doing to help sick and wounded Servicemen and the widows and children of deceased Servicemen'.[64] These arguments were part of an increasing criticism of war by a generation who interpreted its commemoration by their elders as simply an opportunity to imbibe alcohol to excess, gamble, and mindlessly endorse Australia's passive involvement in the wars of other countries. Geoffrey Serle, who had grown up during the height of the British Empire, observed in 1969 how the 'young

---

[62] Geoffrey Bolton, *The Oxford History of Australia. Vol. 5: 1942–1988* (Melbourne, 1986), p. 79.

[63] Katharine Brisbane, 'One Day of the Year', in Phillips Parsons, ed., *Companion to Theatre in Australia* (Sydney, 1995), p. 418.

[64] *Sydney Morning Herald*, 23 November 1960.

Australian now has no sense of conflict in his [sic] loyalties, sees himself naturally as an independent Australian'.[65]

From 1965 onwards, the commemoration of Anzac Day entered into a markedly different era of commemorative practice. This was the year when the RSSILA dropped the 'I' for 'Imperial' from its masthead, and was renamed the 'Returned Services League' (RSL). It was also in that year that the Empire Day celebrations of 24 May were formally 'merged' with the Queen's Birthday holiday in June, having limped along since 1958 as the renamed (and barely observed) 'Commonwealth Day'. And 1965 also marked the 50th anniversary of Anzac Day, which was honoured with the first significant pilgrimage to the battlefields since the war took place. There was extensive coverage of the landing at Gallipoli of some seventy-odd original Anzacs and veterans from Australia and New Zealand, who came ashore in lifeboats from the cruise ship Karadeniz. The media reportage stressed the heroics of the men on the beach that day: 'The landing brought vivid memories of the bloody, brutal fighting 50 years back when the Anzacs fought desperately to tear this small strip of land from the Turks.' The Queen's message also stressed the sacrifice of nations rather than those of Empire: 'every generation of Australians and New Zealanders must grieve for the human sacrifice and will remember with gratitude the valor and devotion of those who lost their lives.' The turnout of servicemen was large: 32,000 in Melbourne; 40,000 people cheering in the crowd. The contribution of nurses and matrons was remembered.[66]

The year 1965 also signalled the entry of Australia into another war—Vietnam—where, for the first time, Australian troops were committed to a conflict where Britain was not also involved. Initially, the war had the support of a majority of Australians, as witnessed by Harold Holt's landslide victory at the 1967 election. But by the end of the decade, Vietnam had come to signify and represent the subservience of Australian foreign policy to another Empire. With Australia's involvement in Vietnam—America's dirty war, as its critics labelled it—there was a further shift in war commemoration. Vietnam veterans were involved in the 1970 Anzac Day commemoration, but controversy would cloud the war and there was an enduring sense from them that their contribution was undervalued in a war that was lost. A new

---

[65] Geoffrey Serle, 'Australia and Britain', in Richard Preston, ed., *Contemporary Australia: Studies in History, Politics, and Economics* (Durham, NC, 1969), p. 18.

[66] *The Age*, 26 April 1965.

generation of protestors and conscientious objectors emerged criticizing any connection with Empires, be they British or American.

One consequence of the Vietnam controversy was a subtle shift of emphasis, whereby the qualities of Australian soldiers in wartime were decoupled from the cause for which they fought. In 1970, for example, it was the heroic qualities and sacrifices of Australian soldiers that was remembered. The *Age* editorial was moved to reflect:

What we celebrate are the human qualities of our countrymen who died in the wars, qualities of courage and sacrifice and comradeship. We remember them with gratitude, and we identify ourselves with those men; for they were our kinsfolk and our friends, men like ourselves. We would like to think that we have something of the same stuff of manhood in us that they had.[67]

Yet even these values and qualities were becoming vulnerable to vociferous attack and critique by a new generation. This took place in the 1970s in the context of an Australian radical nationalism which began overtly to challenge any British connections and celebrated an independent Australian culture and identity. This new mood was symbolized by Prime Minister Gough Whitlam, who ensured the withdrawal of Australian troops from Vietnam. Whitlam also promoted Australian literature and the arts, and became a spokesperson for the new nationalism which was defined by a political, cultural, and military self-sufficiency.[68]

By 1975, the commitment of Australians to the Anzac memory and tradition were called into question. In that year in Melbourne, the police estimate was a mere 20,000 people who had assembled for the Anzac parade, in contrast with the 77,000 football fans who gathered to watch the local football game. There were calls for Australians to show more respect to the fallen. Governor General Paul Hasluck, in one of his last Vice-Regal speeches, castigated his fellow Australians for 'ridiculing the traditional festivals and days of commemoration' and 'neglecting to honour those who had served and died for Australia'.[69] But war and commemoration were not high on the community's sense of obligation and pride. In 1980, one correspondent to the paper wrote that, 'The attitude now prevailing towards Anzac Day is a disgrace and tragedy.'[70] The numbers remained low again in that year. *The*

[67] *The Age*, 25 April 1970.

[68] Stuart Macintyre, *A Concise History of Australia* (Cambridge, 1999), p. 231.

[69] National Library of Australia, Hasluck Papers, Vice-Regal Speeches, 1969–74, 'The Pioneering Virtues', Bairnsdale, 28 March 1974, MS 5274 Box 38.

[70] *The Age*, 25 April 1980, p. 10.

Age in Melbourne reported that 20,000 had gathered (although 5,000 up on the previous year) amidst 'fears that the holiday is losing its significance'. In his regular column, the journalist Ron Tanner observed in *The Age* how Australians were 'much more concerned with the Olympic games, Iran and various elections'.[71]

The theme of inclusion and exclusion was vociferously debated in the commemorative events during the 1970s and early 1980s. The omission of the contribution of Indigenous soldiers from memorialization began to emerge as an issue and the Vietnam soldiers themselves began a legal push for recognition and compensation. By the 1970s and 1980s, feminists offered scathing critiques of masculinity, war, and violence. Organizations such as Women Against Rape in War challenged war as an uncontested part of Australian identity; Anzac Day became the rallying point against the futility of violence of men in war.[72]

The view that Anzac Day had lost its significance was even further endorsed by a lead article in *The Bulletin* in 1980, entitled 'Last Post for Anzac', that argued that young people had little understanding of the meaning of Anzac and that the 'spirit of Anzac' was dying if not dead. The psychologist and cultural commentator Ronald Conway observed that few schoolchildren were aware of its meaning and significance. Australia's wartime experiences were perceived as 'irrelevant and boring'. For Conway, Anzac Day had lost its significance because of four factors: a shifting attitude to war; an increased dislike of patriotic rituals and commemorations; the adverse effect of recent wars on the Anzac legend; and the basic paganism of the whole Anzac commemoration. Conway was even moved to consider whether the spirit of Anzac had 'outlived its historical moment', and suggested that 'we can surely find something a little better than a carping pacifism and indolence to take its place'.[73] The article attracted a range of responses, but critics and supporters alike argued that Anzac day needed to be made more relevant and significant once again to younger people.[74]

Conway's death knell was, however, premature. From 1980 to 1984, the South African War and the two world wars were cinematically restaged for a new generation, with the Empire and the British being positioned as the villain. *Breaker Morant* (South African War, 1980), *Gallipoli* (First World

---

[71] *The Age*, 26 April 1980, p. 13.

[72] Adrian Howe, 'Anzac Mythology and the Feminist Challenge', *Melbourne Journal of Politics*, Vol. 15 (1983–4), pp. 17–18.

[73] *The Bulletin*, 29 April 1980, pp. 55–9.   [74] *The Bulletin*, 20 May 1980, p. 11.

War, 1981), and the television mini-series *The Last Bastion* (Second World War, 1984) all drew on radical nationalist interpretations of Australians being duped into fighting British wars, which remained the central interpretation of Australian involvement by the post-imperial generation.

Perhaps more than any other political leader, Paul Keating, Prime Minister of Australia from 1991 to 1996, took great delight in popularizing this interpretation of Australia's relationship to Britain during the Second World War. At a time when moves towards a Republic were afoot, Keating promoted an Australian nationalism which emphasized the need for severing the ties with the Monarchy. He thus not only emphasized Britain's betrayal at Singapore, but also looked to the Second World War for a more unequivocally national site of commemoration. This he found, ironically enough, in Australia's former colony of Papua New Guinea. The Kokoda track, where Australians had fought a fiercely pitched battle with the Japanese from July to November 1942, had long been integral to Australian military folklore. Keating, however, saw in Kokoda a symbolic departure from Australia's imperial instincts. On the first Anzac Day of his Prime Ministership in 1992, he chose the Australian memorial at Kokoda to deliver his address to the nation. In contrast to 'the many conflicts where we felt pangs of loyalty to the Mother Country', he declared, Australians at Kokoda had fought to repel a foreign invader—for 'the Australian way of life'. For Keating, there could be 'no deeper spiritual basis to the meaning of the Australian nation than the blood that was spilled on this very knoll, this very plateau, in defence of the liberty of Australia'.[75] As James Curran suggests, Keating sought to anoint Kokoda as a 'new foundational myth', in contrast to the more distant conflicts in Europe and the Middle East in the defence of Empire.[76]

While there is evidence in recent years of a renewed interest in Kokoda as a distinctive moment in Australia's emergence from Empire, the Gallipoli campaign nonetheless remains central to Australian commemorative culture. Keating's successor, John Howard, did not feel the same urge to emphasize the defence of the homeland. On the contrary, he stressed the need to maintain loyalty to past military alliances and remained a staunch monarchist. Under Howard, a new Australian and New Zealand commemorative 'Peace Park' was opened at Gallipoli in 2000.

[75] Quoted in James Curran, *The Power of Speech: Australian Prime Ministers Defining the National Image* (Melbourne, 2004), p. 220.
[76] Ibid.

A few years later in November 2003, a new Australian War Memorial was dedicated by Howard and Queen Elizabeth II in the heart of London at Hyde Park Corner. Where Keating sought to reorient Australia's commemorative cartography towards South East Asia, Howard clearly sought to restore the compass to its traditional bearings. This in itself was a process fraught with post-colonial ambiguity. While in London to dedicate the new memorial, Howard made no less that four references to Australia's 'independence' in his public speeches—something that might otherwise have seemed anomalous from the leader of a foreign, sovereign government.[77]

In the twenty-five year period since the publication of 'Last Post for Anzac', the commemoration of Anzac Day has been transformed; the enthusiastic involvement of younger people in the event has been startling. But this new enthusiasm for pilgrimages to war graves has not evoked a new understanding of Empire or of the history of Australia's participation in war. Just as there has been less contestation of war itself and of Australia's involvement in it, so too, any sense of the role of Empire has now dissipated. The rage of earlier generations—informed by a radical nationalism and an acute understanding of the politics of war—has now been replaced by an ahistorical celebration of the heroism of those men who sacrificed themselves for the Australian nation, rather than for Empire. This is exemplified by the new generation of pilgrims who descend on the Gallipoli peninsula in their thousands each year to find the touchstone of their national distinctiveness. In many respects, the Gallipoli battlefields are an unlikely marker of national distinction. The monuments erected in the 1920s were the work of the Imperial War Graves Commission, and in their design, materials, and symbolism the Australian monuments and cemeteries are barely distinguishable from their British and New Zealand counterparts. As a physical reminder of the Anzacs' common cause with Empire and the 'British race', this could hardly be bettered. But this is lost on the average backpacker, who is guided through the battlefields on tours emphasizing the sense of community that developed between the Australian soldiers and their erstwhile Turkish foes, as fellow victims in the tragedy of great power politics. As one recent pilgrim remarked at tours' end, 'It all just seems so pointless after hearing that both sides were fighting a war that wasn't truly their problem to begin with, you know ... now Britain have become the

---

[77] See Stuart Ward, 'Fellow Britons?' in *Meanjin*, Vol. 63, no. 3 (2004), pp. 56–64.

enemy.'[78] While this is no doubt good for contemporary Australian–Turkish relations, it also serves to distance Australians from the more dubious imperial connotations of the Gallipoli invasion. As in C. E. W. Bean's day, the Gallipoli experience underlines the vital role of commemoration in adapting and defining a usable past.

Select Bibliography

C. E. W. BEAN, *Anzac to Amiens* (Canberra, 1946).

JOY DAMOUSI, *The Labour of Loss: Mourning, Memory and Wartime Bereavement in Australia* (Cambridge, 1999).

BILL GAMMAGE, *The Broken Years: Australian Soldiers in the Great War* (Canberra, 1974).

STEPHEN GARTON, *The Cost of War: Australians Return* (Melbourne, 1996).

JOHN GILLIS, ed., *Commemorations: The Politics of National Identity* (Princeton, NJ, 1994).

K. S. INGLIS, *Sacred Places: War Memorials in the Australian Landscape* (Melbourne, 1998).

MICHAEL MCKERNAN, *Here is Their Spirit: A History of the Australian War Memorial 1917–1990* (St Lucia, 1991).

JOHN RICKARD, *Australia: A Cultural History* (London, 1988).

MICHAEL ROPER, T. G. ASHPLANT, and GRAHAM DAWSON, eds, *The Politics of War Memory and Commemoration* (London, 2000).

CRAIG WILCOX, *Australia's Boer War: The War in South Africa, 1899–1902* (Melbourne, 2002).

JAY WINTER and EMMANUEL SIVAN, eds, *War and Remembrance in the Twentieth Century* (Cambridge, 1999).

---

[78] Quoted in Brad West, 'Independent Travel and International Civil Religious Pilgrimage: Backpackers at the Gallipoli Battlefields', in Brad West, ed., *Down the Road: Exploring Backpackers and Independent Travel* (Perth, 2005); Bruce Scates also confirms that, among Gallipoli pilgrims, the 'Australian spirit' is 'usually defined in opposition to the British'. See *Return to Gallipoli: Walking the Battlefields of the Great War* (Cambridge, 2006), p. 200.

13

Gender and Sexuality

ANGELA WOOLLACOTT

In 1868 the first Australian cricket team to tour England acquitted themselves quite well, winning as often as they lost. But what is remarkable about this team is that the players were all Aboriginal. Although these Aboriginal cricketers were erased from Australian public memory by the early twentieth century—to the extent that in 1938 an Anglo-Australian team that toured in 1878 were called 'The First Australian Cricket Eleven in England'[1]—in the late 1860s they drew a great deal of attention in both Australia and Britain. On 26 May 1868, *The Times* asserted: 'No truer test of the interest taken by the public in the performance of this team from the antipodes can be afforded than that of 7,000 persons congregated at the Oval yesterday, when the first match of a series projected to be played in the three kingdoms came off.'[2] Over the following months, *The Times* continued to report on the Aboriginal cricket team's tour, publishing detailed accounts of the matches and scores. Some of these reports listed the Aboriginal players by name, noting the different colours of the sashes worn by the Black players, apparently in order for the English spectators to distinguish them individually. The paper also reported the additional entertainment the Aboriginal men provided, demonstrations of their traditional weapons, or what *The Times* called 'an exhibition of native Australian sports'. At the match at Bootle, Liverpool, in September 1868, such an exhibition resulted in one of the onlookers receiving 'a severe wound across the brow' from a boomerang that had been caught by the wind.[3] Reports of the Aboriginal team, most of whom were from western Victoria, pointed out that they were 'perfectly civilized', because they spoke English and had 'been brought up in the bush to agricultural

---

[1] Frontispiece, *United Empire* [Journal of the Royal Empire Society], Vol. 29 (May 1938), p. 189.

[2] 'Eleven Aboriginal Black Australians v. Eleven Gentlemen of Surrey Club', *The Times*, 26 May 1868, p. 5.

[3] *The Times*, 14 September 1868, p. 5.

pursuits under European settlers'.[4] One commentator made explicit the question of gender, noting that 'it was observed that in all of them there was a manly and dignified bearing.'[5] The Aboriginal cricketers of 1868 are a good example of how ideas of gender have been constructed historically between Australia and Britain, or at least in a British imperial context. Able both to play cricket and thus demonstrate quintessential latter nineteenth-century British manliness, and to show their equally masculine prowess with their own weapons, the Aboriginal team illustrate historically shifting and culturally contingent ideas and practices of gender. Part of a widespread wave of enthusiasm for cricket among Aborigines in the latter decades of the century, much this same team had also performed to great excitement in Australia, including at the Melbourne Cricket Ground on Boxing Day 1866. In the Australian colonial context, the team's matches were racially driven contests of masculine prowess. In the English context, there was an added layer of investment and interest on the part of the team's Anglo-Australian managers. In both places, issues of race and gender were shaped by the politics of colonialism.

Historical understanding of gender and sexuality in Australia since British occupation is sharpened when those topics are viewed through an imperial lens. Post-colonial and imperial perspectives on Australian history consider how Australianness was formed in relation to both the British metropole and the Asia-Pacific region. An imperial lens allows us to see Australia as part of a broader White-settler historical formation, and at once to identify the peculiarities of gender and sexuality in the Australian context. This chapter considers these issues in relation to the topics of frontier masculinities; interracial sexuality; women's struggles for inclusion in national citizenship and for equal rights; and the latter-twentieth-century connections between rethinking Australia's geopolitical location and gender, sexual, and racial inclusiveness.

In 1995, the sociologist R. W. Connell argued in his influential analysis of masculinities that Euro-American definitions of masculinity have evolved in specific long-term historical contexts, particularly those of global capitalist imperial expansion, the process of colonization, and the violence of frontier warfare. Masculinity and violence have been connected at both the individual level and the global level; modern imperialism has been a gendered enterprise

---

[4] 'Eleven Aboriginal Black Australians', *The Times* 26 May 1868, p. 5.

[5] Quoted in John Mulvaney and Rex Harcourt, *Cricket Walkabout: The Australian Aborigines in England* (South Melbourne, 1988), p. 74.

in which men who used force on the colonial frontier came to be considered exemplary masculine heroes, from the Spanish conquistadors in Latin America, to nineteenth-century settler colonialism, to the twentieth-century cultural genre of the Wild West film.[6] This important argument has not been fully explored by scholars in relation to the context of Australian colonialism, but enough work has been done to recognize its salience. While some connections have been made between masculinity and violence, and masculinity and militarism, the full meanings of racial conquest and the frontier for Australian definitions of masculinity are a rich topic still to be properly understood. The very notion of frontier, a concept with transnational valences articulated by scholars from many different locations, propels us to confront the intersections of colonial conquest, violence, and masculinities. It also forces us to focus on the foundational struggle over land, a struggle driven by British imperial annexation that would determine much else in this settler society.

Historical work on Australian masculinities encompasses a number of significant aspects of the Australian past since British invasion. Raymond Evans and Bill Thorpe have produced a beautifully nuanced analysis of the class- and violence-based inter-constitution of masculinities through the convict system. They coined the notion of 'commanding masculinity' to denote the gendered authority of 'the ruling male order—governors, magistrates, commandants, employers, state officials and supervisors'.[7] These mostly middle-class men created a masculinist system of discipline and punishment on Australian soil, a system with direct roots in the enterprise of the military-minded British gentry to control the labouring classes of the British Isles through a system of imprisonment, transportation, corporal punishment, and hanging. Evans and Thorpe posit the formation of subversive and resistant masculinities among the dominantly male convict population in early nineteenth-century New South Wales, and point to the competing and connected interactions of these varying definitions of manhood. Central to these interconnected definitions, they show, was the violence of flogging, a practice that went beyond the punishments of exile and labour to inscribe the power of 'commanding men' directly onto the convict body through wounds and scarring. Convict men were lashed far

---

[6] R. W. Connell, *Masculinities* (Berkeley, 1995), pp. 185–95.

[7] Raymond Evans and Bill Thorpe, 'Commanding Men: Masculinities and the Convict System', in Clive Moore and Kay Saunders, eds, *Australian Masculinities: Men and Their Histories* (Brisbane, 1998), p. 18.

more than convict women. In a more violent inversion of the bodily and psychological punishment of head-shaving meted out to convict women, flogging had the effect of feminizing men convicts by forcing them into submission and vulnerability—a helpless and humiliating state, not least because it was often performed as a spectacle to intimidate other convict men. The vicious and bloody process of flogging reinforced the authority of male officials, including the surgeons who supervised the procedure, in direct correlation to the weakened state of the lashed body. If one of the purported aims of the system was to reform transported men, according to the tenets of respectability touted by humanitarian reformers who competed with militaristic commanding men to define bourgeois British masculinity, it was a signal failure.[8]

A fundamental imperative for the study of masculinity in the context of colonial Australia is, of course, the sheer demographic sexual imbalance. European men far outnumbered European women in the penal colonies and after transportation ended, from a ratio of about three to one in 1788, to five to one in 1822, then gradually evening out although not in fact becoming balanced until into the twentieth century.[9] That demographic imbalance along with the economic importance of the pastoral industry enabled the masculinist romanticization of the bushman, most influentially articulated by Russel Ward in 1958 as *The Australian Legend*.[10] The mythology of the stoic, egalitarian bushmen and their ethos of mateship has served to obscure the violence of Australia's frontier history, especially the significance of that violence for nineteenth-century Australian masculinities. Other places around the nineteenth-century world also gave rise to notions of frontier masculinity linked to nature and freedom. What is distinctive about the Australian mythology of the bushman is that, in contrast to frontier masculinities that valorized heroic individualism, it has had at its heart the male homosocial bonding romanticized as the egalitarian culture of mateship. Making mateship central to masculinity underscored the need for social approval and conformity among Australian men, while also excluding women and ethnic others, revealing the class tensions in which privileged men were considered not truly masculine, and of course elevating the masculine bush above the feminized city. As several scholars have noted, the

[8] Evans and Thorpe, 'Commanding Men', p. 30.

[9] Clive Moore, 'Colonial Manhood and Masculinities', in Moore and Saunders, eds, *Australian Masculinities*, p. 37.

[10] Russel Ward, *The Australian Legend* (Melbourne, 1958).

sentimentalized bushman was the progenitor for the heroic Anzac whom C. E. W. Bean would immortalize in the wake of the First World War, and in whom the conjunction of masculinity and violence is made overt.[11] Needless to say, in representing these iconic male figures as *the* true Australians, both the bushman and the Anzac legends have excluded women and non-White people from national belonging.

In the most important work to date on the historical construction of Australian masculinities, Martin Crotty has argued that in the late nineteenth and early twentieth centuries physicality, violence, and militarism were essential ingredients. Middle-class Australian manliness, Crotty argues, was constructed against 'others' including Aborigines, bushrangers, larrikins, women, the English, and Asians.[12] Between 1870 and 1920, definitions of bourgeois Australian manliness moved away from religious morality and came to centre on physical strength, sporting prowess, and patriotic and military preparedness. Militarism was linked to boyhood and manliness as Australians fretted that their men should be able to handle 'the hot and harsh Australian wilderness',[13] protect the nascent nation from Asian invasion, and simultaneously serve the Empire of which Australia was a proud and maturing part. That militarism was a key component of this new configuration of manhood is evident from the compulsory military training system introduced in June 1911, three years before the Great War from which the Anzac mythology stems and with which Australian soldierly masculinity is usually associated. In this multifaceted definition of particular manliness, Australians' experience with the harsh extremities of the bush, their lust for sporting competitions and good sportsmanship, and their perceived natural abilities as soldiers were all interlinked.[14] While Crotty is focused on the gendered dimensions of culture within Australia's shores, he pays attention to the ways in which Australian manliness was conceived in relation to British definitions, and other external factors such as the imagined Asian threats.

Topics in Australian history particularly studied through the lens of masculinity have included sport, and the First World War. Sport developed

---

[11] Linzi Murrie, 'The Australian Legend: Writing Australian Masculinity/Writing "Australian" Masculine', in Moore and Saunders, eds, *Australian Masculinities*, pp. 68–77. C. E. W. Bean was a war correspondent who became Australia's official historian of the First World War. See Chapter 12 in this volume, pp. 293–5.

[12] Martin Crotty, *Making the Australian Male: Middle-Class Masculinity 1870–1920* (Melbourne, 2001), pp. 6–7.

[13] Ibid., p. 12.   [14] Ibid., p. 26.

in the Australian colonies from the mid-nineteenth century through the immediate post-Federation period, and became central to conceptions of masculinity, and vice versa. The imperial context was integral to the development of Australian sport, as the 1868 English tour of the Aboriginal cricket team illustrates. If, at first, colonial men did not expect to win against touring English teams, their improving performances sparked commentary in both colonies and metropole about vigorous colonial manhood. Intra-imperial competition, as is still true among the former colonies and Dominions and Britain itself, was from the mid-nineteenth century a critical context for the growth of first cricket and later rugby.[15] And of course, scholars have considered the First World War as a crucible of Australian masculinity, although in fact of the vast amount of work on the war and Australian men's participation, only a tiny fraction has actually used gender as a category of analysis. Noteworthy here are analyses of moving oral history interviews with old soldiers, who responded to the Anzac myth with feelings that varied from reassurance, to alienation and inadequacy as a man and a soldier; and of the fraught contests over Australian masculinity in the immediate post-war years.[16]

There is a growing body of work on the frontier in Australian history, such as the suppression and slippages of communal memories of violence on the nineteenth-century South Australian frontier, in which Indigenous oral traditions and local settler memories testify to violent episodes omitted from official histories.[17] We have something of a picture of Indigenous men's extensive contributions to the cattle, pearling, and other industries, as well as their work as trackers and troopers, in all of which the close working relations between Black and White men must surely have been mediated through ideas and practices of masculinities.[18] But despite the extant work on the Australian frontier, a detailed evaluation of how racially based

[15] Daryl Adair, John Nauright, and Murray Phillips, 'Playing Fields Through to Battle Fields: The Development of Australian Sporting Manhood in its Imperial Context, c. 1850–1918', in Moore and Saunders, eds, *Australian Masculinities*, pp. 51–67.

[16] Alistair Thomson, 'A Crisis of Masculinity? Australian Military Manhood in the Great War', in Joy Damousi and Marilyn Lake, eds, *Gender and War: Australians at War in the Twentieth Century* (Cambridge, 1995), pp. 133–47; Stephen Garton, 'War and Masculinity in Twentieth Century Australia', in Moore and Saunders, eds, *Australian Masculinities*, pp. 86–95.

[17] Robert Foster, Rick Hosking, and Amanda Nettelbeck, *Fatal Collisions: The South Australian Frontier and the Violence of Memory* (Kent Town, SA, 2001).

[18] Henry Reynolds, *Black Pioneers: How Aboriginal and Islander People Helped Build Australia* (Ringwood, Vic., 2000); Ann McGrath, *'Born in the Cattle': Aborigines in Cattle Country* (Sydney, 1987).

masculinities were integral to the context of frontier labour and frontier violence is still needed, both to excavate what was common knowledge in nineteenth-century Australia, and to apprehend fully the role of gender.[19] Some work has already been done in this direction, most notably on the drover-cum-explorer Edward John Eyre's masculine subjectivity as expressed in his account of his 1840–1 expedition across the Nullarbor Plain: his imagined heroic yet restrained authority in relation to his men and the Aborigines they encountered, especially his prevention of violence and abuse.[20]

That masculinity *was* a huge factor on the frontier, and demands further investigation, is clear from historical sources. The turn-of-the-twentieth-century novelist Rosa Praed makes clear in her autobiographical reflections on race relations in Australia that the European men had all the advantages and set most of the terms for constructing masculinity. Yet Indigenous men responded as best they could, recognizing the stakes. Praed's childhood was spent on the Queensland frontier of the Lower Logan River in the 1850s and 1860s. The violence of territorial conquest and murder was so pervasive in those years that, writing in London in the 1880s, Praed claimed, 'I have not ceased to dream that I am on an out-station besieged by Blacks; and during many a night do I fly through the endless forests, and hide in stony gullies, pursued by my aboriginal as ruthlessly as was ever De Quincy by his Malay.'[21] Praed recalled that the White men she grew up among were always armed, and the fear and anticipation of attack and reprisals shaped life for both settlers and Aborigines. Caught between the migratory bands of Indigenous people and the White invaders were the 'black boys' who found employment on the stations. The 'boys' on Praed's father's station were 'Bean-Tree, Dick, Freddy, and Tombo'; Praed notes that they 'had adopted, as far as possible, the customs of the white men'. They

would not do menial work, but rode among the cattle, looked for lost sheep, and brought up the horses. Their moleskins were always white. They wore Crimean

---

[19] Over ten years ago Raymond Evans called for more research in this area in his thoughtful brief survey of masculinity and violence in Australian history. Raymond Evans, 'A Gun in the Oven: Masculinism and Gendered Violence', in Kay Saunders and Raymond Evans, eds, *Gender Relations in Australia: Domination and Negotiation* (Sydney, 1994), pp. 197–218.

[20] Kay Schaffer, 'Handkerchief Diplomacy: E. J. Eyre and Sexual Politics on the South Australian Frontier', in Lynette Russell, ed., *Colonial Frontiers: Indigenous–European Encounters in Settler Societies* (Manchester, 2001), pp. 134–50.

[21] Mrs. Campbell Praed, *Australian Life: Black and White* (London, 1885), pp. 27–8.

shirts, with coloured handkerchiefs knotted above one shoulder and under the other, and sang songs in their own language set to operatic airs.[22]

After Indigenous people attacked one of the station homesteads and killed the European family, a revenge party comprising, of course, only men set out to conduct reprisals on those responsible. Significantly, the party included three of the 'black boys', who were armed like the White men. The trust and manly status that these Aboriginal men held as part of the reprisal party were earned partly through their declared preparedness to kill, articulated during the excursion planning. Praed reports that her father instructed the others to kill only the adult men, but some in the group argued for killing the women and children too—including Tombo. Praed's father, however, 'held firm to the traditions of English warfare',[23] in an assertion of rational and protective European masculinity.

According to Praed, like the Europeans, the itinerant Aborigines saw connections between combat and masculinity. In the ensuing unequal fight in which numbers of Aborigines died but no White men, according to her father, one particular Aboriginal man 'stood forth bravely and fought like a man'[24]—a gendered stance that did him little good against the White men's guns. If it is remarkable that the settler men could actually take pride (as Praed suggests they did) in the unequal contests between themselves and Aboriginal men armed mostly with spears and boomerangs, the significance of violence for shaping frontier masculinity is most apparent in Tombo's willingness to argue for killing Aboriginal women and children. It is unclear whether Tombo was sincere in this argument, or whether he mounted it for rhetorical effect with which to stake a gendered claim. From evidence such as this, mediated and fragmentary though it is, it is possible to piece together how Indigenous and other subordinated men constructed masculinity in colonial Australia. If issues of guilt and responsibility for frontier violence haunt Australian history and politics, an imperial framework reveals broader patterns of which our history is a part, even as it compels us to look for its specific contours.

Fundamental to ideas of masculinity shaped on the frontier were interracial sexual relations. Katharine Susannah Prichard's 1929 novel *Coonardoo* was highly controversial at the time of its publication because it confronted the reading public with the troubling reality of sex, and even love, between White men and Black women. Set in outback Western Australia, in the

---

[22] Ibid., p. 35.   [23] Ibid., p. 80.   [24] Ibid., p. 84.

Kimberley region, the novel tells the story of station owner Hugh Watt and his Aboriginal housekeeper Coonardoo. A relationship that grew from childhood friendship to sexual love cannot survive the racism of the outback, and ends in violence and misery.[25] *Coonardoo* was first serialized in *The Bulletin* in 1928, and the protest that greeted it was so fierce that Prichard felt moved to defend its authenticity. In her 1929 foreword, she quoted from Ernest Mitchell, the Chief Inspector of Aborigines for Western Australia, whom she had asked to read the manuscript. Mitchell told Prichard that 'he could not fault the drawing of aborigines [sic] and conditions, in *Coonardoo*, as he knew them'.[26]

Interracial sexuality was integral to colonial and outback Australia. Historical sexual relationships across racial barriers in Australia need to be seen on a spectrum running from marriage, through concubinage, to prostitution, and ultimately rape. Arguably, the spectrum should be viewed as a loop, with evidence that women's experiences ran in both directions. For Indigenous women, relationships with colonizing men have been fraught and precarious, usually involving abuse and exploitation, but also survival, children, and occasionally, the possibility of emotional support. Significantly, Australian history has not shared in the British imperial mythology of a golden age of interracial sex between colonizing men and colonized women before White women arrived and spoiled everything.[27] The colonization of Australia occurred late enough that the supposed golden age in other colonial sites was at or beyond its peak, yet the demographic imbalance of colonial Australia and the relatively prolonged if shifting frontier might imaginably have given rise to belated or diluted versions. The absence of any such myth suggests that the realities of interracial mixing were often so harsh as to elude romanticization; rather, relations between Indigenous women and colonizing men became part of what anthropologist W. E. H. Stanner called 'the great Australian silence'.[28]

Ann McGrath's pioneering work on Aborigines in the pastoral and mining areas of the Northern Territory in the early to mid-twentieth century reveals the pervasiveness and complexities of cross-racial sex and relationships.

---

[25] Katharine Susannah Prichard, *Coonardoo* (Sydney, 1990).

[26] Ibid., p. xiii.

[27] At its pithiest, this myth was stated by the British film-maker David Lean: 'It's a well-known saying that the women lost us the Empire. It's true.' Quoted by Helen Callaway, *Gender, Culture and Empire: European Women in Colonial Nigeria* (Urbana, Ill., 1987), p. 3.

[28] The phrase was the title of one of Stanner's Boyer Lectures delivered in 1968.

McGrath shows how difficult it is to separate concubinage from prostitution, and prostitution from rape. Aboriginal groups and families used European men's demands for access to their women as a survival strategy; women were bartered for money, food, and goods. Such negotiations could be for one go, or they could be for living arrangements of weeks, months, or even longer. Scholars have debated whether Aboriginal women had any agency in this process, or whether they were exploited by their men. As McGrath demonstrates, this is not easy to decide, because there is contradictory evidence, including some evidence that women found sexual gratification, economic survival, and perhaps even emotional satisfaction in these arrangements. Respectable European society regarded these relationships as morally degenerate and men who engaged in them as social outcasts, yet their very pervasiveness fed the taboo. Aboriginal women suffered from the moral and eugenicist lines drawn against interracial relationships, because they were unable to attain social respectability and their illicit status aggravated men's emotional and physical abuse. It was also difficult for the men, not least those who established a long-term family but had to accept their social isolation. This Creole society soon developed its peculiar hierarchies, including the ambiguous status of 'half-castes'; 'half-caste' men had some of the same sexual prerogatives as European men. It was a violent culture, in which prostitution easily blended with rape.[29] And, as we are now painfully aware, it became part of the context for the Stolen Generations, the removal of children from Aboriginal mothers in order to be raised and thus 'assimilated' in White society.

In most of Australia, especially in the north from the mid-nineteenth century onwards, ethnic diversity, of course, went beyond Black and White, as Chinese, Afghan, and Japanese men sought economic opportunities, and Pacific Islanders were kidnapped as labourers for the sugar industry. Interracial relationships included this broad diversity, from Aboriginal women working as prostitutes for Japanese pearlers in Broome, to European women marrying Chinese men in eastern Australia. Arguably, prostitution presents the mixing of colonial and early national Australia more vividly than any other topic. The history of prostitution in Australia stretches back to its inception, with the prostitution of convict women part of the early social fabric. Moreover, it points towards the changing intersections of race, class, and sexuality, particularly changing

---

[29] This paragraph is based on McGrath, *'Born in the Cattle'*, ch. 4 'Black Velvet'.

attitudes towards non-Anglo-Saxon prostitutes. In colonial Queensland, authorities welcomed Japanese prostitutes because they supposedly averted the racial horrors of non-White men being sexually serviced by White women. And in Western Australia, Japanese, French, and Italian prostitutes also helped preserve the fiction of a pure White nation secure from racial contamination. In the twentieth century, however, attitudes shifted, and authorities deployed the dictation test barrier of the Immigration Restriction Act to keep out prostitutes, men linked to the sex trade, and others considered sexually dubious such as those suspected of homosexuality.[30]

Interracial sexuality was one vector through which Australia positioned itself as a regional imperial power, an extension of the British imperial structure in which White-settler Dominions became colonizing powers in their own vicinities. When J. S. Griffiths declared in *The Lone Hand* in 1913 that 'Australia must govern Fiji', his article, entitled 'Fiji: The Eastern Outpost of Australia', carried as its first illustration a photograph of a bare-breasted 'Fijian belle'. Griffith used the metaphor of domesticity to make his case: Britain was 'finding her extensive house so difficult to keep in order that she is not only willing but exceedingly anxious to have the assistance of her older children'. The implicit suggestion was clear: if only Australia was willing to take on the work of ruling Fiji, like patriarchal heads of households with servants, Australian men could find ample sexual rewards for their colonial administrative responsibilities.[31] While the sexual dimension to Griffith's exhortation was at the level of suggestion, at times this dimension to Australia's regional imperialism was both real and violent. Historical evidence is emerging of an Australian resident magistrate in Papua in 1909–10 who was found to have raped local women systematically in the area under his command, forcing local men to bring women to him for this purpose.[32] Links between violence and sexuality were fundamental to the imperial frontier, connected of course to frontier masculinities. A study of bestiality in late nineteenth- and early twentieth-century Queensland

[30] Rae Frances, 'Sex Workers or Citizens? Prostitution and the Shaping of "Settler" Society in Australia', *International Review of Social History*, 44 (1999) Supplement 7, pp. 101–22.

[31] J. S. Griffiths, 'Fiji: The Eastern Outpost of Australia', *The Lone Hand*, Vol. 12, 1 April 1913, p. 508.

[32] Patty O'Brien, 'White Australia and the Brown Pacific: National Interest and Colonialism in Australia's Island Frontier' (2004), unpublished paper cited with the author's kind permission.

suggests that this relatively pervasive rural practice should be seen as part of male sexual violence, and thus as linked to the sexual assault of women.[33]

An area of relatively new research that promises to force us to rethink received assumptions about race and gender in colonial Australia is that on relationships between White women and non-White men. Fascinating stories are emerging from this research, such as that of Selina Johnson, the 19-year-old daughter of a settler in the Acheron River area in Victoria, who in September 1861 ran away with her Aboriginal boyfriend Davy, who had been in her father's employ. She gave birth to Davy's child, and when she was brought back to her father's homestead it became clear that she and Davy considered themselves to be married. On 23 September 1861 the Guardian of Aborigines wrote to the secretary of the Central Board responsible for Aborigines that he had heard from a reliable settler that Selina Johnson's pregnancy had not been the result of a 'forced act on the black's part, but mutual frequent connection between the two'.[34] The local understanding that the relationship was one of mutual consent, and not of rape, contradicted the dominant cultural paradigm for sex between an Aboriginal man and a White woman. Indeed, the fear and exaggeration of Aboriginal rape of White women was such that of the fourteen men executed for rape in Queensland between 1860 and 1910, ten were Aborigines.[35] We now know of intermarriage involving Aboriginal people,[36] as well as relationships and marriages between European women and Chinese men in late nineteenth- and early twentieth-century Australia. In locations ranging from Perth and Fremantle to northern Queensland, such matches were not uncommon. There were 213 marriages between Europeans and Chinese in the state of Queensland up to 1901, mostly in the rural north.[37] Court documents show, however, that White women who lived with or married Chinese men were often seen as deviant and morally transgressive, were harassed by the police,

[33] Ann-Maree Collins, 'Woman or Beast? Bestiality in Queensland, 1870–1949', *Hecate*, Vol. 17, no. 1 (1991), pp. 36–42.

[34] Liz Reed, 'White Girl "Gone Off With the Blacks"', *Hecate*, Vol. 28, no. 1 (2002), p. 10.

[35] Ross Barber, 'Rape as a Capital Offence in Nineteenth Century Queensland', *Australian Journal of Politics and History*, Vol. 21 (April 1975), p. 35.

[36] For example, Katherine Ellinghaus, 'Absorbing the "Aboriginal Problem": Controlling Interracial Marriage in Australia in the Late 19th and Early 20th Centuries', *Aboriginal History*, Vol. 27 (2003), pp. 183–207.

[37] Sandi Robb, 'Myths, Lies and Invisible Lives: European Women and Chinese Men in North Queensland 1870–1900', *Lilith*, Vol. 12 (2003), p. 97.

and sometimes incarcerated or had their children removed from them. Thus women made choices that challenged the White masculinist sexual order, but could be, and were, punished for them.[38]

Central to the history of White women in Australia is their relatively early achievement of the right to vote. Beaten only by Wyoming (1869), Utah (1870), New Zealand and Colorado (both 1893), South Australia granted the franchise to women in 1894, Western Australia in 1899, and federally the new Commonwealth of Australia in 1902 in an Act with a clause excluding Aboriginal people from the vote unless they already held it under state law (as in South Australia). In contrast, women in Britain waited until 1918 for the partial suffrage, and until 1928 for the full version, Canadian women received the vote in 1918, in the United States women's federal suffrage was granted in 1920, and in South Africa White women only were enfranchised in 1930. It might seem paradoxical that in the late nineteenth century, White-settler societies, where cowboys and bushmen were mythologized and women's lives were often characterized by physical and material hardships and social marginalization, became pioneers in granting suffrage to women. A comparison of western American states and Antipodean colonies shows that frontier suffrage politics were largely driven by pragmatism, and a liberal feminism tied closely to the moral purity movement led by the Woman's Christian Temperance Union (WCTU). In frontier and White-settler cultures where men were considered to behave in wild and immoral ways, middle-class women readily adopted a feminism built on temperance. The legal and political status of Indigenous people varied among settler colonies that enfranchised women in the 1890s, including their rights to vote, and the tension between feminist politics and attitudes towards the rights of non-White men played out variously. Pat Grimshaw shows that whereas Colorado feminists became relatively supportive of the rights of non-White men, and New Zealand suffragists learnt during their campaign to be more inclusive of Maori women, in South Australia the rights and interests of Aboriginal people were ignored in debate despite their legal inclusion.[39]

In her history of Australian feminism, Marilyn Lake contends that precisely because of the masculinist culture of Australian nationalism as it coalesced

---

[38] Jan Ryan, ' "She Lives with a Chinaman": Orient-ing "White" Women in the Courts of Law', *Journal of Australian Studies* (March 1999), 149–59.

[39] Patricia Grimshaw, 'Reading the Silences: Suffrage Activists and Race in Nineteenth Century Settler Societies', in Joy Damousi and Katherine Ellinghaus, eds, *Citizenship, Women and Social Justice: International Historical Perspectives* (Melbourne, 1999), pp. 30–42.

in the late nineteenth century, for women inclusion in the Australian polity was critically important. The gendered debates leading up to Australian Federation had a bitter edge, as the 'Woman Movement' was largely based on the rapid growth in Australia of the WCTU and an ideology of maternalist and reforming feminism. The movement sought specifically to use women's reforming influence to counteract men's drinking, gambling, violence, and sexual indulgence. With a philosophy of abstinence, chastity, sobriety, purity, and uplift, the movement raised the ire of male writers, such as those who used the pages of *The Bulletin* to mock feminists in both text and cartoons. It was a cultural war in which the status of women, the gendering of citizenship in the new nation, and ideas of Australianness were all at stake. In its adherence to essentialist notions of women's moral superiority, and to maternalism, the Australian 'Woman Movement' was in accord with feminist thought internationally.[40]

It has been suggested that we need to explore further the ways in which maternalist feminism in Australia was shaped by the fact that 'throughout the early decades of the twentieth century the most common relationship between individual Aboriginal and white women was that of mistress and servant.'[41] The class and authority axis embedded in the mistress–servant relationship imbued maternal feminism with racially based notions of superiority and power that we need still to evaluate. Little scholarship has focused on the quotidian relations of White and Black women in the context of domestic service, the inequalities between White and Black women, and the gross oppression of Aboriginal women in state- and mission-sponsored systems of domestic labour, despite the existence of first-hand accounts.[42] Here is another area where Australian history could benefit from looking elsewhere in imperial historiography for the similarities between Australia and other colonial regimes in which race relations were structured in part by household labour. Interestingly, one of the few studies to consider Aboriginal women as part of the whole story of domestic service in Australia is written

---

[40] Marilyn Lake, *Getting Equal: The History of Australian Feminism* (Sydney, 1999), chs. 1 and 2.

[41] Victoria Katherine Haskins, 'The Women's Movement and Aboriginal Citizenship, Sydney, 1937–1940', in Damousi and Ellinghaus, eds, *Citizenship, Women and Social Justice*, p. 45.

[42] Jackie Huggins and Thom Blake, 'Protection or Persecution? Gender Relations in the Era of Racial Segregation', in Saunders and Evans, eds, *Gender Relations in Australia*, pp. 53–6. A significant new study in this area is Victoria K. Haskins, *One Bright Spot* (Basingstoke, 2005).

by a historian of Caribbean slavery, a connection he points out in his preface.[43]

Turn-of-the-twentieth-century Australian feminism was engaged with, and a product of, nationalism, yet it was also tightly connected to the international women's movement, shaped by its intellectual currents and in turn itself a shaping force. The WCTU, an organization founded in the United States that rapidly became international and had numerous branches across Australia, played a central role. Australian feminists were influenced by the works and speeches of Americans Frances Willard and Charlotte Perkins Gilman, British liberal philosopher John Stuart Mill, and South African Olive Schreiner among others, and had organizational connections to both the British and American suffrage movements. In 1902, for example, Vida Goldstein attended the International Woman Suffrage Conference in Washington. It has become increasingly clear from recent work that we need to see the early twentieth-century Australian feminist movement in its broader international context, especially in its leading roles in both the British Commonwealth League and the Pan-Pacific Women's Association. The British Commonwealth League, founded in 1925 as an organization of feminists across the British Empire and Commonwealth that held annual conferences in London, had its roots in the Australian and New Zealand Women Voters' Committee. This committee had formed in London, during a lecture tour by Vida Goldstein, to represent the political interests of women from Australia and New Zealand who were effectively disenfranchised by living in London, where women did not yet have the vote, in contrast to the progressive Dominions. The intermediate organization, from 1914, was the British Dominions Woman Suffrage Union (BDWSU), formed to promote international suffrage activism, and specifically so that Australian and New Zealand women could lend a hand to their Canadian and South African sisters. The BDWSU stayed active during the war, increasingly including Indian feminists in its meetings, and thus reaching for broader imperial representation. In 1922 the Union became linked to the International Woman Suffrage Alliance, and in 1925 this reformed group finally emerged as the British Commonwealth League, whose successor organization, the Commonwealth Countries League, still exists. From 1925 the League held annual conferences in London for decades, creating a forum for Empire-wide feminist issues that became racially inclusive even though the organization

---

[43] B. W. Higman, *Domestic Service in Australia* (Melbourne, 2002).

was dominated by White women. Australian feminism, then, contended with issues in a transnational, and particularly an imperial, framework.[44]

Fiona Paisley has documented and analysed the changing attitudes of Australian feminists towards Aboriginal women's issues in the 1920s and 1930s, when a small but vocal cohort of White women drew attention to Aboriginal women's multifaceted subordination, and sought to improve their status. One important contribution Australian feminists made was to use international feminist platforms to focus a global spotlight on the status of Aborigines, both through the British Commonwealth League and the Pan-Pacific Women's Association. This latter association, founded in Hawaii in 1928, became an important venue for Australian feminists to extend their activism to the Pacific arena, to express their own modern, transnational, and professional subjectivities, and to debate Australian issues of gender and race in relation to the Asia-Pacific region.[45]

The overseas, especially the metropolitan, arena was an important context for the formation of Australian femininities, beyond feminist movements and thought. From the late nineteenth century, growing numbers of Australian women travelled to London and beyond in search of adventure and opportunities, and used a wider global stage to define Australian femininities. While the assertively nationalist circa 1900 'Australian girl' was represented as bold, sporting, forthright, and self-possessed, in the interwar decades connections between modernism and femininity changed Australian culture. Even though nineteenth-century Australia had been a largely urban society despite the cultural dominance of the bush, it was in the twentieth century that Australia embraced urban life and culture, while in the 1920s to 1930s the feminine became prominent in the arts. Women artists who had studied modernism overseas, such as Margaret Preston, Thea Proctor, Dorrit Black, and Ola Cohn, led a wave of painting, printing, and sculpture that appropriated Aboriginal motifs, represented Australian flora, fauna, and landscapes, as well as female figures and modernist abstractions, and consciously sought

---

[44] For more on the history of the British Commonwealth League and its significance, see Angela Woollacott, *To Try Her Fortune in London: Australian Women, Colonialism, and Modernity* (New York, 2001), ch. 4, and Fiona Paisley, 'Citizens of Their World: Australian Feminism and Indigenous Rights in the International Context, 1920s and 1930s', *Feminist Review*, Vol. 58 (Spring 1998), pp. 66–84.

[45] On the Pan-Pacific Women's Association see Fiona Paisley, *Glamour in the Pacific: Cultural Feminism in the Women's Pan-Pacific, 1920s–1950s* (forthcoming), and Angela Woollacott, 'Inventing Commonwealth and Pan-Pacific Feminisms: Australian Women's Internationalist Activism in the 1920s–30s', *Gender & History*, Vol. 10 (November 1998), pp. 425–48.

to widen the Australian cultural lexicon. At the same time Australian women writers such as Miles Franklin, Henry Handel Richardson, and Katharine Susannah Prichard (all of whom lived overseas for extended periods, indeed the rest of her life in Richardson's case) gained recognition for their contributions to a national literature, and contested men's dominance in Australian writing. In these diverse ways, women regendered Australian culture and broadened national identity, especially towards White women's inclusion, while a few raised issues of racial inclusiveness as well.

Yet in the late nineteenth and early twentieth centuries only a minority of the Australian women who sojourned in London or joined imperial organizations sought to challenge social or imperial hierarchies, and even many feminists were overt imperialists. Women participated in multiple leagues and clubs that accepted imperial rule, that were pro-Empire, or that actively demonstrated Empire loyalty. The Imperial Order Daughters of the Empire was founded in Canada in 1900 and remained a primarily Canadian organization, although it had some support from Australian women. Probably the largest women's organization in Australia, the Country Women's Association, openly proclaimed its conservative and loyalist politics. Individual Australian women who travelled to London for social or career purposes aspired to be presented at court. For example, in 1933 Miss Gwen Hughes of Melbourne attended the international Rural Women's Conference in Stockholm, then spent several months staging cooking demonstrations in England and Scotland. On 23 June 1933, as a highlight of her time in the metropole, she was presented at court.[46] From the end of the nineteenth century to the middle of the twentieth, London was full of clubs, societies, and leagues, many of which were connected to the Empire. Australian women, including many who never left Australia's shores, joined these clubs or their Australian branches, such as the Lyceum Club for professional or well-educated women which had branches in most Australian capital cities. The pro-Empire end of feminist politics in this period is illustrated by journalist Margaret Baxter, from Sydney, who arrived in London in 1904, the same year that the feminist-leaning Lyceum Club opened. Baxter became a fixture of the Lyceum, one of its first Australian members, Australian vice-president of its United Empire Circle which organized Empire-related talks, and the Australian representative on the club's international board. Baxter was also a stalwart of the

---

[46] *The British Australian and New Zealander*, 20 July 1933, p. 9.

Royal Colonial Institute, which changed its name to the Royal Empire Society in 1928. She served on one of the Institute's committees, wrote a regular women's column for its journal, and in 1933 became the first Australian woman elected to its council. Baxter was living proof of the compatibility between feminism and pro-imperialism, regardless of the more complex politics of the British Commonwealth League.[47] Perhaps the clearest evidence that most Australian women supported the Empire in the first half of the twentieth century is that most supported Australia's involvement in imperial wars, particularly the South African War of 1899–1902 and the two world wars.

Various intertwined strands of change from the 1960s onwards suggest that Australia has been struggling with its past and present positioning within the British Empire. My contention is that shifts in gender and sexuality over the past forty years in Australia have been directly linked to shifts in racial thinking, and to a broad cultural re-evaluation of Australia's geopolitical location. Australia cannot yet claim to be a 'post-colonial' nation, both because it is still constitutionally tied to Britain, and because colonialism still shapes its race relations and the status of Indigenous people. The movement for reconciliation between Black and White has high-level political opposition. Yet because post-colonialism is best seen as a process of engagement with colonialism and its legacies, moves towards gender and sexual inclusivity, as well as racial and ethnic inclusivity, are integral to such a grappling with Australia's colonial history.

From the 1960s, a newly assertive Australian nationalism condemned the 'cultural cringe' of deferring to the English canon and ways, in a wave of social change that included the women's liberation movement, and the movement for homosexual rights. The social revolutions of the 1960s and 1970s were, of course, a transnational phenomenon that carried particular valences and centred on different issues in different places. In Australia, both the anti-Vietnam War movement and to a lesser extent the Aboriginal rights movement were catalysts. Australia's participation in the Vietnam War stemmed directly from its post-Second World War foreign policy of dependence on the United States rather than Britain, as well as the home-grown version of the fear of Communism. The Freedom Ride in New South Wales in February 1965, for example, shows the

[47] Woollacott, *To Try Her Fortune in London*, ch. 4.

extent to which the Indigenous rights movement in Australia has found inspiration in the American Civil Rights movement.[48] In the late twentieth century, as it had earlier at key moments of Australian history such as the pre-Federation period, the United States served as both an object lesson and a model for those seeking new formulae. Arguably, turning to the United States has become a new form of imperial relations for Australia, but it reflects a marked turning away from Britain. In a historically interesting way, Australia has replaced the British metropole with America, the British Empire's first settler society and first independent republic.

This shift was apparent in the strong influence the American Women's Liberation movement had on that in Australia. If the United States had been a secondary influence on the first wave of feminism in Australia, subordinate to that of Britain, for second wave feminism it was the primary referent. Lake shows in her comprehensive history of Australian feminism that some 1960s activists were well aware of the history of English militant suffragettes, echoing their actions with media-targeted spectacles of chaining themselves to parts of buildings. Yet it was predominantly American feminist thinkers in whom they found contemporary inspiration, and whose writings they read and circulated. Australian Women's Liberation, however, had its own agenda and its own distinctive issues. One of the celebrated feminist protests that sparked the movement was in March 1965 when Rosalie Bognor and Merle Thornton chained themselves to the footrail of the public bar in a Brisbane hotel, using an iconic site of Australian sexist segregation to protest discrimination.[49]

Second wave feminism in Australia had a significantly different agenda from the turn-of-the-century women's movement, in good part because it built on that movement's successes. Rather than moral purity and sexual abstinence, the new feminism emphasized women's sexual desire and expression, and fought for abortion rights and women's access to contraception. Some issues continued, such as women's education and employment, but here too there were new emphases, such as on equal pay and child care. Rather than casting women as inherently maternal and essentially different from men, the 1960s to 1970s movement claimed women should be as free as men to indulge themselves in physical pleasures and provocative behaviour,

---

[48] Ann Curthoys, *Freedom Ride: A Freedom Rider Remembers* (Sydney, 2002).
[49] Lake, *Getting Equal*, pp. 214–22.

and condemned the sexual objectification of women as well as the confines of the family. Women should rid themselves of constraining underwear, shoes, and clothes, feminists urged, and indeed many young women dressed in what became a new androgynous style. By the early 1970s, lesbian rights and separatist feminist thought comprised an important part of the movement.

Perhaps the intertwining of issues of gender and sexuality with a broad re-evaluation of Australia's geopolitical position, and issues of Indigenous rights and multiculturalism, is best seen in the dramatic political and cultural upheaval in South Australia in the 1970s. Under the Premiership of the charismatic and media-savvy Labor leader Don Dunstan, South Australia became a beacon of progressive social reform and its capital city Adelaide, formerly known as the city of churches, became celebrated for food and the arts. Dunstan, who was Premier in 1967–8 and then from 1970 to 1979, did much to realize his vision of a democratic and multicultural South Australia that led the nation in social and legal reform, urban planning and environmental awareness, Indigenous issues, the arts and culture. He saw himself as part of what in 1981 he called 'a king tide of change' that swept the nation from 1967 to 1977.[50] During this tide of change, he believed, Australia reached a new level of cultural maturity partly facilitated by the wave of post-Second World War migration from Europe that prodded Australia to question British cultural patterns, to recognize and enjoy Australia's climate that enables outdoor living, and to celebrate the related pleasures of gardening, eating, and social mixing. For Dunstan, this recognition was bound up with an acknowledgement of the rights of Aboriginal people, and of Australia's place in Asia, and the needs of Asian refugees.

Dunstan's reforms were prodigious. As Minister for Aboriginal Affairs and then as Premier, he oversaw legislation that prohibited racial discrimination, set up an Aboriginal lands trust, and paved the way for land rights law. He outspokenly criticized the White Australia policy, promoted Adelaide as 'a centre of Australian multiculturalism' with its newly relaxed alcohol licensing and outdoor cafes, and urged Australians to recognize their responsibility within the Asian region, and to accept refugees from South East Asia.[51] Dunstan also helped South Australia to lead the nation on women's issues: he established a women's adviser and an equal opportunity

---

[50] Don Dunstan, *Australia: A Personal View: The Dunstan Documentaries* (Kenthurst, NSW, 1981), p. 70.

[51] Don Dunstan, 'This Is Where I Want to Be', in Derek Whitelock, ed., *A Sense of Difference* (Kew, Vic., 2000), p. 210; Dunstan, *Australia*, pp. 105–6.

unit in his government; and introduced reform to outlaw discrimination and promote the status of women. The Dunstan government reformed rape law, controversially establishing the legal basis of rape in marriage, one of the first governments anywhere to do so.[52] It also took the national lead on decriminalizing homosexuality, spurred by the 1972 drowning of a gay man in the River Torrens in which the police vice squad was implicated. Dunstan's ability to capture attention lay partly in his merging of the personal and the political. His political stance on Australia's integration with Asia was personified by his second marriage in 1976 to Malaysian journalist Adele Koh, and later by his homosexual relationship with his partner in his 1990s restaurant Steven Cheng. Dunstan's eventual homosexuality can perhaps be seen to tie together these diverse strands of political reform and cultural change. Certainly, in Dunstan's view Australia's preparedness by the 1970s 'to question and confront its own previous assumptions' was directly related to its coming to terms with its geopolitical location in Asia, its Indigenous inhabitants, the environment and landscape, and its distance from Britain.[53]

Australian cities had homosexual subcultures and sites for much of the twentieth century. Even earlier, homosexual behaviour among the convicts in early colonial Australia is well documented, as are prosecutions for homosexuality in the latter part of the nineteenth century.[54] Only in recent years has Australian historiography taken up research into the homosexual past, but we are now beginning to apprehend the significance of the urban beats, pubs, and other spaces where homosexual men located each other, and the ways in which they survived in a hegemonically heterosexual environment.[55] Similarly, we have learnt to read episodes of gender anxiety for hidden layers of meaning about sexuality, such as the Second World War anxiety that uniformed women in the armed services would lose their femininity, which cloaked worries about lesbianism.[56] Australian lesbian and gay rights movements of the late 1960s and the 1970s resulted in the decriminalization of male homosexual activity, beginning in South Australia in 1973 and enacted state by state, with Tasmania the last to do so in 1998.

---

[52] Helen Jones, *In Her Own Name: A History of Women in South Australia From 1836* (Kent Town, SA, 1994), pp. 229–30.

[53] Dunstan, *Australia*, p. 10.

[54] Robert Aldrich, *Colonialism and Homosexuality* (London, 2003), ch. 7.

[55] Garry Wotherspoon, 'Comrades-in-arms: World War II and Male Homosexuality in Australia' in Damousi and Lake, eds, *Gender and War*, pp. 215–17.

[56] Ruth Ford, 'Lesbians and Loose Women: Female Sexuality and the Women's Services during World War II', in Damousi and Lake, eds, *Gender and War*, pp. 81–104.

This wave of legislation was followed by another prohibiting discrimination against homosexual women and men in employment and elsewhere.[57] The growing public visibility and acceptance of homosexuality has had special significance for Australian culture. Not only has Sydney become recognized internationally especially for its annual gay Mardi Gras festival, but in a culture where masculinism has long been anchored by myths of the bushman and the Anzac, alternative sexualities and their associated gender transgression have resonated profoundly.

From the 1970s, legislative and government policy changes have also affected the status of Australian women. In 1969 South Australia was the first state to overhaul abortion law. Other changes in the 1970s were tied to feminists' success in gaining access to and positions in the Commonwealth government, not least because of the feminist alliance with the Labor Party that swept into power in 1972 after decades of Liberal Party rule. In a distinctively Australian development noted internationally, leading feminists gained powerful positions, to such an extent that the term 'femocrat' was coined to describe them. In April 1973 Elizabeth Reid became the first adviser to the Prime Minister on women's issues. Reforms included Federal government commitment to day care facilities; a December 1972 Arbitration Commission ruling for equal pay for women; the provision of community services such as women's refuges and rape crisis centres; a 1976 study of sexism in schools; and state by state legislation to prohibit sex discrimination.[58]

Gay rights and improvements in the status of women were part of a broad sweep of social and cultural changes in Australia, changes that included progressive reform on issues of race. Led by government policy, Australian attitudes towards non-Anglo-Saxon immigration shifted. Countering racist views about 'New Australians', official policy now celebrated Australia's 'multiculturalism'. In the late 1960s the White Australia policy was finally rejected, and a proposal for the Federal government to take over Aboriginal affairs was approved by national referendum, which paved the way for Aboriginal people's inclusion in citizenship. Increased immigration especially from South East Asia was linked to Australians' ambivalent recognition of themselves as an Asia-Pacific nation rather than a European outpost. The 1990s renewed movement to create an Australian Republic, by replacing the

[57] Australian Lesbian & Gay Archives Inc., *Homosexual Law Reform in Australia* (Parkville, Vic., 1993).

[58] Ann Curthoys, 'Doing It For Themselves: The Women's Movement Since 1970', in Saunders and Evans, eds, *Gender Relations in Australia*, pp. 435–7.

Queen with an Australian head of state, failed to win majority support at a national referendum, but the campaign, the passionate national debate, and the referendum itself showed Australians rethinking their 'Britishness' and global positioning.

Recent historical reappraisals of Australia as a White-settler society, both comparable to and distinctive from other settler countries, are contributing substantially to British Empire and global history. At stake is not only how Australian history can benefit from transnational frameworks such as the imperial and post-colonial, but how work on the Australian context can help to frame the broader history and study of White-settler societies and European empires. The topics surveyed here—frontier masculinities, interracial sexuality, women's struggles for national inclusion and political rights, and latter-twentieth-century post-colonial struggles that connect gender, sexual, and racial inclusivity—depend upon transnational frames. We cannot grasp the significance of the frontier for the construction of masculinities in Australia without understanding it as a transnational historical formation. Inversely, identifying the full significance of the frontier for the history of racialized gender relations in Australia, and how it has fed into masculinist and militarist national mythology here, will contribute to global scholarship on this topic. The histories of invasion and immigration are of course integral to that of interracial sex in Australia, so that it is impossible to view this topic within closed borders. It is both an empirical and an analytical necessity to consider issues of sex between Indigenous people and Europeans, between Indigenous people and Asians, and between Asians and Europeans in Australia as thoroughly tangled together. The history of Australian feminism can only be fully understood in a transnational framework, because it was influenced by British, American, and other feminists, and because of Australia's early place in the worldwide history of women's suffrage. Australian women were instrumental in British Empire and Commonwealth feminisms, as well as in the Asia-Pacific region, even as they struggled to regender the Australian polity and culture from within and beyond Australia's shores. And seeing the links between struggles over women's status and homosexual rights on the one hand, and Indigenous rights and multiculturalism on the other, reveals the full complexity of the Australian variant of the wider process of challenging legacies of colonialism. Ideas and practices of gender have evolved historically in both the bush and the city, in ways quite specific to Australia even as they were part of and contributed to broader transnational shifts. Focusing on gender and sexuality shows that it is no longer adequate to consider Australia only from within its colonial or national borders, and points instead towards the significance of a reconfigured history of Empire and colonialism.

Select Bibliography

MARTIN CROTTY, *Making the Australian Male: Middle-Class Masculinity 1870–1920* (Melbourne, 2001).

PATRICIA GRIMSHAW, MARILYN LAKE, ANN MCGRATH, and MARIAN QUARTLY, *Creating A Nation* (Ringwood, 1994).

MARILYN LAKE, *Getting Equal: The History of Australian Feminism* (St Leonards, 1999).

ANN MCGRATH, *'Born in the Cattle': Aborigines in Cattle Country* (Sydney, 1987).

CLIVE MOORE and KAY SAUNDERS, eds, *Australian Masculinities: Men and Their Histories* (Brisbane, 1998).

KAY SAUNDERS and RAYMOND EVANS, eds, *Gender Relations in Australia: Domination and Negotiation* (Sydney, 1994).

14

Popular Culture

RICHARD WHITE AND HSU-MING TEO

On 11 May 1934, a bust of Adam Lindsay Gordon, 'National Poet of Australia', was unveiled in Poets' Corner, Westminster Abbey, by the Duke and Duchess of York, a moment replete with imperial pomp and circumstance. It was the work of the celebrity sculptor Lady Hilton-Young, whose first husband, Captain Scott, had died in the name of Empire at the South Pole twenty-two years earlier: 'The features are strong and rugged,' the *Daily Mail* pronounced, 'the wind seems to be blowing through the plentiful hair, and there are restlessness and disappointment in the face.'[1] The Abbey's organist (Dr Bullock) composed a short Voluntary for the occasion.[2] The Archbishop of Canterbury gave the panegyric. The audience, that floating population of the Anglo-Australian establishment at home in London, sang 'Let the whole creation cry' and 'Advance Australia Fair', which reminded the Mother Country that her Australian sons still kept 'a British soul'.[3]

The crowning of Gordon as Australia's 'national poet'—and as the first and only Empire representative in Poets' Corner—is curious: a national culture being given the Empire's blessing, the heart of Empire authorizing nation. It runs counter to conventional trajectories of Australia's cultural history as a story of creeping nationalism. Nor does it fit securely as an argument for the survival of imperial loyalty, despite the moment being the solstice of what John MacKenzie has called the 'extraordinary Indian summer in the popular culture of Empire'.[4] Gordon was neither a son of

---

[1] *Daily Mail*, 12 May 1934.   [2] On 'The Flowers of the Forest', the Gordon clan's air.

[3] Westminster Abbey, Order of Ceremony at the Unveiling of the Memorial to Adam Lindsay Gordon in Poets' Corner. This third verse of what the Order of Ceremony called 'the National Song' was excised when it displaced 'God Save the Queen' as the Australian national anthem in 1984. See Chapter 15, pp. 363–4.

[4] John M. MacKenzie, 'The Popular Culture of Empire in Britain', in Judith M. Brown and Wm. Roger Louis, eds, *The Oxford History of the British Empire. Vol. 4: The Twentieth Century* (Oxford, 1999), p. 229, cf. p. 225.

Empire like Kipling, nor by 1934 generally recognized as Australia's greatest, best, or most prolific poet. He was something of a rake, 'a rather wild youth' as the *Sydney Morning Herald* coyly put it.[5] Unlucky in love and an embarrassment to his respectable family, he set off for South Australia in 1853, aged nineteen. There he began to publish poetry in between his other occupations: policeman, horse breaker, member of Parliament (briefly), champion steeplechase rider. His thin output, which ranged from horsy ballads to more serious work and overblown dramatic compositions, included some great poems often (though unfairly) labelled Swinburnian. He specialized in sentimental melancholy. In 1870, the day his second collection was published, he shot himself on Melbourne's Brighton Beach. He was thirty-seven. His horsemanship became a subject of masculine myth, his suicide of feminine sentiment. But his claims remained thin. Some letter writers in Australia argued the greater claims of Kendall and Lawson; others more widely or highly regarded did not have the advantage of being dead. He could be made respectable. His more disreputable qualities were put down to youthful high spirits, appropriate to a new nation that persisted in seeing itself—as Mother England saw it too—as young, exuberant, even irresponsible. The Archbishop put the Dean's mind at rest over the suicide question: if there were sufficient literary support 'and if, as you say, there were really fine elements in his character, the mere fact that he gave way to the impulse of suicide need not stand in the way'.[6] His greatest champion, Douglas Sladen, who made the promotion of Gordon his life's work, recruited sufficiently positive testimonials to Gordon's worth from the literary establishment, noted his 'high birth', identified his godmother as 'an Empire-maker in South Africa' and lobbied the British and Australian governments for support.[7] It helped that Gordon (briefly), Sladen, and the Dean of Westminster Abbey were all Old Cheltonians. And the timing was propitious, not only Gordon's centenary but a moment of crisis in imperial relations. The breach between British and Australian cricketing authorities over the 1932–3 'Bodyline' controversy still rankled.

[5] *Sydney Morning Herald*, 14 October 1933, cited in *Adam Lindsay Gordon The Poet of Australia. Unveiling of the Memorial in Westminster Abbey* (London, 1934), p. 8.

[6] Cosmo Lang, Archbishop of Canterbury, to Foxley Norris, Dean of Westminster, 28 December 1932, Westminster Abbey Library, 58893.

[7] Douglas Sladen, 'A Sketch of Adam Lindsay Gordon', in *Adam Lindsay Gordon*, p. 10; Douglas Sladen, *My Long Life: Anecdotes and Adventures* (London, 1939), pp. 330–39; 'Memorials. Adam Lindsay Gordon—Memorial Tablet in Westminster Abbey', National Archives of Australia (hereafter NAA), Prime Minister and Cabinet, A461/8, C370/1/8.

But there was also one more positive quality that Gordon represented that was seen as marking him out as the supreme poet to represent Australia at the heart of Empire, agreed to by his biographers, by his supporters at the time, and by the establishment. He was popular.

Popularity was never an essential prerequisite for entry to Poets' Corner. Others there were better or more elevated poets. And while Gordon was widely read in Australia and through the Empire, his popularity did not necessarily convert into cash: the Lyons government paid the 350 guineas the memorial cost after a public appeal raised only £13. 2s. 6d., three guineas coming from the members of the Commonwealth Literary Fund Committee who had advised an appeal would be 'highly popular amongst Australians'.[8] But at the heart of Empire, popularity—or a reputation for being popular—did seem to be a necessary qualification for a colonial, an Australian national poet. As the Archbishop put it, 'amid the cares and burdens of that office I have found refreshment and exhilaration in his songs of swift and eager action in the open air ... Whatever a stern criticism may say as to the abiding merit of his works, at least there can be no doubt as to the value which the heart of Australia sets upon it.'[9] Though comparisons with Swinburne were always a saving grace, Gordon's fame rested on fame itself: the necessity that in an imperial context Australian culture be popular.

This chapter seeks to examine both the extent of a 'popular culture of Empire' in Australia, and the role that popular culture played within the imperial relationship. That popularity should be the supreme test of the quality of Australianness goes to the heart of the relationship between Empire and popular culture in Australia. From Peter Dawson (styling himself 'a singer of the people'[10]) to Kylie Minogue, the Empire's notion of cultural distinction, held by the children of the periphery as well as the metropolitan centre, took it as given that high cultural capital was English and the culture of the colonies could only appeal to a lower common denominator. Many

[8] Professor W. A. Osborne to Secretary, Prime Minister's Department, 12 July 1933, NAA, Prime Minister and Cabinet, 'Memorials. Adam Lindsay Gordon—Memorial Tablet in Westminster Abbey', A461/8, C370/1/8. Originally the plan was for a mere tablet costing 150 guineas, with 200 guineas going to Abbey fees; when the Abbey waived its fee, Sladen managed to up-size the tablet to a bust.

[9] Lang's typescript, 'Adam Lindsay Gordon. Unveiling of Memorial in Westminster Abbey on May 11th 1934', p. 1, tipped into Westminster Abbey Orders of Service, 1934, p. 163. Westminster Abbey Library.

[10] Autobiography cited in Jeffrey Richards, *Imperialism and Music: Britain 1876–1953* (Manchester, 2001), p. 497.

educated Australians would have cringed at, but not necessarily disagreed with, Sir Thomas Beecham's 1940 judgement that Australia was 'much the most backward portion of the Empire' and was 'too complacent and self-satisfied even to begin to understand its actual condition'.[11]

It was a conviction that ignored a great deal of the richness of colonial culture, and of the way in which the notion of the popular is itself an artefact of cultural history. But there are three reasons for a cultural attachment to the popular having some sort of reality in settler societies, reasons determined by the structure of the imperial relationship.

First, there was the tyranny of the market. The market that sustained cultural production in a settler society was (with the exception of the United States) necessarily small. Survival meant not only appealing to a higher proportion of a smaller population than in Britain; it also meant finding means of distinguishing the local product as superior to the imported, of making claims for the greater capacity of the local product to speak to the local audience. Just as local car manufacturers would later claim their vehicles were built 'for Australian conditions', local writers and artists argued that only they could see Australia 'through Australian eyes'. The result was an inevitable interweaving of the popular with the national. The alternative was to aim at the wider global—or more realistically the imperial—market, and greater success (*vide* Kipling) could attend that. Henry Lawson's famous 'advice to any young Australian writer' was 'to go steerage, stow away, swim and seek London, Yankeeland, or Timbuctoo—rather than stay in Australia till his genius turned to gall, or beer'.[12] But once there, in the attempt to be noticed, the colonial writers' comparative advantage lay in their colonial origin so they found themselves popularizing an image of Australia for an Empire audience.[13]

Secondly, the conscious effort to transmit a culture from one generation to another took on added meaning in settler societies, where the older generation saw the 'old' culture as a bulwark against the popular barbarism of

---

[11] *Age*, 4 October 1940, cited in Stephen Murray-Smith, *The Dictionary of Australian Quotations* (Melbourne, 1984) p. 16.

[12] Henry Lawson, 'If I could paint', in Colin Roderick, ed., *Henry Lawson: Autobiographical and Other Writings* (Sydney, 1972), p. 115.

[13] 'The great drawback to the artistic life is the limited market for products ... The attitude of the old world if any attempt to bring artistic work from Australia before it [was made] would infallibly be a can-any-good-thing-come-out-of-Galilee air.' Edward Kinglake, *The Australian at Home: Notes and Anecdotes of Life at the Antipodes Including Useful Hints to those Intending to Settle in Australia* (London, 1892), p. 92.

the new. This was not just teaching the young what the older generation knew, but inculcating the value of the imperial connection and of maintaining a relationship with Home. 'Home' became a central motif reinforcing a connection between England as a feminized domestic hearth, and a more masculine realm of adventure in the colonies. The result was that in a great deal of the popular culture produced for the young, school texts and popular children's writing in particular, a didactic imperialism predominated, a didacticism not found in other forms of popular culture in those same societies. It was always in these works, as we will see, that a popular culture of imperialism was most explicit. The inculcation of Empire loyalty was conceived as good for you: particularly by those with authority over schools and libraries, but probably equally by maiden aunts and godparents looking for suitable gifts for children.

Thirdly, modernism itself is a working out of the separation of centre and periphery, depending as it does on the gravitational pull that gathered artists and writers, intellectuals and bohemians into the metropolis. Its corollary was the necessary view of the mass of society being philistine and provincial, and nowhere more so than in the provinces themselves, a view necessarily propagated by those expatriates who left the provinces behind. The modernist myth created its own reality as it drew an educated, artistic elite away to the centre. Australians mistook London for the world's cultural centre—sustaining London as an art centre, for example, long after it was overtaken as the imagined modern centre progressively by Paris, Berlin, and New York.

These three structural elements point to significant differences in the culture of Empire as it came to be expressed in the Dominions. British scholars have rediscovered a culture of Empire sustaining Britain's imperial reach by the end of the nineteenth century. Their response to the post-colonial turn has been to find a culture urged on them by 'propagandists' and thoroughly permeating British culture.[14] Australian scholars have responded to the post-colonial moment differently. They have rejected—by default—an older 'radical nationalist' perspective that had celebrated the distinctiveness of Australian popular culture from the dominant culture of Empire, and have tended to turn their attention particularly to the fraught relationship between Indigenous Australians and an undifferentiated 'European' culture

---

[14] There is now of course a vast literature: see for example John MacKenzie's Studies in Imperialism series with Manchester University Press.

(where the national and the imperial are conflated). They have tended to evade the question that has occupied so many British historians: how far did an ideology of Empire penetrate popular consciousness? There is no doubt Australians were implicated in Empire, supported it, entered imperial adventures, and shared much of the culture. Britain was 'Home' and Australia a frontier of civilization. If—despite the vast new scholarship—it remains possible for Bernard Porter to argue that Britons remained essentially ignorant of Empire, it could never be said that Australians were ignorant of Britain.[15] But how far were ordinary Australians 'steeped' in the values of Empire or of nation? Much of their popular culture had an explicitly imperialist message, but was that message heeded or did it simply wash over the recipients? When Australians voluntarily marched off to war in 1914, was it a popular culture of Empire that made them do it? When it came to the decision to enlist, Empire certainly provided the public rhetoric to justify it, but most Australians seemed to join up not from a sense of imperial duty but for good pay, a chance to travel, or vague notions of adventure.[16]

* * *

The 1890s has acquired a reputation as being the high point of cultural nationalism in Australia, so it might be a useful place to begin an investigation of popular culture and Empire. The 'Heidelberg school' of painters were using *plein-air* techniques and vaguely impressionist notions to capture the Australian landscape in a new, sentimentally naturalistic way, seeing it, they claimed, for the first time 'through Australian eyes'. Their work began to find an outlet in the new public art galleries.[17] Similarly, writers associated with the Sydney *Bulletin* and other new publishing enterprises also claimed to be writing in an Australian idiom and aimed for a national readership. They made a virtue of cocking a snook at the more imperialistically minded establishment and celebrating democratic vulgarity. The undoubtedly prominent role of the *Bulletin* writers and the Heidelberg painters has been read as radical nationalism—since Vance Palmer and Russel Ward writing

---

[15] Bernard Porter, *The Absent-Minded Imperialists: Empire, Society, and Culture in Britain* (Oxford, 2004), pp. x–xi, 133.

[16] Richard White, 'Motives for Joining Up: Self-Sacrifice, Self-Interest and Social Class 1914–1918', *Journal of the Australian War Memorial*, October 1986, pp. 3–16.

[17] See Chapter 5 pp. 115–22.

in the 1950s.[18] Like other modernists the writers and artists of the 1890s emphasized their break with the past, but in their case that break became both a nationalist one (their work was 'Australian' whereas others were 'British') and a popular one (they were writing for the Australian *people*, as many of them as possible, not a small elite). It was a position that, on both counts, had obvious economic value. More recently, revisionists such as John Hirst have questioned the radical nationalist interpretation in order to assert a more conservative culture. In revisiting Federation, previously seen as the product of a lack of popular interest, they have argued for a 'sentimental nation', a culture structured around a more conservative set of values, in popular patriotic poetry for example, that ultimately were embodied in the constitution.[19]

It is indeed the case that a considerable body of self-consciously Australian work emerged in this era. Assertive Australian nationalism was a force in all sorts of unpredictable ways. There was enough of a national culture to be called into service in songbooks and pantomime, and being 'thoroughbred Australian' was counted a recommendation in popular entertainment. More widely, advertising was making use of an already rich range of national symbolism, and the overt pursuit of 'local colour' was a feature of literature, art, and music. Bush ballads still celebrated bushrangers, native flowers were incorporated into interior design, emu eggs had long had collector status with elaborate nationalist decoration, cooee songs were sung around the piano, and 'The Man from Snowy River' was breaking local publishing records. The artists and writers of the era turned to what they saw as distinctively Australian subjects for their work, the culture of the shearers and drovers associated with the wool industry, the tales of lost children, lonely homesteads, and battling pioneers thrown up by the harsh landscape. They populated their stories and their art with distinctive gum trees, bush characters, colloquial expressions, and popular sentiment.

But that national culture—even the sort that the *Bulletin* stood for—was created against imperial culture and was determined by it. When they invented Australia they did so within an imperial framework. The more 'radical nationalist' culture overtly resisted British culture, but that very resistance was a product of the imperial relationship. The 'distinctiveness' of

---

[18] The classic 'radical nationalist' cultural histories are Vance Palmer, *The Legend of the Nineties* (Melbourne, 1954); Russel Ward, *The Australian Legend* (Melbourne, 1958); and Geoffrey Serle, *From Deserts the Prophets Come: The Creative Spirit in Australia 1788–1972* (Melbourne, 1973).

[19] See John Hirst, *The Sentimental Nation* (Oxford, 2001).

the bush depended on an implicit acknowledgment that an English landscape was somehow more normal. Young Australians asserting the virtues of being 'native-born' were often in rebellion against their British-born parents, just as popular images of Australia as a strapping youth made sense only in relation to a fatherly John Bull. The most vociferous republicans of the 1890s were often recent immigrants from Britain and they drew heavily on British republican literature.[20]

That assertive Australianism could be surprisingly compatible with a loyalty to Empire, summed up in stance of the 'independent Australian Briton'. So when Australian troops marched off to fight an imperial war in South Africa, they claimed a distinctive origin as 'bushmen' and adopted a sheep dog, 'Bushie', as mascot, along with a wallaby, a dingo, and a ringtail possum.[21] The composition of 'Waltzing Matilda', that most 'Australian' of songs, came about through a marriage of the English version of an Irish melody with a celebration of distinctive outback life. The pastoral industry supplied much of what was considered distinctively Australian, but it did so as a contribution to an imperial economy. When Dorothea MacKellar wrote Australia's most popular overtly nationalist poem in 1908, her beloved 'sunburnt country' could only be conceived as a contrast to English 'field and coppice'.

It annoyed the *Bulletin*, which complained that too many Australians were simply not Australian enough. The unfurling of the new flag design for a federated Australia in 1901, for example, produced a typical tongue-lashing: 'That bastard flag is a true symbol of the bastard state of Australian opinion, still in large part biased by British tradition, British customs, still lacking sufficient years to the sufficiency of manhood.'[22] On the other hand there were those who complained of a lack of British sentiment, and insisted on the need to instil British values into the populace—and their children—through the overt celebration of monarchy, imperial military might, and, from 1905, Empire Day. The elaborate celebrations in Sydney for Queen Victoria's diamond jubilee in June 1897 were typical. The *Sydney Morning Herald* was relieved to report a 'wave of patriotic impulse' as proof 'that whatever may be the differences of class and party, in the sentiment of common citizenship of

---

[20] Mark McKenna, *The Captive Republic* (Cambridge, 1996), pp. 133–5; C. N. Connolly, 'Class, Birthplace, Loyalty', *Historical Studies*, Vol. 18, no. 71 (October 1978), pp. 210–32.

[21] R. L. Wallace, *The Australians at the Boer War* (Canberra, 1976), pp. 235–6.

[22] *Bulletin*, 28 September 1901, quoted in Sylvia Lawson, *The Archibald Paradox: A Strange Case of Authorship* (Ringwood, Vic., 1983), p. 209.

a great Empire we are one and undivided'.[23] The sheer spectacle of Empire, as David Cannadine has reminded us, should not be overlooked, and there were suspicions that the crowds were moved more by spectacle than sentiment.[24] In 1900, for example, while the Citizens' Bushmen Corps—a popular patriotic initiative for the South African War—was being drilled and trained on Kensington Racecourse, the public could pay 6d. to watch on non-racing days, and during one race meeting two races were given over to riders from the contingent racing in uniform.[25] Empire was entertaining. But there was also a natural reversion to British standards as the norm, a more mundane kind of loyalty whose power derived precisely from the fact it was not overt, the precise opposite of spectacle. Australians' sports were British, they preferred to 'buy British', their institutions paid deference to British models. Perhaps most telling is the fact that when they travelled overseas, they imagined stepping into a world they already knew through fiction: their imaginative worlds were British by default.[26]

In that regard we can ask to what extent was popular culture an active agent in the processes of Empire maintenance and of nation-making? How far did a popular culture of Empire create the enthusiasm for Britain and Empire consciousness that guided colonial policy? And importantly, how much did that sense of nationhood itself emerge out of a popular culture that was framed by a British imperial order? Consider how Empire and national distinctiveness were mutually constitutive in Adam Lindsay Gordon's presence in Poets' Corner. Even to the limited extent Australian popular culture can be seen as distinctive (and it often obsessively searched for marks of distinction), it was usually distinctive within a context of an international (very often imperial) consciousness. The bush of the popular imagination was always as much the gift of Empire as it was of the nomad tribe.

However, what also becomes very apparent in any overview is how limited it is simply to look at popular culture as a battle between imperial and national loyalty. The notion that popular culture in Australia was necessarily positioned on a spectrum from Empire to nation, hovering between lion and kangaroo, is a reading that is itself a product of an imperial relationship. It cannot be readily assumed that culture is defined above

[23] *Sydney Morning Herald*, 23 June 1897.

[24] David Cannadine, *Ornamentalism: How the British Saw Their Empire* (London, 2001).

[25] Wallace, *The Australians at the Boer War*, pp. 234–5.

[26] Richard White, 'Bluebells and Fogtown: Australians' First Impressions of England, 1860–1940', *Australian Cultural History*, 1986, pp. 44–59.

all by a national orientation, an expression of national identity. On the contrary, a lot of popular culture was conceived outside the Empire–nation framework—audiences and participants 'consumed' it from an infinite variety of perspectives. American minstrels, French restaurants, German music, and Chinese decorative arts found a ready response in Australia, along with a host of activities that defied national stereotyping, from beachgoing and picnics to shopping and dancing. But our purpose here is to consider how popular culture in Australia related to a culture of Empire. The rest of this chapter explores this problem, first through a close study of popular literature, where arguably a popular culture of Empire held more sway; and secondly through the lens of sport, which was arguably the most prominent 'arena' in which the tensions between imperial patriotism and colonial nationhood were played out. Finally we consider the limits of British and imperial influences in everyday life by surveying other popular cultural forms in the twentieth century which were less defined by language, tradition, and economic constraints, and which consequently followed different trajectories. While there was a significant 'imperial' presence in the popular culture of Australia even at this high point of cultural nationalism, we need to keep in mind how circumscribed that presence often was.

*   *   *

The most familiar—and obvious—test case is popular literature, where we can clearly identify the power of Empire in Australian popular fiction: children's, men's, and women's literature. Much of this was overtly jingoistic, but even those works that did not have an imperial agenda were nonetheless influenced by the economic effects of imperialism because of the international structure of anglophone book publishing. The production, dissemination, and popularization of all types of Australian fiction has been shaped and influenced by the Publishers Association of Great Britain, founded 1896. This publishing cartel had an imperial attitude towards the Australian book market which it viewed as its colonial inheritance. Historically, Australia was crucial to the fortunes of the British publishing industry because it was the largest colonial market outside Britain for the better part of the twentieth century.[27] British book publishers fostered a view of the Australian

---

[27] Martyn Lyons, 'Britain's Largest Export Market', in Martyn Lyons and John Arnold, eds, *A History of the Book in Australia 1891–1945: A National Culture in a Colonised Market* (St Lucia, 2001), p. 22.

market as a dumping ground for remaindered British books sold at vastly discounted prices, knowing they spoke to an Australian audience that shared the same imaginative geography and social or imperial values. When British publishers set up in Australia later in the twentieth century, there remained a 'branch office' mentality guiding their activities. Nevertheless, this state of affairs benefited Australians because without the British publishing and trading infrastructure Australia would not have had any book trade.[28] Yet it also meant that those Australian authors who wanted to see their books in print had to comply with the three influential concerns pushing fiction writing towards the realm of the popular described above: the national or cultural distinctiveness of the local product; the pedagogic need to maintain or reinforce the ties with Home, especially for the younger generation; and the assumption that London was the international literary centre.

When it came to Australian literary production, the two axes of anglo-phone publishing—London and New York—meant that, especially where popular fiction was concerned, the requirements of overseas metropolitan readers either shaped the stories that Australians could tell or determined which stories would be published. Imperial themes and the consciousness of a British metropolitan market are easily discernible in Australian chil-dren's literature: W. H. Fitchett's bestselling *Deeds that Won the Empire: Historic Battle Scenes* (1897; 1900; 1928) and *King's Empire* (1906), articles published in popular children's periodicals (*Boy's Own*, *Girl's Own*, and *Magnet* magazines), and 'reward' fiction for children which had the peda-gogic purpose of maintaining imperial ties and knowledge of Britain. The British influence on Australian children's literature, especially throughout the nineteenth and early twentieth centuries, may be seen in the derivative nature of Australian children's genres—settler literature, adventure novels, the generally unsuccessful imitations of boarding school stories—as well as the types of characters deliberately developed as 'colonial Australians' in contradistinction to their imperial relatives.[29] By the 1890s a general shift towards the naturalization of Australianness in scene, style, and characters is evident in children's literature, but it was a shift not incompatible with the needs or colonial fantasies of the British metropolis. Mary Grant Bruce's immensely popular *Billabong* series located the Australian bush as the source of national identity and character, but it also represented continuity with

---

[28] Richard Nile, *The Making of the Australian Literary Imagination* (St Lucia, 2002), p. 89.

[29] Brenda Niall, *Australia through the Looking-Glass: Children's Fiction 1830–1980* (Melbourne, 1984), pp. 1–2.

a half-century-long tradition of colonial settler/imperial frontier children's stories.[30] It took Ethel Turner's bestselling *Seven Little Australians* (1894) to celebrate suburban Australian life in children's literature. Turner was one of the *Bulletin* school, drawing from and contributing to the literary nationalism of the 1890s. But in children's literature, it was a nationalism that complemented and reinvigorated the tired centre of Empire: the young, vigorous, robust nation which gallantly came to the rescue and shouldered the burdens of 'Mother England'. When the Great War broke out, Turner and Bruce promptly asserted imperial loyalties and sent their young male characters rushing over to rescue 'little Mother England' in novels such as Turner's *The Cub* (1915) and Bruce's wartime trilogy: *From Billabong to London* (1915), *Jim and Wally* (1916), and *Captain Jim* (1919).

Along with settler novels, nineteenth-century children's authors also produced numerous adventure stories. By the late nineteenth century, popular romances had largely split along gender lines—at least as far as authorship was concerned—into female domestic romances and social comedies, and male quest or adventure romances. In Australia the adventure story was unquestionably a male preserve after the 1870s when Marcus Clarke's convict romance, *His Natural Life* (serialized between 1870 and 1872), and Rolf Boldrewood's bushranger tale, *Robbery Under Arms* (serialized between 1882 and 1883) were published. Studies of the impact of British imperialism on literature have focused overwhelmingly on the adventure novel as a conduit for jingoistic imperial ideas—an imaginative space where imperial conquest of far lands and foreign peoples was mapped out; where imperial masculinity was forged and found superior to that of other races. Australian authors were greatly influenced by British romance literature: the novels of Walter Scott, Robert Louis Stevenson, and Henry Rider Haggard.[31] The production and reception of Boldrewood's work occurred within the context of imperial adventure fiction produced in the imperial metropolis. *Robbery Under Arms* evolved as a serial during the same period as Stevenson's *Treasure Island* (serialized in *Young Folks* in 1881–2) and Rider Haggard's *King Solomon's Mines* (1885), *Allan Quartermain*, and *She* (both 1887).

However, the international context for adventure novels changed in the early twentieth century. It is generally agreed that the British adventure novel underwent a crisis especially after the bloodbath of the First World

---

[30] Niall, *Australia Through the Looking-Glass*, p. 116.

[31] Robert Dixon, *Writing the Colonial Adventure: Race, Gender and Nation in Anglo-Australian Popular Fiction, 1875–1914* (Melbourne, 1995), p. 15.

War, and the Australian adventure novel started weaning itself away from its British publishing lifeline. This was partly due to the greater publishing opportunities for Australian adventure tales offered by local publishers such as Angus and Robertson, New South Wales Bookstall Company, Horwitz, or Cleveland who, between them, published popular adventure, war stories, crime, Pacific island stories, and biographical tales of outback travels and adventure, and westerns. London firms continued to re-issue or publish fiction by Guy Boothby, J. M. Walsh, and Dale Collins during this period, but bestselling authors such as Louis Becke, Beatrice Grimshaw, Arthur Upfield, William Hatfield, Frank Dalby Davison, Frank Clune, and Ion Idriess, among others, managed to find Australian publishers for their works. The 1950s and 1960s became a 'vintage' era for Australian male writers of popular fiction who were placing substantially more manuscripts with Australian publishers than with British publishers, finding or creating their own popular mass market within Australia.[32] Another notable change in male popular fiction was the way in which the imaginative world became Americanized after the Second World War, even as imperial and economic power shifted from Britain to the United States. By the 1950s, Australian male writers of popular paperback fiction such as Gordon Bleeck, Alan G. Yates ('Carter Brown'), or Richard Wilkes-Hunter were solidly ensconced in the world of American pulp fiction, churning out corny westerns, war stories, sordid tales of 'hard-boiled' crime, Cold War espionage thrillers, American science fiction, and 'executive' pulp stories which reflected anxieties over the masculine identity of the white-collar 'corporation man'. Australian publishing companies issued magazines such as *American Detective* and *American Crime* during this period.[33] Where men's popular fiction was concerned, therefore, the British Empire had ceased to be the imaginative locus for male genres by the mid-twentieth century. It was superseded by Australian or American genres, and future direction and influence would come from these mass markets. In this regard, the conditions of writing and publishing differed widely for male and female writers of popular fiction.

Women's popular fiction also rehearsed imperial themes and emphasized imperial ties in its romantic intrigues. Throughout the late nineteenth and twentieth centuries, Australian authors such as Rosa Praed, Mary Gaunt, Marie Bjelke Petersen, Alice Grant Rosman, Joyce Dingwell, Lucy

---

[32] See Graeme Flanagan, *The Australian Vintage Paperback Guide* (New York, 1994); Toni Johnson-Woods, *Pulp: A Collector's Book of Pulp Fiction Covers* (Canberra, 2004).

[33] Flanagan, *The Australian Vintage Paperback Guide*, p. 117.

Walker (Dorothy Sanders), Jennifer Ames/Maysie Greig (Jennifer Greig Smith), Margaret Way, Colleen McCullough, Valerie Parv, Miranda Lee, and Emma Darcy, among many others, have acquainted readers all over the world with tales of burning love in the Australian bush. Especially in the early twentieth century, the 'Australia' represented in Australian women's romances was filtered through the prism of the British publishing industry and the need to cater to the fantasies of British readers. Writers in the first half of the twentieth century, such as Alice Grant Rosman, centred their romances around English characters, often setting the story in Britain, in order to appeal to the British market and ensure the publication of their novels. Indeed, many of Rosman's romances are indistinguishable from contemporary British romances even though she took care to import the occasional Australian character for exotic background colour. Standard plot devices for other female romance writers included the upper-middle-class English hero or heroine who found love and redemption in the Australian outback, which remained the most popular locus for romance despite the fact that Australia was overwhelmingly urban by the end of the nineteenth century. For Marie Bjelke Petersen, Rosa Praed, I. A. R. Wylie, and many other popular Australian romance novelists writing for Mills and Boon and, later, Harlequin Enterprises, publication and success in the British or American markets were necessary prerequisites to their works appearing in their own country. Therefore, they had to cater to the desire of their metropolitan publishers and readers for what Alan Boon of Mills and Boon called 'Great Open Space' romances set in the colonies.[34] The ties between British publishing and the Dominions remained strong in the post-Second World War period, when many new Mills and Boon authors were recruited from Australia and New Zealand during the 1950s and 1960s.

It is impossible to overestimate the importance of London publishers such as Mills and Boon, Hodder and Stoughton, Hurst and Blackett, Hutchinson, or Collins in providing international and lucrative publishing opportunities for Australian women's writing. Although New York rivalled London as a centre of romance publishing by the end of the twentieth century with romance publishing firms such as Bantam, Doubleday, and Avon, with rare exceptions, the American romance market remained closed to Australian writers because of New York publishers' demands that contemporary romances be American in focus, characters, and setting. By contrast, British

---

[34] Joseph McAleer, *Passion's Fortune: The Story of Mills and Boon* (Oxford, 1999), p. 258.

publishers offered Australian writers the opportunity to romance the colonial as well as the decolonized world. This meant that London as *the* centre of
publishing for women's romance novels held sway throughout the twentieth
century and persists even today.

Where adult popular fiction is concerned, therefore, gender and genre differences meant that Australian women's popular romantic fiction remained
tied to the apron strings of the British Empire—both ideologically as well
as through the publication process—long after this had ceased to be true
of male popular fiction. In women's romance novels, an emphasis on the
civilizing mission as well as the recurring plot device of marriage between
English and Australians reinforced imperial ties and urged the natural fit of
imperial–colonial interests throughout the twentieth century.[35] The problems of masculinity and adventure, fear of domesticity and feminization
(read: 'Englishness' as well as urban/suburban lifestyles) which occurred in
men's adventure novels and created ambivalence or conflict between nationalism and imperial identity were far less likely to appear in women's fiction.
This was partly due to the structural requirements of the different genres of
popular fiction produced by men (adventure, crime, thriller, westerns) and
women (overwhelmingly romance). And once again when even romance
fiction emphasized national distinctiveness, it was under the imperial gaze,
as in contemporary romances which incorporate Aboriginal culture as a
touristic sign of the faux-post-colonial nation.

*   *   *

As with popular literature, sport was also an arena where pockets of imperial
sentiment persisted, and proved surprisingly resilient. Three elements in the
very nature of sport contribute to the longevity of Empire connections. First is
its structure around contest. Spectators take sides: their involvement derives
from identification with one side rather than the other, and the development
of national competitions reinforced notions of national unity. Second is its
ritual nature, where the repetition of contests, and the acquisition of tradition
and ever lengthening statistical series, of record scores and 'historical' firsts,
add considerably to its enjoyment. Thirdly, men's sport was peculiarly
steeped in the imperial ideal of martial masculinity, and even women's sport

---

[35] See Hsu-Ming Teo, 'The Britishness of Australian Popular Fiction', in Kate Darian-Smith,
Patricia Grimshaw, Kiera Lindsey, and Stuart Macintyre, eds, *Exploring the British World:
Identity–Cultural Production–Institutions* (Melbourne, 2004), pp. 721–47.

promoted the idea of sport as a proving ground for the nation. Thus it was particularly well suited as a popular gauge of the tensions between imperial loyalties and local sentiment.

Cricket is the obvious case where a popular culture of Empire endured. England–Australia games continue to have special meaning. The 'test' of nationhood that a test match implies continues to echo nineteenth-century validations of sport as character-building, developing those manly traits of leadership, obedience, determination, loyalty, and courage. These notions were themselves the product of changes in Empire ideology and social Darwinist racial thought that began to take root in Australia from the 1870s. Prior to that time, direct sporting ties with England were few, and those that existed merely served to emphasize a feeling of community with the home country. Thus, the first visiting English cricket team in 1861 was greeted by the local press in Sydney with the words: 'In inviting you to visit us we had no idea of testing our skill against yours—that would be simply absurd; but we were desirous of having you here to witness British skill in the noble game of cricket. It is a comfort to know that we are beaten by our own countrymen.'[36] In subsequent decades, however, these sporting encounters became increasingly filtered through anxieties about the resilience and vigour of a race of transplanted Britons. Australians greeted with obvious relief any indication that the race was not degenerating under the Australian sun. Victories over English teams proved that Australians retained 'the manhood and muscle of their English sires', and that there was no longer evidence to support fears about 'the possible physical degeneration of the English race in the bright Australian climate'.[37] Australia's victory in the inaugural 'test' match in Melbourne in 1877 was widely understood not only as a triumph for a new colonial breed, but also as a reassuring sign of the resilience of imperial stock. As the *Australasian* typically boasted: 'The victory of the Australian Eleven over the English cricketers is no ordinary triumph ... The event marks the great improvement which has taken place in Australian cricket; and shows, also, that in bone and muscle, activity, athletic vigour, and success in field sports, the Englishmen born in Australia do not fall short of the Englishmen born in Surrey or Yorkshire.'[38]

[36] *Sydney Morning Herald*, 28 January 1862, quoted in W. F. Mandle, *Going it Alone: Australia's National Identity in the Twentieth Century* (Ringwood, Vic., 1978), p. 27.

[37] See Richard White, *Inventing Australia: Images and Identity 1688–1980* (Sydney 1981), p. 72.

[38] *Australasian*, 17 March 1877, in Mandle, *Going it Alone*, p. 28.

Some historians have tended to see in these contests the earliest popular signs of national self-definition, and it is indeed significant that the colonies fielded 'Australian' teams against England several decades before any signs of national political awareness. In a seminal essay in 1972, W. F. Mandle went so far as to suggest that cricket was crucial to the building of national self-confidence—a necessary cultural precursor to the political project of Federation.[39] True, success on the cricket field could, at times, bring forth bouts of separatist rhetoric that suggested a weakening of imperial loyalties. The *Bulletin*, for example, proclaimed after an Australian test win in 1896: 'This ruthless rout of English cricket will do—and has done—more to enhance the cause of Australian nationality than could ever be achieved by miles of erudite essays and impassioned appeal.'[40] Yet these utterances were by no means typical, and need to be weighed against the powerful associations of cricket as a symbol of Empire unity. As K. S. Inglis writes: 'Intense devotion to the most English of games ... [indicates] how spontaneously and profoundly Australians embraced the culture of the motherland ... real anti-imperial nationalism might have disposed Australians not to play cricket at all.'[41] Just as inter-colonial cricket matches could be seen as intensifying rivalry between the Australian colonies and forging national unity simultaneously, so England–Australia matches worked both to bind the Empire together and to sharpen national differences within it.

The inherent tension between these two coexistent functions was most sharply in evidence at the height of hostilities in the 'Bodyline' series of 1932–3. The series began amicably enough, with the West Australian government welcoming the tour as 'a powerful influence in cementing the bonds of Empire'.[42] But the new English tactics of bowling fast, short-pitched balls at the batsman's head and body (designed to neutralize Australia's Don Bradman) created a popular furore in Australia, both among the crowds and in the press, and culminated in an official complaint against this 'unsportsmanlike' behaviour. No word could have been better calculated to wound English susceptibilities, and the English team managers threatened

[39] W. F. Mandle, 'Cricket and Australian Nationalism in the Nineteenth Century', *Journal of the Royal Australian Historical Society*, Vol. 59, no. 4 (December 1973), pp. 225–45.

[40] K. S. Inglis, 'Imperial Cricket: Test Matches between Australia and England, 1877–1900', in Richard Cashman and Michael McKernan, eds, *Sport in History: The Making of Modern Sporting History* (St Lucia, 1979), p. 171.

[41] Ibid., p. 170.

[42] Quoted in Ric Sissons and Brian Stoddart, *Cricket and Empire: The 1932–33 Bodyline Tour of Australia* (Sydney, 1984), p. 38.

to cancel the tour unless the slur was withdrawn. That the Australian Prime Minister, Joseph Lyons, was called upon to help resolve the impasse is indicative of how much seemed to be at stake, and how close the tour came to a fatal breach in the popular cultural ties of Empire. Yet as much as the Australian team's defiance of the English establishment has become the stuff of nationalist folklore, the fact remains that the burden of Australia's complaint—ultimately—lay in England's departure from a set of common standards and assumptions about 'British' fair play. When the British Cabinet Secretary, Maurice Hankey, visited Australia the following year, he noted that it was because of Australia's 'admiration' for Britain 'that they felt so bitterly about the ridiculous bodyline controversy. They hated to feel that we had lowered our standard of sportsmanship'.[43]

The two rugby codes followed a similar pattern, both the amateur union and the professional league drawing on imperial ideology. Although the early Rugby League 'test' matches were distinguished as much by open brawling as fair play and sporting conduct, it was nonetheless possible to conceive of these contests as imperial encounters. The captain of the 1920 British touring team, Harold Wagstaff, called for the games to be played in 'the British spirit of sportsmanship, for we are Britishers of the old land and you are Britishers of the new land. We're all the same in blood and sport, and know how to lose and, I hope, how to win.' Tony Collins has identified a deep affinity between the working-class origins of the game in Australia, and the northern English heartland of the 'British' League. In both settings, Britishness was understood in terms of a masculine, working-class, egalitarian ethos, sharing a common disdain for upper- and middle-class English mores and values. Thus, it made perfect sense for the President of the NSW League, Harry Flegg, to refuse a merger with the Australian (Rules) Football National Council in 1933 on account of his 'pride in the British tone and atmosphere of rugby'.[44]

Yet other football codes revealed the arbitrariness of the search for either national or imperial significance. Australian Rules flourished in the southern states at the height of Empire, despite its lack of any international competition. Soccer, popular at junior level, never acquired the obsessive fan base of the other Australian codes or the English game, and after the Second World War was associated strongly with non-English migrants:

---

[43] Ibid., p. 107.

[44] See Tony Collins, 'Australian Nationalism and Working-Class Britishness: The Case of Rugby League Football', in *History Compass*, Vol. 3, 2005.

on the other hand its followers are more likely to maintain an adherence to English clubs, and, with the multiplication of sources of migration, to other European clubs. By the end of the twentieth century all four football codes flourished despite their quite different relationships to Empire and nation. Other sports—more individualistic or less imbued with the rhetoric of Empire—carried less of the burden of Empire. In tennis's Davis Cup, sailing's America's Cup, and swimming at the Olympics, the United States was the most significant rival and at moments the contest came to be a battle for national pride against another imperial power. Some historians have seen an Americanizing process at work in the transformations of sport in the later twentieth century, with the dominance of television and the emergence of national leagues. But what can be read as American national influences are more likely to reflect more structural or economic imperatives affecting sport the world over.

The Olympic Games best illustrate the profound shifts in Australian sporting culture over the past hundred years from an imperial to a global framework. Given the extraordinary enthusiasm for the Olympics in recent decades, it seems hard to imagine that the inaugural Games in Athens in 1896 were widely regarded with disdain at the time in Australia. The *Argus* boasted that 'the average Victorian football team, in good condition, could outrun, outjump, outkick, and outlast an equal number of athletes from the age of Phidias and Pericles.'[45] The earliest Australian medal winners did not compete for Australia but for Britain or 'Australasia', and there was periodic debate over the years about whether the Empire ought to compete as one or several nations. In preparation for the 1912 Stockholm Games, the Australian team manager, Richard Coombes, proposed that the Empire teams should meet up in London beforehand and train and travel as a single unit. This, Coombes wrote, 'is surely the very ideal of Empire—the forces of the Mother Country and her children, and Colonies, congregating on the shores of Britain to concentrate the forces of Empire, and then voyaging to the battle-ground of Stockholm to challenge in friendly warfare the best of the world's athletes'.[46] With the advent of the 'Empire Games' in 1930, there was even discussion over whether it was worth bothering with the Olympics. In

---

[45] Quoted in Douglas Booth and Colin Tatz, *One-Eyed: A View of Australian Sport* (Sydney, 2000), p. 114.

[46] *The Referee*, ibid., p. 115. See also Garth Henniker, 'Richard Coombes and the Olympic Movement in Australia: Imperialism and Nationalism in Action', *Sporting Traditions*, Vol. 6, no. 1, pp. 2–15.

the aftermath of the highly politicized Berlin Games of 1936, Australian team manager Harry Alderson recommended that Australia withdraw from the Games in future in order to concentrate on the Empire Games: 'It is only in the British Empire Games that the amateur status of the Olympic Games is genuinely recognized. In most of the other teams, the semblance of amateurism is scarcely maintained.'[47] As Brian Stoddart suggests, prior to the Second World War 'success in British terms against British standards maintained in British Institutions' seemed a sufficient prize to many Australians.[48]

* * *

In the two fields of literature and sport, a popular imperialism was a significant factor in their development in Australia, and elements of it persisted long after the breaking of the formal bonds of Empire. It would be a mistake, however, to leave it at that, and not explore the limits of imperial influence and the impact of other factors in other areas of popular culture. Literature, bound by the English language, has particular power: the meaning of Britain was often expressed in the imaginative (and escapist) world of the reader, and statues to Shakespeare and Burns were tangible memorials to a literary Empire in Australia. Sporting contests also carried a special symbolism because of the peculiar depictions of sport as a proving ground, capable of representing the vigour, character, and moral fibre of a race, an empire, or a nation. Up until the Second World War (at least), Australia's connection to Empire remained relatively unscathed in both of these fields of popular entertainment. Arguably, however, when it came to other popular cultural forms, the Empire had surrendered in the cinemas and the dance halls of the 1920s.

What, for example, is to be made of the impact of the visual world of display advertising? In popular art (poster and commercial art, interior decoration) the reference points were less constrained by language; more wide-ranging European connections were evident in the popularity of art nouveau and mild modernism dominating commercial art and domestic interiors, not just in high modernist intellectual circles where cosmopolitanism could be a sign of cultural capital. In the decades before the Great War, there was also the self-conscious nationalism of (migrants) Lucien Henry and R. T. Baker in their wide-ranging design work promoting the use of Australian flora and

---

[47] Quoted in Booth and Tatz, *One-Eyed*, p. 120.
[48] Brian Stoddart, 'Cricket's Imperial Crisis: The 1932–33 MCC tour of Australia', in Cashman and McKernan, eds, *Sport in History*, p. 126.

fauna, although the more banal decorative design still reproduced Englishness.[49] From the 1920s, advertising agencies themselves, self-conscious in their go-getting modernity, their modern business methods, and popular psychology, increasingly looked to the United States for inspiration.[50] It is not too sweeping a generalization to say advertising in the first two-thirds of the twentieth century consistently imbued Britain and 'British' iconography (cottage gardens, English village life, the fire in the hearth) with positive associations of tradition, enduring values, natural forms. America and its iconography (sky-scrapers, streamlined cars, gadgets in the kitchen) were identified with being up to date, a sign of the future, modern and technological. This pope's line dividing the world of advertising values into English tradition and American modernity was also apparent in both Britain and the United States. Both tradition and modernity had their selling points in a consumerist age, but in the turnover of consumerist fashion, being up to date took precedence over, and was normalized against, any desire for tradition.

In popular music the flow from the Victorian English music hall to the Australian parlour was strong, and the latest in military marches and sentimental romance was soon heard around Australian pianos. But this was interrupted by an Irish tradition and American minstrels.[51] Percy Grainger's attempts to produce 'popular' and 'democratic' music drew on an imperial racial framework. But then the enormous transformation brought by the recording technology to the structure of the music industry and the experience of popular music throughout the twentieth century took place largely outside a British imperial framework. American music became the norm. Even Australian bush ballads transformed into country music, and as Australian performers turned into cowboys, the American connection again became apparent: Slim Dusty's first two copyrighted songs were tributes to Texas and the bush respectively: 'I'm a Yodelling Guy from Texas' and 'Beautiful Aussie Land'.[52]

[49] Ann Stephen, ed., *Visions of a Republic: The Work of Lucien Henry* (Sydney, 2001); R. T. Baker, *The Waratah: The Australian Flora in Applied Art*, Part 1 (Sydney, 1915).

[50] Robert Crawford, 'Selling a Nation: Depictions of Australian National Identity in Press Advertisements, 1900–1969', Ph.D. thesis, Monash University, 2001, pp. 175 ff.

[51] Richard Waterhouse, *From Minstrel Show to Vaudeville: The Australian Popular Stage, 1788–1914* (Sydney, 1990); Emily Pollnitz, ' "A Subtle pow'r in those sweet songs": Romance, family and distinction in the drawing-rooms of middle-class Australians, 1880–1900', History IV thesis, University of Sydney, 2005.

[52] Chief Examiner Copyright to D. G. Kirkpatrick (Slim Dusty), 25 January 1943, NAA, C37939; Graeme Smith, *Singing Australian: A History of Folk and Country Music* (Melbourne, 2005), pp. 85–7.

Admiration of America was also evident in the newly emerging popular cultural forms of radio, cinema, and later television. Australians took to the new culture of the cinema with enthusiasm. As members of a wealthy and urbanized society, most Australians had access to a local cinema, and by the 1920s they were the most avid filmgoers in the world—more so even than Americans. And their diet was 90 per cent American: Australia was Hollywood's most important export market.[53] British films competed for the rest with German and French imports (well-received before the talkie revolution) and the small but, for a time, vibrant Australian industry. A story would later be told of a struggling national industry snuffed out by the dominance of the Hollywood juggernaut, using commercial monopoly power to overwhelm any local competition. There was some truth in this: Hollywood's role as the international centre of movie-making drew Australians there as surely as London's West End drew those wanting to crack 'legitimate' theatre, and systems of block-booking made it difficult for Australian films to get shown.[54] But just as significant was the power of Australian distributors and their preference for Hollywood's product: there was such profit in distribution to the Australian market, little if any in production, and popular culture was treated as business not art.

Empire was a serious issue in the world of the 'pictures' between the wars. Many cinematic adventures took place in the Empire, and the values of the Empire—boys' own adventure, the celebration of civilized 'whiteness'—transferred readily to the screen. Hollywood shared many of MacKenzie's 'ideological cluster' of hero-worship, racial superiority, militarism (and even monarchism curiously), but they harked back as much to Theodore Roosevelt's 'strenuous life' and the American frontier as to Kipling and Baden-Powell.[55] Australian authorities were as suspicious of Hollywood's version of a specifically British Empire as they were about Hollywood's sexual morality. Some vigilant loyalists could identify insidious American propaganda in depictions of British characters, and alerted authorities of the need to control such works especially where inferior races, easily swayed by such cheap tricks, were concerned. The Royal Commission into the film industry, established by the Australian government in 1927, was

---

[53] John Tulloch, *Australian Cinema: Industry, Narrative and Meaning* (Sydney, 1982), p. 34.

[54] Angela Macdonald, 'Hollywood Bound: A History of Australians in Hollywood to 1970', Ph.D. thesis, University of Sydney, 2001, p. 4.

[55] John M. MacKenzie, *Propaganda and Empire: The Manipulation of British Public Opinion, 1880–1960* (Manchester, 1984), p. 2.

an opportunity to address the concerns of these 'Empire moralists'; what Diane Collins has characterized as 'club women, Empire loyalists, clergy, educationalists, and sections of the press'.[56] They deplored the fact that the masses in Australia seemed to fritter away their time at the beach, at the races, at the cinema, beyond the reach of the gospel of imperial duty and loyalty. While arguments were made in favour of supporting local Australian production, the main recommendation of the commission was for an 'Empire quota'. When it came to the crunch, Empire counted for more than nation. But this was not so much a sign of the strength of Empire feeling, as an acknowledgement of its weakness in the face of Hollywood's popularity. In the end, because of limited federal powers and industry lobbying, the recommendation was not acted upon: commercial considerations were more important even than imperial ones.[57]

Commercial imperatives also ensured limited space for an Empire culture in the development of new broadcasting technologies in Australia. While Australian governments greeted the advent of wireless in the 1920s and television in the 1950s with trepidation, equating commercialism with a lowest-common-denominator Americanization that would threaten British values in Australia, they ultimately surrendered to the demands of the commercial broadcasting industry. The Australian compromise between the British and American models of broadcasting was to have both: a publicly funded system (eventually run by the Australian Broadcasting Commission—later Corporation) and a commercial system funded by advertising. In broad terms (with significant exceptions) it meant two cultures, a popular commercial culture that tended to be dominated by American entertainment, and an 'ABC' culture identified strongly with Reithian uplift and instilling British civilized values: though even here the ABC was as much influenced by the imperative to ensure outback Australia had access to the joys of radio and television. The one significant development was an increasing interest in the ABC of developing a distinctively national culture from the 1940s (when its preference for English accents began to weaken), and this was further stimulated by the introduction of local content quotas for commercial radio and television. By the 1970s the local popular music, television drama, film-making, and advertising industries were thriving and—because they were popular—began to find lucrative markets in Britain.

---

[56] Diane Collins, ' "More than Just Entertainment" (1914–1928)', in Ina Bertrand, ed., *Cinema in Australia: A Documentary History* (Sydney, 1989), p. 73.

[57] Ibid., pp. 73–5, 116–20.

In contrast to popular literature and sport, in many of those other cultural fields the dominant 'imperial' cultural relationship was apparently with the United States, but it would be oversimplifying to suggest that Australians merely switched from one popular cultural Empire to another. It is important to note that Britain was itself succumbing to the seduction of 'American' popular culture. Where films were concerned, Hollywood appropriated British stories such as *The Sheik, Mrs Miniver*, or *Gunga Din* and transformed them into transatlantic popular culture which found its way to Australian screens. Can the final product then be judged 'American' or 'British'? Such examples are salutary reminders as to the limitations of national understandings of popular culture in an age when technology and increasing ease of travel and communication facilitated a variety of complex transnational exchanges. Cultural flows between Britain and Australia, as well as the United States, ebb, eddy, and wash back to this day.

The popularity of Slim Dusty in Britain in the 1950s and then Rolf Harris, the Australian pop bands of the 1960s drawing on the children of post-war British migrants, the popularity of Australian television soap and radio personalities (Jonathan Coleman, Mike Carlton) in Britain, London's power to lure the sons (usually) of Empire into playing significant roles in Fleet Street, theatre, or public and independent broadcasting—all demonstrate that there is no simple trajectory from the heart of Empire to the outback or New York or anywhere else. Popular culture, so rich and complex and polyvocal, continues to resist generalization, but in a transnational, consumerist world where commercial imperatives increasingly determine cultural production, both imperial and national considerations matter less than ever. And yet … residual sentiment remains.

*   *   *

In 2001 Australians celebrated the centenary of Federation. As a prelude, Westminster again became a site for the working out of Australia's cultural relationship with Empire. To celebrate the 100th anniversary of the passing of the Commonwealth of Australia Act through the British Parliament, the then Prime Minister John Howard led a large official delegation of ex-Prime Ministers, state leaders, other MPs and dignitaries to London for a four-day trip on 3–7 July 2000. Though overshadowed by preparation for the Sydney Olympics, the $2 million 'junket' caused a stir in Australia with many in the media deploring the waste of taxpayers' money, especially at the very time when a consumption tax was being introduced. Paul Keating, Howard's immediate Labor predecessor, refused to participate, though the event itself was the brainchild of a Labor politician with a flair for history. Most opposition focused on the expense of the trip, yet there was enough vestigial anti-imperial sentiment for James Terrie, the national director of the Australian Republican Movement, to complain:

this is just a throwback to the old cultural cringe when Australians needed to go to Britain for approval and acceptance. I'm sure the British people must find the prospect of all these Australians coming to London a little bit strange. And it will strike many Australians as a return to the days when we were expected to tug our forelocks at Britain—and those days have long gone.[58]

Outside official metropolitan circles, 'the British people' took little notice. In this regard they were perhaps following historical precedent. Even in July 1900, the passing of the Commonwealth of Australia Act by the British Parliament took place with little fuss, followed immediately by a more pressing debate over the south Lancashire tramways bill. A century later, 'Australia Week' received scant coverage in the British media. The centrepiece of the trip, a special sitting of the House of Commons on 5 July, was scarcely remarked upon except to record rather gleefully the British Prime Minister Tony Blair's enthusiastic announcement of a war memorial to be erected to American rather than Australian servicemen. The Australian press gave widespread coverage to the 'historic Service for Australia in London's hallowed Westminster Abbey', noting how the chamber was 'filled with the ancient sounds of the didgeridoo' as the Aboriginal arts performer and theatre director Richard Walley performed a traditional Nyoongar/Yamitji piece, followed by the mostly expatriate congregation singing 'God Save the Queen' and joining in the chorus of the popular song 'I am Australian'. It was a way of asserting, at the heart of Empire, an Australian cultural independence—through a colonial appropriation of Indigenous culture.

London's *Daily Telegraph* devoted an article, 'Britain pays tribute to Australian centenary', to Australia Week, but other British media were less interested, idly noting the vague exoticness of what the *Times* columnist Giles Coren called 'some arcane Commonwealth anniversary'.[59] Where Australians were happy, even gratified, to have Adam Lindsay Gordon inserted

[58] Mark Chipperfield, 'Australia's London Party Outrages Republicans', *Daily Telegraph*, London, 25 June 2000.

[59] Christopher Lockwood and Andy McSmith, 'Britain Pays Tribute to Australian Centenary', *Daily Telegraph*, London, 6 July 2000; *The Times*, 6 July 2000.

into the hallowed halls of Westminster Abbey in 1934, by 2001 they wanted more than popular culture taken seriously in the old imperial metropolis. The Australia Week celebrations emphasized Australia's contribution to 'high' culture: the classically trained opera singer Christina Wilson's solo performance of 'I Am Australian' in Westminster Abbey; an Arthur Boyd art exhibition at Australia House; the performance of a few Australian dramas, including Jane Harrison's 'Stolen'—a play about the removal of Aboriginal children from their families; interviews conducted by the Australian-born journalist Phillip Knightley with Germaine Greer and award-winning novelist Frank Moorhouse; and an exhibition of Penny Borland's photographs at the National Portrait Gallery. All to no avail. In the absence of Kylie Minogue or other popular *Neighbours* stars, more attention was paid by the British media to the fact that 'Australian tennis ace' Patrick Rafter would be playing American André Agassi at Wimbledon—a match rife with symbolism of Australia's changing imperial loyalties played out on the common ground of a shared British heritage. And most Australians looked forward to the opening ceremony of the Olympics, a popular extravaganza that negotiated a melding of a nationalist bush legend of the land with Aboriginality and multiculturalism, in which the Empire was little more than a footnote.

Select Bibliography

JOHN ARNOLD, PETER SPEARRITT, and DAVID WALKER, eds, *Out of Empire: The British Dominion of Australia* (Melbourne, 1993).

TARA BRABAZON, *Tracking the Jack: A Retracing of the Antipodes* (Sydney, 2000).

IAN CRAVEN with MARTIN GRAY and GERALDINE STONEHAM, *Australian Popular Culture* (Cambridge, 1994).

SUSAN DERMODY, JOHN DOCKER, and DRUSILLA MODJESKA, eds, *Nellie Melba, Ginger Meggs and Friends: Essays in Australian Cultural History* (Malmsbury, Vic., 1982).

ROBERT DIXON, *Writing the Colonial Adventure: Race, Gender and Nation in Anglo-Australian Popular Fiction, 1875–1914* (Melbourne, 1995).

JOHN FISKE, BOB HODGE, and GRAEME TURNER, eds, *Myths of Oz: Reading Australian Popular Culture* (Sydney, 1987).

PETER GOODALL, *High Culture, Popular Culture: The Long Debate* (Sydney, 1995).

SYLVIA LAWSON, *The Archibald Paradox: A Strange Case of Authorship* (Ringwood, Vic., 1983).

JOHN RICKARD, *Australia: A Cultural History* (New York, 1996).

GAVIN SOUTER, *Lion and Kangaroo: The Initiation of Australia* (Melbourne, 2000).

PETER SPEARRITT and DAVID WALKER, eds, *Australian Popular Culture* (Sydney, 1979).

JON STRATTON, *Race Daze: Australia in Identity Crisis* (Sydney, 1998).

HSU-MING TEO and RICHARD WHITE, eds, *Cultural History in Australia* (Sydney, 2003).

GRAEME TURNER, *Making it National: Nationalism and Australian Popular Culture* (Sydney, 1994).

RUSSEL WARD, *The Australian Legend* (Melbourne, 1958).

RICHARD WATERHOUSE, *Private Pleasures, Public Leisure: A History of Australian Popular Culture Since 1788* (Melbourne, 1995).

RICHARD WHITE, *Inventing Australia: Images and Identity 1688–1980* (Sydney, 1981).

15

'In History's Page': Identity and Myth

NEVILLE MEANEY

'Britishness' resonates throughout Australian culture and has been incorporated, either directly or indirectly, into every major representation of Australia's modern history.

Following the United Kingdom's entry into the European Economic Community in 1973, which signalled Britain's intention to seek its future in Europe and its abandonment of 'Greater Britain', Australians had no choice but to give up their British identity and with it their British rites and symbols. Searching for substitutes they chose in a 1977 national poll 'Advance Australia Fair' as their new anthem. It convincingly defeated the bush ballad, 'Waltzing Matilda' and 'The Song of Australia' both of which, in contrast to 'Advance Australia Fair', had a distinctly Australian flavour.

Indeed it might be said that Australians were comfortable with 'Advance Australia Fair' because it was more central to their idea of themselves, or at least a remembered idea of themselves. A hundred years earlier when Peter McCormick was moved to write the words for 'Advance Australia Fair' he penned a hymn celebrating Australia's Britishness. His invocation that 'history's page' should 'at every stage advance Australia fair' was informed by the only history Australians in the race patriot era could imagine, namely a history that would show them to be worthy members of the British race and Empire. As a stanza, excised from the latter-day sanitized version of the anthem, put it,

> Britannia then shall surely know
> Beyond wide oceans' rolls
> Her sons in fair Australia's land
> Still keep a British soul.

That the Australian people should have preferred 'Advance Australia Fair', even while drawing a veil over its origins, is emblematic of the continuing, if now almost unacknowledged, influence of the British past upon the present and of Australians' difficulties in coming to terms in the post-nationalist era with that past.

Australia's representations of the British Empire and of Britishness have been central to the stories giving meaning to the country, and it is the purpose here to offer an overview of the changes that have taken place in the character of these representations and their meaning for Australia's relations with Britain and the Empire from the beginnings of self-government in the 1840s.

The chapter identifies three distinct periods; first the era of liberal republicanism, covering the initial period of colonial self-government, 1840s to 1860s; secondly, the British national or race patriot era, which lasted from the 1870s to the 1950s; and thirdly, the post-national or what is sometimes called the 'multicultural' era which, after a brief gestation in the 1960s, came into its own in the 1970s.[1]

In the first period it was political leaders and newspaper editors who, often also filling the role as cultural leaders, gave voice to colonial self-consciousness and defined the relationship to Britain and the Empire. The colonists constructed their new political system in the classical period of British liberalism. After the struggle to stop transportation of convicts and end despotic military rule they took as their ideal for this 'new Britannia in another World' a British-derived view of ordered liberty and an Enlightenment belief in universal human progress.[2] Identifying with the Whig history of the English Civil War and the 'Glorious Revolution' they turned to the most advanced reform movements in Britain, especially the Chartists and Utilitarians, to find the inspiration for their Antipodean commonwealth. As the *People's Advocate*, the most radical newspaper in New South Wales, put it, 'If we wished to look for a "Model" it is to the Constitution of England we should look modified so as to suit the wants and requirements of the present age.' In its opinion England 'enjoyed a larger store of personal liberty and rational freedom than is perhaps enjoyed by any other country

[1] In this chapter I am developing a theory-based sketch of 'Britishness' in Australia which was published as 'Britishness and Australia: Some Reflections' in the *Journal of Imperial and Commonwealth History*, Vol. 31 (May 2003), pp. 121–35. This article was a sequel to another published as 'Britishness and Australian Identity: The Problem of Nationalism in Australian History and Historiography', *Australian Historical Studies*, Vol. 32 (April 2001), pp. 76–90.

[2] For the background to Enlightenment influences in the Australian colonies, see John Gascoigne, *The Enlightenment and the Origins of European Australia* (Cambridge, 2002). The phrase 'a new Britannia in another world' is taken from William Charles Wentworth's 1823 poem *Australasia*.

in the world, not excepting even America'.[3] Upon the basis of these ideas they drew up their constitutions and proceeded to extend the boundaries of self-government, giving the suffrage almost immediately to all men and by the end of the nineteenth century also to women.

Freed from the limiting prescriptive privileges of the Old World the Australian colonists undertook to carry forward and develop further this inheritance of liberty. They were intent on producing a most advanced form of the British polity in which the people's will would prevail. Public meetings were held to protest against the conservatives who, led by William Charles Wentworth, wished to establish a hereditary upper house in the New South Wales constitution. Newspaper editorials denounced these attempts to incorporate this aristocratic principle in the new political order. Henry Parkes, who more than any other colonial politician embodied the radical liberal fervour of the era, saw this dispute as a continuation of the struggle for parliamentary democracy which had brought about the English Civil war. Writing in his newspaper *The Empire*, he used the words of the English Whig historian T. B. Macaulay to chastise Wentworth for betraying the colonial cause. He cited Macaulay's scathing attack on an earlier Wentworth, Sir Thomas Wentworth, a renegade parliamentarian who had taken the side of King Charles I: 'His earlier prepossessions were on the side of popular right. He knew the whole beauty and the value of the system which he attempted to deface. He was the first of the Rats, the first of those statesmen [in Australia (sic)] whose patriotism has been only the coquetry of political prostitution'.[4]

Likewise the colonists, in so far as they interested themselves in the distant conflicts agitating the western world in the mid-nineteenth century, saw Britain as the standard-bearer for the historical process by which peoples everywhere were freeing themselves from tyranny. Commenting on the failure of the 1848 revolutions in Europe, *The Empire* asserted that the British people 'remained the representative of that mighty progress which, in spite of such impudent pretenders as Louis Napoleon and such impassioned sots as the Parisian citizens, is still safe from the assaults of tyranny—and will still increase in light and power, and finally triumph in the happiness of our race'.[5] Accordingly dominant opinion in the press, the public, and the Parliament depicted the Crimean War as an Anglo-French crusade on behalf of liberty against Tsarist Russia, the most reactionary power in Europe. At a

---

[3] *People's Advocate*, 21 April 1849 and 13 November 1852. [4] *Empire*, 22 April 1851.
[5] *Empire*, 24 March 1852.

demonstration of loyalty in Sydney, Henry Parkes, echoing the sentiments of many others, maintained that the war was 'so far as England and France were concerned … a most righteous one, and merited the co-operation of every lover of liberty'. The Victorian Legislative Council in adopting a resolution of support for the British cause similarly declared the war to be one 'of freedom against despotism'.[6]

In this early period, although the colonies were creating their 'new Britannia in another world', a world in which the Indigenous people were being supplanted and Asian peoples were pressing upon their borders, they did not for the most part define their Britishness in exclusive race terms. During the Crimean War the political leaders could speak of the British as 'their brave fellow countrymen' who had 'the same blood, the same feelings and the same interest as Englishmen',[7] while still holding to the Enlightenment view of the unity of humankind and the British liberal doctrine of the equal rights of all under the Crown. The greatly respected historian of early Tasmania, John West, writing as editor of the *Sydney Morning Herald*, repeatedly expressed the view that 'humanity is broader than nationality and substantial progress is not to be sacrificed to what, after all, is a sentiment.'[8]

When, in the 1850s and early 1860s, European miners, angered by Chinese competition on the Victorian and New South Wales goldfields, forcibly expelled the 'Celestials' from the diggings and called for restrictions to be placed on them, the colonial legislators were very reluctant to enact such measures. The Parliaments in adopting such laws encountered spirited objections from those who regarded the poll taxes and limits on free entry into the colonies as contrary to Enlightenment ideas of liberty and British ideas of justice. Butler Aspinall, who represented a goldfields electorate in Victoria's Legislative Assembly, declared the colony's proposed actions against the Chinese to be 'unEnglish and discreditable'. Furthermore these Acts, which only applied to Chinese, were defended more frequently as unhappy expedients intended to meet a particular problem of law and order than as a means to protect a White or Anglo-Saxon race. And so, after the gold-rush fever dissipated, the colonies rescinded their discriminatory legislation. The Reverend John Dunmore Lang, a fiery advocate of republican independence, who had voted for the New South Wales legislation, took the lead in 1867 in seeking its repeal, arguing that the Chinese were as moral,

[6] *Sydney Morning Herald*, 23 May 1854; *The Age*, 12 January 1856.
[7] *Argus*, 19 December 1855 and 12 January 1856.
[8] *Sydney Morning Herald*, 5 July 1860.

able, and civilized as their British neighbours and that therefore there were no grounds for continuing to make these invidious racial distinctions.[9]

The colonists also accepted the British liberal idea of Empire, namely that the settler colonies would eventually seek and obtain their independence from the Mother Country. Though there were differences of opinion over whether separation and a republic should be sought immediately, it was generally agreed that complete self-government, probably accompanied by a federation of the colonies, was their destiny and that this would be accomplished with British goodwill and leave a legacy of mutual sympathy and a shared heritage.[10] The Melbourne *Argus* predicted that 'The day will assuredly come when Victoria will become a nation, and when her citizens will transfer to her their allegiance.' Likewise *The Empire* editorialized that there was 'nothing unseemly in entertaining the idea of separation—nay, it is rather a truly English piece of wisdom to look at the event as a prospective certainty'. And the Hobart *Courier* expected that 'bye and bye, in the progress of the years, and it may be at no distant period, the political ties may be gently and kindly unloosed.' Australians would then be willing 'to accept our own responsibilities to make ourselves as a federation of Australian states'.[11] This independence was not to come about through violent revolution. The Australians were not to follow the American example. Indeed it was claimed that achieving control over their own destiny would make Australians more inclined to be Britain's close friend and ally.

By the 1870s, however, Australia was undergoing rapid modernization and, in response to this, the colonists, like other western peoples caught up in this same social maelstrom, were seeking psychological security by redefining community in more intense, exclusive terms. It was a process which equated nation with race, thus defining each people by fusing the cultural with the biological. At the end of the century Charles H. Pearson, an English liberal intellectual who had for the sake of his health migrated to Victoria, concluded that Australia was in the vanguard of this movement towards a collectivist identity. Summing up his experience in *National Life and Character: A Forecast* he pointed out that the colonies' newness, egalitarian democracy, and proximity to Asia had produced the most intense

---

[9] *Proceedings of the Legislative Council and Assembly of Victoria*, First Session, 1856–1857, p. 269; D. W. A. Baker, *Days of Wrath: A Life of John Dunmore Lang* (Melbourne, 1985), pp. 487–8.

[10] Mark McKenna, *The Captive Republic: A History of Republicanism in Australia, 1788–1996* (Cambridge, 1996), chs 3 and 4.

[11] *Argus*, 13 July 1854; *Empire*, 13 February 1851 and 5 February 1856; *Courier*, 25 February 1854.

reaction to the trauma of modernization.[12] National sentiment, which West had so lightly dismissed, became the all-encompassing social cement of the new order. Peter McCormick's anthem in praise of Australia's own Britishness might well be seen as an early expression of this new sensibility, an expression of a White British identity which considered the Aborigines a dying race,[13] banned 'coloured' people from migrating to the country, and denied those already within its borders basic civil rights, including naturalization, the franchise, and employment in some occupations.[14]

At this time a school of English historians, including Sir John Seeley, E. A. Freeman, J. R. Green, and J. A. Froude, influenced by the spirit of the age, took for their central theme the unique character of the Anglo-Saxon, Anglo-Celtic, or British people and their peculiar tradition of parliamentary government. This new nationalism celebrated the trinity of race identity, imperial power, and individual liberty. Seeley's *Expansion of England,* published in 1883, was particularly important in giving these works an imperial dimension, and creating an image of a global Greater Britain in which all those of British race and culture were united as one people.[15] Popularized through a thick texture of cultural practices, through newspapers, school readers, adventure stories, and public rites and ceremonies, this history gave the colonists a vivid and pervasive representation of these new ideas of social belonging.[16] The Australian settlers proudly thought of themselves as bonded with all those who shared the same 'crimson thread of kinship'. Talk of independence and a republic was banished to the fringes of political debate.

In this process Henry Parkes, the leading nineteenth-century colonial statesman, was the bellwether. By the 1880s he had turned his back on ideas of separation and embraced Seeley's vision. Celebrating the centenary of the arrival of the First Fleet, Parkes, the then Premier of New South Wales, announced that he sought 'no separation' from Britain but rather hoped 'that

---

[12] (London, 1893), pp. 17–26, 98–111, 187–92, 220–6.

[13] Henry Reynolds, *Dispossession: Black Australians and White Invaders* (Sydney, 1989), ch. 4; Richard Broome, *Aboriginal Australians: Black Response to White Dominance* (Sydney, 1982), pp. 90–4.

[14] Matthew Jordan, 'Rewriting Australia's Racist Past: How Historians (Mis)Interpret the "White Australia" Policy', *History Compass,* Vol. 3, July 2005.

[15] J. W. Burrow, *A Liberal Descent: Victorian Historians and the English Past* (Cambridge, 1981), especially pp. 2–4, 34–5, 102–6, 124–5, 172–3, 188–92, 200–5, 248–9, 281–5, 290–6; Deborah Wormell, *Sir John Seeley and the Uses of History* (Cambridge, 1980), pp. 154–5.

[16] D. E. Roberts, 'The Role of State Education in the Development of National Identity, 1872–1918', Ph.D. thesis, Monash University, 1999.

the red line of kinship' would unite the colonies to Britain 'for generations to come'. As he rallied his fellow Australians to support new and more absolute laws aimed at keeping out all Chinese, he did not argue the necessity of civic order but the imperative of race. These alien Asians were a threat to the 'British character' of the colonies. Explaining the new discriminatory Acts to London, Parkes said that 'blood' was all, that there could never be any sympathy or peace between the two races. The Australian colonists were determined 'to preserve the British type in the population'.[17] By the mid-1890s the colonies had agreed to legislate to prevent the migration of all natives of Asia, Africa, and the Pacific islands. When the Commonwealth Parliament in its first major piece of legislation adopted the so-called White Australia policy, leaders of all parties defended their actions on these same grounds.

Even as they adopted this British race identity, many colonists still had what Parkes described as a 'local patriotism' or 'the feeling of a warm Australian patriotism'.[18] That is, there had grown up, especially among the native-born, an affection for the bush and the land. There was a sense, derived from experience, of belonging to a country which possessed its own distinctive fauna and flora, its own seasons and character. The Reverend W. H. Fitchett, the author of *Deeds that Won the Empire*— a very popular work dedicated to 'the Imperial race'—was critical of those who, looking back nostalgically at the 'Old Country', failed to appreciate the different beauty of their new home. Though Australians were 'of purely British stock', their country had its own natural grandeur. It was his view that 'for resonant, far-running and thrilling sweetness, an Australian magpie, heard in the keen air of a spring morning is equal' to 'Shelley's Lark' or 'Tennyson's brook'.[19] Imbued with this spirit, education departments began to include Australian geography, literature, and history in school curricula and the New South Wales government instituted an annual 'Wattle Day'.

Yet this love of the land did not replace the pride in race. As Parkes noted, Australia's folk songs and folk culture were comparable to those which had appeared in other colonies of settlement or were to be found in the different parts of the British Isles, including the counties of England. Despite

---

[17] New South Wales, *Parliamentary Debates, Legislative Assembly*, 1887–1888 Session, Vol. XXXII, 3 April 1888.

[18] 'Our Growing Australian Empire', *The Nineteenth Century*, January 1884, p. 141.

[19] *Deeds that Won the Empire: Historic Battle Scenes* (London, 1903), p. v; and *The New World of the South: Australia in the Making* (London, 1913), pp. x–xi.

such differences, generated by place of birth or land of adoption, all were united by 'blood' as one people, and it was this national myth above all else which made them British. For Australians indeed the superior virtues of the land they had occupied often led them to proclaim that they were better Britons. Australia was, in Fitchett's words, 'the very happiest example of the colonising genius of the British race'.[20]

There were among the English, Scottish, Welsh, and Irish Australians different degrees of support for the Empire and Britishness, those of English and Ulster Irish Protestant descent being generally the most enthusiastic and those of Irish Catholic origin the most reserved. Indeed just as Seeley in his *Expansion of England* used English as synonymous with British so many English migrants like Parkes, much to the chagrin of the Celts, especially the Irish, persisted with the practice in Australia.

The Irish Catholics could not easily forget English oppression. Irish Catholics were in the forefront of the colonies' few and limited instances of armed resistance to British authority, whether Vinegar Hill in 1804, Eureka Stockade in 1854, or among the bushrangers, most notably Ned Kelly. Yet even though historic grievances against the English did play a part, to a greater or lesser extent, in these acts of defiance, they could not be considered to represent Irish Australians' attitudes to the Empire. While Peter Lalor, the leader of the miners at the Eureka Stockade, grew up in an Irish patriotic family, neither he nor other major figures among the multi-national body of diggers who took up arms urged Australian independence in their camp meetings or their list of complaints. It is true that Ned Kelly in justifying himself did make much of the wrongs done by the English to the Irish peasantry, but it is equally true that Irish Catholics were well represented in the Crown's constabulary which hunted him down and captured him.

In the latter part of the nineteenth century all the colonies when introducing compulsory education made their own contribution to the Irish Catholics' persecution mentality. Following the example set by Victoria in its 1872 Education Act the colonial governments, at the same time as they established public schools to cater for all pupils, withdrew state funding from Church schools.[21] Since the Catholic bishops believed the state system to be a Protestant or, even worse, an irreligious institution, they regarded this denial of state aid as a great injustice and called on their Irish flock to pay for

[20] *The New World of the South*, p. xii.
[21] A. G. Austin, *Australian Education 1788–1900* (Melbourne, 1961); Dennis Grundy, *'Free, Secular and Compulsory', The Education Act of 1872* (Melbourne, 1972).

separate parish schools. Indeed the clergy linked the education question to the Irish national cause, and the teaching orders, monks and nuns primarily drawn from Ireland, attempted to give this substance by balancing British history with Irish history and imperial loyalty with Australian loyalty. If the public schools' readers gave children a history of the British race centred on England and its military, imperial, and parliamentary heroes, the Catholic readers gave prominence to Irish patriots and martyrs who had fought against their English overlords.[22]

There is doubt, however, about the strength of Irish Catholic antagonism towards the idea of being British. The Irish, even more than Australians of Scottish and Welsh descent, may have carried with them memories of England's past wrongs and resented English pretensions to superiority, but they for the most part had little trouble in identifying with the British or Anglo-Celtic race and the British Empire. William Bede Dalley, a son of Irish convicts and a devout Roman Catholic, was the first colonial leader to commit Australian troops to fight in an Imperial cause. As acting Premier of New South Wales in 1885 he sent a military contingent to assist Britain in the war against the Madhi in the Sudan, arguing that 'British blood—Australian blood', the two being identical, had been shed in defence of the Empire.[23] Cardinal Patrick Francis Moran, the Archbishop of Sydney, approved of Dalley's action and sentiment, and in 1888 he set out what became the orthodox Irish Catholic position declaring that 'whilst the Australians are then one in heart and in hand with their brothers of the dear mother country, we are not less loyal to the empire of which we are proud to form part ... The freedom which we enjoy is the mainstay of the empire's strength, and we desire that Ireland should, to the fullest extent, enjoy the same freedom without which the Empire cannot stand.' On this latter point Moran was speaking not only for his flock but also for the majority of Australians who favoured self-government or 'home rule' as the solution for the Irish problem.[24]

Irish Catholics were roughly a quarter of the population and were spread fairly evenly within and across all the colonies. They had little choice but

[22] Brother Ronald Fogarty, *Catholic Education in Australia 1806–1950* (Melbourne, 1959); Roberts, 'The Role of State Education', pp. 47–100; S. G. Firth, 'Social Values in the New South Wales Primary School, 1880–1914: An Analysis of School Texts', in A. G. Austin, ed., *Melbourne Studies in Education* (Melbourne, 1970), pp. 123–59.

[23] New South Wales, *Parliamentary Debates*, Legislative Council, 1884–1885 Session, Vol. XVI, pp. 5–9, 17 March 1885. See also Chapter 12 in this volume, pp. 290–1.

[24] Patrick O'Farrell, *The Irish in Australia, 1788 to the Present* (Sydney, 1993), p. 163.

to accept their minority status and to come to terms with the ethos of the dominant society. Moreover, under democratic self-government, convict and free settlers from Ireland, as from other parts of the British Isles, were able to aspire to the highest political offices in the land. It is Patrick O'Farrell's judgement that, despite everything, 'the Irish in Australia identified proudly with the power and prestige of the Empire' and looked forward to Ireland being 'as free as they were in Australia'.[25]

However, with the rise of mass nationalism and the Australian adoption of the British race myth, the meaning of freedom under self-government came under question. In the nationalist era each distinct western people accepted that its destiny could not be fulfilled and that it could not be culturally or morally whole until those who shared the myth were united within a common polity. Seeley himself looked forward to the creation of an Imperial Federation, and to this end was a foundation member of, and leading figure in, an English-based Imperial Federation League. Though the precise form that this Federation might take was never very clear, the impulse which had brought the subject to the centre of imperial thought and argument remained powerful. At its core was the conviction that somehow or other the British race should be able to develop common policies which would enable its scattered branches to face the world as one.

From the outset, Australian leaders, even many of those who had imbibed most deeply of the British race sentiment, had difficulties in accepting the Imperial Federationists' proposal for a political union. Parkes, enmeshed in the fabric of Australian public life, felt the dilemma most keenly and tried to find language and institutions by which to solve the national problem. Swept along by a vision of Greater Britain, he was convinced that if 'the English people'—and here he slipped into Seeley's confusing nomenclature—'held together in one world-embracing-Empire' they would be 'destined for a historic mission beyond that of all previous nations'. Writing in an English journal he said that should this come to pass the people of the British Isles would have to adopt a different attitude towards the colonies of settlement. Australians were 'more purely British than any other [people] outside the shores of Britain'. To counter the English perception that the Australians were but colonial dependencies of the Mother Country and therefore not entitled to be treated as equals, he claimed that they were in some key respects better Britons showing the way to the future regeneration of the

---

[25] *The Irish in Australia*, p. 163.

race. Referring especially to the Australasians' democratic constitutions and equal liberty he asserted that this 'Young England' was 'in all the best characteristics of the race, more English than Old England itself'. If Australians were to participate in the common destiny then, as Seeley had argued, the English people had to accept the overseas British as belonging to Britain as 'one part of the nation belongs to all other parts in the United Kingdom'. Australians had to be treated not as subordinate colonists but as equal partners sharing 'in all the glory of the British Empire'.

For this purpose, Parkes contended, as the passions of nationalism required, that the Empire had to find the means of binding the British peoples together 'in one great self-sustaining, consanguineous political organism'. Yet this could not be achieved through colonial representation in either the British Parliament or the British Cabinet. Not only were there constitutional objections but, even more, it was clear that, since the colonists would always be in a minority, these schemes could not be relied upon to protect their peculiar vital interests, such as their claim to annex eastern New Guinea or more broadly their assertion of an 'Australasian Monroe Doctrine for the South Pacific'.[26]

Parkes' only suggestion was that after the colonies federated as 'The British States of Australia'—the name presumably adapted by analogy from the United States of America—the new body should establish a Council of Australia in London which would have responsibility for dealing with the British government. At different times he asserted, without understanding the distinction, that the ultimate solution should be, on the one hand, an organic union or, on the other, a 'great alliance' of powers meeting on 'equal ground'.[27] Race culture and state interests were not easily reconciled, and so the centripetal attractions of mythic history could never overcome the centrifugal pressures of divergent geography.

The achievement of Australian Federation did nothing in itself to resolve the issue. It neither rejected a possible imperial union nor endorsed such a future. Nevertheless it was meant to embody the most advanced form of the Anglo-Saxon tradition of parliamentary government. Parkes, in giving

---

[26] Roger C. Thompson, *Australian Imperialism in the Pacific: The Expansionist Era 1820–1920* (Melbourne, 1980), pp. 84–6 and 104–6.

[27] 'Our Growing Australian Empire' and 'Australia and the Imperial Connection', *The Nineteenth Century* (January 1884), pp. 132–49 and (May 1884), pp. 867–72; New South Wales, *Parliamentary Debates, Legislative Assembly*, 1890 Session, Vol. XLIV, p. 57. See also Bruce Mansfield, *Australian Democrat: The Career of Edward William O'Sullivan, 1846–1910* (Sydney, 1965), pp. 257–65.

the new structure the title of Commonwealth, showed his reverence for this tradition which the Australians had done so much to advance. From the sixteenth century this distinctively English word had been used to describe the ideal polity, that is, a form of government responsible to the people and committed to the common weal or common good. Very well read in the Whig history of the English Civil War he saw it as a noble struggle by the people and parliament in defence of liberty. The Australian colonists had inherited a form of government which had been 'fought for, died for, by our ancestors'. Parkes' fellow Australians in creating the Federation were admonished 'to honour the heroic Englishmen of the seventeenth century who must ever command the homage of the students of our constitutional history ... The magnificent fabric of freedom ... which the Stuart kings had laboured so strenuously to destroy, rose from their ashes with renewed splendour; and every age since has produced wise and enlightened men to enlarge its foundations'.[28]

Until the 1960s, Australian politicians, intellectuals, and historians continued to wrestle with the problem of racial unity and imperial consolidation. They continued to puzzle over how their Commonwealth could be connected in a lasting and equal union with the other British peoples. Alfred Deakin who during the movement for Australian Federation had opposed all British initiatives for Imperial Federation, saw no contradiction in subsequently accepting the Presidency of the Victorian Imperial Federation League. In his Presidential Address he reiterated Parkes' theme that 'The same ties of blood, sympathy, and tradition which make us one Commonwealth here make the British of today one people everywhere.' In the Address, Deakin referred six times to the British Empire as 'nation' and only once to Australia.[29]

Indeed it was in the two decades immediately following Federation that the most serious efforts were made to find some agreed form of Empire-wide political cooperation which, while protecting the distinct geopolitical interests of the diaspora, would unify the British race in the face of external threats. Against the background of a growing competition of the great western nations for survival or supremacy a group of British intellectuals,

[28] Sir Henry Parkes, *Fifty Years in the Making of Australian History*, Vol. 2 (London, 1892), pp. 400-4.

[29] Cited by James Curran in his John Curtin Ministerial Library Visiting Scholar Public Lecture on 19 April 2004 at the Curtin University of Technology, Perth, Western Australia. <http://john.curtin.edu.au/events/speeches/curran.html>.

infused with a missionary zeal, established the Round Table as a secret organization to study how the organic unity of the Empire should be accomplished. These apostles of the new imperialism understood that if they were to succeed they would need to win over the self-governing Dominions, and so they formed branches throughout Greater Britain.

For the members of the Australian branches, who, like those of all other branches, were recruited mainly from the ranks of academics, lawyers, and senior government officials,[30] the approach of the Round Table came at a most propitious time. It was the high era of British race patriotism. In 1905 the Australians instituted an Empire Day for celebrating what Prime Minster George Reid called 'the grandest and greatest Empire that was ever formed'.[31] Labor and Liberal leaders vied with one another to prove their loyalty to the British race and Empire. With the British government's enactment of the Irish Home Rule bill, Irish Catholics also felt able to give their wholehearted loyalty to the Empire. Accordingly when the First World War broke out all classes and communities were united in their support for the Mother Country. At a great meeting in the Melbourne Town Hall the Liberal Premier of Victoria, addressing the overflow audience as 'my fellow Britishers', called on them to be ready to make sacrifices for the Empire. The leader of the Labor Party declared that if they 'faltered or hesitated they would be less than Britishers'. And John Gavan Duffy, speaking as 'an Irish Catholic Nationalist', urged the Irish Australians to 'stand shoulder to shoulder, knee to knee' to fight 'the battle for an empire whose flag flew over all the world, from East to West, the greatest empire the world had ever seen'.[32]

In this atmosphere the Round Table branches or 'moots'—an old Anglo-Saxon word with connotations of free men meeting in a common assembly—applied themselves with great enthusiasm to the task. Indeed Australia probably made a greater and more thoughtful contribution to this search for organic unity than any of the other Dominions. Under the patronage of Alfred Deakin, the Melbourne 'moot' was the most active and reflective, and the powerful intellect of its secretary, Frederic Eggleston, did not allow members to indulge themselves in emotional fantasies. Eggleston cautioned that 'Imperial Union is not an end in itself. It may be the means to an end. That end is the realization of the unity of the British race and

---

[30] Leonie Foster, *High Hopes: The Men and Motives of the Australian Round Table* (Melbourne, 1986), Appendix A, 'Members of the Australian Round Table', pp. 189–243.

[31] *Sydney Morning Herald*, 25 May 1905.   [32] *Age*, 7 August 1914.

its mission of civilization to the world.'[33] As British race patriots they had high hopes, but like Parkes before them they were compelled to face the difficulties that had condemned all previous schemes.[34]

The First World War brought to the fore the problem with which Parkes, his political successors, and the Round Table had wrestled. Australia's Prime Minister, Billy Hughes, more than any other political leader, felt profoundly and articulated repeatedly the British race vision. As a result of the war, he proclaimed, the British people had been saved from degeneracy and decay and 'had found its soul'. The war had 'drawn all parts of the Empire and all classes closer together'. It had 'welded together, by bonds that time will not dissolve ... the loose federation known as the British Empire into one homogeneous nation'. Therefore he hoped that the word 'Empire' could be given greater meaning and that the experience of the war would cause the British people scattered around the globe to 'cement for ever a Federation-Empire—call it what you might—which will ensure the peace of the world'.[35] When the British Prime Minister David Lloyd George, influenced by leading Round Table members, created an Imperial War Cabinet composed of himself and the Prime Ministers of the Dominions, Hughes welcomed it. Charged with responsibility for framing the trade, defence, and foreign policy of the Empire it seemed the long-sought solution for the problem of reconciling the autonomy of the Dominions with the desire to achieve British unity in the wider world.

While the war gave the movement for British race consolidation a greater urgency it also highlighted the difficulties of the idea. The Imperial War Cabinet was not a cabinet but rather a council of prime ministers responsible to different parliaments. Imperial policy therefore required the consent of all the governments of the Empire. In practice Lloyd George was not willing to be hamstrung in making Britain's world policy. He would not allow Britain's freedom of action to be limited by what in effect was a Dominion right of veto. As the end of the war drew near and the question of peace terms moved to centre stage Hughes saw Lloyd George's unilateral decision-making as a betrayal of the imperial idea, and he complained to his colleagues in

[33] 'Imperial Union', *United Empire*, 4 (January 1913), pp. 91–3.

[34] Warren Osmond, *Frederic Eggleston: An Intellectual in Australian Politics* (Sydney, 1985); Neville Meaney, 'Frederic Eggleston and Australia's Role in International Affairs', *Australian Journal of Politics and History*, Vol. 51, no. 3 (September 2005); Neville Meaney, *The Search for Security in the Pacific* (Sydney, 1976), pp. 258–60.

[35] W. M. Hughes, *'The Day'—and After: War Speeches*, arranged by Keith Murdoch and introduced by the Rt. Hon. Lloyd George (London, 1916), pp. 12, 16, and 61.

Melbourne that there was 'no imperial Government in this great crisis, although there may be an Imperial War Cabinet'.[36] When Lloyd George failed to consult him about the armistice terms which contained the basis for the peace and involved specific Australian concerns, Hughes recognized the inadequacy of the Imperial War Cabinet. Having learnt his lesson he followed the Canadian lead and insisted that Australia at the Paris Peace Conference should be represented not only on the British Empire Delegation—the symbol of race solidarity—but also in its own right on the same terms as other small allied nations—an expression of its own separate interests.

The war had cast a shadow over Australian expectations about the imperial idea. Three of the most able members of the Melbourne Round Table moot, John Latham, Robert Garran, and Frederic Eggleston, who were in Britain at the time of the dispute over the armistice, saw great danger in Lloyd George's behaviour. John Latham spoke for them all when he wrote to the British Round Table:

The consultative principle embodied in the Imperial War Cabinet is supported by no legal or even conventional sanctions. It depends upon an assumed basis of common loyalty and good faith ... The neglect to consult the Dominions at this critical juncture, whether due to design or indifference, causes me the most grave apprehension as to the future of the Empire.[37]

The Australian Round Table never quite recovered from this blow, but its members still could not face abandoning a goal, the achievement of which would alone make them whole.

Australians' difficulties in coming to terms with these developments showed up in the universities' treatment of the history of Britain and the British Empire. From early in the twentieth century the teaching of history had come under the control of the universities, and thus the modern intellectual discipline began at this point to play a formal role in the making of Australia's 'history page'. Professors of history not only designed the university syllabi and educated the teachers of the subject but also often presided over school syllabi and wrote the textbooks. Though the academy offered history as a science concerned with the systematic collection and analysis of documentary evidence, most of its practitioners, like their

---

[36] Cable, Hughes to Watt, 23 October 1918, W. M. Hughes Papers, National Library of Australia (hereafter NLA), MS 1538/23/233.

[37] Copy of letter, Latham to Philip Kerr, 9 November 1919, Latham Papers, NLA, MS 1009/19/23–25.

counterparts in other western universities, could not escape the romantic impulse to place the national story at the centre of their teaching and writing. And for Australian historians, many of whom were members of the Round Table, this meant primarily the story of the British peoples and their Empire with Australia as a modest appendix to the grand narrative.

These historians, like the Round Table and the country as a whole, expressed different though overlapping views of Britishness and the Empire. The overwhelming majority would have accepted Keith Hancock's much cited description of Australians as 'independent Australian Britons' in which, while all the words were important, 'most stress' was laid upon the last.[38] Beyond this, however, they could be said to divide into four schools, each of which addressed one of the main elements in the Australian conception of Britishness and the British Empire. For convenience these schools might be labelled conservative imperialism, liberal imperialism, liberal humanism, and radical nationalism.

The most important conservative imperialists were Ernest Scott, Professor of History at Melbourne University (1913–36) and John M. Ward, Professor of History at Sydney University (1939–79). Both Scott and Ward were sympathetic to the Round Table's aims but were able to adapt to the changes which during the period in which they held their chairs saw first the transformation of the British Empire into the British Commonwealth and then the latter's transformation into the Commonwealth of Nations.

In his *A Short History of Australia*, Scott, commenting on Germans' expectations that at the outbreak of the First World War Australia would seize the opportunity to separate from the Mother Country and set up a republic, wrote that the Germans might have as 'truthfully prophesied that Yorkshire would declare its independence or that Manchester would become a republic'. He went on to add that Australians were 'proud of their race' and that British history, which was their history, was the source of the 'racial genius' which had enabled them to conquer and develop their new land.[39] During the First World War the challenge to the British race was so great that he even urged the establishment of an Imperial Federation through the mechanism of an Imperial Parliament,[40] an institutional answer to the problem of imperial union which nearly all Australians had long since rejected.

---

[38] Keith Hancock, *Australia* (London, 1930), p. 66.

[39] Ernest Scott, *A Short History of Australia*, 6th edn (Melbourne, 1936), p. 363.

[40] Stuart Macintyre, *A History for a Nation: Ernest Scott and the Making of Australian History* (Melbourne, 1994), p. 85.

When, however, with the coming of peace, that objective proved chimerical he accommodated himself to the Canadian- and South African-led demand for autonomy which was given formal expression in the Balfour Declaration and the Statute of Westminster. An epilogue to the 1936 edition of the *Short History* revealed his acceptance of this reality. The language of race disappeared and he explained that the Dominions were now 'freely associated' with Britain and each other, and that the British government had given up all claims to legislate for the Dominions unless at their request. Nevertheless these innovations were the final stage in the search for a resolution of the problem of the self-governing Dominions' relationship to the Mother Country. They had 'brought to a conclusion a process of historical development within the British Empire'. And the effect of autonomy, especially in the case of a foreign war, was played down. The formation of the British Commonwealth did not separate the Dominions from the Empire. It merely indicated that they occupied 'a distinctive position within it'. The British Commonwealth was 'a great confederacy of nations', and even though the Dominions were 'independent within their own spheres … the whole is not only mightier than its parts, but grander'.[41]

Ward, though of a later generation, was in many respects still made in the same mould. He idealized the British Empire, believing that it 'had brought civilisation and order to the world'. He respected the role of power in international relations and had no pressing desire to seek reform of the Empire. On the other hand his adherence to the Burkean tradition of English liberty allowed him, like Scott, to adjust to necessary changes and their incorporation into the evolving British and British Imperial constitutions. The inevitability of the Asian and African dependencies achieving self-government had to be faced, and the conversion of the British Commonwealth into the Commonwealth of Nations managed so as to cause the least friction. For him, British liberty was formed from the accretion of precedents arising out of the interplay of historical and cultural forces. Australia might have its own interests and character but Australians from their colonial foundations were British 'in social origin, culture and political inheritance as much as in status, law and institutions'.[42]

Foremost among the liberal imperialists were George Arnold Wood, Professor of History at Sydney University (1891–1928), and Sir Keith Hancock,

---

[41] Scott, *Short History*, pp. 374–5.
[42] J. M. Ward, *Empire in the Antipodes: The British in Australasia, 1840–1860* (London, 1966), p. 1, and *Changes in Britain, 1919–1957* (Melbourne, 1968), pp. 254–6.

Professor of History at Adelaide University (1926–34), at Birmingham University (1934–44), and at the Australian National University (1957–61). These historians, while sentimentally attached to Britain, nevertheless understood British liberty as a principle for critiquing Empire and bringing about progressive reform.

Wood, born into an English Dissenting family, admired the British Liberal Prime Minister W. E. Gladstone for keeping Britain out of European power politics and opposing imperial expansion. Like many Liberals in England, Wood spoke out against Britain's role in the South African War and came close to being dismissed by the University for taking this stand. Since Britain in the First World War was fighting German militarism and autocracy in defence of small countries, Wood had no hesitation in supporting the Empire, briefly endorsing conscription and even Imperial Federation. In an article for the *Australian Worker* he suggested that such a union of the British peoples would be the best way both to defend White Australia and 'increase the power of British workers in all parts of the world to fight for justice and peace'. Like most liberals, he was, however, disillusioned by the peace terms imposed on Germany, and quickly lost interest in the question of Empire.[43]

Much affected by the great human suffering of the First World War, Hancock was suspicious of the arrogance of nationalism, especially when it appeared in the guise of imperialism. Unlike Australian Prime Minister S. M. Bruce, who feared that the 1926 Balfour Declaration would lead to the disintegration of the wider 'British nation', Hancock saw the principle of autonomy as a wise application of the British liberal tradition to Empire. It seemed natural to him that, though devised to meet the problem of the White Dominions, it should eventually be extended without regard to race or culture to India and the dependent colonies.

In the introduction to his *Survey of British Commonwealth Affairs 1918–1939*, Hancock argued that free association in a Commonwealth was the British answer to the conundrum of Empire. It did not loosen the ties between its members; rather, since the nations of the Commonwealth cooperated voluntarily out of respect for shared ideals, it would make for a greater harmony and unity than any attempt to impose an imperial sovereign, whether the British government itself or some form of Imperial

---

[43] 'Should We Have Imperial Federation?', *Australian Worker*, 18 January 1917; Max Crawford, *"A Bit of a Rebel": The Life and Work of George Arnold Wood* (Sydney, 1975), Prologue and chs X–XIV.

Federation.[44] Hancock's biography of Jan Smuts was intended, by showing how this had worked for the Afrikaners in South Africa, to illustrate that this answer was equally valid for all the colonies whether European-settled or Asian and African dependencies.

The liberal humanist school was primarily the creation of Max Crawford during his long tenure as Professor of History at Melbourne University (1937–70). Crawford had little interest in either the hegemonic or fraternal Empire. As a student of Wood's he had been exposed to the liberal tradition in British history, especially the great moral and political issues involved in the 'Puritan Revolution'. At Oxford these interests had been expanded to include the European Renaissance and the problems of freedom and necessity. Nevertheless, he placed at the core of Melbourne's course structure the English Civil War.

A rich source for debates on fundamental questions about liberty and authority, power and morality, religion and truth, free will and determinism, the study of the English Civil War offered an insightful perspective on the ideological conflicts of the 1930s, 1940s, and 1950s. If it did not directly convey an intellectual and historical justification for British and therefore Australian social democracy—any imposed orthodoxy was anathema to the liberal spirit of enquiry—the spirit of the Department tended by its very openness to support that end. While it gave full scope to Marxist analyses of the inequality and injustice of capitalism, it, like one of its heroes, R. H. Tawney, looked to an English parliamentary answer; that is, as Tawney himself put it, after a public discussion and debate all issues would be brought to the House of Commons for resolution.[45]

The 'radical nationalists', led by Brian Fitzpatrick, Russel Ward (Professor of History, University of New England, 1967–79), and Robin Gollan (Professor of Australian History, Australian National University, 1976–89)—the latter two for relatively brief periods being members of the Australian Communist Party—derived from a resentment of both the British ruling classes' treatment of Australia as a subordinate colony and the London-centred Empire's supposed exploitation of its resources and people.[46]

---

[44] *Commonwealth Parliamentary Debates*, 1926 Session, Vol. CXIV, pp. 4772–6, 3 August 1926; W. K. Hancock, *Survey of British Commonwealth Affairs*, Vol. 1 (Oxford, 1937), ch. 1.

[45] R. H. Tawney, *The British Liberal Movement* (New Haven, Conn., 1925), p. 147.

[46] Brian Fitzpatrick, *British Imperialism and Australia, 1788–1833* (London, 1939) and *The British Empire in Australia* (Melbourne, 1941); Robin Gollan, *Radical and Working Class Politics:*

Russel Ward's classic work, *Australian Legend*, argued that an authentic Australian nationalism with its roots in the nomadic working class of the bush had been thwarted by the imperial authorities acting in collusion with a local Anglophile bourgeoisie. When, however, the radical nationalists are examined more closely it would appear that they did not deny Australians' sense of loyalty to Britain and the Empire or the pervasiveness of Britishness in Australian culture.[47] The focus for their work was an internal quarrel inside Australia about class and social justice and inside the Empire about the relations of the Dominions to the Mother Country. Their prime concern was that Britain should treat Australia as an equal partner and recognize Australia's distinctive values and interests. They were particularly hostile to conservative Australians' 'cultural cringe' or 'groveldom'.[48]

It was Irish Catholics and trade unionists, with their legacy of bitterness from the conscription controversies, who were most attracted to radical nationalism. Yet when the Empire was threatened by an external enemy most radical nationalists rallied to the common cause. They too were captive to Australia's Britishness. During the Second World War and the immediate post-war years, Labor Prime Ministers John Curtin and J. B. Chifley, who were of Irish Catholic descent and had been deeply involved in the First World War anti-conscription movement, proclaimed again and again that Australians belonged to the 'British-speaking race' and were guardians of British civilization in the South Pacific. In 1954 at the time of Queen Elizabeth's first visit to Australia the *Age* marvelled that:

Labor premiers with Irish names, who could not for the sake of their careers be seen even holding a top hat, behaved as correctly and spoke as warmly, if not as elegantly, as the chancellors of ancient universities.

The Irish Catholic Labor Premier of New South Wales Joseph Cahill, in welcoming the Queen to Sydney compared her landing at Farm Cove to Captain Arthur Phillip's arrival on the same spot in 1788. 'It was', he said 'from that very point that our British Civilization fanned out to encompass a continent'. And he continued, reciting what might be thought of as

---

A Study of Eastern Australia, 1850–1910 (Melbourne, 1960); Russel Ward, *The Australian Legend* (Melbourne, 1958).

[47] Russel Ward, *Australian Legend*, pp. v, 52, 212–13 and also *Australia Since the Coming of Man* (Melbourne, 1987), p. 165.

[48] Interview with Russel Ward for National Library of Australia Oral History Project, 8 November 1986; C. M. H. Clark, *A History of Australia. Vol. IV: The Earth Abideth For Ever, 1851–1888* (Melbourne, 1978), p. 406.

Australia's then national creed, 'our origin is British, our soul is British. We think British, we act British.'[49]

In more recent times, however, Peter McCormick's 'British soul' has withered on the vine. Neither Prime Ministers nor Premiers make this kind of speech any more. Courses on the British Empire or Commonwealth of Nations have disappeared from the history syllabi. British history itself has been absorbed into European history. The histories of Asia, Africa, and America are no longer treated as subordinate parts of British imperial expansion but rather as subjects in their own right.

Since the 1950s, historical circumstances have conspired with social changes to undermine Australians' desire and ability to keep their British identity. Like other peoples who were in the vanguard of modernization, Australians, as they became inured to the permanence of change, no longer felt the extreme psychic trauma which had caused them to embrace race nationalism. Moreover, following the defeat of Nazi Germany and the rebellion of African and Asian peoples against European imperialism, the West's race nationalism was widely condemned and became a source of great embarrassment in the international arena.

Against this background Australia's White British self-definition began to lose its virtue. This process was given a specific impetus as a result of the remaking of the British Empire and the sundering of ties with Britain. The British Commonwealth being transmuted into a multicultural, multi-racial Commonwealth could no longer serve, even nominally, Australia's national purposes. As British power waned so did its role as a great power protector and a market for exports. Perhaps the final blow was the United Kingdom's decision in the 1960s to turn its back on 'Greater Britain' and to seek its future in Europe.[50] Australia's British myth had come undone and as a result the Australian people were confronted with a crisis of identity.

This was recognized at the time. It was probably Donald Horne who was the first to discern what these changes portended. In 1968 the editor of *The Bulletin* wrote: 'There is a commendable emptiness in Australians about their place in the world, the need for a new rhetoric, a new approach,

---

[49] *Age*, 2 April 1954 and 'State Dinner Speech by the Premier of New South Wales…', 4 February 1954, National Archives of Australia, A9708 RV/AK Part 3. I am indebted to Oliver Jones for these quotations.

[50] Stuart Ward, *Australia and the British Embrace: The Demise of the Imperial Ideal* (Melbourne, 2001), ch. 10.

as if Australia were beginning again.'[51] Politicians, pundits, journalists, and scholars all remarked on this emptiness. The Australian historians' response was as awkward as the question. Those still seeking a nationalist answer hoped to fill the void by writing an exclusive Australian history page and so offer the people an 'Australian soul'.[52] Others urged Australians to define themselves anew by developing close ties with East Asia, opening their doors to migrants from all countries, and creating a multicultural society.[53] More frequently scholars, repelled by nationalism's record of exclusion and oppression, turned their backs on the question of national community and sought instead to uncover the sufferings of the victims of that social idea. Their aim was to restore the outsiders to their proper place in the story of the making of Australia.

None of these different paths have, however, produced a viable myth for the contemporary community. The nationalists have failed to strike a responsive chord in the public imagination. Australians, like western Europeans, have lost the appetite for atavism. 'Advance Australia Fair' may have echoes of an older British nationalism but even in its new guise it cannot evoke the quasi-religious emotions of 'God Save the Queen' or 'Rule Britannia'. Indeed the difficulties that the authorities encountered in trying to find an anthem to replace 'God Save the Queen' showed how nationalism had lost much of its appeal. The public competition launched by the Whitlam government in 1973 was a fiasco. Though over 2500 entries were received none were found to be plausible. A number of eminent literary and musical figures grasped, even if only intuitively, the reason for the failure. Australia's leading composer, Peter Sculthorpe, commented that what was being sought was 'a national anthem that's stirring and heroic—and I don't think things are like that any more'. In his opinion, 'the thought of that kind of anthem being written is laughable—society's changed too much.' Similarly Judith Wright, one of the country's most distinguished poets, explained that it was

[51] *The Bulletin*, 20 January 1968.

[52] Most notably C. M. H. Clark in the last three volumes of his *A History of Australia*: Vol. IV, *The Earth Abideth For Ever, 1851–1888* (Melbourne, 1978); Vol. V, *The People Make Laws, 1888–1915* (Melbourne, 1981); and Vol. VI '*The Old Dead Tree and the Young Tree Green*', *1916–1935* (Melbourne, 1987).

[53] Stephen Fitzgerald, *Is Australia an Asian Country? Can Australia Survive in an East Asian Future?* (Sydney, 1997), especially pp. 14–15 and 176–9; S. Castles, M. Kalantzis, B. Cope, and N. Morrissey, *Mistaken Identity: Multiculturalism and the Demise of Nationalism in Australia* (Sydney, 1992).

'an impossible task to write a national anthem in the twentieth century when we are starting to believe that nationalism has its limitations'.[54]

The most general term now used to describe Australia is multiculturalism. The professed pride in cultural diversity is as much a reaction against nationalism itself as against Australia's former White British race identity. But, whatever other role they may play, neither Eurasianization nor multiculturalism can, by its very nature, offer a myth for an Australian community. In avoiding this question it is as though the culture makers and perhaps even the public at large have been fearful that if any attempt should be made to look for a unifying social idea the only answer would be some form of nationalism with all its potential for reviving the evils that multiculturalism has endeavoured to eradicate.

The problem of a unifying social idea will, however, not go away. Communities cannot exist without them. Lacking any other alternative the legacy of Britishness has kept surfacing, and sometimes in surprising places. Indeed founders of feminist and Aboriginal historical studies, whose early works have tended either directly or by inference to dismiss past national orthodoxies as the cause of intolerance and oppression, are in different ways beginning to express concern about this lack of attention to what Miriam Dixson has called the Anglo-Celt 'core culture'.

In *The Imaginary Australian: Anglo-Celts and Indentity—1788 to the Present* Dixson, one of the pioneers of the 'new wave' feminist movement, makes a heartfelt plea for an explicit reaffirmation of British culture as a necessary barrier against social and political disintegration. While admitting that this 'core culture' has in the past legitimized prejudice and caused injustice, she also sees it as the source of the ideas which have empowered those who have fought for equal rights for all citizens and all cultures. In her view the preservation of this national heritage is a precondition for modern democracy and its renewal in Australia.[55]

Likewise Henry Reynolds, in a series of path-breaking works on Australia's autochthonous people, has over time moved the focus of his work from the Aborigines themselves to British colonial policy. In *The Other Side of the Frontier* he has dealt with Aboriginal resistance to the European invasion,

---

[54] *Age*, 14 April 1974 and *Sydney Morning Herald*, 4 July 1973.

[55] *The Imaginary Australian: Anglo-Celts and Identity—1788 to the Present* (Sydney, 1999), especially pp. 162–5. See also Miriam Dixson's *The Real Matilda: Women and Identity in Australia, 1788 to the Present* (Ringwood, Vic., 1976).

in *Frontier* with the settlers' racial attitudes towards the dispossessed, and then in *The Law of the Land* and *This Whispering in Our Hearts* with the legal and moral principles which underpinned British authorities' attempts in the first half of the nineteenth century to safeguard the rights of the Aborigines to their traditional lands.[56] These latter two works were inspired by the unspoken assumption that a re-examination of Australian colonial experience as part of the British Empire might offer the only historical basis for reconciliation. They convey the message that though the British reformers of the 1830s and 1840s failed in their efforts to protect Aboriginal land rights the principles upon which they acted might well provide the Australian heirs to that British heritage with a new starting point for settling this vexed question.

Whether the specific arguments of Dixson and Reynolds are valid is beside the point. What they do suggest, however, is that the major issues preoccupying contemporary historians seem inescapably, even if often unwittingly, to lead back to a study of Australia's British past and to a reconsideration of that past in the light of Australia's changing circumstances. None of the new directions have in themselves been able to give meaning to the post-nationalist community to which all belong and which in many ways all share. None have met the need of connecting the present to the past, of dealing with the problem of continuity and discontinuity, or of constructing a history of Britishness in Australia which would help to make sense of the new era.

'Postmodern' playfulness—the last refuge of the desiccated intellectual—which sometimes appears in the scholarly treatment of this subject, is a ludicrous response to the problem of understanding human society. In his *Quarterly Essay*, 'Made in England: Australia's British Inheritance', David Malouf has by contrast recently offered a measured reassessment of the British inheritance and by so doing has underscored its importance for any future discussion of Australian culture.[57] At the least the essay is a reminder that this is a subject which Australians can only ignore at their peril. Without a study of Australia's Britishness, conducted free from the emotional trammels of the past, Australians will not be able to escape fully from McCormick's history page and find a more certain way of legitimizing the

---

[56] *The Other Side of the Frontier* (Melbourne, 1982); *Frontier* (Sydney, 1987); *The Law of the Land* (Ringwood, Vic., 1988); *This Whispering in Our Hearts* (Sydney, 1998).

[57] David Malouf, 'Made in England: Australia's British Inheritance', *Quarterly Essay*, 12 (2003).

values and institutions which in practice hold the commonwealth together. Only such a study can provide an intellectual grounding for treating and evaluating Australia's present problem of social identity.

Select Bibliography

DOUGLAS COLE, 'The Problem of "Nationalism" and "Imperialism" in British Settlement Colonies', *Journal of British Studies*, 10 (May 1971).

JAMES CURRAN, *The Power of Speech: Australian Prime Ministers Defining the National Image* (Melbourne, 2004).

W. K. HANCOCK, *Australia* (London, 1930).

JAMES JUPP, ed., *The Australian People: An Encyclopedia of the Nation, Its People and Their Origins* (Cambridge, 2001).

STUART MACINTYRE and JULIAN THOMAS, eds, *The Discovery of Australian History, 1890–1939* (Melbourne, 1995).

MARK MCKENNA, *The Captive Republic: A History of Republicanism in Australia, 1788–1996* (Cambridge, 1996).

DAVID MALOUF, 'Made in England: Australia's British Inheritance', *Quarterly Essay*, 12 (2003).

NEVILLE MEANEY, ed., *Under New Heavens: Cultural Transmission and the Making of Australia* (Port Melbourne, 1989).

PATRICK O'FARRELL, *The Irish in Australia, 1788 to the Present* (Sydney, 2000).

RUSSEL WARD, *The Australian Legend* (Melbourne, 1958).

Epilogue: After Empire

DERYCK M. SCHREUDER AND STUART WARD

Nothing reveals more clearly the scope and complexity of Australia's Empire than the nature of its demise. For the best part of two centuries, the Empire had functioned variously as a justification for conquest and dispossession, an anchor for settler-colonial identities, a model for colonial governance, a cause to rally men and women for overseas service, a safeguard against external threats, a rationale for industry and investment, and a whole lot more besides. One might have expected, then, that the rapid pace of imperial decline in the post-Second World War era would have torn away at the very fabric of Australian civic culture, leaving a lasting legacy of political turmoil, economic stagnation, and social dislocation.

Yet this was clearly not the case. As in Britain, where it is often said that the Empire was lost in a 'fit of collective indifference',[1] so too in Australia there are few indications that the broad mass of the population was particularly concerned about the break-up of the British world. With the notable exception of the fall of Singapore in 1942 (where Australians had far more at stake than the integrity of the Empire), the quickening pace of imperial decline in the 1940s and 1950s gave rise only to a few qualified reservations in Australia. By the early 1960s, the process that had been dubbed 'decolonization' had acquired a sense of inevitability. While the passing of Empire could prompt feelings of nostalgia and regret in certain quarters, at no time did it prompt any widespread, concerted appeal to have the process reversed. Nor did it register significantly in any Australian Federal election campaign between 1949 and 1963.

This in itself might suggest that the Empire was never quite the needle in Australia's compass that it was purported to be—or at the very least that it

---

[1] This is, however, debatable; see Stuart Ward, ed., *British Culture and the End of Empire* (Manchester, 2001), pp. 2–5; Bernard Porter, *The Absent-Minded Imperialists: How the British Really Saw their Empire* (Oxford, 2004); Wendy Webster, *Englishness and Empire, 1939–1965* (Oxford, 2005).

had long since lost its significance and appeal by the 1950s. But this would not so much explain the demise of Australia's Empire as explain it away. There are a number of compelling reasons why an Empire that had been so fundamental to the Australian outlook could be eclipsed within a short space of time without so much as a public demonstration.

First, there was no single, decisive body-blow to the imperial idea. Even the 'loss' of India could be understood at the time as an aberration—while the rest of Britain's colonial mission continued around the world unabated. The same can be said of the Suez crisis of 1956—generally regarded in Britain, both at the time and since, as a bellwether of imperial decline. In Australia, the British humiliation at Suez (and its widely touted 'lessons') did not reverberate to anywhere near the same extent. Similarly, the wave of decolonization across Africa in the years 1957 to 1964—although a momentous event in hindsight—provided no singular event or upheaval that might focus attention on the end of Empire. Kwame Nkrumah's breakthrough in securing independence for Ghana in 1957 barely registered in public awareness in Australia. And this pattern was repeated as the decolonization process gathered momentum into the 1960s. It was the piecemeal nature of these developments that cushioned the impact of what was, in reality, a major redrawing of the imperial landscape. It took an extended tour of Africa by a British Prime Minister—Harold Macmillan in early 1960—to bring Africa onto the front pages of Australian newspapers. Yet even Macmillan's celebrated 'Winds of Change' speech in Cape Town was greeted by a relatively low-key response in the Australian press—as though its significance for Australia was only marginal. The 'End of Empire' tended to acquire meaning and significance in retrospect; it was never the stuff of 'breaking' news.

Even more important, however, was the persistent idea that the 'British' Commonwealth would provide continuity as a natural successor to Empire. It is significant, for example, that Indian independence caused far fewer misgivings in Australia than the more vexed question of whether India should be allowed to join the Commonwealth as a Republic. The Australian Labor government acquiesced in the former but dug its heels in on the latter. It was Australia's Foreign Minister, H. V. Evatt, who insisted that India should only be permitted to join the Commonwealth if the key principles of 'kingship, kinship and practical comradeship' were respected and preserved.[2] From the

---

[2] Frank Bongiorno, 'Commonwealthmen and Republicans: Dr. H.V. Evatt, the Monarchy and India', *Australian Journal of Politics and History*, Vol. 1, no. 46 (2000), p. 46.

point of view of the Australian government, Britain's colonial Empire was regarded as dispensable whenever it threatened to disrupt the ties of common allegiance among fellow 'British' nations. Evatt lost out on this point and India was duly admitted, but this in no way dampened Australian insistence on the core values of the 'old' Commonwealth. Despite a 1949 resolution that the association should henceforth be termed the 'Commonwealth of Nations', Australians of all political persuasions persisted in referring to the 'British' Commonwealth. Evatt went so far as to deny—perversely—that a change of nomenclature had occurred, declaring in January 1949:

There has been a great deal of loose talk about the omission of the word 'British'. It has never been omitted ... To omit the word 'British' causes confusion. It is the British Commonwealth ... The name 'British' doesn't mean that every nation in the group is British in race, because they are not. But it does mean that there is a central feature of the Commonwealth deriving from Britain and the traditions of Britain, and that means to Australia the most intimate relationship—with the King. So it is the British Commonwealth.[3]

This tortured logic, in itself, suggests that Australia's Empire was fundamentally about Australia and Britain. While the cartographic projection of a worldwide British Empire—chequered in swathes of red—had long served to reinforce the timelessness and durability of Australia's self-styled Britishness, it was never its primary source or inspiration. There persisted throughout the decolonization era the belief that Australia would somehow remain British, whatever the global political landscape and whatever the fate of Empire in Asia and Africa. H. V. Evatt's insistence on the enduring Britishness of the Commonwealth echoed down through the 1950s and 1960s at every significant juncture where the ties of Empire and Commonwealth appeared to be loosening. It surfaced most prominently during Australia's support for Britain at Suez, when Robert Menzies privately reassured Anthony Eden: 'You must never entertain any doubts about the British quality of this country.'[4] And it was repeated on other occasions when Australia's Britishness seemed to be in doubt, such as the signature of the ANZUS Alliance in 1951; the opening of the Australian–American War Memorial in Canberra in 1954; the renegotiation of imperial trade preferences in 1956; and the completion of

---

[3] 'Extract of a Broadcast by Dr. H. V. Evatt, 16 January 1949', National Archives of Canada, Ottawa: RG25, series A-3-b vol. 4234, file 6065–40 Part 1.

[4] Menzies to Eden, 1 November 1956, quoted in W. J. Hudson, *Blind Loyalty: Australia and the Suez Crisis* (Melbourne, 1989), p. xii.

the Australia–Japan Trade Agreement in 1957.[5] The Menzies government persisted in treating the Commonwealth as a 'two-tiered' grouping—with the inner 'Crown Commonwealth' representing the common instincts, values, assumptions, and ethnicity which had typified the virtues of the old association.[6]

*   *   *

Yet this insistence on the durability of Australian Britishness in the face of the realities of imperial decline could not withstand the logic of a different set of realities, namely the changing attitudes in Britain towards the value and utility of the Commonwealth. In particular, the Prime Ministership of Harold Macmillan (1957–63) inaugurated a major reappraisal of British priorities and interests in the post-war world. Immediately upon assuming office in January 1957, Macmillan called for 'a profit and loss account of our colonial possessions, so that we may be better able to gauge whether ... we are likely to gain or lose by its departure'.[7] Although the initial Whitehall response to this was inconclusive, it nonetheless signalled the beginnings of a conceptual shift, allowing the possibility that Britain's commitment to Empire and Commonwealth might be a major liability rather than an asset. This impression gained ground as Commonwealth trade failed to deliver the necessary growth to sustain Britain's global aspirations, and the much-lauded 'New Commonwealth' failed to perform its anticipated role as a mouthpiece for British policy and influence. Far from speaking with a concerted voice, the new, multiracial Commonwealth was deeply divided on a number of key issues, not least the inclusion of members like South Africa who did not share the multiracial ideal. By the end of the decade, Macmillan had appointed Iain Macleod and Duncan Sandys to the posts of Colonial and Commonwealth Secretary respectively—each of whom set about the task of jettisoning Britain's moral, political, and economic responsibilities in the colonial world.

---

[5] Witness Menzies' comment to Japanese Prime Minister Kishi on the eve of the negotiations: 'It is part of the tradition in British countries that when you have had a fight you shake hands and have friendly relations.' Quoted in Alan Rix, *The Australia–Japan Political Alignment* (London 1999), p. 31.

[6] See articles by Menzies in *The Times*, 11, 12 July 1956.

[7] Quoted in A. G. Hopkins, 'Macmillan's Audit of Empire, 1957', in Peter Clarke and Clive Trebilcock, eds, *Understanding Decline: Perceptions and Realities of British Economic Performance* (Cambridge, 1997), p. 234.

For Australia, it was this unmistakeable downgrading of the Common-wealth—far more so than decolonization per se—that raised questions about Australia's aspirations and orientation in the post-imperial world. A series of events in 1961 brought the extent of these changes fully to light. In March of that year, South Africa was forced to withdraw its application to remain in the Commonwealth as a republic in the face of mounting criticism of its apartheid system. Opinion in Australia was divided between those who applauded the triumph of 'New Commonwealth' principles over South Africa's racist laws, and those who persisted with the more conventional view that Commonwealth countries should not interfere with each other's domes-tic policies. This latter position was adopted by the Menzies government, and advocated forcefully at the March 1961 Commonwealth Conference by the Prime Minister himself. Menzies, like Evatt before him, was roundly defeated in his efforts to preserve the 'core values' of the Commonwealth as he conceived them—an outcome which he put down partly to the treachery of the Canadians in siding against South Africa, and more importantly to the cunning duplicity of Harold Macmillan, whose 'apparent preference for a Brown face' (Pandit Nehru) represented for Menzies a betrayal of the old, white, British family.[8]

Only a few months later, an even greater challenge to Australia's Empire emerged when the Macmillan government decided to seek membership of the European Economic Community. This move was prompted by Britain's relative decline in the post-war world—politically and economically—and the need to arrest that process by finding new means of securing British prosperity and influence. Although Macmillan went out of his way to reassure the Commonwealth that membership of a closed European trading bloc would not signal a downgrading of imperial and Commonwealth interests, this was precisely what emerged as negotiations between Britain and the EEC unfolded over the ensuing eighteen months.

For Australia, the prospect of British membership of the EEC carried far more immediate and wide-ranging implications than the pace of decolo-nization or the composition of the Commonwealth. Not only did it signal that the days of privileged access to the British market for Australia's pri-mary industries were severely numbered, it also carried the more symbolic message that Britain would in future look to its regional neighbours and

---

[8] David Goldsworthy, *Losing the Blanket: Australia and the End of Britain's Empire* (Melbourne, 2002), p. 104.

networks rather than fellow 'British' countries overseas. In presenting Britain with such a stark choice, the EEC had the capacity to redefine Britishness itself—setting Britons of the new world firmly apart from the old. Although the membership negotiations were cut short by General de Gaulle's 'veto' in January 1963, it was already clear by this stage that the Macmillan government was committed to entry on terms that would bring an end to Australia's traditional economic rationale as a supplier of raw materials and foodstuffs to Britain. As *The Australian* editorialized in its inaugural issue in July 1964, Britain's EEC membership was the 'one event' that brought home the changes in Australia's place in the world: 'The burning desire of Mother to leave us to our own affairs was a shock. It was a salutary shock. For it helped to make us understand that now, as never before in our short history, we stand alone.'[9]

It was also in 1961 that the British government resolved to clamp down on the principle of free inward migration from the British subjects of the Commonwealth. The Commonwealth Immigrants Act (passed in April 1962) was designed primarily to limit the flow of migrants from India, Pakistan, and the West Indies, but it was considered imperative that the new regulations should be seen to apply equally to citizens of the 'white' Commonwealth in Canada, Australia, and New Zealand. In practice, the British adopted a voucher system that privileged 'skilled' (read 'white') workers, enabling Australians to continue to live and work in Britain as they had always done. But the significance of the Act lay in the departure from the principle of free entry into Britain as of right, and the Australian government complained bitterly about the infringement of their status as British subjects. Coming immediately on the heels of the EEC membership bid, the implications for Australia seemed clear. As the *Sydney Morning Herald* indignantly intoned: 'We are, or thought we were, the same people—simply the British overseas. Now, it seems, we are not.'[10]

These tensions had, in many ways, been inherent in the ambiguous nature of 'Dominion status' from the very beginning, but it was the peculiar pressures of imperial decline that brought the divergent interests of the successor states of Empire into such stark conflict. Socially and culturally, Britain had experienced its own brand of decolonization

---

[9] *The Australian*, 'Facing the Challenge of Adulthood', 15 July 1964. See generally Stuart Ward, *Australia and the British Embrace: The Demise of the Imperial Ideal* (Melbourne, 2001).

[10] *Sydney Morning Herald*, 23 April 1962.

which reflected fundamental changes in community attitudes, not least through inward migrations from the very Empire it had once controlled. John Darwin suggests that Britain itself had become one of the 'successor states' to the Empire, and it was precisely the attempts of successive governments to fashion a post-imperial role for Britain that brought the wider implications of the end of Empire into focus in Australia.[11] The recurring shocks of the early 1960s, then, were the effects of a much deeper sea change in the meaning and significance of 'being British'.

This is borne out by one lesser known initiative of the Macmillan government (also in 1961)—namely, to repatriate the language of Britishness for diplomatic purposes. Hitherto, the term had been understood (in its official usage) to refer to all 'British' governments around the world, with the more cumbersome adjective 'United Kingdom' reserved for the Mother Country. But in the light of the profound changes in the Empire and Commonwealth, Macmillan moved to reclaim usages such as 'British government', 'British ministers', and 'British interests' to mean 'Great Britain' alone.[12] He instructed his Commonwealth Secretary to seek the approval of the governments of Canada, Australia, and New Zealand to make this subtle switch—which was duly granted, apparently without any fuss or press comment.

The fate of 'Empire Day' also symbolized the transition. Created imperially in 1904, and celebrated annually in Australia (and other Dominions) on the anniversary of Queen Victoria's birthday (24 May), its mortality had to be recognized by 1958—when Australia followed Britain's lead in converting it to the more ethereal 'Commonwealth Day' (albeit with some initial confusion as to whether the term 'British' should be included). Yet when this failed to take hold in the popular imagination, it was decided (again in Britain) in November 1965 that the occasion should henceforth be celebrated in conjunction with the Queen's birthday, thereby ushering 24 May gently (and deliberately) into obscurity. It limped along for a few more years in Australia as 'cracker night', but when the crackers themselves were abolished in the early 1970s the occasion was stripped entirely of significance. For most Australians today, Empire Day jolts only

[11] See John Darwin, *Britain and Decolonization: The Retreat From Empire in the Post-War World* (London, 1988), p. 324.

[12] Macmillan to Sandys, 1 May 1961; 20 June 1961, Macmillan Papers, Bodleian Library Oxford, dep. C. 351.

faint memories of sparklers, throwdowns, thunder bungers, and Catherine wheels—not imperial patriotism.[13]

*   *   *

It is the creeping obsolescence of Britishness that reveals the more subtle—but no less profound or lasting—effects of the end of Empire in Australia. It was not a traumatic phenomenon in the sense of widespread consternation or popular distress, but it nonetheless provided a formative context for the way Australians performed, articulated, argued about, and acted upon their sense of nationhood in the post-imperial era. Australians may not have experienced a process of 'decolonization' in the same way as India or Nigeria, but it is possible to detect a dawning awareness that Britishness was no longer credible, nor even particularly meaningful, in the absence of the political and material underpinnings of Empire. What Jim Davidson has termed 'de-dominionization' demanded a thoroughgoing overhaul of the time-honoured symbols, sentiments, rites, and rituals of Australian civic culture.[14]

But this was never a straightforward matter of mopping up the imperial debris. Although Australians had, for generations, evolved a rich archive of symbols of a cherished Australian homeland, they had tended to draw on the wider British myth when it came to conveying their sense of themselves as a distinctive people. Britain had long served as the imagined source of a shared history, language, culture, ethnicity, and civic institutions, as manifested in school curricula, public rituals, oaths of allegiance, notions of citizenship, traditions of governance, national symbols, and so on. Redefining these concepts in a more limited, national frame would raise as many questions as it answered.

This was borne out by the widespread calls for a 'new nationalism' that became the subject of media attention and political rhetoric from the late 1960s. It was Donald Horne who coined the term in 1968, referring specifically to Prime Minister John Gorton's plea to his fellow Australians to 'help me in the years ahead to foster this feeling of real nationalism'.[15] But it was taken

[13] Stewart Firth and Jeanette Hoorn, 'From Empire Day to Cracker Night', in Peter Spearritt and David Walker, eds, *Australian Popular Culture* (Sydney, 1979).

[14] Jim Davidson, 'The De-Dominionisation of Australia', *Meanjin*, Vol. 63, no. 3 (September 2004), pp. 75–84; See also Davidson, 'De-Dominionisation Revisited', *Australian Journal of Politics and History*, Vol. 51, no. 1 (March 2005), pp. 108–13.

[15] *The Bulletin*, 5 October 1968.

up in a variety of contexts to describe the many ways Australians attempted to place their nationhood on a new, post-imperial footing. Debates about the Australian flag, the national anthem, the Monarchy, and the appropriate observance of Anzac and Australia Day were the most obvious signs of the mood for national renewal. As Governor General Paul Hasluck implored his fellow Australians on Australia Day 1973: 'Our patriotism has to be patriotism for the Australia of today—the Australia that exists—not to an Australia of a different kind that no longer exists.'[16] But these issues were animated more by memories of what Australia had left behind, rather than any clear, consensual vision of what the new nation should become. Moreover, the public inclination was to ridicule any attempt at instilling new patriotic values and sentiments. In 1973, for example, Immigration Minister Al Grassby sought to promote a 'new awareness in our national heritage' by way of a major overhaul of the rites and rituals of Australia Day (26 January). He proposed an annual 'national pageant' in Canberra, enlisting the combined efforts of 'artists, poets, trade-unionists, industry, Government and the Armed Forces'. His reference to 'poets', however, was widely misquoted as 'pets', prompting a round of guffaws from the *Sydney Morning Herald*:

[Mr Grassby] would need considerable skill to disentangle the Afghan hounds from the Siamese cats, the galahs from the goldfish and the blue-tongued lizards from the budgerigars. The occasion, in fact, might well be more of a shambles than a pageant. No; let the pets stay at home, as the vast majority of Australians do on Australia Day, which has never been observed in more than a perfunctory way and is universally regarded as being no more than an excuse for a holiday.[17]

The problem was twofold: nationalism seemed somehow old-fashioned and inappropriate for a newly emergent Australia, offloading its nineteenth-century colonial baggage; and 'Australia' itself seemed a highly elusive concept when stripped of its British and imperial origins. As one of the entrants in the 1973 National Anthem Quest, Bob Ellis, confessed, 'you've got to leave out all the gum trees and wallabies, and you can't talk about defending the country against the yellow hordes, so there's not much to talk about except an independent stance and belated pride in ourselves. Anything else would embarrass the audience.'[18]

---

[16] 'Patriotism and Loyalty', Governor General's televised Australia Day address, 26 January 1973, National Library of Australia, Hasluck Papers, MS 5274 Box 38.
[17] *Sydney Morning Herald*, 31 January 1973.   [18] *Sydney Morning Herald*, 4 July 1973.

There was more to the problem than national symbols, however. The unravelling of the British myth removed the *raison d'être* of arguably the foundation stone of twentieth-century Australia—the White Australia policy. From the moment of its inception in 1901, Australians had been prepared to withstand overseas criticism of their racially discriminatory immigration programme, because they believed that it was vital to preserving a stable, homogeneous British community in the Southern Hemisphere. But as the credibility of Australian Britishness was called into question, the onslaught of overseas opinion (and an increasingly vocal domestic opposition) became irresistible. First the Australian Labor Party in 1965, and then later the conservatives under Harold Holt, began officially to back away from the tenets of White Australia. Yet in casting around for alternative ethnic markers of the nation, Australians simply found it easier not to have any—opting instead for the official endorsement of multiculturalism in the 1970s. The irony of a society built up over generations on the principle of racial exclusiveness suddenly embracing—indeed celebrating—its unique ethnic diversity is inescapable. Unsurprisingly, Australians have been arguing ever since about securing a 'balance' between tolerance and inclusiveness on the one hand, and respect for 'core Australian' values and institutions on the other—that is, the very values and institutions that the White Australia policy was designed to protect and preserve. This was particularly apparent under John Howard, who claimed during his Prime Ministership that 'we've come back from being too obsessed with diversity to a point where we are very proud and conscious of those ongoing, distinctive, defining characteristics of being an Australian which we tend to identify with what I might call the old Australia.'[19] There remains an ambiguous legacy of Empire in the problem of disentangling the 'defining characteristics' of the 'old Australia' from the original racial determinants of the national complexion.

Similarly, Australians have found it difficult to shed the mantle of a colonial power in the Pacific, particularly in Papua New Guinea where, despite more than thirty years of independence, Australians continue to play key roles in financing, administering, and—briefly in 2004–5—policing the region. This is partly because the timing and nature of New Guinean independence were determined by factors extraneous to the territory itself. As early as 1961, the pace of decolonization in Africa had begun to raise questions about the future of Australia's own colonial territory. For one

---

[19] Quoted in Curran, *The Power of Speech*, p. 241.

senior External Affairs officer, on tour in Africa in 1961, the rapid progress of constitutional change pointed inexorably to the need for Australia 'to do some solid pressure-cooking of technically and administratively competent Papuans'.[20] The climate of world opinion would not long tolerate Australia's status as a middle colonial power, and time was clearly running out to equip the territory for self-government.

By the end of the decade, the issue of independence for Papua New Guinea had become entangled in Australia's own search for a 'new nationalism'. Opposition Leader Gough Whitlam made several visits to Port Moresby and became convinced that Australians would be unable to present a new, 'mature' face to the world until they had buried the last 'remnants of colonialism'. Meanwhile the Australian administrators of the territory had set about devising and promoting the idea of a unified New Guinean nation-state—complete with the necessary trappings in the form of a new flag, a national day, a national song, and so on.[21] At a time when Australians were debating the need to overhaul their own national symbols, this was a curious twist—decolonization in New Guinea had become part and parcel of Australia's route towards 'de-dominionization'. By the time of Whitlam's election in December 1972, independence was a foregone conclusion. The main obstacle was overcoming the deep anxieties in many districts—particularly in the Western and Southern Highlands—that independence would mean the withdrawal of Australian protection against rival internal political groupings. In some parts of the country, Whitlam's offer of independence was turned down flat, as in the following letter to the Prime Minister from the island of Karkar off the northern coast of New Guinea in February 1973:

Mipela pipel bilong KarKar ino bin laikim or askim long long kwik Political Independence, olsem mipela pilim mipela ino redi gut yet … Mipela pilim olsem hariapin Papua New Guinea long independence em wanpela hamamas or gutpela samting bilong nupela gavaman bilong Australia tasol, em ino laik tru bilong pipel bilong Papua New Guinea.

[The people of Karkar do not want nor have we asked for early political independence which we consider highly premature … We feel that early independence for

[20] Mick Shann, quoted in Goldsworthy, *Losing the Blanket*, p. 85.
[21] See James Griffin, 'Papua New Guinea', in W. J. Hudson, ed., *Australia in World Affairs, 1971–75* (Sydney, 1980), pp. 349–50.

Papua New Guinea might suit the political ambitions of the present government of Australia but is not in the best interests of Papua New Guinea.][22]

The Karkar Islanders' analysis of Australia's motives was not wide of the mark. Yet seen in a broader, global context, it remains true that Whitlam had no real choice but to push for rapid independence. The emergence of Michael Somare as a credible 'national' leader provided the Labor government with the necessary means of divesting itself of the formal trappings of colonial power. At the Independence Day celebrations of 15 September 1975, Australian Governor General Sir John Kerr emphasized that 'both Papua New Guinea and Australia have been fortunate that during the long period of colonisation we managed to avoid policies and relationships which have proved tragic elsewhere.'[23] But while Independence might perform the function of cleansing Australia's colonial record, it cannot be said to have brought an end to the underlying colonial dynamics of Australia's ties with its former territory.

Of all Australia's post-imperial legacies, the question of Aboriginal 'reconciliation' remains the most prominent, complex, and divisive. Here again, the issues have their origins in the end of Empire era. In 1933, Ernest Scott, writing in the *Cambridge History of the British Empire*, offered the conventional account of the means whereby British settlers dispossessed the indigenous peoples of Australia. The Aborigines were 'troublesome but not dangerous. They were not capable of organized warfare, as were the Indians who menaced the first colonists of North America, or the fierce Bantu tribes of South Africa.' In short, 'the natives were never a serious impediment to colonisation'.[24] The idea that the colonization of Australia was uniquely peaceful, involving the tragic but inevitable reduction of the Aboriginal population by 'natural' causes, was a mainstay of imperial culture in Australia for generations. It performed an indispensable civic function, legitimating the British occupation of the continent and, in turn, reinforcing the sense that Australia and its settler inhabitants were inextricably tied to the British world.

History itself—not unlike other civic emblems such as the anthem, the sovereign, the flag—became caught up in the post-imperial search for

---

[22] Sibon Luang (President of the Karkar Council) to Whitlam, 9 February 1973, National Archives of Australia, A452, 1973/205. English translation in file.

[23] Quoted in Griffin, 'Papua New Guinea', p. 347.

[24] Ernest Scott, ed., *Australia: Cambridge History of the British Empire*, Vol. VII, Pt I, (Cambridge, 1933), pp. 67, 90.

national renewal. From the late 1960s, historians began to examine more carefully what the anthropologist W. E. H. Stanner termed 'the Great Australian Silence', and produced histories that challenged the foundations of Australia's Empire story.[25] The most confronting aspect of the new histories was the persistent theme of frontier violence. Evidence of armed conflict and fierce Aboriginal resistance abounded, suggesting that the settlers' claim to the continent was based, not on peaceful acquisition, but on an (ongoing) process of oppressive occupation.

Despite the insistent logic of the new research, Australians remain divided and disoriented over what to make of these findings—whether they reveal little more than an unfortunate 'blemish' on an otherwise respectable record of national achievement (for which a simple apology would suffice), or an entirely new foundation for understanding Australian civilization, past and present. Recent years have shown a growing inclination to reject outright the new research as the reckless machinations of a cohort of 'black armband historians', hell-bent on miring the country in an enervating and counterproductive guilt complex. In 2002, deep divisions in the community were exposed by Keith Windschuttle's impassioned denunciation of an entire generation of historians. Echoing Ernest Scott, he insisted that 'the British colonization of this continent was the least violent of all Europe's encounters with the New World ... The notion of sustained "frontier warfare" is fictional.'[26] As in so many other contexts, the eclipse of Empire has opened unlimited scope for redefining the nation, but yielded little in the way of common ground. The persistence of the peaceful settlement narrative amid the crossfire of the so-called 'history wars' suggests that many Australians still avail themselves of the founding myths of Australia's Empire in order to make sense of their past and present.

What all of the above examples have in common is that they represent processes that are yet to be played out. There remains an enduring tension between a deep attachment to the familiar contours of a 'settled' past, and an aversion to the colonial taint that comes with so much of that territory. The history wars are perhaps the most visible arena where the dilemma of how to make sense of a colonial past in a post-colonial world occupies centre stage (and it is significant that most of the issues at stake in the history wars are

---

[25] W. E. H. Stanner, *After the Dreaming* (Sydney, 1968), pp. 18–29.
[26] Keith Windschuttle, *The Fabrication of Aboriginal History*, Vol. I (Sydney, 2002), p. 3.

inherently 'post-colonial' issues—even when they are debated outside their imperial context).

Moreover, many of these contested issues are framed in the future tense: 'reconciliation', 'multiculturalism', regional 'engagement', and the republic, are invariably debated as post-colonial goals that Australians are yet to attain fully. But their end point may never fully emerge because they are themselves the product of an imperial past that can never be fully discarded. Stuart Macintyre suggests that 'not until the lingering effects of the colonial condition are finally expunged to Australian satisfaction is the Empire likely to find acceptance in its future historiography.'[27] But eliminating the legacies of Empire may prove to be more than a passing phase—indeed it may well be the very condition of post-coloniality that history has bequeathed Australia. The idea of 'Australia' was forged out of imperial processes that were, as Alan Atkinson says, at once both destructive and regenerative.[28] While Australians might rightly disavow Empire and seek new ways of anchoring their sense of civic community, they will never be able to renounce completely the political and social legacies of Empire that remain inextricably woven into their civic fabric.

---

[27] Stuart Macintyre, 'Australia and the Empire', in Robin Winks, ed., *The Oxford History of the British Empire. Vol. V: Historiography* (Oxford University Press, 1999), p. 181.

[28] See Chapter 2, p. 53.

INDEX

Note: Page numbers in **bold** indicate illustrations